RUSSIAN FRONTIERS

Russian Frontiers:

Eighteenth-century British Travellers in the Caspian, Caucasus and Central Asia

Beatrice Teissier

First published in 2011 by
Signal Books Limited
36 Minster Road
Oxford
OX4 1LY
www.signalbooks.co.uk

A catalogue record for this book is available from the British Library.

ISBN 978-1-904955-80-1 Paper

Production: Dorothy Martin
Cover Design: Baseline Arts
Cover image: courtesy of the Bodleian Library, Oxford
Images: courtesy of the Bodleian Library, Oxford
Maps © David Sansom
Printed in India by Imprint Digital

CONTENTS

Acknowledgements

I am greatly indebted to the Iran Heritage Foundation for making the publication of this book possible. I am particularly grateful to Alexander Morrison for his comments on the manuscript and to Roger Tomlin for photographing many of the illustrations. I also wish to thank most warmly the many other people who have contributed to this project through help, comment or encouragement. In Britain: Galya Appleby, Roger Bartlett, Laura Cracknell, Stephanie Dalley, Marina Fennel, Teresa Fitzherbert, Kara and Phillip Hattersley-Cooper; Ro and Michael Giedroyč, Margaret Gordon, John Gurney, Jennifer Griffiths, Professor Edmund Herzig, Sheila Honigsberg, Jill Hughes, Arthur MacGregor, Chris Maton, Alec Rainey, Anne Rosenshield-Paulin, David Sansom, Vanessa Winchester, Tamara Zilber and Professor Andrei Zorin. In Kazan: Alsu Arslanova, Guzel Ibneeva, A. Garzavina, R. Khairutdinov, Natalia Makarova, Leonard Nedashkovsky, R. Salikhov, Sergei Sanachin, Professor Elena Vishlenkova (now in Moscow) and I.K. Zagidulin, and from Astrakhan, Victor Victorin. I am most grateful to Michael Bird for his editorial skills and to the Taylorian Main and Slavonic Libraries, Oxford, for being so generous over illustrations.

Thanks to Oriental Research Partners, Newtonville, MA, for permission to quote from A.L. Fulllerton's 1997 edition of John Cook's *Voyages and Travels* and to Mr Drummond-Moray for permission to quote from GD 24 in the National Archives of Scotland.

i.m. C.B.

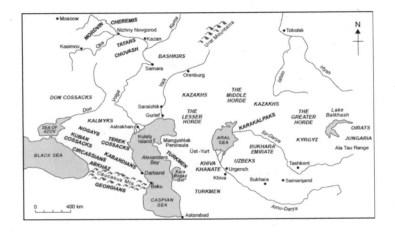

Map 1. Main centres to the south and east of Moscow and distribution of peoples in the eighteenth century

Introduction

The 'large and powerful' Russian Empire 'is inhabited by no less than 16 different nations', states the *Encyclopaedia Britannica* of 1797. After listing the 'nations', or peoples, from Slav to Thoutktchi, the *Britannica* continues: 'Besides these ... there are scattered through the Russian empire vast numbers of Bukharian Tatars, Persians, Georgians, Indians, Greeks, Servians, Albanians, Bulgarians, Moldavians, Valekians, Armenians and Jews.'[1] To western observers, such a variety of peoples contained within one vast empire seemed both bewildering and remote, and to this day remains the domain of specialists.

This anthology of eighteenth-century British travellers focuses on the peoples and places of 'Western' and 'Circassian' 'Tartary', as the central and southern Volga and the north-east Caucasus were known in western geographies, with forays into Azerbaijan (when briefly under Russian rule in the early eighteenth century), Kazakhstan and 'Independent Tartary' (Central Asia).[2] The reasons for this focus are straightforward. First, then as today, the history of the Russian Empire cannot be fully understood without an awareness of its frontier regions and some of the areas that once constituted the lands of the Golden Horde, which were so crucial to Russian expansion.[3] Secondly, the histories with which this book deals are far less well known than nineteenth-century narratives of the 'Conquest of the Caucasus' or the 'Great Game', yet they reveal geopolitical issues that still deeply affect these areas today. Travel writing can only be a partial source for the history of these peoples and places in the eighteenth century; while needing to be evaluated, it nevertheless provides an accessible introduction to them and an important supplement to archival material. Thirdly, the consolidation and expansion of the Russian Empire during the eighteenth century meant greater contact for its different peoples, not only with academicians working for the St Petersburg Academy of Sciences but with other travellers, among whom the British were a significant group. The history of British travellers in eighteenth-century Russia has tended to concentrate on their experiences in 'European' or western Russia,[4] partly because there were far fewer travellers to 'Asian' Russia and events in these areas were considered marginal. Since the break-up of the Soviet Union in 1991, however, the peoples of Russia's frontiers have been the subject of a growing scholarly literature,[5] which this anthology is intended to complement. Finally, an anthology focusing on British travellers offers a cohesive body of work, allowing changes in perception and style to be gauged in relation to a single indigenous writing genre across the century.

1

With the exception of Central Asia, Russia made significant inroads into the regions discussed in this book throughout the eighteenth century. The former khanates of Kazan and Astrakhan (annexed by Russia in the sixteenth century) were still populated by a mixture of indigenous peoples. Kazan province contained sedentary Muslim and Christianised Tatars, including the Chuvash, and animist and Christianised Finnic groups, such as the Mordvins and Cheremis. Nomadic, Buddhist, western Mongol Oirats (known as Kalmyks to the Russians) were found west and east of the Volga in the Caspian steppe. Other Tatar groups, such as the Nogays, inhabited the Astrakhan region and the Caucasus. All these areas experienced upheavals in the eighteenth century, including forced Christianisation, in particular from around 1730 to 1750, and a mass migration of Kalmyks to Dzungaria in 1776, encouraged by China and driven by oppression. Russia erected fortification posts against 'Tartar' incursions, oversaw the settlement of foreign colonies along the Volga and instituted regional reforms, such as increased powers for governors. Tension with Persia led to instability on the west coast of the Caspian and Daghestan.

The southern route to Persia (and ultimately India) via the Volga and the Caspian had been opened up to Muscovy after the conquest of the khanates of Kazan and Astrakhan. The latter also created access to the northeast Caucasus. This was to remain an intractable area for Russian expansion in the eighteenth century, despite the annexation of Crimea in 1783 and the establishment of Russian and European colonies. Russia's advance through Daghestan and its brief occupation of Shirvan and Ghilan in the early eighteenth century, and again later in the century, were even less successful. Russia's encroachment on the Kazakh steppe, originally brought about by expansion into Siberia and by volatile relations with the Lesser and Middle Kazakh hordes, was also pivotal to eighteenth-century imperial interests in the east. The Central Asian regions south-east of the Caspian, known as Independent Tatary, or the Khanates of Khiva and Bukhara (now Turkmenistan and Uzbekhistan), were still free of Russian presence, despite strong Russian (and British) interest, and extremely hazardous for travellers.

During the eighteenth century intense state-sponsored exploration in Russia was carried out by Russian and foreign scientists, under the auspices of St Petersburg Academy of Sciences. These expeditions involved mapping, recording (natural resources, geology, flora and fauna, ancient remains), ethnography and assessing potential for Christianisation and development. They fall into three main phases, the first of which began with expeditions to Siberia and Central Asia under Peter the Great. The second phase is represented by the second Kamchatka expedition of 1733–43, which produced several publications,[6] and the Orenburg expedition of 1734–37. The third phase, under Catherine II, produced the famous expeditions of Ivan Ivanovich Lepekhin to the Urals and western Siberia; Peter Simon Pallas, whose travels took him north of the Caspian to the Urals, the Altai, Lake Baikal and the

Amur; and Johann Gottlieb Georgi and Johann Peter Falk, who travelled
with Pallas. The former had a particular interest in Lake Baikal, the latter
covered the Urals from Orenburg to Ekaterinburg. Samuel Gottlieb Gmelin
travelled in the Caucasus, Persia and the Caspian, and Johann Anton Güldenstädt in the Caucasus and the Caspian.[7] In 1793–94 Pallas travelled to
the Crimea and in the Black Sea region.[8] The later academic scientists' travels
followed set routes and instructions, [9] although systematic questionnaires
had been used earlier under Peter the Great and in the 1730s, notably by
Vasilii Nikitich Tatischev in exploring Siberia and on the Orenburg expedition.[10] The Caucasus and Crimea were also visited late in the century by
travellers, some of whom, such as Jacob Reineggs, Marschall von Bieberstein
and Maria Guthrie, were in Russia for professional reasons, while others,
such as Jean Potocki, were private travellers.

In London in 1780–83 William Tooke, chaplain of the English
Factory at St Petersburg, published his translation of Georgi's *Beschreibung
aller Nationen des Russischen Reichs* ... (St Petersburg 1776-80) as *Russia:
or a Compleat Historical Account of All the Nations which Compose that
Empire....* . The sources Tooke listed in his introduction to the first volume
(on Siberia) demonstrate the type of research possible at the time.[11] In
1799 Tooke published his own *View of the Russian Empire during the Reign
of Catherine 2nd*, which drew on the findings of the various academic expeditions. In a formal, pedagogical manner he brought together much dispa-
rate material for an English reading public.

The British travellers whose accounts compile this anthology followed
no such scholarly agenda. They fall into two main types: those (the
majority) who worked in Russia and travelled in the course of their duties:
the doctors John Bell and John Cook; the merchants Jonas Hanway, John
Elton, Mungo Graeme, Reynold Hogg, Captain Thomas Woodroofe;
the hydraulic engineer John Perry, and the soldier–engineer Peter-Henry
Bruce. They also include John Parkinson, the tutor who accompanied
Edward Wilbraham-Bootle (the future Lord Skelmersdale), for whom
Russia (with Crimea) was part of an extended Grand Tour.[12] An extract
from the orientalist and civil servant George Forster's journey from Bengal
to England via Khorasan has also been included.

These travellers were aware that they were visiting lands that were little
known or, in the case of Central Asia, virtually unknown to western Europeans. In eighteenth-century western Europe the term 'Tartary', probably
a thirteenth-century derivation from the classical 'Tartarus' (Hades), had
lost its medieval mythical aura. This had been replaced by an awareness of
the variety of remote peoples and places, which deserved 'observation'. The
term 'Tartar', rather than the correct *Tatar*,[13] nevertheless continued to be
used. The travellers' observations reflect the norms of eighteenth-century
travel and memoir writing, with the inclusion of ethnographic, scientific, historical and/or antiquarian commentary in narratives profoundly

coloured by contemporary Eurocentric ideas of progress. Yet their observations also reflect their different characters and experiences. They rarely acknowledged sources in their books, although, as demonstrated by Tooke and other scholars, these were potentially plentiful. Bell referred to scientists and academicians simply as 'serious Germans'. They did, however, cite accounts by earlier travellers, such as Anthony Jenkinson of the Muscovy Company, Adam Olearius or Cornelius le Bruyn,[14] as well as borrowing freely from each others'. Hanway, for example, relied on Cook's notes, leaving Cook bitter at what he came to see as plagiarism.

Two further factors coloured travellers' observations: their attitude to Russia, and their awareness of the history of the areas they were traversing. Attitudes in Britain to Russia had been, since the time of Anthony Jenkinson and Giles Fletcher in the sixteenth century, generally ambivalent or negative.[15] The spectacular growth of Russia's empire in the eighteenth century prompted feelings that veered from admiration to alarm. Russia's late rise from 'impenetrable obscurity' and 'barbarism' under Peter the Great and Catherine II was lauded by thinkers for whom progress through stages from 'rudeness' to 'refinement' was the defining achievement of civilised society.[16] This view was counterbalanced by stereotypes found in geographies and travellers' and diplomats' accounts. These often portrayed Russia as a land of despotic and arbitrary rulers, corrupt nobles and governors, and ignorant, brutal and drunken people and clergy,[17] although other stereotypes concerned the fortitude, courage and strength of the Russian people. Negative attitudes towards Russia in general coloured travellers' perceptions of the non-Slavic ethnic communities they encountered. Such perceptions were caught between several tensions: deliberate or inadvertent comparison with Russians; the classification of peoples according to western European ideas of progress; and sympathy for a disappearing way of life.

The travellers knew that the Russian Empire's south-eastern regions had a rich history, including as they did parts of ancient Scythia, Sarmatia, areas colonised by the Greeks or conquered by Alexander the Great, and the lands of the Golden Horde, Timur and their successors. Most British travellers were ill equipped to disentangle fact from legend – they were not orientalists and linguists, and they had no access to indigenous sources – yet they did not view historic remains as mere curiosities. Ancient sites not only symbolised the passing of great conquerors and empires, and the triumph of a threatening new one; they also resonated with eighteenth-century discourses on the origins of civilisation. Scythia (here comprising peoples living at 49° latitude) was for Europeans such as Jean Sylvain Bailly the source of the '*lumières des sciences*' for the rest of the world.[18] Others, such as the orientalist William Jones, dismissed this idea as fanciful, maintaining that all 'Tartary' had been 'unlettered' before the coming of Islam. Jones anticipated that more information on the subject would be provided by Pallas and other 'indefatigable men employed by the Russian court'.[19]

For yet others, notably Scottish jurists, orientalists and social historians of the Enlightenment, the feudal heritage of the supposed Scythian ancestry of northern Europeans (Goth and Gael) was argued to be a better model for liberty than absolute monarchy, which was seen to be tyrannical.[20]

Classical sources had different resonances for Russians and Europeans. For Russians, areas written about by Classical authors, such as the Caucasus, or colonised by the Greeks, such as Crimea, helped to legitimise their territorial claims. For an educated western public brought up on the Classics, Central Asia resonated as much with the conquests of the Persian Empire or Alexander as with the greatness of Samarqand and Bukhara under Timur. For others, however, 'learning in these once flourishing countries' had been brought to decay by the 'Rapines and Oppressions' of the Uzbeks.[21] The theme of decay was thus added to that of past and present conquest, of ancestry, loss of innocence, savagery and of potential for development. The Tartaries visited by European travellers therefore evoked multi-layered responses. For the Russians, on the other hand, the word 'Tartar' was fraught with negative associations, such as the Tartar 'yoke' under the Mongols, which were never completely shaken off.[22]

This anthology spans approximately a hundred years. It introduces the reader to these areas regionally, thematically and chronologically, as well reflecting the travellers' different voices. It has four sections: the Volga region from Kazan to Astrakhan; the Caspian; the north-east Caucasus; and Central Asia. The material for each region is divided, where appropriate, into themes such as 'Towns and Settlements' or 'Peoples and Customs'. In order to contextualise the British travellers' observations, introductions to the anthology sections refer to academicians' and other travellers' works as well as to modern scholarly literature and published archival material. This will enable readers to compare and contrast sources and scholarship. The span of this book has meant that only fundamental works of modern scholarship are referred to. The Conclusion discusses the reliability and contribution to knowledge of the travellers' observations and compares them to the academicians'. It also examines the travellers' attitudes to Russia and assesses the reception of their work in Britain at the time.

Editorial note

The spellings and the capitalisation of the texts have been left as originally printed. Where there might be confusion, the modern spelling has been given in brackets. In some sections, entries have been separated from their original context and grouped together in chronological order for convenience. In other sections, chronological order is still followed but the entries have been left entire. The travellers often measured distances in versts – 1 verst = ¾ English mile. In the anthology sections travellers' notes are placed within parentheses, editor's notes within square brackets.

ENDNOTES

1 *Encyclopaedia Britannica*, vol.16, p.650.

2 *Encyclopaedia Britannica*, vol.18, pp.314ff. 'Eastern Tartary' was Chinese (Manchuria).

3 Kappeler, p.204: 'Russian expansion in Asia was to some extent a continuation of the gathering of the lands of the Golden Horde.' The 'Golden Horde' (sometimes known as the khanate of Qipchaq or the Ulus of Jochi) is the name given to the appanage (provision) of Batu (a son of Jochi, son of Chengiz Khan). It consisted of the western part of the Mongol Empire and was based at Sarai on the Volga. At the height of its powers, this empire extended from Siberia to the Danube, incorporating Kazakhstan, southern Russia, Khorezm, the Caucasus and Ukraine.

4 E.g. Putnam; Cross 1997; Garrad. I intend to address areas not included in this anthology but relevant to the project, such as the traditionally Bashkir southern Urals, Kazakhstan, Crimea and parts of Siberia, in future publications.

5 E.g. Bennigsen-Broxup; Khodarkovsky 1992; Khodarkovsky 2002, pp.394–430; Barrett 1995, pp.578-601; Slezkine 1994; Dunlop; Frank 2001; Kappeler 2002; Werth pp.543-69; Sunderland; Crews; Pollock. See also the following collected papers and colloquia: Kemper, von Kügelgen and Yermakov 1996; Bower and Lazzerini; von Kugelgen, Kemper and Frank 1998; Dudoignon, Is'hakov and Mohammatshin; Dudoignon and Komatsu; Geraci and Khodarkhovsky, eds, 2001; Gammer and Wasserstein; Levi and Sela.

6 E.g. Gmelin 1767; Krasheninnikov.

7 Lepechin; Pallas 1771–76; Pallas 1776, 1801; Georgi, 1775; Georgi 1776–77; Gmelin 1770–84 (vol. 4 ed. P.S. Pallas); Güldenstädt; Falk.

8 Pallas, 1799, 1801; Fr. trans. Leipzig 1799, 1801; Eng. trans. London 1802–03.

9 Tooke 1799, vol.1, p.xvi; see also Slezkine, in Bower and Lazzerini.

10 Tatischev, pp.99–209; Grau, pp.173ff; see also Slezkine 1997.

11 The sources he gives are extensive, including Ebulgazi Bahadur Khan, *(*1729–30), as well as French and British orientalists and most travellers to the region, ranging from the thirteenth-century with John de Plano Carpini to those of the Russian academicians.

12 For example the adventurer John Ledyard (*John Ledyard's Journey through Russian and Siberia 1787–1788*, ed. Watrous 1966); the notorious socialite Lady Elizabeth Craven (*A Journey through the Crimea to Constantinople*, 1789); and the antiquarian E.D. Clarke (*Travels in Various Countries of Europe, Asia and Africa*, 6 vols, London 1816). Maria Guthrie (*A Tour of the Taurida, or the Crimea ...*, London 1802) was the only one to have firm links with Russia, having been acting directress at the Smolnyi Institute and later married to Matthew Guthrie, a Scottish physician, scientist and antiquary working in Russia, who was State Councillor to tsars Paul and Alexander I. Her book was heavily edited by her husband. These later travellers saw Russia at a comparatively safer and more settled time, but all except Ledyard witnessed the great changes in the Crimea after it was annexed.

13 Golden, pp.370–71.

14 E.g. 'The First Voyage made by Anthony Jenkinson ... towards the land of Russia ... The Voyage of Anthony Jenkinson made from Mosco to Boghar in Bactria in the yeare 1558,' in Hakluyt, 1598, and in Purchas, 1625; Olearius, Eng. trans., London 1669; le Bruyn, 1737; *The Compleat Geographer*, 1709, 1723; Derrick, 1762.

15 For example Jenkinson's first trip (1557) and Giles Fletcher's *Treatise*. See Harris,

pp.516, 542–50. For other early travels to Russia, see Harris *passim*.

16   For an introduction, see Berry.

17   E.g. Cross 1997 and 2000 *passim*; Perry 1716; Gordon; MacCartney; Chappe d'Auteroche; Richardson; Sinclair 1787; *Encyclopaedia Britannica* 1797, vol.16, pp.650ff.

18   Bailly, 1777.

19   Jones 1790, pp. 88–114; Ibn Arabshah (1392–1450) wrote a famous life of Timur, first translated into Latin by Golius in 1636, see Pedersen, p.71; Toomer, p.49.

20   E.g. J. Richardson, *A Dissertation on the Languages, Literature and Manners of Eastern Nations*, Oxford 1777–78; Berry; Kidd.

21   Forster, p.91.

22   Ostrovski, *passim*, with bibliography.

Map 2. The Lower Volga region

Part I: The Volga

1 Journeys by River and Land

The river in Russia known as the Volga was considered one of the most 'famous in Europe'. Yet its other names – the Rha of antiquity, the Itil or Etil of the Tatars, and the Rhau of the Mordvins – represented different histories.[1] In their journeys the travellers discovered non-Slavic peoples, such as Tatars, Kalmycks, Mordvins and Bashkirs, who had long considered parts of the river as theirs. The Volga was renowned for its extraordinary length (about 2239 miles, 3582 km) and breath, its numerous turnings and islands, and the proliferation of its tributaries when reaching the vast delta (over 7000 sq. miles, 0000 sq. km) and the Caspian.[2] From its source in the Valdai Hills north-west of Moscow, the river doubles in width after the confluence of the Oka to Kazan, but becomes even mightier after the confluence of the Kama above Samara. In Georgi's day the river's broadest point was considered to be the stretch between Tsaritsyn and Astrakhan.[3] Travellers were often obliged to winter in Kazan, after which they still had a journey of some 970 miles (1552 km) before reaching Astrakhan. Saratov was approximately the voyage's half-way point.

Bell compared the Volga to the Nile because of the fertilising effect of the spring inundations:

> In the spring, when the snow melts, the VOLGA overflows all the low grounds, sometimes to a great distance; the consequence is the same with that produced in EGYPT, by the inundations of the NILE; for the mud, carried down by the stream, fertilizes the country to a great degree; so that on the islands in the VOLGA, some whereof are very large, and overgrown with tall trees, I have found plenty of asparagus.[4]

Most travellers were struck by the 'fruitfulness' of the banks of the upper Middle Volga, sometimes observing their lack of cultivation. The many references to the sight of liquorice growing are due to its high value as a medicinal plant in eighteenth-century Europe. Bruce observed that:

9

Forty wrests [versts] below Czaritza, this great river casts out her second branch, which joins the first, and with it falls into the sea. From hence, on both sides of the Wolga, as far as the sea, grow vast quantities of liquorice of a very large size, its stalk being as thick as a lusty man's arm, and sometimes above four feet high, the seeds lying in cods upon the stalk.[5]

Although in Bruce's opinion, this liquorice was, 'inferior, both in size and sweetness, to that which grows near the river Araxis in Asia'.

Travellers were also struck by the river's diversity of geographic zones, from the dense forests of the north down to Kazan, then forest steppe to Saratov, then steppe to Tsaritsyn, and finally the semi-arid lowlands stretching to Astrakhan. But the Volga, together with the Caspian, was above all famed for its fish. European travellers from the sixteenth century onwards describe the extraordinary varieties of fish to be caught in both summer and winter.[6]

Recording his voyage of May 1715, Bell wrote:

As to fish, no river in the world can afford greater variety, better of their kind, nor in larger quantities.
Here we tasted the sterlett, a fish much and generally esteemed, it is of the sturgeon kind but seldom grows above thirty inches long. It is found in other rivers of RUSSIA; but the VOLGA produces the best and in greatest plenty. The caviare, or spawn, is very good to eat raw, after being cleaned and dressed.[7]

From St Petersburg or Moscow, the most expedient way to travel to Astrakhan, especially if loads were heavy, was by river, embarking at Kazan, Saratov or Tsaritsyn. Those who had read Jenkinson's or Olearius's earlier accounts would have had some inkling of what lay before them. It was only in the brief summer months that large vessels could sail easily, taking advantage of the swollen river to avoid sandbanks, shallows and small islands. Spring floods, caused by melting snow and ice, rose at different times and places, but mostly from late March to the end of June, when the waters subsided rapidly. In the south, when the waters rose from late April to early June, the floods could be apocalyptic: valleys looked like vast oceans and animals were swept away and drowned or swooped upon by birds of prey.[8] Though winter travel was less affected by floods, it was frequently more dangerous, and travellers constrained by officialdom or pressed to link up with other merchants' vessels or caravans had no choice but to attempt it.

The return journey, which circumstances often dictated to be in the autumn, was more arduous still. As Bell recounts, it typically combined river and land travel:

September 7th [1718], leaving ASTRACHAN, we sailed up the VOLGA. Our progress, contrary to the course of the river, was very slow and tedious. In calms the boats were drawn up by men, who went upon the banks; but in hard gales we were obliged to hale them near the side and lye still.
October 12th ... we arrived [at] SARATOFF ... The winter drawing on prevented our farther progress by water. We therefore unloaded, and discharged the boats, being resolved to remain here till the snow fell, when we might proceed by land in sledges.[9]

If the traveller was not forced to winter in disagreeable places, the journey could take three months. Bruce observed how attempts to speed matters up by travelling by sledges on the frozen river could be extremely hazardous:

On the 8th of January [1723] I set out from Astrchan in sledges on the ice, in company with several others ...
On the 11th ... one of our horses dropt through and was drowned ... The next day [14th] it rained, and the ice became so full of rents, that we were often put to shifts to extricate ourselves: two of our sledges and horses fell in, which we saved with great difficulty ... We got to Kamusinka ... on the 22nd; and here getting fresh horses, [we travelled] under constant rain ... we took up our quarters on a woody island ... On the 25th ... we found the ice so full of large rents, that it was impossible for us to proceed farther upon it, and in endeavouring to make the shore, seven of our sledges fell in through the ice, and five of our horses were drowned: the rest we saved with extreme danger to ourselves, as the ice was continually yielding and breaking under us ... our sledges and baggage lay six hours in the water, and must have been lost but for the lucky assistance of a party of men who were passing this way ... about half an hour afterwards, the river broke up with a thundering noise, and nothing but water was to be seen ... By the overturning of my sledge, I lost a whole suit of Tartarian armour, a blunderbuss, a pair of brass barrelled pistols, a silver-hilted sword, a little trunk in which was my pass ... and some money for my travelling charges.[10]

Traffic on the Volga was constant from spring to summer. Great *lotka*s or flat-bottomed barges, manned by crews of up to 200 men, brought meal and other necessities down to Astrakhan, while others loaded with fish, rock salt and caviar made their way in the opposite direction. In summer, silk and other Persian and Indian luxuries were also transported upstream. The Volga was, after all, an ancient trade (and raiding) route, used by Arabs, Khazars, Rus and Vikings. In his attempts at 'procuring a proper vessel to convey my caravan to Astrakhan', Hanway was unimpressed with the quality of the shipping on offer, while also conceding how substantial the trade carried out in these boats was:

> Their [the *lotkas*'] decks are only loose pieces of the bark of trees; they have no knees, and but a few beams: hardly any pitch or tar is used; in place of it are long slips of bark, which they nail over the gaping beams ... The method of keeping them clear of water, is by a large scoop which is suspended by the beam ... Notwithstanding these vessels appeared as so many wrecks, the trade carried on by means of them is very considerable. The ARMENIANS ... load goods on large barks of 2 or 300 tons, at the rate of 50 copeeks [kopecks] per bale.[11]

For the merchant travellers, their amount of goods and their standing with the Russians determined their vessels. These ranged from purpose-built merchant ships, to unspecified 'boats' and leaky craft. Bell's circumstances were easier than the merchants'; his voyage to Persia via Astrakhan was made in a convoy of barques adapted for either sail or oars, large enough to accommodate baggage and carriages. Bruce was protected by sailing in a galley as part of the fleet.

Burlaki, or oarsmen and haulers, were essential for towing vessels upstream.[12] Most were peasants hired cheaply during the winter. Their work was closely linked to trade along the Volga–Astrakhan stretch. Other areas of operation were along the Dnieper and from Moscow to Archangel. As professional boatmen, they managed up to 50 or 60 versts (37.5–45 miles, 60–72 km) per day.[13] Elton and Graeme thought these men were untrustworthy: 'we heard these Fellows, when they have an opportunity, do most of the mischief that is done on the Volga.'[14] Their views, however, do not seem to have been substantiated by other travellers' experiences.

Piracy was a very real threat on the Volga,[15] as were ambushes by Kalmyks. Armed escorts, usually in the form of Cossack guards, were considered essential. Most attacks happened in spring, taking advantage of the floodwaters, and the greatest danger spots were the stretch from Kazan to Tsaritsyn and the mouth of the Caspian. Pirates worked in large groups; when boarding they announced themselves and ordered everyone to lie down and stay still until they had taken what they wanted. En route along the Volga from Saratov to Astrakhan, Graeme and Elton were detained by contrary winds which 'obliged us to go near the entrance of Zolotova Inlet':

> We had scarce opn'd this Inlett, e'er we came on a sudden in sight of at least forty People, who were within pistol shot of us ... and by them was five or six large Boats ... Several such sorts of Alarms we had before we reach'd Astracan, sometimes occasioned by the Russians, sometimes by the

Calmucs ... it was a fortnight e'er we arrived at Astracan, and we were
thoroughly fatigued. For when we were in the Boat, whosoever's Turn it
was to sleep, there was no Room to lye down ... and when at Night we
made fast to the Shore, the Danger of being surpriz'd by Villains gave us
but painful Sleep.[16]

Pirates showed no mercy to any resistance. The *burlaki* were terrified of
them, but the well-armed Armenians had a reputation for fighting back
bravely. Hanway spared no detail in his account of the barbaric punishment meted out to captured pirates:

These robbers appear mostly in the spring, when the banks of the VOLGA
being overflowed, they have a greater field, and can the more easily escape
a pursuit. The soldiers who are occasionally sent after them, are ordered to
take them alive ...

As their cruelties are very great, so is the punishment inflicted on them
when they are taken. A float is built, in size according to the number
of the delinquents, and a gallows erected on it, to contain a sufficient
number of iron hooks, on which they are hung alive by their ribs. The
float is launched into the stream, with labels over their heads signifying
their crimes; and orders are given to all towns and villages on the borders
of the river, upon pain of death, not only to afford no relief to any of these
wretches, but to push off the float, should it land near them. Sometimes
their partners in wickedness meet them, and, if there are any signs of life,
take them down, otherwise they shoot them dead; but if they are catched
in these acts of illegal mercy they are hung up without the ceremony of a
trial, as happened about eight years ago.[17]

Travel by river did not always involve hardship and danger, however. There
were pleasures to be enjoyed along the way too, as Bruce attested in his
description of an encounter near Arbuchim, where he 'overtook three
gallies and one store ship'.

[T]hey had lost three of their anchors, and had three soldiers and one
gunner drowned. Being the senior officer, I took them under my
command, and this meeting made the remainder of the voyage so much
more agreeable, as there were some officers ladies and a band of music on
board the store ship, passing our time with dancing in the evenings, and
with fishing and fowling by day ... and as we had good store of all sorts
of liquors on board our vessels, we passed our time altogether in the store-
ship ... very agreeably.[18]

The steppe route was generally less sensational than the river voyage, but it had a reputation as a desolate place where travellers could lose their way and perish. Lack of habitation, fear of robbers and poorly stocked post houses compounded the travellers' apprehension. Travel on the steppe and by road was cumbersome, involving horses, sledges, covered wagons or *kibitki* and carts, and the land transport of trade goods was burdened with bureaucracy. Hanway described the problems faced by trade caravans:

> The caravans generally set out about 12, both in the night and day, except in the heat of summer … from MOSCO to ZARITZEN, [they travel] only 40 or 50 werst [in 24 hours]: in summer the stages are shorter. Great part of the last mentioned road being through an uninhabited country, makes the carriers cautious not to jade their horses. Every time they set out, the conductor ought to count the loads … It is most eligible to stop in the field, where the usual method is to form the carriages in a ring, and bring the horses as well as the men within it, always observing to keep in such a position as best to prevent an attack, or repulse an enemy. The KHALMUCKS on the banks of the VOLGA are ever ready to embrace an opportunity of plundering and destroying passengers; therefore when there is any occasion to travel on those banks … an advanced guard of at least four COSSACKS is of great use; especially to patrol at night …[19]
> A hundred carriages take up two thirds of a mile in length, so that when no horseman is at hand to spread the alarm, the rear might be easily carried off. They have not even a trumpet, horn … for this purpose; they trust in providence …[20]

Parkinson, on the other hand, travelled for most of his leisurely journey in a *kibitka* with the benefit of court patronage and experienced none of the merchants' problems, although some of their discomforts.

Observation of the life of the Volga was de rigueur for western travellers writing on Russia, whose accounts are thus frequently repetitive.[21] It also occasionally featured in scientific papers of the Royal Society.[22] Eighteenth-century academicians, geographers and naval officers of various nationalities in Russia had the more rigorous task of assessing, mapping and exploring the river.[23] The hydraulic engineer John Perry, who made the first known scientific measurements of the river, falls into this category. A mathematical knowledge of the flow of the lower course of the river was essential to his work. His further speculations as to what happens to the waters as they flow into the Caspian, as well as on the climate of northern Russia, were presented with professional thoroughness and with a Royal Society audience in mind:[24]

About 3 Miles below the Town of Camishinka, in a narrow Place where the Stream runs free without any Eddy ... Firstly ... I reckon'd the Course of the Stream to be about 23 Fathom, or 138 English Feet in a Minute. Secondly, I sounded the River quite cross from Side to Side, and the mean Depth, reckoning one place with another, I computed to be at least 17 Foot. Thirdly, the Breath of the River, which I took by making an Observation with a Theodolet [theodolite], I computed to be 5860 Foot (Fractions not regarded;) and multiplying these 3 Sums, the Course of the Stream, with the Depth and Breadth of the River by each other, gives 13747560, the Number of cubical Feet that runs down the Wolga in the said time, and divide the said Sum total by 36, which is the Number of cubical Feet contained in a Tun of fresh Water, and the Quotient will be 381876 Tons of Water that runs down the River Wolga in one Minute of Time.[25]

Perry's observations on the uninhabited banks of the Volga, echoed by Bell, are symptomatic of contemporary Eurocentric views on progress. It was, wrote Perry, 'a thousand times to be lamented, that so rich and noble a Countrey, situated on the Side of the great River Wolga ... should now lye in a manner waste without Inhabitants, whilst the Samoiedes ... pass their Days in Misery; and even many of the Northern Russes I have seen for want of Sun to ripen their Harvest, mingle Roots of Grass and Straw with their Corn to make Bread.'[26] In later eighteenth-century Britain such ideas became formalised into social theory.[27] Russian settlement policies in these areas were also part of its drive to develop the empire; their results were witnessed by later British travellers.

A comparatively light-hearted engagement with the Royal Society is evinced by Cook's account of the search for the legendary zoophyte (half-animal, half-plant) called 'baronetze' near Astrakhan, a creature that had intrigued the 'curious' of Europe since the seventeenth century:[28]

All the world has heard of the wonderful baronetze [borometz]. Philosophers and naturalists were divided in opinion about it, they could not adjudge it to be an animal, nor properly a vagetable. It was said that the baronetze grew in the kingdom of Astrachan, upon a stalk of two foot high, from the top of which grew a lamb-like fruit, covered with a fine fur every way resembling a young lamb! Who are ignorant that the Armenian or other merchants sold one to the late king of Prussia, which he as a very great curiosity, made a present of it to the Royal Society, who suspecting a fraud ... obtained leave from the king to dissect it: within the skin, they discovered saw-dust or some other materials with which it was stuffed, and the navel pierced with a stick, which was so fixed, as to appearance, looked like a stalk ... [We] made search, we also asked all the different Tartars who inhabit the desarts of Astrachan, and were ridiculed and laughed at,

15

as we very well deserved, these people justly wondering that men who were said to be very learned, could ... be so easily imposed upon; and from this inferring, how properly I shall not say, that much of our learning was certainly chimerical.[29]

The travellers' conclusions, spurred by the mocking Tatars, enabled them to poke fun at 'serious Germans' who persisted in the hunt.[30] Serious scientific discoveries nevertheless continued to be made. In his account of a late eighteenth-century information-gathering tour of Russia's southern provinces, Parkinson introduced one of the most prominent academicians in Russia, the German botanist and zoologist Peter Simon Pallas:

Dr Pallas called upon us in his Droosky [*droshky* or carriage] and conducted [us] to the top of the hills at the back of this plain where he showed [us] a quantity of concretions on the edge of these heights which have evidently been cast up by the waves of the sea, when the desert made part of the Caspian. He had dug here himself for the purpose of making this experiment ... We coasted the brow of the hills a considerable way enjoying a fine view of the serpentine Wolga, of the wooded plain on the other side of it, and of the desert beyond, not to mention the plain below us, the town of Sarrepta, the Calmuc Tents, Zarizin, and on the right the Sarpa with the Desert at the back of that river.[31]

The *Encyclopaedia Britannica* of 1797, aware of the academicians' work, noted that concretions and shells, such as those found near Sarepta, demonstrated that the Caspian and the Black Sea had once been joined.[32]

ENDNOTES

1   See Bell; also Hanway, vol.1, pp.140–41; Tooke 1799, vol.1, pp.272–73; Spuler 1978, p. 280–81. Carpini was the first European to use the name Volga for the river in his thirteenth-century account: Rockhill, p.8 n.2.

2   E.g. Georgi 1780–83, vol.4, pp.384–424.

3   Ibid., p.386.

4   Bell, p.21.

5   Bruce, p.244.

6   Postnikov in Speake ed. 2003, pp.1250–54. Bruce and Cook mention some simpler local fishing methods: in summer with ropes and nets from the shore, in winter with nets through poles and a net lowered through the ice (Bruce, pp.235–37; Cook, vol.1, p.276); academicians such as Gmelin (1770–74, vol.2) and Georgi (see n.2 above) explained the various traps used. See also Tooke 1799, vol. 3, pp.153ff.

7   Bell, p.10.

8   Georgi 1780–83, vol.4, pp.390–92.

9   Bell, pp.154–55.

10 Bruce, pp.337-340.

11 Hanway, vol.1, p.103.

12 Also Cook, vol.1, pp.290–91; Hanway, vol.1, p.139.

13 Cook, vol.1, p.290.

14 Spilman, p.6.

15 Also Cook, vol.1, pp.291–95; Woodroofe in Hanway, vol.1, p.147.

16 Spilman, pp.5–6.

17 Hanway, vol.1, pp.105–6.

18 Bruce, p.235.

19 Hanway, vol.1, p.89.

20 Hanway, vol.1, p.89.

21 E.g. Cook, vol.1, pp.282–86; Hanway, vol.1, pp.140–41; Tooke, vol.1, p.274.

22 For example, entries no.33 by J. R. Forster in *Philosophical Transactions*, vols 57 and 58 (1768, 1769).

23 Postnikov ed. Speake 2003, pp 1251–52; see also Tardy; Goldenberg and Postnikov, *passim*. Such work had begun in Russia in the seventeenth century, Postnikov ed. Speake 2003, p.1251.

24 Perry 1716, pp.70–74, 100–3, 105–35.

25 Perry 1716, p.101.

26 Perry 1716, p.93.

27 e.g. Berry 1997.

28 Appleby 1997, pp.23–34.

29 Cook, vol.1, p.266–67.

30 Bell, p.43.

31 Parkinson, p.146.

32 *Encyclopaedia Britannica* 1797, vol.4, p.225.

Introduction

Two towns, Kazan and Astrakhan, and one foreign settlement, Sarepta, stand out among the centres described by the travellers in their voyages down the Volga. To their observations have been added, when relevant, accounts by the geographer Ivan Kirilov; the administrator and Corresponding Member of the Academy Piotr Ivanovich Rychkov; the academicians Gmelin, Falk, Georgi and Pallas; and the chaplain to the British Factory in St. Petersburg, William Tooke.

Kazan

Kazan had always been symbolically, strategically and economically important for Russians, and its *guberniia* (province) was vast.[1] It included the Volga region south of Nizhny Novgorod, the western Urals, including Ufa, up to Bashkir lands.[2] The early travellers found Kazan impressive as a trading and manufacturing centre and shipyard. In the late eighteenth century, following Catherine II's visit in May–June 1767,[3] it became a showpiece. Besides its famous 'Russia' and 'Maroqin' leathers, Kazan's industries were textiles and soap-making, flax-growing, saltpetre extraction, and the production of hazelnut oil, wax and honey.[4] The shipyard was established on the Casanka west of the citadel under Peter the Great in 1718, to take advantage of the area's ample oak forests and its strategic position on the route south down the Volga to the Caspian. In the 1720s Kazan had its own admiralty school.[5]

Stranded in Kazan waiting for the Volga to thaw in 1715, Bell enjoyed the company of Swedish officers captured at Poltava.[6] Captain Woodroofe reported that ships were built in Kazan for use on the Caspian against the perceived threat from Nadir Shah of Persia (1736–47). As a British captain, he noted the difficulties of working in Kazan's shipyard (Kirilov listed a meagre thirty-nine 'professionals' there, such as carpenters, caulkers etc.).[7] His entry also highlights an important period in Anglo-Russian trade relations. The British signed a treaty of commerce with Russia in 1734, and in 1741 the British Russia (Muscovy) Company obtained permission to build two ships, to be manned half by Britons, half by Russians, for 'the navigation of the Caspian'. The latter was chiefly due to the efforts of John Elton, who had gained Persian agreement for the Russia Company to trade with Resht. One ship (*Empress of Russia*) was built and duly sailed to Astrakhan under the command of Captain Woodroofe, but then the enterprise was scuppered when Elton agreed to work for Nader Shah as chief ship-builder for a Caspian fleet. This antagonised both the Russians and the British, who foresaw damage to the Russia Company. Trade relations between Russia and Britain were duly suspended by Empress Elizabeth in 1746.[8]

Kazan had three distinct areas:[9] the Kremlin, with adjacent markets, shops and taverns; areas south of the Kremlin towards Lake Kaban, with administrative buildings, churches, seminaries, a cathedral and a gymnasium;[10] and, beyond the old city walls around Lake Kaban, Tatar suburbs west of the lake and factories on either side. In the eighteenth century the city evolved rapidly.

The French traveller and scientist Chappe d'Auteroche, who visited Tobolsk in Siberia to observe the transit of Venus in 1761 and subsequently wrote a controversial, negative memoir about Russia, praised Kazan for its well-built wooden houses and 'society' living.[11] Major buildings were two-storey, either in the Baroque or (in the second half of the century) the Neo-Classical style, distinguished by local 'Tatar' touches, such as floral and vegetal decoration.[12] There had always been an emphasis on church and monastic building here; by the late 1760s Kazan had one hundred and two churches, a cathedral, eight men's monasteries and three nunneries.[13] The town (without the Tatar suburbs, see pp.54–55) consisted of some 3069 households and more than 800 merchants.[14] In the 1770s, after the Pugachev uprising of 1773–5,[15] much of the city was rebuilt in brick, and regular blocks of buildings intersected by straight roads replaced the old rambling roads and alleys. By the end of the century its population was about 22,000 Russians (with Europeans), including, according to Parkinson, 3–4000 Tatars,[16] with other minorities such as Chuvash, Cheremis and Mordvin peasants and workers. Being a trade centre it also had a transient population of Persians, Kirghiz, Kalmyks and presumably Armenians.[17]

The conquest of the Kazan khanate by Ivan IV was noted by earlier travellers, but Parkinson made no mention of its earlier history, as if the city's 'Russianness' were now sealed and its former Tatar identity reduced to a curiosity.

Bell's visit in November 1715

CAZAN is about seven hundred and thirty five versts to the north of the VOLGA, on a high bank of the rivulet CAZANKA, which is navigable from this place to the river. The town is strong by situation, and defended by a castle, fortified with walls of brick. Within the citadel are the cathedral church, the palaces of the archbishop and governor, and the apartments for the courts of justice. The town is fenced with a ditch and palisades. The suburbs are inhabited chiefly by mechanics, except a street or two possessed by MAHOMETAN TARTARS, the posterity of the ancient natives.

The country adjacent is very pleasant and fertile; producing wheat, rye, barley, oats and several kinds of pulse. The woods to the south and west consist of stately oaks, sufficient to supply all the navies in the world; and from hence to St PETERSBURG is abundantly furnished with timber, for all the purposes of ship-building, by an easy conveyance, all the way by water. The woods to the north and east, which are of prodigious extent, consist of trees of all sorts.

...

There is a considerable manufactory of RUSSIA leather; the hides here reckoned the best in the empire. Great quantities of this leather are exported to LEGHORN, and other parts of EUROPE, and may be considered among the staple commodities of this country. The strong smell of this leather is acquired in the dressing; for instead of oil, common in other places, they use a kind of tar, extracted by fire from the bark of the birch-tree; which ingredient the RUSSES call deuggit, and which tree is here in greater abundance than in other parts of the world; and then they dye them with logwood.

...

We found two SWEDISH generals, HAMILTON and ROSEN, and many other officers of distinction, taken prisoners at POLTAVA, who were no farther confined than by having a soldier of the garrison to attend them at their lodgings; and by generosity of the governor, lived as easily as circumstances would allow. These gentlemen were invited to all public diversions; and by their polite and agreeable behaviour, contributed not a little to our passing the winter with a good deal of pleasure, in such a remote part of the world.

Upon the banks of the CAZANKA stands a monastery [Zilantov], very pleasantly situated. I accompanied our interpreter to visit the abbot, who received us in a very friendly manner. He would not however give the interpreter his blessing, nor admit him into the church, during divine service, unless he pulled off his wig. He, professing the communion of the GREEK church, expostulated a little with the priest, telling him that learned bishops made no such scruples. The abbot replied, that it was contrary to the rules of discipline, to allow any man to enter the church with his head covered.[18]

...

I think the cold here is more intense than at St Petersburg, though it is five or six degrees farther south, in going about three miles from town, in a clear day, I had my face, fingers and toes frozen, notwithstanding I was not half an hour on the road. I applied the common cure, that is, rubbing the number parts with snow, which I found perfectly effectual.[19]

(Bell, November 1715)

Captain Woodroofe takes stock of Kazan's shipyards

[January 1741] We arrived at CASAN, having been 58 days in travelling 1300 wersts, occasioned by the badness of the roads. Captain ELTON was already arrived at this place. Here is a considerable admiralty yard: they had then on the stocks five fly-boats of about 250 tons, five smacks of 180 tons, and five small damscoots of about 25 tons, which were to be launched the ensuing spring, and might be ready in case of any necessity to employ them on the Caspian. The master builder having already received orders to build a ship for the ENGLISH merchants, had therefore dispatched people into the woods to cut timber

...

The timber used for the RUSSIAN navy is cut down in the neighbourhood of this city; it is of excellent quality, but they do not distinguish sufficiently the trees which are on the decay: they also cut the timber at the leaf as well as at the fall, and often suffer it to lay too long on the ground. They are generally two summers in conveying it to St PETERSBURG, which is done in low flat bottomed vessels, taking the advantage of the rising of the river to go up to TWERE, and from thence into the canal by the LADOGA lake

...

[April 1742] As a compliment to Mr Elton we laid the ship's keel, which was 65 feet in length, and fixed the stem and stern posts ... He left the sole care of building the ship to me, but I had neither boat-builder, rigger or sail-maker. May 30th, the ship was launched, though her upper works were yet unfinished; for the waters fell away so fast that we were afraid of being aground ... [we transported her] three miles into the great Volga down a small river, upon which the admiralty yard stands.[20]

This is the greatest magazine in Russia, except MOSCO and St PETERSBURG for all kinds of merchandize. It is advantageously situated for the commerce to the south east parts, even to CHINA; the province itself reaching quite to SIBERIA ... Here are markets for horses, sheep, and all other kinds of cattle: provisions in general are very cheap, and great quantities are sent down to ASTRAKHAN, and to all the towns and settlement on the VOLGA.[21]

(Captain Woodroofe in Hanway, 1741–1742)

Sightseeing in the governor's carriage

Casan, what we have seen of it yet, appears handsomely and regularly built of stuccoed white. This was owing to the destruction of it by Pugatcheff. I enquired the number of inhabitants and was told they amounted to twenty-two thousand, of whom the Tatars composed between three or four.

The Governor [Prince S.M. Baratiev][22] as he had promised to do the evening before, sent us his carriage to carry us about the Town for the purpose of seeing its curiosities. An officer, whom we had met at his house the preceding evening accompanied us. We went first to the General Governor's [M.L. Golenischev-Kutuzov][23] house in the castle ... Being the Governor's carriage we were taken for him, the guard turned out everywhere and we were received with the greatest possible distinction. We were taken afterwards to see a hospital for old people, which certainly was not worth seeing; then the suburb inhabited by the Tartars.[24]

(Parkinson, March 1793)

Between Kazan and Astrakhan

The towns between Kazan and Astrakhan were seen by the travellers as little more than fortified garrisons where fresh transport and provisions could be obtained. Bell remarked on the fertility of the land below Samara, and lamented, in true Eurocentric style, its lack of cultivation. This problem was to be addressed by settlement, notably by foreigners (especially Germans), along the Volga during the century. The scale of Peter the Great's trading and shipping ambitions is shown by the attempt to build a canal from the Don to the Volga at Kamusinski. As a soldier, Bruce focused on towns' defences and garrisons. Cook mentioned the Tsaritsyn line of forts built between 1694 and 1718 to defend Russia's southern frontier and check nomadic raids.[25] The threat to the towns of the middle and lower Volga was not only attack by Kalmyks or 'Tatars'; a sense of vulnerability can be felt in references to destruction by fire, to rebellions, such as Pugachev's, and robbers.

Pallas's and Georgi's accounts show the development of these garrison towns. They had mixed populations, including Russians, Cossacks, Tatars, Kalmyks (Christianised or not[26]) and Europeans. Samara and Saratov developed through trade and river traffic in fish, melons, mutton and skins supplied by the Kalmyks and Kirghiz.[27] In winter Samara was the main rendezvous of Tatars from Kasimov trading in skins, which were made into coats and capes.[28] In spring a bridge was thrown over the River Samara to facilitate the movements of caravans towards the River Yaik (Ural).[29] 'Manufactures', such as soap or leather products, which were seen by eighteenth-century observers as a mark of enlightened development, were still only small-scale in these regions in the early eighteenth century. By the 1770s Saratov was increasingly built of stone; its prosperity grew with the settlement of some 300 German Lutherans below the town from 1764 onwards.[30] Pallas described a rich town.[31]

Tsaritsyn (Volgograd) remained essentially a fortress town. In the early 1770s the interior of the fortress was still badly built, with few good houses and only the churches built of stone.[32] Its trade with the 'Kalmyk horde', however, was thriving.[33] The town was almost destitute of good artisans, lamented Georgi, which proved to be an advantage to the neighbouring colony of Sarepta.[34]

Sarepta was founded as a colony in 1765 by members of the Renewed Moravian Church from Herrnhut in Saxony. The settlement of colonies of foreigners in order to populate and bring technical skills became Russian state strategy under Catherine. It followed in the wake of Russian, Cossack and Kalmyck settlers down the Volga from the reign of Peter the Great onwards.[35] Sarepta was portrayed by Parkinson as a beacon of orderly, industrious civilisation. A map in Gmelin[36] shows the almost military layout of its buildings and kitchen gardens within a fortified rampart (fig.1).

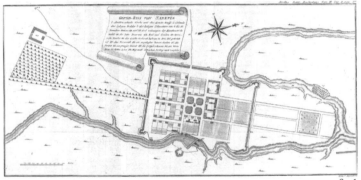

fig.1

Due to its situation near the Sarpa, and some difficult escarpments, Sarepta was stronger than many steppe towns, although it did not escape plunder and destruction by 'rebels from the Yaik' during the Pugachev uprising in 1774.[37] The colony's industries included weaving, tobacco and soap making and brandy distillation. The community was closely regulated in all matters from finance to religious observance. It had received a loan of 40,000 roubles from the government, to be repaid in thirty years, otherwise it benefited from very light taxation.[38] By the time Parkinson and Pallas visited, Sarepta was considered a symbol of a successful colony, which had flourished where others had failed.[39] Pallas also mentioned Russian and partial Tatar colonies established in 'the desert of Astrakhan' on the banks of the Volga or the Sarpa, specifically to develop silk production. These were unsuccessful – mostly, Pallas argued, because of Russian resistance to working with silkworms.[40]

Samara and environs

The 20th [June 1716] we arrived at the town of SAMARA, situated to the left, in a fine plain. The place is but small, and fortified only with ditches and palisades, with wooden towers at proper distances, mounted with cannon, sufficient to defend it against the incursions of the TARTARS, called KARAKALPACKS, or BLACK CAPS, who inhabit the desert to the eastward of this place ...

The 21st, having provided fresh hands for the navigation of our barques, we departed from SAMARA; and the weather being calm rowed down the river, which is here very broad. The western bank is very high, but the eastern quite flat. The fields on both sides are very fruitful; but especially to the west, where the grass grows very high, intermixed with sage, thyme and other herbs; there are also some woods of oaks. A few hundred acres of such land would be of great value in England, tho' here it is waste and uncultivated.[41]

(Bell, June 1716)

Fortifications and fine dining at Saratov

We came on the 25th [July 1716] to the ISMEYOVI-GORY, or SERPENT-HILLS, so called from the windings of the river at this place; and after passing several towns, and many villages, we landed at SARATOF, a large town on the same side, about eight hundred and fifty wrests from CAZAN. It is but slightly fortified with a ditch, wooden walls, and towers mounted with cannon, and defended by a garrison of regular troops and Cossacks.

We dined the next day with the governor,[42] who entertained us with great variety of provisions, particularly fish and very fine mutton.[43]

(Bell, July 1716)

Saratov and the Kalmyk threat

The city of Saratof is situated on a very fair large plain, about four wrests from the main river, on a branch of the Wolga; it is inhabited, or rather garrisoned, by a great number of Russian soldiers and Cossacks, who are put here as a guard against the incursions of the Kalmuck Tartars, inhabiting, a vast territory lying between the Wolga and the river Jaick, towards the Caspian sea, and possess the left side of the Wolga from hence near to Astrakhan ...[44]

(Bruce, June 1722)

A canal project near Kamusinski ...

I was sent directly to Mosco, with orders for my being immediately dispatch'd from then into the province of Astracan ... to survey a Work, which his Czarish Majesty had before design'd, and another person been employed for the ... Communication Ships of War, as well as trading Vessels of Burden, to pass between the Caspian and the Black Sea, by way of the said two great rivers, the Wolga and the Don ... The Distance of which Communication between the said two Great rivers is about 140 Russ miles by way of other two small Rivers, the one called the Lavla, which falls into the Don; the other the Camishinka; upon these small River Sluices were to be placed to make them navigable, and a Canal of near 4 Russ Miles to be cut through the dry Land where the said two small rivers come nearest together; which work, if finished, would be of very great advantage to the Czar's Countrey ...

The said Work was first begun by one Colonel Breckell a German, who was a Colonel in the Czar's army ... but he had very little understanding of this business ... and made his escape out of the country ...

I went and surveyed [the Work] ... I shew'd [His Majesty] the Reasons why the said Work ... was not properly design'd ... His Majesty was pleased to order me to take it upon me, and to begin the canal in a new place, that I proposed as more practicable ...

Upon which work I was employed three Summers successively, having demanded 30000 Men for it, but never had half that number, and the last Year not 10000 Men given me, not the necessary Artificers and Materials that were wanting ...

In the latter end of 1701, I received orders to let that work stand still for a while ... (there being several Sluices near finish'd, and the Canal half dug) ... I was sent to do another work at Veronize ...[45]

(Perry, 1698–1701)

... is finally abandoned

Kamusinski ... is a well fortified town, situate on the river Kamus, and has a numerous garrison of soldiers and Cossacks. A canal was begun here to make to make a communication between the rivers Wolga and Don, or Tanais, and after being greatly advanced, was at last found impracticable by the vast quantity of hard rock lying in the way, which could only be removed by blowing at such an immense expense of time and treasure that the attempt was dropt.[46]

(Bruce, July 1722)

Tsaritsyn, a garrison town

Czaritza ... is fortified with several bastions and towers, but all of wood, and inhabited only by soldiers and Cossacks ... All about here, even as far as Astrakhan, the island of Zerpinsko excepted, which being twelve wersts long, supports the cattle belonging to the garrison, the soil is so very barren, that it affords no manner of corn: this defect, however, is easily supplied by the help of the river, the fertile land of Casan furnishing those parts, and even the city of Astrakhan, with wheat and rye, at a very moderate price. Forty wrests below Czaritza, this great river casts out her second branch, which joins the first, and with it falls into the sea.[47]

(Bruce, July 1722)

The Tsaritsyn line

We at last arrived on the west end of this much famed line, which runs betwixt the rivers Don and Volga, a work of the great Peter's, fit only for such a prince to have made. It is a ditch and rampart reaching the whole length of 60 versts; the ditch is 20 yards broad, well formed, and proportionately deep. The rampart is very high, and the south side, towards the Kalmucks ... country, or the desert of Astrakhan, is planted with high and strong pallisadoes made of fir trees, drove into the ground, and fastened together with cross beams, so close that a man cannot get thro' anywhere, except I think, at two places, through which brooks of water run, and these are fortified as far as art hath hitherto been able.

There are four strong forts built upon this line at equal distances, well stored with canon, and betwixt the forts are many houses, where only soldiers live ...

The name of the forts from the west to the east, are called in the same order, viz. Donskaya, Osokor, Graczi, Meczotnaya, and Tsaritzin ...

The design of building this line, is to restrain the incursions of the Kalmucks into the Empire of Russia, and, although it has the effect of curbing great bodies, yet small parties have made their way thro' where the brooks run, and done considerable damage ...

The city of Tsaritzin is neat and compact, the streets well laid out, but the houses are all of timber; it is surrounded with a very deep dry ditch and high ramparts with bastions, well stored with great cannon.[48]

(Cook, February 1740)

October in Tsaritsyn

The sun was yet warm, and the weather delightful. On the plains, near ZARITZEN, they feed dromedaries, which are not unlike camels.

Zaritzen is situated in the latitude of 47 (and a half), at the distance of 1042 wersts from MOSCO, on a high bank of the VOLGA, of which it commands a delightful prospect. The buildings are mean, nor are there many inhabitants: the place is defended by a deep ditch, a rampart garnished with artillery, and a garrison of 3000 men.[49]

(Hanway, October 1743)

Sarepta

Parkinson in Sarepta, June 1793

Before our breakfast was over the Master of the Police called upon us to accompany us to the house where the Sisters or unmarried women live altogether. They were at different kinds of work in separate rooms and in small parties: some spinning, others sowing, some embroidering, others weaving. The Children divided into two classes were with their respective School Mistresses. The whole number including the children is about seventy and without them fifty. The children sleep at home.

Besides the rooms where they work [we] went into their chapel, their eating room, their bedroom, the Bakehouse and the kitchen, in every one of which we were struck with their great neatness and comfort. [In the chapel] they have prayers every evening at seven, and at nine the Children go to prayers in the Church. They breakfast at six, dine at eleven, sup at six, go to bed at ten, rise at five. The garden is managed by two of the Sisters. Here the little society walk, breakfast and drink their coffee. We sat for a considerable time in one of the arbours with our obliging conductors. There were a great many Water Melons coming up; to which, as well as to fruit in general, the gentle rains with which they have been blessed are likely to be very favourable.

We went from the Sisters' house to the Shop, which contains articles of every kind and particularly a great many from England. The profits belong to the Society.

The next thing we saw was the Brothers' house, where we found them divided into a number of little parties according to their respective trades, for instance of Shoemakers, Weavers, Taylors, joiners etc. These little [parties] dine as the whole society does in the Hall or Eating room; but they breakfast and drink their coffee in their own apartment. They received us everywhere with great civility and a sort of unaffected politeness which was very pleasing and which reminded me of the manners of the people at Chaux de fonds and Locle. It was curious to recognize among the Taylors and the Shoemakers, for instance, several of the faces which we had seen at the concert on Sunday evening. The whole Number including the Children may be a hundred and without them eighty.

18 June I think Dr Pallas told us this evening that [the] original design of establishing the Society was the Conversion of the Calmucs. The May[or] was employed as a Missionary and lived with them two years, at the end of which time it was found that the Scheme was not practicable.

On our return it being nine o'clock, their hour of Prayers, we stepped into the Church. The Service consisted of a hymn accompanied by an Organ, in which the whole congregation joined and which lasted about quarter of an hour.

Mad^e Pallas observed to-day that the People of Sarrepta when treated civilly will do anything to serve you; but when treated otherwise will do nothing in the world.

19 June Their water at Sarrepta comes from the hills two miles off and is conveyed to no less than twenty Wells; the most delicious water imaginable. The Square in the middle of Sarrepta is composed on the North side of the Brothers' house, the Church and the Sisters' house, on the South by the Inn and the shop; on the East by the Widows' house and the Candle Manufactory, and on the West by the Comptoir and the ----. A single row of Poplar trees and Aspern are planted near the buildings all round; and there is an enclosure planted with trees of the same kind, but not kept in very nice order.

The Germans came into the country 29,000 men and now the number is increased to 32,000. The Kirghese and Pugatcheff destroyed and carried off about 2,000.

...

We ... walked in the afternoon to Dr Sedler's [50] Garden. As well as several others it is situated on the Sarpa. He has planted a good many trees and Vines enough to furnish last year two hundred Eimer[51] of wine; each of which contains sixteen bottles. We drank tea at Dr Pallas's and accompanied him and Madame Pallas in the evening to the Mineral waters, eight versts off on the way to Zarizin. The building consists of a long covered walk which leads to the wells of the Baths and [a] few cottages besides. If the Colony could have obtained a grant on the spot, they would have put themselves to some expense to prepare it for the reception of company. But ... they have not been able to obtain a grant. There has however now and then been a considerable concourse of strangers who are obliged to live in tents. The waters have a brakish taste ...

22 June There were twenty-eight degrees of heat in the course of this day...I don't know whether it was because the next day was Sunday; but the Town today was crowded with Calmucs, who on account of the heat wore their upper garments turned down and had nothing on their body but their shirt.[52]

(Parkinson, 1793)

Chorny Yar and environs

[W]e arrived before Zornayar, seated on the right side of the river, on a high shore, near a vast plain, without trees or eminences; the form of the place is square, fortified with wooden towers and ramparts, and garrisoned with soldiers and Cossacks, all horsemen. A few wersts below is a third branch of the Wolga, called Buchwostowa, which falls into the two preceeding; and at twenty wrests down she sends out her fourth branch called Donitoska, which does not mingle with the other three, but flows by a particular channel into the Caspian sea. In passing this last shore, we frequently visited the Kalmucks in their kibbits or tents, which we always found pitched on the most delightful places I ever saw ...[53]

(Bruce, July 1722)

A stopover at Chorny Yar

Finding our convoy did not keep up with us, we stopped at CHERNO-YARE. This is the first town from ZARITZEN, at the distance of 200 wersts, generally called midway to ASTRAKHAN. It is defended by a ditch, with some canon and cheveaux de frize. They trade with the KHALMUCKS, KOOBANS and other TARTARS, in a quarter distinct from town.[54]

(Hanway, October 1743)

Parkinson visits Chorny Yar

The banks of the Wolga are lofty and steep where Czernoyar is situated, which causes the town, the buildings whereof, except the churches, are all of wood, to look handsome as one approaches. It being a holiday the People were all in their best cloaths and I could [not] help comparing the goodness and neatness of their cloaths with the rags and tatters of the populace in Italy. While we were waiting for horses, it seemed to be the appointed time for all the young Girls in the place to fetch water from the Wolga. As they were in their national dress and very neat it was a very agreeable and picturesque sight.[55]

(Parkinson, June 1793)

Enatavski Krepost

On the 26th [September 1744], we arrived at the fortification called ENA-TAFSKI KREPOST, 120 wersts from ASTRAKHAN: here is a village in which two regiments of infantry, and one of dragoons were quartered. The fortification consists of a deep ditch, focused with a breastwork, and well provided with artillery. Though this settlement had been made only the summer before, yet it was well supplied with the necessaries of life, and from its situation promised great improvement. It stands on an eminence, about half a werst from the VOLGA, a small branch of which runs into the valley just below it, and forms a peninsula; the adjacent country is well wooded, and the soil rich. These settlements are of great advantage to the RUSSIAN empire, for at the same time as they awe the TARTARS, and prevent their incursions, they open a trade with them for sheep and horses; and in some places for richer commodities.[56]

(Hanway, September 1744)

Astrakhan

Astrakhan emerges from travellers' accounts as a difficult, ramshackle town. Visiting in spring 1739, Elton and Graeme reported, 'Before we had seen Astrakhan we were very much prejudiced in its Favour, and concluded from its Situation (so commodiously, as we imagined) it must be very beautiful, etc., but we did not find it so.'[57] The town was a major port, trading centre (see Part II) and garrison, and a melting pot of nationalities, including Cossacks, Russians, Europeans, Tatar groups, Kalmyks, Armenians, Georgians, Indians and Persians. It had suffered from plague, fire, occupation and rebellion, and was almost permanently on alert because of its proximity to Persia and Ottoman interests in the Caucasus. In the 1770s its vast province stretched south from below the Terek and west to encompass the Kuban steppe; to the east it looped around Saratov, followed the Volga to Samara and almost joined the River Yaik (Ural).[58] In Cook's day the inhabitants had no idea of the extent of the 'kingdom' to the east.[59] Bruce, following Olearius,[60] named the eastern Volga as the dividing line between Russia and Asia. Other rivers, such as the Don, Kama and Ob, had in the sixteenth and seventeenth centuries been mooted as boundaries. In the eighteenth century the officer Phillip Johann von Strahlenberg and the historian, ethnographer and governor V.N. Tatishchev identified the Urals as the natural boundary between Russia and Asia.[61]

Astrakhan's climate was extreme. It was plagued by insects, and dogs apparently roamed the streets feeding on unburied corpses. But it was also famous for its vineyards and gardens, fisheries, salt-works,[62] saltpetre mines,[63] distilleries[64] and wildlife. In such travellers' descriptions there is much repetition, although opinions occasionally differed, as, for example, on the quality of the wine. Cook worked in Astrakhan as a chief naval surgeon in the 1740s; his descriptions are the most thorough. Hanway visited on his way to and return from Persia, during the 'Elton affair', and suffered as a result at the hands of governor, Tatishchev. This governor had an eventful career before coming to Astrakhan. Under Peter the Great, he had travelled to Germany and Sweden. He had been involved in the iron industry of Perm and Siberia, had founded Ekaterinburg, quelled the Bashkirs and was now responsible for Kalmyk affairs. By the time he was in Astrakhan he was renowned as a scholar but also as an embezzler and bribe-taker.[65]

The city of Astrakhan resembled an island, being built on marsh and salt-lake islands where the Volga divides into numerous branches flowing into the Caspian. It was encircled to the north and east by the River Kutum, which itself had numerous branches, and to the south by the River Ilmen. A canal ran east–west through the city. Half-filled salt lakes were everywhere. The city consisted of five main areas: the citadel or Kremlin, with the most important buildings, such as the arsenal, magazines, chancelleries, the cathedral church and the governor's, archbishop's and bishop's residences; and town within the city walls. There were also the area between the city walls and the canal; settlements and suburbs beyond the canal; and finally gardens, orchards and watermills to the south and east.[66]

fig.2

The citadel occupied the city's highest point. Outside the Kremlin, but within the city walls,[67] were the caravanserais (Russian, Indian and Armenian), surrounded by shops and storehouses. The Nikolski port (fig.2), where goods from the Volga arrived, and the exchange buildings were opposite the citadel; to the south was the Admiralty, and beyond it the Tatar market. The English were said to live on the west side of the Admiralty.[68] To the east of the Kutum were military and naval hospitals. Cook's description and a plan of about 1774 in Gmelin show the separation of the different nationalities in Astrakhan.[69] The Russians had their own space east of the Kutum, where there was also a botanical garden.

Beyond the canal were the Armenian and Tatar suburbs, with further 'towns' populated by Tatars, Bukharans, Ghilanians and Tatars descended from Indians.[70] Trade, political events and natural growth meant that the population fluctuated, particularly its Armenians, Indians, Persians and different Tatar groups. Cook estimated the population at more than 100,000 in the 1740s, but acknowledged that official censuses were inaccurate. After extensive fire damage in 1768, a large sum was set aside for rebuilding in brick, but progress was so slow that, according to Georgi[71] it would take several generations to complete. The city then had twenty-five Russian churches, two Armenian ones, a Catholic ('Papist') and a Lutheran one, and an 'Indian Temple' (for mosques, see p.62).[72] Georgi reported 2541 houses in the 1780s, including those in the Kremlin and the soldiers' barracks, but it is unclear whether his figure includes the households of the suburbs and only stone-built buildings.[73] When Pallas visited at the end of the century, he noted improvements in Astrakhan and the 'elegant' 'commercial halls' (one Tatar, another for the Persians built by Armenians).[74]

Parkinson's wide-ranging account vividly conveys Astrakhan's atmosphere at the end of the eighteenth century. It also reports opinions on 'the corruption of those in power'; far from St Petersburg, liberties could be easily taken by officials. Parkinson contrasted this with the 'oppression' of peasants and the lower ranks of the military, poignantly illustrated by an episode involving a deranged soldier. He also mentioned economic drawbacks, such as the exorbitant price of wood (confirmed by Pallas[75]).

A prosperous city

ASTRAKHAN is ... fortified by a strong brick-wall, with embrasures, and square towers at proper distances. In the citadel are the cathedral church, governor's palace, and the public offices. There is a creek, or haven, for ships that navigate the river and the CASPIAN sea. The houses are generally built with wood, conveyed in rafts along the river; for the neighbouring country produces nothing, being all a barren desert. To the westward there is no water to be found for many miles. The islands, however, adjacent to the town are very fruitful, and produce excellent grapes, transplanted hither from PERSIA and other parts; also water-melons, esteemed the best in the world; and various kinds of musk-melons, peaches, cherries, pears, apples and apricots.

Here are several large vineyards, belonging partly to the court, and partly to private persons; there is a FRENCHMAN who superintends them. The wines are very good when drunk on the spot; but cannot bear carriage, for the lest motion renders them insipid. Were it not for this circumstance RUSSIA would be able, not only to supply itself abundantly with wine, but even other parts of EUROPE. This pernicious quality is attributed to the nitrous particles of the foil where the vines grow. I have myself seen in the furrows, made for watering them, a whitish crust of salt: But the grapes, notwithstanding, are very sweet, without the least tincture of tartness.

About a mile below the town are collected great quantities of common salt. The people dig pits, into which they introduce the water; which being exhaled by the heat of the sun, the fall is left upon, the bottom: after gathering, they transport it along the river, in large barques of about five or six hundred tun. The gun-powder manufactory is a little above the town; in which, and in the mines of saltpetre, near this place, are employed a great number of workmen for the service of the government.

The climate is healthy, though very hot. The weather is generally calm, during which great numbers of gnats and muskitos infest the inhabitants. These vermine indeed are sometimes dispersed by a breeze from the sea, which renders this place very pleasant. They are hatched and sheltered in the marshes toward the sea, which are so overgrown with strong tall reeds that they are altogether impassable.

The MAHOMETAN TARTARS here live without the town; and have the same privileges as in other places.

Astrakhan is a place of considerable trade to PERSIA, CHIVA, BUCHARIA and INDIA. The people of these nations have a common caravansery, where they live and expose their goods to sale.

The ARMENIANS carry on the greatest part of the PERSIAN trade; for the PERSIANS themselves seldom go out of their own country. There are a few INDIANS, or BANIANS, at this place, who have a streak of yellow down their forehead, made with saffron or sume other vegetable. They are a good natured, innocent kind of people, and live mostly on fruits.

The market is plentifully supplied with provisions of all kinds; but especially fish, of which no place that I know abounds with such variety. After the file is over, which is usually about ten o'clock, what remains of the common forts is thrown to the dunghill, where the hogs and poultry feed upon them; and hence it happens that their very pork and fowls taste of fish. It would be tedious to mention all the different kinds this place affords: I cannot however omit the carp, which for size exceeds all of that name I ever heard of. I have seen some of them of more than thirty pound weight, very fat and luscious. Those caught in autumn are carried to MOSCO frozen ...[76]

(Bell, July 1716)

'The seat of an immense trade'

> Astrakhan being situate on a navigable boundary, between the two most considerable quarters of the globe, is naturally the seat of an immense trade …
>
> I was quartered, in this city, at the house of a widow, who had a maid servant that had been purchased as a slave from the Tartars …[77]

(Bruce, July 1722)

Compliments for Mr Elton

> [W]e arrived at Astrakhan, where we anchored opposite to the governor's house, after a voyage of 1445 wersts (963 miles) from CASAN to this place, which we performed in 28 days … [T]he governor, vice-governor, and commander of the garrison, came on board and congratulated Mr Elton on his safe arrival, assuring him that he had the honour of being the first who had spread ENGLISH colours in that part of the world, and that this was the first ship that had ever sailed the Volga perfectly equipped. After paying these compliments, they drank success to the British-Persian trade …[78]

(Captain Woodroofe in Hanway, May 1742)

Cook's visit in March 1740

The city and its population

The city of Astrakhan is built upon an island called the island of Hares, that island lying east and west, having the famous river Volga on its north side, it makes a pretty appearance to strangers at their arrival from Russia: because they have a view of its length and the steeples of all its churches with a very high brick wall, which surrounds both it and the citadel: Mr Hanway has been misinformed. He says it contains about 70,000 inhabitants. It certainly contains many more than a hundred thousand, but this in Russia, is not to be certainly known, as they keep no register of women and very young children …

The citadel is built upon the west end of the city on a hill, the wall surrounding it is brick, 30 feet high at least, and very thick, having many high strong bastions, mounted with a great number of large cannon: But it is not a regular fortification, though strong enough for any enemy in that country: Astrakhan lieth 60 versts from the Caspian sea: In it are contained magazines of all kinds, the governor's and archbishop's palaces, the government's chancery where all affairs, civil and military, are judged of, and all the records are kept. The metropolitan church, a large monastery, all built with white freestone, guard-house, and several other buildings, are within the walls of the citadel: There are only three gates into the citadel, one from the city, another from the south opening into the Tartar suburbs, a third from the north towards the Volga. The wall of the city takes its beginning from the north cast corner of the citadel, and runs eastward three quarters of a mile, then turns south a quarter of a mile, and proceeds from the south cast corner west, till it again joins the south-east corner of the citadel ...

On the inside of the walls, betwixt them and the houses, there is a void place, where none are allowed to build 20 fathoms broad, quite round the city. There are three long streets from east to west, and many cross-streets intersecting the former three. There are within the walls two large stone churches, and one of wood. I think the length of the city and the citadel is equal to an English mile. The houses are built with timber, and the streets are laid over with timber also, so that a fire happening in this city must be very dangerous. The suburbs are many, and extend wide. They contain many more inhabitants than the city. There are two churches on the east, and a large monastery of stone, one wooden church on the south, and one betwixt the river and the city of the north, all for those of the Greek persuasion; besides which, the reformed have one built with timber, the Romans have a monastery, and the Armenians have a fine church, these two are built of stone.

The hospitals are built without the suburbs on the east, beside the large monastery, both for the army and fleet, through the admiralty is built on the west end of the citadel, enclosed with a deep ditch and rampart, with bastions mounted with cannon. The Russian and Armenian merchants inhabit the eastern suburbs, the Russians only the south and north, but the ancient Tartar inhabitants live in the suburbs next to the admiralty. Within the city none of the Tartars are permitted to live.

The Indians, and some Armenians, are permitted to live in two spacious caravanseras, which have only two ports, at which guards are kept day and night; they are enclosed with high stone walls.

The kingdom of Astrakhan on the south is confined by Circassia, and 44 degrees 10 minutes north latitude, on the west by 62 degrees 30 minutes east longitude, on the north by 52 degrees north latitude, and on the east by 69 degrees east longitude, as they compute: for the inhabitants have no certain knowledge of the extent of this great kingdom to the east, possibly it may reach the Jaik river, or further.[79]

...

Russians, in our days, are the natural, and the greatest number of the inhabitants of the city of Astrakhan, but the kingdom is inhabited by Kalmucks and Nagai Tartars; the last of which are the descendants of the ancient inhabitants, who were conquered by Ivan Vasilitch the tyrant. They at this day, pay very much respect to their chiefs, who are called by them Murzas.

The city is inhabited by great numbers of Georgians, who embrace the Greek religion, and serve in the army, as also Armenians. They do not seek much after any other glory than merchandise and are as cunning as the Jews, though they all profess the Christian religion ...

There are many Persians, and various kinds of Tartars, which I do not rank among the inhabitants, because they plead dependence upon their own proper countries.[80]

...

They sow many different kinds of melons and pompions[81] which they eat with bread. The water melon, I was told by our countrymen who had been in the West Indies and Italy, is far preferable to any growing in these countries ... when I could get the water melon, it is extremely healthy, but the other melons are very dangerous, producing agues accompanied with dysentries. Astrakhan produceth the largest grapes I ever saw and very agreeable to eat, though the wine has a sharpness uncommon, which I believe proceeds from the salt of the earth. There are two kinds of mulberries here, the red and the white, of a particular kind of white mulberries, had almost killed some of the Prince's servants by vomiting excessively ...

Astrakhan gardens produce very many vegetables, but they must be frequently watered for the heat and drought is very great, and showers are seldom seen here ... For an hour after sun-rise, the salt lies upon the surface of the earth.

The inhabitants of Astrakhan are blessed with all kinds of tame animals which we have, and by a far greater of wild than we have, or that I can describe: the following is a sample, wild swine, deer of different kinds ... and the antelope, which in the desart roam in herds to the number of some hundreds

Hares are in great plenty: I never saw in Astrakhan, nor heard of either bears or wolves ... for there are no woods, except in the islands, and in the time of high water the islands are all covered over ... There are wild horses in Astrakhan as I was informed, but I never saw any of them alive, they are run down, and hunted like other wild animals ... I have eaten what was called wild horse but it is much preferable to any beef.

The plumed inhabitants of Astrakhan are too numerous for me to give an account of them ...[82]

[The island of Hares] in a true sense is not a large island, for a branch of the Volga washes it from the north round the cast side, and, at the distance of two miles south, it casts off a small branch which runs straight west and falls again into the Volga, about a mile or two south from the city. The soil, not only of this island, but of the rest, and also of the desart, is very light and sandy, but it is so very much mixed with salt, that it produceth only, naturally, a great variety of Kals, vast quantities of liquorice, reeds, genista aculcata, an herb call Astrakhania, nitraria, and others of the like nature. The earth will produce no grain, unless it has, during the winter season, lain under water, wherefore the Tartars have great dikes, which they open or shut, as they intend to have grain, or wash out the salt, when they intend to sow a piece of ground, they cut through the dike on the lowest end of the valley, and let out the water which formed the lake in the preceeding year, and, in two or three days, from the excessive heat and drought of the climate, it is fit for tilling, then they dress it, and sow it with what grain they please, and it is incredible what increase it produces, whether grain or fruits.[83]

Garrison and government

The garrison of Astrachan consists of six regiments, five of infantry and one of dragoons. The immediate chief commander of the garrison is the commandant, who is commonly a brigadier, though I have known a colonel, but then he cannot command a senior colonel: But orders issued from, and in the name of the cantoir or office belonging to the garrison, where all their affairs are transacted by all officers of superior rank, must be obeyed. Each regiment has a separate hospital, though in very bad condition ... Besides the proper garrison, three or a greater number of field regiments commonly winter here, and 2 or 3000 Cossacks, besides the Tartar militia: For the Kalmucks are not, in Astrachan especially, much to be trusted.

The use of this regular garrison is to keep watch about the city and citadel: there are also a detached number of 3 or 400 sent to Kizleer, and a few to Tchornayaz [Chorny Yar], but none to Tsaritziin: It being garrisoned by the field forces. The irregulars, are never made use of, but in conjunction with the regulars, and to scour the desart in troublesome times, and bring certain advice of the operations, places of resort, and numbers of these wandering barbarians who disturb their neighbours.[84]

This garrison of Astrachan seems to have more fatigue, and no better pay than any other garrison in Russia. They are frequently obliged to march into the desarts in the greatest frosts, by which many are frozen to death, they are also obliged in the summer to fell and bring to Astrachan wood for use in the garrison hospitals, but chiefly for their officers, as also hay: This mal-practice will not be redressed till they get another sovereign like Peter the Great ... When these poor recruits are ordered to march for Astrachan, they are sent by water to save charges and the more effectually to keep them together. They therefore are sent in the summer season, and, by the time they arrive in Astrachan, the different fruits are all ripe, on which these poor half starved creatures fly with great voraciousness, and in a very short time, from a fish diet upon the Volga for six or eight weeks, a warm moist air still increasing as they advance nearer Astrachan, and being lodged in very ill contrived wet barracks, and surcharging their bodies with, which before their arrival they had never had seen, far less eaten, they contract malignant quartans, and fluxes of all kinds, which soon reduce their numbers ...[85]

Precautions against the plague

As orders were sent from the admiralty, appointing me to take care of the sick belonging to the port, I had much time on my hands, and thought it my duty to give my opinion about the proper way to prevent the plague from making its appearance in Astrachan. I therefore gave in a petition to the precawse or government's chancery, and sent a copy of it to the medicine-chancery, chiefly representing, that we could not be free of the danger of getting the plague in such a very hot kingdom as Astrachan, unless the inhabitants were ordered to keep every thing as clean and free from putrefaction as possible, both without and within doors, which I imagined would not be difficult to be done, if the following rules were carefully attended to.

I observed that the common people buried their dead in the church-yards, both within and without the city, very superficially, scarcely covering the coffin half a foot with earth; which, considering the looseness of the soil, gave the greatest chance to promote the disease we were so much afraid of; and that many were buried in churchyards not fenced about, so that horses and carriages drove frequently over the graves, and, in this dry climate, rendered the earth finely pulverized, which was easily carried away by the first gust of wind, exposed the coffins to view a very few days after interment: that the noisome smell, and a visitation of the church-yards, would prove what I had asserted, to be true. I therefore desired, that, without loss of time, this might be altered, by Ordering the churchyards to be fenced in, or by preventing wheel'd machines or horses ever to pass through these places, and lastly, to order the graves to be made very deep.

I next represented the loathsome manner in which the Kalmucks exposed their dead, not only in the neighbourhood of Astrachan, but under the walls of the city, where dogs, crows, and swine were daily to be seen feeding upon them, to the great shame and danger of a well regulated government. I therefore required, that, since it was contrary to their law to bury, they should be obliged either to burn them, or cast them into the Volga.

I next took notice of the dead-house being not a verst distant from the city, the putrid exhalations of which, when the wind blew, might be observed to be very offensive, on the Iceside, at the distance of three versts. This being an unanswerable proof that the inhabitants of the city, were daily obliged to respire air much saturated with one of the well known causes of the plague, I begged that, whatever the archbishop and his priests might alledge to the contrary, the present dead house should be filled up, and a new one erected at a reasonable distance from the city.

My petition met with all the success I could expect from the governor of Astrachan, and also from the medecine chancery ... None objected to anything but the archbishop and Kalmucks ... but both were forced to submit to these regulations. The proud bishop bore me a grudge for this ever after ...[86]

Astrakhan's environs

There are very few fresh water lakes in the neighbourhood of the city, but a great many brackish, very salt, or even covered over with salt, like to ice; upon some of them I have walked and if the salt is broken ... where it is not deep, the moisture beneath is black as ink, and emits a most disagreeable noisome smell, though the salt is of the best kind ... At a distance of 60 versts south-west from Astrachan, there is a large salt lake, about 50 versts long and 20 broad, so thick crusted over, that some hundred horse and carts are constantly at work, carrying salt to be put on vessels riding on the Volga, not only for the use of the kingdom of Astrachan, but the greatest part of the Empire ... These salt-men dig out the lake with great iron gavelocks.[87]

There are a great variety of black snakes, and other serpents, upon the banks of this river: Many flocks of antelopes, hares are here in abundance, a variety of medicinal herbs grow everywhere; but liquorice grows in such plenty, that I am well assured the banks of the Volga alone, betwixt Astrachan and Tchornoyar can produce more than is made use of in all Europe.[88]

(Cook, 1740)

The Elton affair

I was kindly received in ASTRAKHAN by Mr GEORGE THOMPSON, agent to the BRITISH merchants trading to Persia; and also by the governor, general WASSILIE NIKIETISH TATTISCHEFF [V.N. Tatishchev] to whom I carried a valuable present on account of the merchants. I had much discourse with him, and he gave me many assurances that nothing on his part should be wanting to promote the interest of the merchants trading to PERSIA; he proposed to me some schemes ...[89]

I was several times with the governor, whose discourse ran continually on ELTON; the sum of it was 'that NADIR SHAH having conceived an high opinion of this gentleman's capacity, had made him presents, and either engaged him for a salary to build ships for him, or required his assistance to superintend such an undertaking: that ELTON had already met with great difficulties, the timber being knotty, and the roads to the shipyards hardly passable. He observed moreover that the PERSIANS were extremely ignorant of maritime affairs ... so that it would require much time to bring them [plans for the fleet] to maturity; but such enterprises ... could not but alarm the RUSSIAN court.[90]

(Hanway, October 1743)

40

Hanway's return from Persia in 1744

The 27ᵗʰ [October 1744], we arrived safe in ASTRACHAN [after a quarantine of 6 weeks on CARAZA island], where I received information ... in relation to ELTON and our unhappy CASPIAN trade. The next day I waited upon the governor, whose behaviour was now very different from it had been twelve months before ... I did not appear before him with an empty hand, yet his behaviour was hardly within the limits of civility.[91]

The City

[Astrakhan] contains about 70,000 inhabitants, among whom are many ARMENIANS and TARTARS of various denominations, with a few PERSIANS and INDIANS. The manners and customs of all these different people exhibit an epitome of ASIA. The city is about 2 and a half miles round, but including the suburbs near five miles. It is surrounded by a brick wall in a ruinous condition, being about 200 years old. Here was a garrison of six regiments of the bell: RUSSIAN troops: and in the adjacent plain they had erected a great number of small batteries, which were intended to sweep the country, and to prevent the approach of an enemy, NADIR SHAH having lately given some alarm on this side.

The houses are of wood, and most of them very mean; the higher parts command a prospect of the VOLGA, which spreads itself here near three miles, giving pleasure and convenience to the inhabitants. In the summer the people are generally sickly, which is owing to the marshy lands near it. The earth being impregnated with salt, which appears on the surface, is extremely fertile, bearing fruit in abundance, the immoderate use of which creates many distempers among the common people.

The government of ASTRACHAN extends as far as SARATOF. The city is surrounded by gardens and vineyards, which lie about two miles from it. These produce almost every kind of garden-stuff known in ENGLAND, except potatoes, collyflowers and artichoaks ... OLEARIUS commends the fruits of ASTRACHAN, but I met with none extraordinary, except the water-melons; though the court find the grapes delicious enough to bear the great expence of land carriage, as already mentioned. The wine of ASTRACHAN is also very indifferent. As their summers are generally dry, they are obliged to water their gardens; this is done by large wheels, some of which are moved by horses, others by the wind, These wheels are of a sufficient height to throw the water into the highest part of the garden, from whence it runs in trenches to the root of every tree and plant. The gardens and vineyards are generally watered in this manner, from the middle of May to the middle of September. The chief game in the neighbouring country is hares and partridges; and in summer there is plenty of quails. Here are also water and wild fowl of all sorts in great abundance.

About ten miles below ASTRACHAN is a small island called BOSMA-KOFF, remarkable for its large storehouses of salt, which is made about twelve miles to the eastward of it, and being brought thither in boats, is conveyed in large flat bottomed vessels up the VOLGA. With this all the country is supplied, as far as MOSCO and TWERE. They dig annually some millions of poods, the exclusive property of which is claimed by the crown, and brings in a considerable revenues; for the common food of the soldiery, and of the bulk of the people, is bread and salt. In this place also are large fisheries, to which the neighbourhood of the saltworks is of great advantage. These extend even to the sea, reaching south eastward as far as YAEIK, and also 100 miles above ZARITZEN. From these fisheries all the country is supplied as far as St PETERSBURG: the vessels are loaded with salt fish, and sent away in the spring; but as fresh fish keeps good for long as it is frozen, the winter is no sooner set in, than it is transported by land as far as MOSCO and St PETERSBURG.

Captain WOODROOFE, who was for some time at ASTRACHAN, assured me, that from the latter end of July to the beginning of October, the country about that city is frequently infested with locusts, which fly in such prodigious numbers as to darken the air, and appear at a distance like a heavy cloud. The account which the inhabitants give of them is, that generally as the cold weather comes on, they are seen in their flight from the northward to the southward. Whenever they fall, they eat up every thing that is green. In this season therefore all the gardeners look out for them, and upon their first appearance endeavour to keep them off, by making as much smoak and as great noise as possible; but in spite of all their art, these destructive insects, after flying as long as they are able, sometimes fall in their gardens, on the tops of houses, and even into the fires. Their bodies, compared with the smallness of their wings, are very large. Their size is generally from two to two and a half inches long, and about three-quarters of an inch in diameter, and their shape near the same as the largest sort of green grasshopper.[92]

(Hanway, October 1743)

Parkinson in Astrakhan, June–July 1793

Heat and dust

We called this evening upon the Governor [P.M. Skarijinski][93] with whom as he speaks no language but Russ we were obliged to converse by means of an interpreter. He was extremely civil, remarking that Astracan was seldom visited by such strangers as ourselves, and offering us all the services in his power.

With regards to the trade of Persia they told me that there had been five Persian Ships here this year and that the goods which they brought to

Astracan from that country were chiefly silks, half silks and Cottons. The way which they take to have good water here is to let it stand for several days in a cellar and to keep it in Ice. The Sand or whatever it is loaded with settles then and leaves it perfectly good. We begged some water of this kind last night from the Master of the house. N.B. When there is no wind here what renders the heat insupportable are the Saline Particles which rise out of the earth and load the Air. These ... penetrate into the skin and cause fevers. The heat of day was universally complained of though the Thermometer was supposed to be up only to 30 and it rises sometimes to 36. The People resident here are only here for a time and therefore do not adopt the Methods observed in other countries to guard themselves against the heat. They also come from a part of the world where these precautions are not necessary and not practised and therefore they go on here as they have been used to do in a very different climate. They ought to do as the Italians do at Venice and Naples, i.e. turn night into day; shut their doors and windows in the former and open them in the latter.[94]

...

Astracan not being paved the streets are deep in dust which the wind blows about and renders very unpleasant. Yet they are still worse, the Ober Commandant says, after rain, for then it is not possible to conceive how dirty and nasty they are. The houses in general are of wood and make a very shabby appearance. The Churches, however, as well as a good many houses, are of brick stuccoed white and in the style of Petersbourgh embellished with architectural ornament. A good part of the street is now and then built in this way and looks handsome; though as the stucco is become dirty and begun to peel off everywhere more or less, those buildings have at the same time a ruinous, neglected slovenly Appearance.[95]

The great number of Mills which one sees about this town are for the Purpose of watering their gardens. I have just counted near thirty which I can see from the window of our apartments. All their wood for building and burning comes from Casan and Viatka, which causes it to [be] very dear. It costs, I think he [the Over-Commandant] said six roubles a month to heat a single stove. And yet I think he said at another time that though he dines at home every day and has generally ten persons to dine with him, his table costs him no more than twelve roubles a month. All the necessaries of life are so cheap that his income of 3,000 roubles will go farther, he says, than 20,000 at Petersburgh.[96]

Power and corruption

I had a visit early this morning [30 June 1793] from Mr Kelly, an American Englishman in this service, who though a wild impetuous man, threw a good deal of light on the corruption of those who are entrusted with power, on the rascality of the Naval officers in Russia, and in some respect on the nature of military rank.

Nothing can be sold without the Governor's permission. He permits them to sell their commodities for more or less according as they are paid. Hence the high price of many of the common Articles of life at Astrachan. Meat which ought to be no more here than one Copeck a pound is three or four, and so on. The Boats that come from Moscow are drawn up close to his own house in order that they lie the more at his Mercy.

At the first foreign port they [the naval officers] come to they sell the Cables, Sailcloth and Anchors, which they bring out with them to serve in case of emergencies ... A Russian Vessel upon arriving in Copenhagen, was actually obliged to purchase an anchor in consequence of really having lost one after having sold all the rest ...

As an instance of Oppression he mentioned that if a Peasant has the misfortune to lose half a dozen Brothers, and as many children, he must pay himself the Capitation Tax for them all, till I suppose a given time. Or was it the tax to the Lord? Another instance was that if a Peasant has a handsome daughter, it is in the power of the Lord to take her and treat her as he thinks proper. The Question always is, [Agathi] says, what rank has a Man; the character of a Scavant or anything of that sort is not in the least regarded.[97]

We drank tea at the Governor's and called afterwards on the O[ver] Commandant where I begged leave to bath. The Governor makes 100,000 roubles of his place [fisheries, salt]. The Vice G[overnor] 40,000. Though two millions of roubles worth of salt is made here in the year, the revenue receives no more than 400,000 roubles. The Over Commandant told this [to] Bootle, adding: I have written an account of all this to Petersburgh.[98]

Out and about in Astrakhan

We dined at the O[ver] Commandant's very uncomfortably, devoured almost with flies, stupefied with the Noise and fooleries of a Russian soldier who had lost his understanding, and in the midst of spectators who having already dined themselves, came in and sat by while we ate dinner. I could not help observing that the Russians and others submitted to pull off their hats at the requisition of this fool and especially while he was preaching.[99]

I walked out this morning [2 July] to the Cathedral (where I loitered for some time on the terrace), through the Persian shops and into the Indian Caravansera. There is a long square of one floor, covered after the manner of the East with Soil.[100]

Upon traversing the town one finds a great many stone houses interspersed among the houses of wood ... The evening was fine and the shipping looked beautiful with a rosy western sky behind it. It had been settled that we should go along with M. Agathi to see the Indian form of worship. But when we came ... it was too late. Their service commences always at Sunset.[101]

We were present this morning [7 July] at the public examination of the young persons who are educated in the schools of Astracan. I was surprised to see four girls in the first class. The Governor and a great crowd of people attended. The Examination was held in the refectory of an old dissolved convent near the Cathedral. They are about two hundred in number and divided into four classes, of which the first said their cathechism, the second was examined in Arithmetic and Grammar, the third in Geography and ancient history and the fourth in Geometry, Fractions, Algebra and Fortification ... This examination takes place twice a year and not only in the Capital but wherever schools are established ... The examination lasted from nine to near twelve and concluded with a little collation given by M. Agathi the director of the Schools.

The Tartar shops are built at their own expense. It is contemplation to erect a new Caravansera for the Indians with the public money ... What they call the Russian Shops, those I mean opposite to the Shops of Moscow and decorated in front with arcades, are handsome and have a good effect. The Walls of the Kremlin and the Bielogorod[102] are of brick and in many places fallen to decay.[103]

(Parkinson, 1793)

ENDNOTES

1 See the 1779 map of Kazan province by T. Tschernoi in *Atlas imperii russici*, p.25.
2 Bushkovitch, p.277.
3 Ibneeva, p.78ff.
4 Rychkov, p.183; Tooke 1799, vol.3, pp.282, 346, 388, 464, 521; Kalinin, pp.70–72; Kahan, p.99; Alishev, pp.54–63; Kirilov and Falk in Garzavina and Novitskaya, pp.49, 54–55.
5 Kirilov in Garzavina and Novitskaya, pp.40–50 and n.5.
6 The battle of Poltava (1709) between Russia under Peter the Great and Charles XII of Sweden turned the tide against the Swedes in the Great Northern War of 1700–21. The Swedes were severely defeated, which ultimately ended their dominance of the Baltic, and Russia was established as a serious military power.
7 Kirilov in Garzavina and Novitskaya, p.49.
8 Greaves, p.352
9 Kazan University Library, MSS, plan no.4062; Kalinin, *passim*; Ostroumov, *passim*.
10 Rychkov (pp.183–84) lists Kazan's main roads and buildings, excluding the suburbs.
11 Chappe d'Auteroche, p.559.
12 Ostroumov, pp.59–60, 73ff, 83.
13 Rychkov, p.182 (both wooden and stone); Falk in Garzavina and Novitskaya, p.55,

mentions thirty-five good stone churches and the monastic buildings.

14 Falk in Garzavina and Novitskaya, p.54. This number had dropped from the 2028 people involved in trade in the 1720s (ibid., p.49). Numbers fluctuated, but for the growth of Tatar merchant trade see pp.54–55 in this book.

15 E.I. Pugachev (1740s–1775) was the leader of a large-scale uprising against the Russian state. The mutiny took place between 1773 and 1775 and involved disaffected Cossack groups (e.g. Yaik, Orenburg), Old Believers, Kalmyks, Bashkirs and other Tatars, and peasants. The rebels attacked and/or besieged Orenburg, Yaitsk, forts on the Urals, and the Volga from Samara to Kazan (Kazan and Saratov were plundered in 1774). They were finally defeated at Tsaritsyn. Pugachev was betrayed and executed in Moscow in 1775 (Alexander, pp.72–79).

16 Kalinin (p.87) suggests around 25,000 in the early nineteenth century.

17 Falk in Garzavina and Novitskaya, p.49.

18 Bell, pp.19–26.

19 Bell, p.24.

20 Hanway, vol.1, pp.111–13.

21 Hanway, vol.1, p.112.

22 Lysenko, p.291.

23 M.L. Golenischev-Kutuzov (Lysenko, p.291).

24 Parkinson, p.110.

25 Khodarkovsky 1992, p.163.

26 Pallas 1788–93, vol.1, p.228.

27 Ibid., pp.228–29.

28 Ibid., pp.229–30.

29 Ibid., p.228.

30 Pallas 1788–93, vol.5, pp.264–65; Bartlett, pp.73–76; Brandes, p.21.

31 Pallas 1788–93, vol.5, pp.264–65.

32 Georgi 1780–83, vol.1, p.264.

33 Ibid.

34 Ibid.

35 Bartlett, pp.1–30 and *passim*; Brandes *passim*.

36 Gmelin 1770–74, vol 2, tab.2.

37 Georgi 1780–83, vol.4, p.318.

38 Ibid., pp.304–18; Bartlett, pp.104–5; Brandes, p.41 and *passim*.

39 Pallas 1812, pp.99–105. For difficulties faced by colonies, see Bartlett, pp.103–4 and *passim*.

40 Pallas 1812, pp.97–98, 106–11, 187–88.

41 Bell, pp.28–29.

42 This governor is not listed in Lysenko.

43 Bell, pp.29–30.

44 Bruce, p.239.

45 Perry 1716, pp.2–5.

46 Bruce, p.243.

47 Ibid., pp.243–44.

48 Cook, vol.1, pp.239–42.

49 Hanway, vol.1, pp.99–100.

50 Parkinson, p.259, Collier (ed.) notes that Dr Sedler might be a Dr Seydel referred to by Pallas.

51 Parkinson, p.259, Collier (ed.) notes that an Eimer is a measure of capacity equivalent to 12.806 litres.

52 Parkinson, pp.143–49.

53 Bruce, p.244.

54 Hanway, vol.1, p.108.

55 Parkinson, pp.152–53.

56 Hanway, vol.2, pp.7–8.

57 Spilman, p.10.

58 *Atlas imperii russici*, no.23 (1774), by J. Trescott.

59 Cook, vol.1, pp.246–47.

60 Olearius 1967, p.324. Much of Bruce's description of Astrakhan follows Olearius and has been omitted.

61 Bassin, pp.6–7 and *passim*. For Tatishchev this geographical division helped ideologically to divide the empire neatly in two, and to root western Russia further in Europe.

62 Kahan, pp.91–95, tab.3.17. Astrakhan was the third most important salt-producing region after Lake Elton and Perm in the eighteenth century. Tooke 1799, vol.3, pp.444–45.

63 These were abandoned by the time Pallas visited at the end of the eighteenth century, due to neglect by the owner and Kalmyk raids. Pallas urged for them to be reopened (Pallas 1812, pp.166–70).

64 Georgi 1780–83, vol.4, pp.380–83.

65 E.g. Cook, vol.2, pp.46–47, 93, 138–44.Tatishchev was a serious scholar. He was the first to compare documentary sources with traditional legends, and to develop the use of instructions and questionnaires for his information gathering in the Urals and Siberia. His great work *Istoriia Rossiskaya*, started in the 1720s, was controversial because of his reworkings and claims to have used chronicles that were subsequently lost. He used this chronicle material to show the antiquity and legitimacy of the Slavs and to justify an autocratic monarchy, which for him was the only way for a growing empire like Russia to be governed. In addition to the *Istoriia* and ethnographic work, he published on law and historical geography, and compiled the first Russian encyclopaedic dictionary. Parts of the *Istoriia* were published only after his death by Müller between 1768 and 1774; Part IV appeared in 1784 and Part V in the nineteenth century. See Hellie, pp.191–96; Thadeu, pp.196–200 (with extensive Bibliography); Black 1986, *passim*.

66 Authors differed as to the area of the city, but what they measured also varied. Hanway gave the area of the city and citadel as 2 1/2 sq. miles, and 5 sq. miles including the suburb. Cook thought the citadel and city (presumably within the city walls) measured about 1 sq. mile. Georgi (1780–83, vol.4, p.372) thought the citadel and principal streets amounted to 2 versts or 1 ½ miles.

67 Georgi 1780–83, vol.4, p.373.

68 Cook, vol.1, p.246.

69 Gmelin 1770–74, vol.2, tab.43.

70 Kahan, p.259.

71 Georgi 1780–83, vol.4, pp.375–76.

72 Ibid., p.283.

73 Ibid., p.383.

74 Pallas 1812, pp.210–11.

75   Ibid., pp.211–12.
76   Bell, pp.36–39.
77   Bruce, pp.245, 251.
78   Hanway, vol.1, pp.114–15.
79   Cook, vol.1, pp.244–47.
80   Ibid., pp.255–256.
81   Fullerton (ed. Cook, vol.1, n.138) notes that a pompion is a pumpkin.
82   Cook, vol.1, pp.262–64, 267.
83   Ibid., pp.261–62.
84   Cook, vol.1, p.287.
85   Ibid., pp.287–88.
86   Ibid., pp.320–22.
87   Ibid., pp.281–282.
88   Cook, vol.2, p.149.
89   Hanway, vol.1, p.117.
90   Ibid., pp.120–21.
91   Hanway, vol.2, pp.5–6.
92   Hanway, vol.1, pp.123–25.
93   Salikhov 2001, p.268.
94   Parkinson, pp.161, 162.
95   Ibid., pp.164–65.
96   Ibid., p.167.
97   Ibid., p.168.
98   Ibid., p.173.
99   Ibid., p.169.
100 Ibid., p.172.
101 Ibid., p.173.
102 Collier (ed. Parkinson, p.261) notes 'the Bielogorod ... the old town immediately south east of the Kremlin. Literally White Town.'
103 Parkinson, pp.177–78.

3 PEOPLES: CHEREMIS, MORDVIN, CHUVASH, TATARS AND OTHERS

Introduction

Unlike Russian academicians, British travellers did not deliberately seek out and question ethnic groups. Curiosity or necessity, however, might lead them to question the peoples they encountered. They were not extensively prepared by research and reading for such encounters, although most had evidently read (and borrowed from) earlier travellers. Much of their knowledge appears to have been picked up en route, whether from Russian officials (e.g. governors such as Tatischev), academicians (e.g. Pallas) or other professionals, and local peoples. The question of subsequent editing also arises, given that many of these journals were published as books some time after they were written.

The travellers generally used the term Tartar or Tatar for all non-Slavic indigenous peoples of the middle and southern Volga, whether of Turkic, Mongol or Finnic descent. They usually defined a group by its name (e.g. Cheremis, Nogay) and/or religion. Bruce offered some information on 'Tatars', rightly stating that they formed several nations 'distinct among themselves', and probably different from the Scythians and Sarmatians of the Classical authors, while sharing the same geography. Academicians tended to divide Russia's non-Slavic peoples into three main groups: Finns, Tatars and Mongols.[1]

While not being social philosophers or *literati*, and often reporting anecdotally, the travellers adhered to certain eighteenth-century Eurocentric norms regarding the observation of ethnic 'peoples' and the nature of progress. These were based on a hierarchical scale of human development from 'rude' to 'refined', defined by the stages of hunting, shepherding, farming, and finally commerce and industry. Moral advances, such as the development of principles and manners, were thought to accompany these stages,[2] which, according to Tooke, were all to be found among the peoples of Russia.[3] Several themes feature repeatedly in the travellers' observations: religion, way of life, social status, diet, cleanliness and physical appearance, particularly of females. They also commented on past history, and made direct or indirect comparisons with Russians.

Cheremis, Mordvin and Chuvash

The Cheremis (also known as Mari) and the Mordvin (or Burtas) were originally Finno-Ugrian groups of the Middle Volga.[4] The former were to be found between Nizhny Novgorod and Kazan up to Perm. The latter were centred below Nizhny. Both had a history of submission to the Bulghars and the Golden Horde. In contrast, the Chuvash, who inhabited the south-west of Kazan, are thought to be of Turkic, possibly Bulghar origin. These peoples were only partly influenced by Islam after its introduction in the area in the ninth and tenth centuries.[5] All groups became subject to Russia after the conquest of Kazan, and some migrated to the lower Volga and the Urals in the eighteenth century. By the late eighteenth century they constituted approximately 4 per cent of Russia's population, of which the Chuvash were the most numerous.[6] They were animist forest peoples who lived in mixed settlements, sometimes with Russians

Черемиска спереди.
Eine Tscheremisin vorwärts.
Teme Tcheremisse par devant.

fig.3

(as Perry observed) if nominally converted to Christianity, or in self-contained groups.[7] The Chuvash were considered the most private. They were a taxed peasant class, with no remaining aristocracy, who lived primarily by agriculture.[8] Some served as conscripts in the imperial forces or were *teptiars* (dependent on the Bashkirs in the Urals). These peoples had been subjected to a brutal, though unsuccessful, policy of forced conversion from the reign of Peter the Great to that of Empress Elizabeth.[9]

In the 1770s even the converted groups were considered 'pagan'.[10] Their religion was essentially a nature one, involving sacrificial rituals performed in open-air sacred places but also such traditions as saints' days or abhorrence of pork variously adopted from Christianity and/or Islam.[11] Domestic customs might be shared with Tatars and Russians.[12] At the end of the century Pallas wrote that the Mordvins were anxious to 'preserve the forests in the countries they inhabit' because their 'veneration' for old and beautiful oak trees had 'continued since the days of paganism'.[13] They still worshipped at their ancient tumuli, which they considered 'the paternal relics' of their ancestors.[14]

Travellers attempted to describe these peoples' religious practices, of which they had piecemeal, second-hand information. Bruce's account of the Cheremis (fig.3), heavily indebted to Olearius, is accurate in its mention of sacrifice, a supreme god, child-naming customs and polygamy, yet there are discrepancies when compared to the academicians' (e.g. marrying of sisters, dress).[15] Bell's association of Cheremis and Chuvash 'Tartars' with an expelled Jewish tribe goes back to the Middle Ages and Giles Fletcher; his contemporary source may have been the writer and patron Aaron Hill.[16]

Although the travellers described these peoples as 'idolatrous' or 'heathen', these terms had various associations in the eighteenth century. Perry and Bell were sympathetic; even though these peoples 'have no learning', they found them 'simple, harmless, inoffensive' (Bell) and 'sincere, honest, ingenious' and 'above' the Rus (Perry). Bruce, in contrast, heightened Olearius' negativity,[17] declaring the Cheremis to be 'barbarous, treacherous and cruel', not so much because they were pagan but because they were undeveloped generally and lived by robberies. With the exception of Bruce's, however, the travellers' views on these peoples contrast with the academicians' generally contemptuous verdicts.[18]

The failure of forced conversions

It is by reason of these foolish and abominable Superstitions, and the Illiterature of the Priests, and the general Perfidiousness of the People, as beforementioned, that not only the Samoieds and those Tartars that border on the Czar's Dominions but also the Murdaw and Morsie, and the Cheremiss Tartars, on this side of the Wolga, who have been conquered above 140 Years since, who live in Villages intermix'd with the Russians, and are immediately under the Government of the Czar (for the most part within the Province of Cazan) absolutely refuse to embrace the Christian Religion in the Form which the Russes represent it to them, tho' they have been many times offered considerable Encouragement and Enlargement of their Privileges, in case they would be baptized into the Russ Faith; and though they daily suffer the Insults and Affronts of the Russes, so much the more for their Obstinacy in not doing of it.[19]

...

When I was employed in making the Communication at Camishinka [1698–1701] above half of the Labourers that were sent to dig the Canal there, were of these Tartars (Mordwa, Mordzee, Cheremiss) and most of the Horse that were sent to cover the Workmen, were composed of the Gentry, or better sort of the same People. I have often taken occasion to ask them about their Religion, and they say, that the Russes using of Images, is a Terror to them to think of embracing their Religion; for that there is but one God, and that he cannot be pictured or described by Men; they look up towards the Heavens, and say, that he resides there, and of whom they are afraid to do Evil; or to change their Religion for fear he will not afterwards bless them. Their Faith is something like the Mahometan; they explain their Notions very rationally, that God is the Eternal Maker of all Things, by whom they receive Life, and to whom they that live uprightly, return again after Death. And because of the Falsity of the Russes in the Practice of their Lives, they tell them to their Faces, (I mean the common People in their Discourse one with the other) that they will not believe there is any good in their Religion; and say to them, That if their Religion be right, why do they not do right? As to these Tartars, I must do them this Justice, that as often as I had occasion to trust, or make use of them, both I and all my Assistants have observed, that we have found them sincere and honest in their Lives, and ingenuous in the Conversation, above what we have in the Russ Nation; and I make not the least doubt, as I have often told these Men when I have discoursed with them, that were the Christian Religion laid down to them, in that Purity as it was delivered by our Saviour and his Apostles, and as it is taught by the Doctrine of the Church of England; and that were they intermixed in a Countrey where there was that Preaching, and where there is that Learning and Exemplariness of Life that is known among the Clergy, and that Honesty and Integrity towards each other, as may generally be said of the People of England, there is no doubt but the said Tartars, as well as the forementioned Samoieds, and other Borderers of Russia, would very readily and gladly, long e'er this, have embraced the Christian Religion.[20]

(Perry, 1698–1705)

At *Kasimov en route to Kazan*

The 17th [November 1715] we left KASSIMOVA, and the 21st arrived at MURUM, a pretty large town and, and a bishop's see. The country produces plenty of corn. About this place there are a few idolatrous TARTARS, who live in dirty cottages thinly scattered. They are a simple and harmless people. How or when they settled here is not known.[21]

(Bell, 1715)

Between the River Oka and Kazan

The 15th [January 1741], we passed the river OCCA, but the ice being very rotten, two of our horses with a load of canvas fell through it. The 24th, we arrived among the CHUWASHIN Tartars, the poorest and most wretched of all mortals; they are descended from the KOOBANS and subject to RUSSIA, but now driven to the eastward. We could not discover what notions the CHUVASHINS have of religion, but observed when they dress victuals, they stick part of it over their doors and windows; and when they kill an animal, which their poverty but seldom permits, their priest takes out the fat, and after eating some of it and greasing himself, he smears over their place of worship, and the dross or refuse he burns: They generally subsist on dead animals, which they devour greedily. The neighbouring TARTARS eat horse-flesh, and dress it like that of any other animal.[22]

(Captain Woodroofe in Hanway, January 1741)

Around Vasilsurask

The Ceremisse Tartars inhabit both sides of the Wolga, from hence to the kingdom of Casan. They are a people barbarous, treacherous, and cruel, living by robberies; their food is wild-fowl, fish, honey, with plenty of milk, which their pastures furnish them with, and they eat the flesh of their horses and cows, when they die of their own accord, for they never kill any for themselves: they have no houses, but most wretched huts. Those on the right side of the river are called Nagarin, or Mountaineers, and those inhabiting the left, are called Lugoivi, from their meadows, which supply them on both sides of the river with hay: they are all heathens, using neither circumcision nor baptism; they give a child its name from the first person they meet that day six months after its birth; they acknowledge an immortal God, the author all good who ought to be adored, but ridicule the immortality of the soul; although they believe not in hell, yet they dread the devil as the author of all misfortunes, and therefore they pretend to appease him with sacrifices: when they offer a sacrifice to God, they kill a horse, cow, or sheep, and extend its skin on a high pole, which they implore to intercede for them with God, that he may increase the number of their cattle. They have a high veneration for the sun and moon, as the authors of the productions of the earth. They make no use of churches, priests, or books: polygamy is used among them, so as to marry two or three sisters at a time. Their women and maids are all wrapped up in a piece of white coarse cloth, and scarce anything to be seen but their faces; the men wear a long coat made of linen cloth, under which they wear breeches: they all shave their heads; the young men that are unmarried, leave a tress of hair to hang down their back by way of distinction. Their language is peculiar to themselves, having no resemblance of other neighbouring Tartars, or with the Turkish or Russian; although some of them that are conversant with the Russians have attained some knowledge of their tongue.[23]

(Bruce, June 1722)

In the Kazan area

Besides the idolatrous TARTARS ... there are two pretty numerous tribes called the TZERIMISH [Cheremis] and TZOOWASH [Chuvash], they speak a language quite different from the MAHOMETAN TARTARS in these parts, who use a corrupted dialect of the ARABIC. The MAHO-METANS likewise have some learning; but the TZERIMISH and TZOOWASH have none. They have a tradition among them, that in former times they had a book of religion; but, as no body could read it, a cow came and swallowed it. They pay great veneration to a bull. From whence they came is unknown; but from their complexion, it is probable they are from ASIA. They live by agriculture, and seem to be an inoffensive kind of people. Their huntsmen offer in sacrifice, to some deity, the first creature they catch. Hence some curious men have imagined these people part of the ten tribes of the JEWS, expelled by SHALMANEZER. I advance this only as a conjecture, which every reader may follow or not as he pleases.[24]

(Bell, November 1715)

Tatars of Kazan

The Muslim Tatars of Kazan (figs.4 and 5) were acknowledged by the travellers to have a special status vis à vis other Turkic Tatars. They were the 'most civilized' of the Tatars (Bruce) and 'live decently' (Bell). They traded, lived by agriculture and grew rich (Bell, Bruce, Parkinson); they lived in houses, were hospitable (Parkinson) and, as Woodroofe reported, 'clean and neat in their persons'.[25] Such views generally coincide with those of the academicians and other observers.[26] Bell and Parkinson visited the Tatar suburbs out of curiosity but gave little detail of their layout, or of life within them. All travellers convey the separateness of the Muslim suburbs from the Russian nucleus of Kazan. Bruce pointed out that Tatars were not allowed into the citadel, although this fact was disputed by Gmelin in the 1730s.[27] Bruce also mentioned that converted Tartars lived in the town, although probably not in the centre.

In the eighteenth century there were two principal Tatar suburbs outside the city walls. The Old Tatar Suburb (*staraia sloboda*) on the south-west bank of Lake Kaban dated back to the seventeenth century. From the 1750s onwards, the New Tatar Suburb (*novaia Tatarskaia sloboda*) grew up on the same side of Lake Kaban, but further south-east.[28] These suburbs would have contained separate areas for 'service' (*sluzhilye*) Tatars.[29] The New Suburb, deliberately removed from the Old, took shape after the church confiscated Tatar land in the Old Suburb and settled new converts

Казанской Татаръ.
Ein Kasanischer Tatter.
Tattare de Kasan.

Татарка казанская спереди.
Eine Kasanische Tatarin vorwärts.
Femme Tattare de Casan par devant.

figs.4 and 5

and Christians there during the time of enforced Christianisation under Archbishop Luka Kanashevitch (1738–55).[30] Academician Gmelin visited the Old Suburb in 1733 and described one of the four wooden mosques there. It was built in the 'local style': square shaped, with a 'tower' and gallery, in line with other houses and accessed through a small door up a few steps. It had many windows and was carpeted.[31]

The politics of Christianisation, which became virulent in the reigns of empresses Anna and Elizabeth and included the destruction of mosques from 1742 onwards, made for a difficult religious life in the *sloboda*s. This changed with Catherine II's visit to Kazan, which aimed to encourage trade with the east and to court powerful Tatar merchants with established trading links to Orenburg, Troitsk, Central Asia and even China.[32] She met local Tatar representatives and approved the building of a two-storey stone mosque in 1767/8 (the still extant 'Marjani Mechet') in the Old Sloboda.[33] A second stone mosque followed in the late 1760s and early 1770s (Ananevska).[34] These mosques were built in a local Baroque style with Islamic detailing (e.g. floral and honeycomb decoration).[35] Funding was from rich Tatar merchants, whose businesses were closely linked to the life and quarters (*mahalli*) of the mosques.[36] When Georgi visited Kazan in the 1770s he mentioned two stone mosques and two wooden ones.[37]

By the early eighteenth century prominent Tatar landowning classes who had converted and become serving (*sluzhile*) Tatars after the fall of Kazan had lost their privileges and positions.[38] An urban merchant and manufacturing class developed in its stead, accompanied by a growth in influence of the religious establishment (*ulama*).[39] From 1784, however, noble Muslim Tatars (princes or noble free men, *murzas*) were given the same prerogatives as the Russian nobility.[40] In Kazan, the affairs of the urban Tatar merchants were regulated from around 1781 onwards by their own Town Hall (*ratusha*). This was run by elected heads from prominent merchant families with a declared loyalty to the crown. It was supported by the Tatar community, who paid annual dues. The enterprise ran into funding difficulties at the end of the century, which caused a split between the merchants.[41] The wealth and sophistication of some merchants and their houses, which might have European-style façades but Tatar interiors,[42] was highlighted by Parkinson. He was introduced as a special favour to the heavily painted women of the house.[43] In 1781 there were apparently 481 families in the Old Tatar Suburb, 470 in the New, and 106 converted Tatars in Zakharevskoi (part of the Old Suburb).[44] Their principal 'manufactories' were the making of Morocco leather, embroidering buskins and soap-making.[45]

Georgi dwelt on another essential aspect of Tatar life in Kazan and its province, not touched on by our travellers but crucial to understanding the respect afforded to some of the settled Muslim population: education. The best religious 'academies' were said to be in Kazan, Tobolsk and Astrakhan, although 'Bukharia' (Bukhara) was then acknowledged as the true centre for advanced theological studies.[46] All Tatar villages had a *mesched* (mosque), a school, including some for girls in the big villages and *slobodas*, a *mullah* (cleric) and an 'abyss'.[47] Of 536 mosques in the province of Kazan, 418 were destroyed in the 1740s. They were gradually rebuilt in the post-Kanashevich era and during Catherine's reign.[48] Instruction was in Arabic, even if some schoolmasters were not very learned and had to earn their living by trade or farming.[49] With this learning came a strong sense of identity. Historical manuscripts, wrote Georgi, were to be found in the simplest of huts, and all Tatars were said to be 'pretty well acquainted' with the history 'of their own people'.[50] The sense of identity of the Volga Tatars has been the subject of much debate (see pp.126–27). Kazan Tatars saw themselves primarily as (Mahomeddan) Tatars of Kazan, while agreeing, according to Georgi, that they had 'sprung' from a 'mixture of warriors', including Nogays and other 'strangers' brought to Kazan by commerce.[51] Efforts to Christianise and educate Tatars as part of the Russian system nevertheless continued. In the early eighteenth century the Silandrovo monastery, for example, had a school where Cheremis, Chuvas, Mordvin and Kazan Tatar children were taught Russian, Latin, 'philosophy' and Christianity.[52] Teaching the Tatar language in the city gymnasium, first mooted in the mid-eighteenth century, came about in the early 1760s as a pragmatic step to help in the training and assimilation of special cadres.[53] A primer for the Tatar alphabet in Russian and Arabic script was published in 1778 by the interpreter Sagit Khalfin, one of the first teachers of Tatar.[54]

In the suburbs of Kazan

The suburbs are inhabited chiefly by mechanics, except a street or two possessed by MAHOMETAN TARTARS, the posterity of the ancient natives. They live very decently, have the free exercise of their religion, and many other privileges. Some of them are very rich by the trade they carry on to TURKEY, PERSIA, and other places.[55]

...

By accident, I met with an ENGLISHMAN at this place. He was by trade a carpenter, and had been in the RUSSIAN service; but, being suspected of deserting, he was condemned to banishment, to this country, for a certain time; and, notwithstanding that was elapsed, the poor man, deprived of all means of asserting his liberty, remained still in the same situations. He bought a TZERIMISH wife, from her father, for six rubles, about thirty shillings Sterling. He brought her to visit me. She was a woman of a chearful and open countenance, and dressed in the manner of her country; of which, for its singularity, I shall give a short description. Her hair was plaited round her head, in many locks, but that on the back part longer than the rest, at the end of which was tied a tassel of red silk, and in the middle a small round brass bell; about her head was a fillet set with small shells, instead of jewels, and hung all round with silver pence; above this was a piece of linen so artfully plaited, and done up, that it looked like a grenadier's cap; at the top was a silk tassel, with another brass bell, which jingled as she turned her head. The rest of her dress was clean though homely, and the whole seemed becoming enough.[56]

(Bell, November 1715)

'The most civilized of all the Tartars'

The kingdom of Casan lies on the left side of the Wolga, and its inhabitants all live in houses, and subsist by agriculture: they supply the southern provinces with all sorts of provisions, and by this means are the most civilized of all the Tartars. They are partly Mahommetans, but most of those who inhabit cities and towns, are of the Greek church; they are forbid, under severe punishment, to enter within any of the fortifications. They are bounded on the south by the Tartars of Bulgaria, and on the north by those of Siberia.[57]

(Bruce, June 1722)

A visit to a rich Tatar household

Several of the Tartars are in affluent circumstances and live in handsome houses. One of these wealthy Tartars shewed us the Mosque, though it happened unluckily not to be at the time of divine service; and afterwards conducted us to his house where he treated us with Eau de vie, with sweetmeats, with Hydromel, with Tea. He also offered [us] coffee, and even carried his complaisance so far as to show us his house, his wife and his daughter-in-law. The ladies before they made their appearance had tricked themselves out in all their finery; and the wife in particular had laid on a whole coating of white and red paint on her face.

We dined at the Governor's, Prince Baratiew's; and in the afternoon about five o'clock set off for Bolghari, an old Tartar Town ...[58]

(See pp.130–31)

(Parkinson, March 1793)

Kuban or Nogay Tatars

From Samara onwards the travellers encountered very different types of Tatars. Some were threatening, nomadic steppe people, the Turkic Karakalpaks; others were the Kalmyks and the people referred to interchangeably as Kuban or Nogay Tatars. These were originally part of the vast Nogay conferederation and were concentrated around the River Kuban and the steppe south-east of the Sea of Azov.[59] Together with branches of the Nogay, they had a long history of struggle with the Crimean Tatars, the Ottomans and the Russians for control of the Sea of Azov. They came under Russian domination when the Crimea was annexed in 1783.

In their sixteenth-century heyday the Nogays roamed over a vast expanse from the River Yaik (Ural) to the lower Volga, then westwards to the north and west of the Black Sea, the Danube and beyond. They were gradually scattered and weakened by Kalmyk advances westwards in the seventeenth century, and they became pawns in conflicts between Russia, Crimea and the Ottomans on Russia's southern frontier.[60] Under Peter the Great some became subject to the Kalmyks. Bruce believed the present-day Nogays to be descended from a thirteenth-century breakaway group. His dating is confused, but his facts are partly right: he could either be referring to the formation of the Nogays when they seceded from the Golden Horde in about the late fourteenth century or to the Small Horde of Kubans, which formed around the Kuban in the sixteenth century. Georgi wrote of the decline of the Nogays around Astrakhan, from 25,000 men in 1715 to 1200 in 1772.[61] There remained four 'pastoral and wandering' hordes of Nogay around the Sea of Azov and between Azov, the

Don and the Kuban. These were first 'under the protection' of Crimea, then briefly declared 'free' in 1774 by the Ottomans, then mostly subject to Russia after Crimea was annexed.[62] In the 1780s, they numbered about 70,000 men (i.e heads of households) when combined with troops from the other side of the Don.[63]

The Kuban and Nogay were generally portrayed as raiders and plunderers in the early eighteenth century. Hanway confirmed that by his time in Russia the Kuban were considerably 'diminished', with the fortified River Kuma as a barrier.

En route to Astrakhan

The next People that I shall take notice of, are the Caban Tartars, who are a very strong bodied, well proportioned People, black Hair and a swarthy Complexion, as generally are all the other Tartars. They inhabit to the Westwards of the River Wolga, along the North-East Coast of the Black-Sea, and between that and the Caspian Sea, from whence they make frequent Incursions into the Out-Parts of Russia, plunder and fire Villages, and often carry off Cattel and Horse and People; by reason of which, there is a great Tract of Land on the West side of the Wolga, all the way between the Town of Saratoff [Saratov] and the Caspian Sea, lies wholly uninhabited, save only the Islands about Astracan, and the People that live within the Town of Camishinka, Czaritza, Ischornico, and Terki, the nearest of which are from 150 or 60, to above 200 Miles Distance from each other, (as the Road lies) where Garrisons are kept at each particular Place, and are always ready for an Alarm. And by reason of the Incursions of the said Tartars, the Russes do not plough and sow in these Parts (though the land is extremely rich) but have every Year Corn brought down to them by the River Wolga, and the same Vessels go back laden with Fish and Rock-Salt, &c. of which the greatest Part of Russia is supplied from a Place 30 Miles below Camishinka: As also from Astracan there is returned every Year some small matter of rich Goods from Persia and Armenia, as wrought Silks, Calicoes, &c.

The said Tartars when they make their Incursions, it is usually in the Summer time, when there is Grass enough on the Ground; and each Man for Expedition sake takes two Horses, which they change as they ride, sometimes sitting upon one, and sometimes upon another. They always travel with Centinels at a convenient Distance from all Sides of their main Body, to prevent being discover'd, it being an uninhabited Countrey, as aforesaid, which the Russes call Step. They come with that Swiftness and Caution, that there seldom is any Advice of them; and immediately fall upon what Booty they can find, and do what Mischief they can, and then return again with the same Expedition as they came on, before the Russes can make any Head against them to cut off their Retreat: And those that happen to be taken, on either Side, are used very barbarously, with seldom or never any Redemption from their Slavery. One of the Advantages therefore which was propos'd for making a Communication between the Wolga and the Don, was to have been a Barrier to prevent these Tartars from advancing farther into Russia.[64]

(Perry, 1698–1701)

A surprise attack near Kamishinka

Whilst I was employ'd at Camishinka, there was an Army every Year of 2000 Gentlemen on Horseback, being most part of them Mordwa and Morzee Tartars, immediate Subjects to the Czar, (of whom I shall have occasion to speak more hereafter) with 4000 Foot, and 12 Field-Pieces, who were sent to cover the Workmen from the Incursions of the said Cabans; and Guards and out Centinels were placed at several Miles Distance, on the Tops of Hills and Proper Places, to prevent our being surprized: But notwithstanding all our Guards and Watches that have been placed, a Party of between 3 and 4000 of these [Kuban] Tartars once came just as it was Day in the Morning, without our having the least Advice of them, up to our very Camp; and when they found that the Alarm was taken, and our Cannon began to play upon them from our Lines, they immediately retired with the same Speed they came on, before our Men could mount or get in any Order to attack them, it requiring some time before they could come to their Horses; besides, that many of their Horses that were at some Distance without the Camp, were surprized and carried off by the Enemy. They carried off in all about 1400 Horses, some of which belonged to the Army, and others to the Workmen; with several People that were looking after the Horses where they were feeding in the Meadows, at some Distance from the Camp; there being no Inclosures in that Countrey.[65]

(Perry, 1698–1701)

What's in a name?

KOOBAN, in the RUSSIAN language signifies a wild hog; which name was given to the these Tartars on account of their fierce and savage nature, having cost IVAN WASSILOWITZ more trouble to subdue them than either the CRIM or NAGAY Tartars: they are loaden with a heavy poll-tax both for themselves and cattle.[66]

(Woodroofe, in Hanway, January 1741)

At Chernoyare

[Chernoyare] is defended by a ditch, with some canon and chevaux de frize. They trade with the KHALMUCKS, KOOBANS and other TARTARS.

The 19th [October 1743] we advanced near 90 versts ... We found the place inhabited by some NAGAY and CIRCASSIAN TARTARS, who ply on the river with open boats, of which there are a few regular stages for the convenience of the government. Here also some settlements of the KHALMUCKS.[67]

(Hanway, October 1743)

Tatars of Astrakhan and region

Astrakhan's population was more complex and mixed than Kazan's, in terms both of different Tatar groups and of other nationalities. Bruce and Georgi cited the Nogays as the region's dominant Tatar group. Academicians and modern scholars have identified several groups, including settled, semi-nomadic, nomadic and transient communities. The main Tatar groups (excluding Central Asian traders) were: urban and 'service' Kazan Tatars, brought to Astrakhan by Peter the Great; Mishar Tatars from Penza and Nizhny Novgorod; small rural groups from Ryazan (Kasimov); different types of Nogays; settled Astrakhan town (*yourtovi*) and village (*aulni*) Tatars; semi-nomadic (Yetisen); nomadic (Koschevi); the nomadic Nogay-Karagash from the Kuban (remnants of Nogays captured by Kalmyks in the early eighteenth century); rural, semi-nomadic Outars (related to the Nogay) around the Caspian, between Astrakhan and the Kalmyk steppe; and semi-nomadic Turkmens of the Lower Volga.[68] Pallas described one such group, the Kundure Tatars roaming by the River Akhtuba (cover illustration), who shared Nogay and Kirghiz customs.[69] Bruce (again following Olearius) described the existence of nomadic Nogays and commented on their interaction with and partial subjection to Russia, as well as rare instances of conversion.[70] Cook described the village life of Nogays, who lived in houses during the winter but tents in summer. Gmelin also mentioned Tatar villages 'in a poor state' around Astrakhan.[71] Hanway noted settled, agricultural 'Crim' Tatars. Tatars from Central Asia were referred to as from Khiva (Chvinzi) and Bukhara.

Astrakhan's Tatar suburbs reflected, as in Kazan, segregation from Russians and Europeans but also greater variety. All suburbs (as shown in Gmelin's map of c.1770) lay to the south of the canal running east–west through the city from the Kutum to the Volga or along the Volga.[72] There was a Tatar quarter immediately beyond the canal, alongside the Armenian one. The main Tatar suburb (Tiek or Zarew), 'with a great number of streets with wooden houses',[73] was further south along the Volga. This too was divided: Kazan Tatars (the richest, presumably because of trade) lived along the large central street, whereas Astrakhan Tatars (fig.6), who were officially forbidden long-distance trade, lived in the other streets. They were the poorest, and lived by minimal local trade, agriculture and manual work, and were used in public services, such as running Crown-carriages to Kizliar.[74] Other communities lay between these two Tatar suburbs: the Agrishan (Tatars descended from Indians); Besrodnaya (literally 'without nation'), a mixed market town;[75] and the Bukharan and Ghilanian

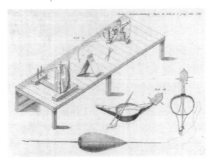

fig.6

suburbs.[76] The eighteenth-century urban Tatar population of Astrakhan has been estimated at about 8000, with some 6000–7000 rural Nogays and migrants from the middle Volga.[77]

The Astrakhan mosques appear not to have had the cachet of Kazan's, although Gmelin mentioned the *Bolshaya Shakarshkaya Mechet*, an unfinished 'Great' wooden mosque on stone foundations in the Tatar sector, between the Bukharan and Agrishan quarters.[78] Each suburb apparently had a different number of mosques, presumably reflecting their wealth.[79] Georgi mentioned fifteen mosques in all and 'good schools'.[80]

The travellers described local Muslim Tatars of Astrakhan as expert agriculturalists and traders, and Central Asian ones as traders. Agricultural production was mainly millet, pulses and melons in the villages and, around Astrakhan, 'garden stuff', which supplied the whole town. The Tatars also traded in their 'manufactures' of cotton, leather, soap and silk;[81] their 'magazine' for goods was a substantial brick building.[82] The travellers wrote approvingly of Tatar hospitality, cleanliness and appearance. Hanway, always conscious of his role as an upholder of the Christian faith, deprecated the 'awful tone' of a Tatar 'priest' during invocations and Tatar 'lack of civilization'. Cook's anecdotes give a more accurate idea of relations between Tatars and Europeans in Astrakhan. Both Bell and Bruce mentioned the distinctive nostril ring worn by Nogay women (fig.7), while Bell's description of a wealthy Tatar lady 'of extraordinary

Hocaickax mamupka.
Eine Nogaische Tatarin.
Feme de Tatares Nogais.

fig.7

beauty' riding an ox conveys an exoticism worthy of nineteenth-century
orientalists. The combination of wealth and physical beauty was presented
as a mark of superiority (and therefore acceptability) distinguishing certain
'Tatars' from others. Georgi, in contrast, stressed the poverty of the Nogays
in the 1770s. The 'wretchedness' of such peoples may have been exaggerated
by academicians to suit imperial motives (see Conclusion). Bruce generalised on the branch of Islam to which the Astrakhan Tatars belonged ('the
sect of the Turks', i.e. Sunni), while Georgi distinguished more precisely
between settled Nogay Tatars of Astrakhan and semi-nomadic ones, who are
'extremely ignorant' and partly pagan.[83] The former were more traditionally
Sunni Islamic, although the Yourtovi practiced certain Sufi rites, such as
worship of saints. Rural and nomadic Tatars were Muslim but also followed
their own traditions. The Karagash-Nogays, for example, had female
shamans.[84] The differences between so-called Muslim Tatar and Kalmyk
Tatar were repeatedly stressed and very much weighed against the Kalmyks.

Bruce on the Nogays

It seems beyond a dispute, the Tartars were unknown to the ancient geographers, who comprehended them under the general appellation of Scythians and Sarmatians; it is evident the Tartars consist of several nations,
distinct among themselves, in their names, language and customs. The
Nagayans, with the Tartars of Casan, and some others inhabiting between
the Wolga and the Don, or Tanais, are said to have Indians, who revolting
from their sovereigns about the year 1212, emigrated and settled themselves on the Palus Meotis, near the Euxine sea, and extending their con-

quests to the river Don, and from thence at last to the Wolga, near which they inhabit at this day. The Nagayans are seated along the shores of the Caspian, from the river Iaick, to the Wolga. Before this country was conquered by the Russians, it was inhabited altogether by Tartars, but now they are neither suffered to reside within this city, nor build a new one, nor fortify any of their towns or villages with walls.

The Nagayans live for the most part in round huts made of bull-rushes, or canes, and seldom exceed twelve or thirteen yards in circumference, with a hole at the top to let out the smoak; yet the least of these huts has a falcon, or hawk, as those Tartars are great masters of this sport: they have hawks of all sorts and sizes, each bred to fly at different kinds of game. The Russians call the Nagayans, vagabonds as they have no settled habitations in the summer, but ramble up and down. They pack up their huts in carts; their wives, children, and goods, on camels, horses, and oxen; and move about from one place to another, where they can find better pasturage for their cattle. When winter approaches, they begin to reassemble with their flocks, to pass it in several troops near Astrachan, where they are furnished with arms to repulse any inroads from the Kalmucks, or other Tartars from the River Iaick; and as soon as the winter is over, they are obliged to return all their arms. They pay no tribute to the Russian emperor, but are obliged to serve him in his wars under their own commanders, as they are, in time of peace, governed by their own petty princes and judges. To secure their obedience to the emperor, he has always some of their princes, or myrzas, hostages in the castle of Astrachan.

Their religion is Mahometanism, of the same sect with the Turks, except some few who have embraced the religion of the Greek church: they are used to dedicate some of their children, like the Nazarites, to God or to some saint or other; they are distinguished from the rest by a ring, which the boys wear in their right ear, and the girls in their nostril. They live upon what their cattle, hunting, and fishing supply them with. They make use of fish dried in the sun instead of bread, although they also make cakes of meal and rice; they eat camels and horse flesh, and they hold mares milk in great esteem: their common drink is milk and water, yet, besides wine, hydromel (or mead), and brandy, they find indifferent good beer in Astrachan: their cattle are much the same with those of the Kalmucks. The Nagayans in their persons are handsomer than the Kalmucks, especially their women; the men wear a loose coat of some coarse cloth, and over that a sort of cloak of sheep skin, the woolly side outwards, with a cap of the same on their heads; the cap is commonly of a black colour. Their women are clad in white linen, with a plaited coif on their heads, both sides of which is ornamented with a great many pieces of silver coin, hanging down.[85]

(Bruce, 1722)

Bell's stay in Astrakhan, 1716

The Mahometan TARTARS here live without the town; and have the same privileges as in other places. I met several of their women in the street with rings in their noses, which were of different value, according to the rank of the person who wore them; some of gold, and other set with precious stones. On enquiring the reason of such a singular ornament, I was told, that it was the consequence of a religious dedication of these persons to the service of God: It is made by the parents, even while the mother is pregnant; in token whereof, as soon as the child is born, they put a ring in the right nostril, which continues there until death. I have seen some with two such rings.[86]

...

One day as I was walking through the streets of ASTRACHAN, I observed a very singular appearance; it was a pretty TARTAR [Nogay] lady mounted astride upon an ox; she had a ring in her nose, and string drawn through the nose of the ox, which served instead a bridle; she was dressed better than common, and attended by a footman; the singularity of the equipage, but particularly her extraordinary beauty, drew my attention. The MAHOMETAN must not be confounded with the KALMUCK TARTARS; the first are a well looked civilized people in comparison of the other.[87]

(Bell, July 1716)

The Nogay way of life

The Nagai and Karacalpaaks are a little swarthy, from their being, I suppose, in the fields during the summer season, but in other respects, they are as well sunned as any man in Europe, and their women are very agreeable. The Nagai till and dress the grounds, in which the sow millet, pulse, oats, and Indian wheat, with a variety of the finest melons in the world. They live in houses in the neighbourhood of Astrachan in the winter season, but dress the land, feed their herds, hunt, and fish during the summer, and, for their greater conveniency, live in tents, not very unlike the Kalmucks, but much more cleanly every way.

No broils happen betwitxt the Nagai and the Kalmucks; for the Nagai inhabit the islands betwixt Astrachan and the Caspian sea, whereas the Kalmucks are obliged to feed their flocks in the desart to the west of the Volga.[88]

(Cook, 1740)

The Crim Tatars

For several miles round this city [Astrakhan] where the soil will admit cultivation, there are settlements of a very civil and industrious people of the race of the CRIM TARTARS, who are tributary to the RUSSIANS. In the summer they improve their land, the chief products of which are manna (seed so called), oats, musk and water-melons; but they reckon that their principal treasure consists in their wives and children, with their sheep, horses and cattle. When any of the daughters become marriageable, they cover her tent with white linen, and put a painted cloth on top, which is usually tied with red strings; they also have a painted wagon on the side of the tent; and this is to be her marriage portion. Those who design to marry observe this signal, and the girl is generally given to him who offers the father the most valuable present. Those people are MAHOMMEDANS, and, contrary to the practice of the KHALMUCKS, extremely nice in their burying places. They dig the graves very deep, and after lining them with bricks dried in the sun, and whitewashing them in the inside, they build a cover over them. They also raise thick walls of mud round each tomb, on the top of which are fixed one or more white flags, according to the character of the deceased.[89]

(Hanway, 1743)

Farming, fowling and a visit to the women's tent

One day walking by a large field of millet ... my dog went among the millet and sprung some quail, some of which we shot. A Tartar, to whom the field belonged, came to us. We imagined ... that he desired to chide us ... and would ... have been glad we had been somewhere else; not that we were in the least afraid of anything the Tartar would do, but the thoughts of having wantonly wronged a harmless kind of people, were very disagreeable.

... when he came to us, he with great courtesy told us that these birds destroyed his millet, and that if we liked the diversion of killing them ... it was probable we would get 100 for one. He said he would go to his tent and provide some delicious melons by the time we should return, not doubting but that we would be very thirsty.[90]

...

Mr Posset was accustomed to hire from the Tartar Muzsas, a number of their men, in the spring time, to dress the vine gardens, for he had fine gardens on his own property, into which he never permitted the labourers belonging to the Empire to enter, lest they might have accused him of employing them in dressing his own gardens ... He therefore was well acquainted with the Tartar Muzsas, who had been many years hospitably entertained in ... his house; they therefore prevailed with him to go with

Mrs Posset, in the summer time, to their camp, to take a dinner, obliging themselves to put no restraint in either of them, which the difference in religion (they being all Mahometans), might ... have occasioned. It is well enough known that the Mahometans are very careful to keep themselves very clean, by bathing, depilation, or taking off the hair which grows about the greater emunctories upon the body, and by daily ablutions, particularly before and after repasts.

At Mr and Mrs Posset's arrival, dinner was served up ... principally mutton and fowls. After dinner was over, Mrs Posset expressed some desire to visit their wives ... She accordingly was introduced into a large tent, where many of the Muzsas wives had assembled, no doubt to see and converse with a Christian, with whom they very rarely, if ever, had any correspondence.

The men had not long retired into their former tent ... till they were alarmed with a great screaming among the women, but Mrs Posset's voice was heard much louder than any of the rest; whereupon Posset, forgetting, that it was dangerous and very rude, immediately ran to, and without any hesitation, entered the womens tent, where he spied the Tartar women sitting opposite to Mrs Posset, exposing what modesty should be hid, and two of them wanted much to explore what Mrs Posset would have kept secret. Mr Posset immediately rescued his wife, and the Tartars were no ways dissatisfied with Posset's going into their wives tent. Mr Posset said, that he frequently went and visited the Tartars, but Mrs Posset never could be prevailed upon to repeat her visits. The old woman acknowledged the truth of this.[91]

(Cook, 1740s)

Perils of trading

This year the Caracalpake Tartars obtained liberty to trade with the people of Astrachan: But they never came into the city, and encamped at a distance of eight to ten versts from it, where the Astrachan merchants and Tartars went, but I was never informed that their commerce was of any advantage. Towards the latter year they decamped and returned homewards: But a body of Kalmucks, altogether unknown to the government of Astrachan, way-laid them, and made boty of a great deal of their cattle and merchandize.[92]

(Cook, 1743)

Tatar devotion

The TARTARS hold ... image worship in the utmost abomination; they will not carry even money which has impression of man, bird, beast, creeping things, or insect, into their temples. Their devotion is in silence and prostrations, except that the priest in an awful tone at certain times utters an invocation to the lord of nature, through the mediation of MAHOMMED. It must be observed, that the TARTARS about this city [Astrakhan] and kingdom, were formerly distinguished under denominations different from the present; for these countries were but little known, nor are they yet sufficiently civilized to admit of that communication, which affords an opportunity for an entire discovery, though the RUSSIANS have made a great progress in it. The NAGAY TARTARS are MAHOMMEDANS, resembling in countenance the KHALMUCKS, but better favoured, for their eyes are not so small; these and the KOOBANS are driven off to the east-ward, and have seldom of late years made any inroads on the RUSSIAN frontiers.[93]

(Hanway, October 1743)

Inside a Tatar house

They [Captain Kelly and his wife] took us into the opposite house which is inhabited by Tartars, as a Curiosity. More than two-thirds of the room was occupied by a Stage or Divan covered with a Carpet. Here they sit in the day and sleep at night. Upon our entering the Women all retired. Every thing was very neat; the bedding was put aside in the day time, two shelves above were filled with a variety of Pottery and China ware; and a row of Cushions were laid along the back of the Divan. The whole Tartar abode appeared neat and particularly the People.[94]

(Parkinson, June 1793)

Persians of Astrakhan

The extracts below highlight three key areas of Russo-Persian relations in the eighteenth century: threat of war, ambivalent diplomacy and commerce. Cook and Hanway observed the alarm induced in Astrakhan by Nader Shah's campaigns in Daghestan and Central Asia. Cook's account telescopes Nader Shah's Central Asian campaigns in 1740 and his 1741 attempt to subdue the Lezghi Tatars in Daghestan.[95] In 1742 Russian troops were sent to fortify Kizliar, rightly fearing that Nader Shah intended to advance there (see p.203).[96]

Astrakhan's situation made it a natural stopping point for embassies to and from St Petersburg. Its defences also made it a place of refuge for Persian exiles, who had been, or might one day be, of service to Russia.

Cook referred to Peter the Great's campaign in Daghestan in 1722–3 and to Ismael Bey, Shah Tahmasp II's envoy, who negotiated the treaty ceding parts of Shirvan and Ghilan provinces to Russia, and was forced to take refuge in Astrakhan for his pains. Cook, who had himself been part of an aborted embassy to Persia in 1746–7, conveyed the excitement and trouble the embassy of Hussein Khan, with his retinue of five hundred men and nineteen elephants, entailed in Astrakhan in the time of Nader Shah. Another important exile and social curiosity, in Parkinson's time, was Murtaza Quli Khan, half-brother of Agha Kuli Khan, the Qajar ruler of Astarabad, who was a contender for the throne of Persia. Catherine II had hoped to use Agha Muhammad Khan by supporting him in exchange for concessions over trade with India via Central Asia. Catherine sent an expedition to create a base in the Gulf of Astarabad in 1781, but the Russians were expelled. Muhammad Khan's rebel half-brother, Murtaza, then gained Russian support and was given a base in Astrakhan and Kizliar.[97]

Parkinson observed the domestic life of the small and mostly transient merchant community of Astrakhan's Persian quarter.[98] Georgi mentioned the Persians as being mostly from the Caspian area (Shirvan, Ghilan) and that they formed 'a particular society preserving the customs of their country'.[99] Other Persian merchants were in the Orenburg region (the biggest community), Ufa, and along the Terek and the Kama rivers.[100] Some in the Stravropol province of Orenburg were Christian converts, but most were of the 'sect of Ali' (Shiites).[101] None of the British travellers defined the religion of the Persians of Astrakhan; Cook and Parkinson did, however, voice contempt when describing the events and customs they witnessed. This was in keeping with European prejudices against Persia in the eighteenth century, to which a fascination and horror with Nader Shah was added.[102] Georgi's judgement of the Persian merchants in Russia is forthright: 'they are courageous, hasty, voluptuous, polite, but very covetous'.[103]

Defending Astrakhan from Nader Shah

After he [Nader Shah] had conquered these inhabited countries [Buchara, Khiva], he could proceed no farther for desarts infested by wandering hoards of Tartars, which inhabit the desert betwixt him and Astrachan … he garrisoned Chiva, and the other towns belonging the principality … and returned to Persia by way of Astrabat, Mezanderan, Casbin and Ardevil, with a design … to punish the rebellious Lesgee Tartars …

The careful Governor lost no time … in causing strong lines to be drawn round the south of Astrachan … He sent into the desert many parties of dragoons and irregulars … to bring him all intelligence.[104]

(Cook, 1740–41)

Preparations for defence

The colonel hearing that I was going to PERSIA, spoke much of NADIR SHAH, who had given great alarms on that side, when he was last winter in the neighbourhood of DERBEND; insomuch that a body of 18,000 RUSSIANS had been ordered to ASTRACHAN and KIZLAR ...[105]

(Hanway, October 1743)

The Persian ambassador's elephants

At this time we had no fewer than four Persian ambassadors at once in Russia ...

Ismael Bey, who had lived in Astrachan eighteen or twenty years: He made peace with Shach Tahmas [Tahmasb] and Peter the Great, granting to Peter, Giland, and all the provinces upon the west side of the Caspian Sea, betwixt it and the borders of Russia; but was afraid ever to return to Persia, and therefore lived at the Russian expence, and kept court like a great prince in Astrachan.

When any ambassador from Persia ... halted at Astrachan, a ... command of ... one hundred and twenty men kept guard upon Ismael Bey ...[106]

...

In the latter end of July [1740], nineteen elephants arrived on the west banks of the Volga, with an ambassador called Hussein Khan, and a great number of attendants, on their way to St Petersburg ... The one [ambassador] who came with the elephants, wanted much to have wintered in Astrachan ... but the Governor let him know, that in Astrachan there was neither provision nor conveniences for his retinue, being five hundred men and elephants ... The only liberty ... this ambassador could obtain, was to be permitted to go to the bagnio ... At last [after many excuses] he resolved to march ... orders were given ... to pass through all the towns and cities in Astrachan, without the ambassadors' being able to view them ... Indeed all sorts of men were glad at the departure of this troublesome man, especially as our markets were beginning to be very costly to the poorer house-keepers.

During his stay ... all care was taken, that neither Persians nor Tartars were permitted to go to him ...

I went over the river to see these monsters ... we went to one who seemed to be the largest, with two smaller female ones, on each side. They were all chained by the hinder legs with strong iron chains. The male elephant made a great noise ...

I saw these creatures go away, conveyed by four regiments: They moved from the south of the hill, northward, up the banks of the Volga. It is incredible how frighted the Russian horses were ...[107]

...

I there [St Petersburg] saw the public entry of the Persian ambassador, and the presents, with the elephants ... which was superb enough ... The unruly elephant was very troublesome ... These great beasts were covered with very silks, brocades, and cloth of gold, some of them reached near the ground. They gave out that King Solomon's tent covered one of them. It was of silk, very large, ancient ... but I scarcely believe it was Solomon's. This however was esteemed a precious present.[108]

(Cook, 1740)

The khan of Astrabad

In the afternoon the refugee Khan from Persia made his appearance accompanied by his Russian interpreter: so that we were obliged to converse with him by means of a third Person. One of his attendants brought him from time to time a pipe in water which after two or three inspirations he returned, or when he meant to pay a compliment, offered to some person near him. We came in each of us for the honour of a whiff. He kept his cap or turban on the whole time; his robe was red cloth tied round with a sash; his slippers were blue, he wore a cloak over his robe when he entered which he afterwards laid aside. His Nose was aquiline, his Eyes full and his Countenance expressive with the most handsome black beard I ever saw. What struck me as much as anything was the inharmonious vulgar tone of his voice. He invited us to go and see him. Several Persian Merchants came and presented him with flowers which he gave to the ladies. One who stuck very close to him was known, the Ober-Commandant said, to carry on a correspondence with his brother.

I understand that he was the Khan of Astrabad and that his eldest brother being desirous of subjecting the whole kingdom to himself had attacked this his younger brother and obliged him to fly for his life. At this moment he is at war with all the other Khans. Several battles have been fought and he has been often wounded. This eldest brother has no children and indeed as I was told by one person has been rendered incapable of having any. On the contrary the younger brother has several.

The Empress makes him an allowance of 12,000 roubles a year. I think he has about sixty Persons with him. It is in contemplation to remove him to Kislar: to which he is very averse because then he would not meet with the same society, he would not be treated with the same respect and he dreads the Climate. The Russian Government neither wishes to offend the brother by taking him too decidedly under its protection; nor to offend him by a want of attention; for fear that one or the other should in process of time be in a situation to revenge the affront.

He and his Persians rise at three in the morning, pay their adorations, smoke, drink their sherbert and go to bed again. They rise again either at six or nine and the rest of the day is divided between smoking and sleeping. To see Women come into society as they do here is a new sight to him and they say he is much amused with it.[109]

The Over Commandant accompanied us after dinner on a visit to the Khan ... who could not immediately receive us. We were treated in the first place with tea ... and half a score dishes of fruit ... These were handed to us one after another. Besides which we had sherbert and a whiff of his Pipe. The Over Commandant says he has been an exile at the courts of different Khans for the last nine years. The young man who handed the Pipe to him is supposed to supply the place of a mistress.[110]

He sat in the eastern manner all this time on his Divan ... Several of his Ministers were in the room, particularly his Mufti and his Visier ... A curtain covered a window which looked into a chamber ... where he kept an Uncle and another Person in chains. As we went out all his attendants were in waiting and formed a lane. Their dress in general was a long outward garment of red Cloth, a close garment of stuff for the most part of some other colour tied with a sash under that, a Turban, Trowsers and slippers. His whole suite is about seventy. Every man has a divan to himself.[111]

...

In the afternoon we took a little walk out with the Ober Commandant to the Persian shops and the quarter of the Indians ... The Persian habitations are very uncomfortable. We went into one consisting of a single Apartment, dark and stinking, two thirds of which was taken up with the Divan on which they sleep. The richest Merchants when unmarried live in this way. When married they have a house and quit their shops.[112]

...

The Over-Commandant told me that ... the Persians are about 100: three or four of them being married and live in convenient houses; but the rest, being here at certain times only for the purposes of trading, content themselves with Cabines such as we saw ...[113]

(Parkinson, June 1793)

Indians of Astrakhan

The Indian presence in Astrakhan was less fraught with tensions than the Persian one, but for all travellers it was an essential curiosity. Indian merchants had been in Astrakhan since the early seventeenth century, if not before, and had been allowed to travel upstream to Kazan, some even settling in Moscow.[114] There was also a long history of failed missions from Russia to India in the seventeenth century. While there was poor demand for Russian produce in India, Russia was keen to receive India's goods (silver, cotton, silk, spices, precious stones) and craftsmanship (masons, textile workers). Initially Indian merchants were exempt from certain trade and travel restrictions. The height of Indian trading success in Astrakhan was during Peter the Great's reign, when they had companies with close ties with the Indian diaspora in Iran and the Caspian.[115] The revenue they brought to the Russian treasury was such that, according to Bruce, the emperor allowed them to hold a *suttee* or funeral pyre for a merchant's widow.

In 1725 there were some 209 Indians living in Astrakhan, but by the 1740s the community was in decline. A 1747 census shows only fifty-

fig.8

one, with most from Multan (now Pakistan).[116] There were also Indians at Kizliar at this period.[117] The decline in the community was brought about by the imposition of bureaucratic strangleholds that prevented them from moving freely outside Astrakhan, as well as competition from the Armenians and the interruption of Russian trade with Persia and India. In the late 1790s the total number of Indians, according to the Vice-Governor, was about a hundred, although Pallas reported only about forty.[118] There may have been confusion over Indians who had renounced their faith and those who had not, or those who had married Tatar women and lived in separate communities. By this time the Indians were chiefly involved in money lending or exchanging. The change in both European and Russian attitudes towards the 'Banyans' (Indian merchants) is well conveyed by the travellers. Responses range from benevolence and respect to the extreme negativity of the Russians at the end of the century. Although targeted at the Multani community in Astrakhan, such antagonism echoes the contemporary negativity of many British in India towards Hindustanis.[119]

The Indian 'temple' was one of the unmissable sights of Astrakhan (fig.8). Travellers stressed either the 'hideousness' of Indian 'pagan' art – a stereotypical European view from the sixteenth century onwards – or its grandiose qualities.[120] Parkinson's more 'enlightened' description resembles that of Pallas,[121] who also noted how the Indians went every evening to the Volga for their 'ablutions'.[122]

'A good natured, innocent kind of people'

There are a few INDIANS, or BANIANS, at this place who have a streak of yellow down their forehead, made with saffron or some other vegetable. They are a good natured, innocent kind of people, who live mostly on fruits.[123]

(Bell, July 1716)

An account of suttee

[T]he Banyans without doubt contribute most to its [Astrakhan's] flourishing condition. They are a sort of Pagan Indians, whose principal pursuit is trade, and have their factory within the city. One of their chief merchants dying at this time, his widow desired leave of the emperor to burn herself with his corpse, according to the custom of their country: but his majesty, unwilling to encourage so barbarous a custom, refused her request, and the Indian factory were so much dissatisfied with it, that they threatened to withdraw from the city with their effects. His Majesty ... at last gave them leave ... The corpse being dressed in his cloaths, was carried to some little distance from the town, where a funeral pile of dry wood was raised, and the body laid upon it: before the pile were hung Indian carpets, to prevent it being seen. The wife in her best apparel ... attended by great number of Indians of both sexes, was led by a bramin or priest, to the funeral pile, which on her approach was kindled: she then distributed her upper apparel and jewels among her friends and acquaintances, of whom she took her last farewell with a great deal of ceremony, and the pile being in full flame, and the carpets taken down, she leaped into the midst of the fire; her friends then poured quantities of oil over her, and reduced both corpses to ashes, which were carefully gathered and put into an urn, to be conveyed to their relations in India.[124]

The Banyans are incomparably more ingenious, subtle and civil, than any of the other Indians: there is no trade in Persia, or the Turkish dominions, which is not principally managed by them ...[125]

(Bruce, July 1722)

An Englishman in the temple

My curiosity carried me to see the devotion of the INDIAN PAGANS in the little temple which they have here. Their priests use beads, incense, caps, prostrations and offerings: they have also small bells with other music, and raise their voices in singing with the utmost vehemence. The object of their adoration was a PAGOD, ugly and deformed to a degree of horror. After the service was over, they presented me some of the fruits which had been offered to this idol; but I thought proper to refuse them, not without some melancholy reflections on the abject state to which human reason is frequently reduced.[126]

(Hanway, October 1743)

Indian community life and religion

The Indians carry on no commerce but live on the interest of their money being literally like the Jews usurers by profession. The Vice-Governor told me that their number was about a hundred: that they burn their dead and regard an interment as a subject of rejoicing. The Ober-Commandant had written to the G[overnor] General that they were a useless sort of people and ought to be driven out of the country. They seem to live within the precincts of one great inclosure ... in the most uncomfortable way imaginable. We entered and walked a good way along alley where we understood that they lived and we were almost suffocated with Smoke. We saw several perched on the walls of their inclosure where they often appear, I understand, perfectly naked.

They eat no meat but subsist on vegetables and have a great respect for dogs, believing that the souls of those who die migrate into the bodies of those animals. We met a party who were well dressed ... I was told that several of them are very rich. I understand that they have no women of their own and their principal expense is in that article.[127]

The Indians, he [Mr Agathi] assured me, are Sodomites and have their boys from Casan. The Governor's lady told me that they lend their money at the enormous interest of five Copecks a rouble per month. At the same time they live at no expense.[128]

...

I walked out early this morning to the Cathedral... through the Persian shops and into the Indian caravanserai. This is a long square of one floor, covered in the manner of the East with Soil. Several windows open to the roof, flowers or plants in pots stand there, and the Indians themselves are frequently to be seen on the roof. There was a schism among them some time ago, they separated, and a part of them removed to another habitation. They live in a very dirty way and are almost devoured by Vermin (which their religion forbids them to kill), especially the Dervises. The wives of those who are married to Tartar women continue to reside in the Tartar abode and their husbands visit them there but never pass the night with them for fear of being murdered.[129]

She [the governor's wife] told me that there arrive Indians here from time to time, very poor at first and obliged to act in the capacity of servants: that they get rich however by degrees, and then follow the trade of the rest, namely that of usury. That some of them are married to Tartar women but that the issue of such marriages are brought up in the Mahomedan religion. That they give two great entertainments, the married people one, and the unmarried another, to all the Town in their respective abodes ...[130]

...

When we entered the Indian place of worship we found a Bramin on his hams before an altar preparing himself. One of his assistants soon after handed a small pot of incense to him, which he continued afterwards to fan. Before he rose to present it I observed him twirling round his hands in the same manner exactly as the Calmuc priests did. A few drops of water were thrown on the incense in order to produce a vapour which is considered as a representation of the air, one of the four elements and that which on this occasion is intended to be offered. The presentation of this element as well as those which came after, was accompanied by the whole congregation chaunting together with the tinkling of Bells and Cymbals. The Dervise next as a symbol of light lighted a row of six wicks and presented them in the same manner as the incense (he raised and lowered it alternately) chaunting and tinkling the bell which he held in his left hands before. To represent water he poured a little on the ground at several different times and to represent the earth he held up a small square piece of doubled linen. When the offering[s] were finished the bells and the Cymbals ceased.

The second part of the ceremony was to taste all the Elements. For this purpose the consecrated water in the first place was sprinkled on each of the Congregation: then the lighted wicks were handed round and each person put his hand into the flame. Afterwards a small spoonful of water was poured into the hand of every one which he immediately sucked up: and lastly by way of tasting Earth a plate of cut cucumbers went round and every one took a little. The Service then ended and we were immediately presented with a plate of Sugar candy.

Sometime during the latter part of the service (this was after the tasting of the Fire) they fell on their faces and remained in that position for some time. After which, rising on their hams, a prayer was said by the Dervise for their country. The rest of the service being chaunted, it was the only occasion that we had an opportunity of remarking the tones of their pronunciation, which struck me as not unlike French.

The congregation consisted of about sixteen Persons who dropped in one after another, and as they entered squatted down first on their hams, and the touched the ground with their foreheads.

The greatest part of the temple was occupied by a matted Divan upon which they all stood. Upon an inclined plane rising from what I call the altar were placed their Idols in two rows, ornamented several of them like the Calmuc with Chains of Pearls. On the middle upper row were I think five of these. The largest in the middle. Their size was that of a doll. Below was a short one with a Baskir cap which had the preeminence. Another was in the form of a dog etc. etc. Another with several arms. Two with goats heads etc. etc. The Idols are in the frame suspended from the ceiling, Their faces are of metal and their garments flowered. On the left hand upon the altar, as well as two black stones lying upon it the genetal parts of the two sexes were represented. [On the left] an upright Penis was in the middle and two representations of the female parts were represented on each side of it. On [the stones] the female parts were represented by white streaks which were[meant] to be natural but probably were artificial. Several of the Utensils employed in the service were on the ground below. We were warned not to touch anything.

They had the complaisance to offer us a dish of tea and behaved to us with great civility.[131]

(Parkinson, June–July 1793)

Armenians of Astrakhan

The Armenians held an exceptionally advantageous position in Russia for most of the eighteenth century. The Armenian trade diaspora was very old, but in 1667 the Armenian merchants of New Julfa (the Armenian quarter of Isfahan established in 1605) brokered an agreement with the tsar to convey all the raw silk from Persia via Russia to Europe.[132] Thus began their control of Persian–Russian and other foreign trade via the Caspian and the Volga, with links east to India, Central Asia and China, and west to the Ottoman lands, the Baltic and Europe.[133] Armenians had been in Astrakhan (and Kazan) since the seventeenth century and had displaced Indians as the main traders in the city by the early eighteenth century.[134]

Persecution in Persia[135] and political events, such as the fall of the Safavid state,[136] also prompted new arrivals throughout the century. Besides Astrakhan, there were Armenian communities in Moscow, St Petersburg, Orenburg, the North Caucasus and Azov, and in 1778–9 virtually a whole town of exiles from the Crimea was created at Nor Nakhichevan (near Rostov on Don).[137] The Armenian community in Astrakhan grew steadily, from about 200 households in 1746 to more than 1280 males (family heads) in the 1770s.[138] The spurt of incomers in the 1740s was mostly due to the state of Persia under Nader Shah, when ties with New Julfa were broken.[139] The community was said to enjoy 'all possible privileges' (i.e. more than Russians).[140] Catherine II 'established a loan-bank, solely for the purpose of facilitating and extending the trade and manufactures' of the Armenians;[141] they had tax benefits, their own court house and judges, 'chiefs of their own election' and their own Town Hall.[142] Herzig has written on the codification of Armenian customary law in Astrakhan (Astrakhan Law Book, eighteenth century), which included multilingual documents and in some ways resembled Islamic practice.[143]

Armenians enjoyed freedom of religion, including the right to processions.[144] Their wealth enabled them to build large stone churches (fig.9).[145] Houses in the Armenian quarter, south of the canal, were either wooden or European-style stone ones.[146] Although trade was their chief occupation, Armenians were also involved in bagnio keeping and barbering, small

fig.9

manufactures such as blacksmithing and clock-making, market gardening and domestic silk production.[147] The last was never as successful as the Moscow-based industry.[148] In 1795 an Armenian printing press relocated from Nor Nakhichevan to Astrakhan.[149]

Such wealth and privilege did not make Armenians (fig.10) popular with Russians. Many reasons were given for this. Their ancient Christian faith was suspect because some of its customs resembled Jewish or Catholic ones[150] (Gmelin went as far as to say he preferred the Jews,[151] whose presence in Astrakhan is not mentioned by the travellers). All the Armenians' faults were attributed to love of 'greedy gain'. Although they were educated, their drive for 'traffic' meant they had no 'remarkably learned men among them'. Even their acknowledged qualities, such as cleanliness, modesty and (except when entertaining) frugality were attributed to prudence.[152] They had the reputation of loyalty to their traditions.[153] The travellers, notably Cook, reflected such views, while contrasting Armenian industry to Russian laziness.

The Georgian community in Astrakhan is barely mentioned by the travellers, although they had their share of exiles,[154] ambassadors and traders there. The last appear not to have had a major role in the city's business,

fig.10

although they were closely involved with Armenian trade with Georgia outside Astrakhan.[155] Cook mentioned them only as army recruits in the garrison. The omission with regards to the Georgians in Astrakhan suggests either that they were not considered influential enough to merit special description, or that here they were seen as part of the Russian community.

A governor grumbles

He [Governor Tatishchev] then spoke of the Armenian traders, who were our great opponents, observing 'that they are the most crafty people in all ASIA, and delight in fraud. Let them, continued he, get 50 per cent in a fair way, they are not contented without cheating five, and the five is sweeter to them than the 50'. Though this is in some measure true, part of it might be carried to the account of the old man's [Tatishchev's] inability, crafty as he was, to get of them all he desired.[156]

(Hanway, October 1743)

Astrakhan's threadbare silk industry

Its [Astrakhan] merchants from very different nations, not only reside here for a time, but many are born in the place, and through length of time, seeing the advantages and privileges [they] declare themselves subjects of Russia, so that at present many Armenians, who, every one knows, are the natural subjects of either Persia or Turkey, deny their allegiance to either of these mighty monarchies; and even, when they reside for a time in either of these empires, boldly claim the protection of the Russian ambassadors, residents or consuls.[157]

... the Armenians are allowed indeed to transport European goods of all sorts, except warlike and naval stores, but they must sell none in Russia, and must buy them with the produce of raw silks of the Persian growth, or jewels.[158]

The city is inhabited by a great number of Georgians, who embrace the Greek religion, and serve in the army, as also the Armenians. They do not seek much after any glory than merchandise, and are reckoned as cunning as the Jews, though they all profess the Christian religion. I have often thought, and am still of the opinion, that they, viz. the Armenians and the Georgians, are the descendants of the Jews who were sent into captivity by Nebuchaddrezzar. They are liker the Jews than any other people I ever saw, and, though they are Christians, yet they have all the cunning and deceit of their progenitors.[159]

...

... the Governor and his family went by water to see a silkworm shade, which an Armenian merchant, had by his knowledge and industry, produced about two or three years ago ... The Armenian had planted the garden with mulberries four or five years before this in less than two acres of ground; and he said, that he hoped this year would produce a bale of good silk ... I overheard them saying that the great emperor Peter had planted a mulberry garden ... I said nothing to any of the Governor's family, but privately caused my servant to hire a boat ... at the distance of two versts from Astrachan I was landed on a very pleasant island, on top of which ... was built a long line of houses ... which I was told was the factory ... I went, in great hopes of being very agreeably entertained: but how much I was disappointed, when ... I found a poor woman, and some miserable children, who told me that, her husband had gone fishing for their dinner; that the great silk-work of Peter the Great was reduced to eight or nine worms, only to keep up the name of it, and give bread to this poor, lazy, indolent and ignorant family of beggars; but I understood, that an annual sum allotted by Peter for propagating silk-worms ... was appointed for the relief of some court beggars.[160]

(Cook, 1740s)

Social life in a cosmopolitan city

I had some conversation ... with a Person now resident here but a native of Achaia. He told me the whole trade of Astracan is in the hands of the Armenians and the Persians. That the Armenians call themselves subjects of Russia at Astracan and subjects of Persia when they are in that country. That the trade is spoilt by being carried on by people who are not resident in the country but who come only to sell their goods. That the Government does not bestow a thought or stir a finger for the benefit of commerce here. That the Russians are wholly occupied by the Fishery.[161]

...

[We] were invited to dine with our Armenian Friend at eleven o'clock ... Our party consisted of the Ober Comandant, three other Russian officers including our crazy countryman Mr ——, a Russian Merchant, and four Armenian Merchants viz. our host, his brother, his son inlaw and an old man who had been in England and Holland. It was remarkable that in this little party there were no less than five languages spoken alternatively, viz. Russ, Armenian, French, German and English. A table was set out before dinner according to the Russian fashion: two sorts of dried Caviar, Eau de vie, and a Persian wine. It is the custom of Armenians to begin their dinner with Eggs. We had a great variety of dishes, some Russian and some Armenian, a great variety of Wines, some Persian (particularly wine of Shiraz and Ispahan) and some Russian, and a great variety of fruits in the dessert which were chiefly Persian: Apples, Citron of great size, Dates, Acid preserved plums etc. I counted twenty-four Articles.[162]

...

We saw several Armenian women in this excursion walking about cloathed in a long white veil.[163]

...

There was also an Armenian Merchant and his wife present in the afternoon, both in their national dress. In general the Armenian Women do not go into company: but the husband of this lady is a fine Gentleman or rather is a lively young man who chuses to break the customs of his countrymen in this respect.[164]

The Over-Commandant told me that the number of Armenian houses here was 1,600 and the number of people not less than 10,000.[165]

...

Two young ladies just arrived from St Petersburg amused the Company by dancing the Russian, the Bohemian and the Cossack dances: and after supper a band of Armenian Music was provided and two Armenians who danced to it the Armenians dances. The horrid custom of drinking toasts was introduced ... and the poor Khan as well as ourselves were obliged to submit to it.[166]

(Parkinson, June–July 1793)

ENDNOTES

1   E.g. Georgi 1780–83, but Tooke (1799, vol.2) has Mongoles, Tartars, Manchures, Nations of uncertain Origin, Dispersed bands of European and Asiatic nations. He includes, but appears to play down, the Finnic element (p.276).

2   For an introduction to this subject see Hodgen; Berry; Porter. In eighteenth-century Britain these issues of progression by stages were particularly the domain of the great Scottish figures of the Enlightenment, including Hume, Ferguson, Millar and Smith.

3   Tooke 1799, vol.2, pp.117–20.

4   Quelquejay, pp.20–21; Barthold and Quelquejay 1960, pp.1337–38; Busigin and Zorin 1984; Iurchenkov 1997; Sanukov in E. Helimski, U. Kahrs, M. Scötsle eds., 2005.

5   Quelquejay, pp.20–21; Benzing. The language has words unrelated to Bulghar or Finnic.

6   Kappeler 2001, p.122, tab.3.

7   For contemporary academicians see e.g. Lepekhin 1774–83 and 1795; Georgi 1775, 1780–83, vol.1; Pallas 1788–93; Müller 1791.

8   Kappeler 2001, p.122; Georgi 1780–83, vol.1, p.68.

9   Werth 2003.

10   Georgi 1780–83, vol.1, p.92 (Cheremis), p.109 (Chuvash); Pallas 1788, vol.5, pp.38–39.

11   Georgi 1780–83, vol.1, pp.82ff, 104.

12   Pallas 1788, vol.1, p.111.

13   Pallas 1812, p.34.

14   Ibid., p.50.

15   Cf. Georgi 1780–83, vol.1, pp.73ff; Olearius 1967, pp.298–300.

16   Hill, ch.50, pp.328–31, uses language very similar to Bell's.

17   Bruce's passage derives much from Olearius (cf. Olearius 1967, pp.298–300).

18   See note 10 above.

19   Perry 1716, p.225.

20   Ibid., pp.225–27.

21   Bell, p.16.

22   Hanway, vol.1, pp.110–11.

23   Bruce, pp.231–33.

24   Bell, pp.22–23.

25   Hanway, vol.1, p.112.

26   Georgi 1780–83, vol.2, p.23; Tooke 1799, vol.2, p.51.

27   Gmelin 1751, vol.1, p.83, makes a point of contradicting Olearius. (See Olearius 1967, pp.328–29.)

28   Kazan University Library (Old Library), MSS 450, 4062, maps from 1768.

29   Gilmanov; Georgi 1780–83, vol.2, p.28.

30   This subject has been much written about. For an overview and bibliographies see Bobronikov, pp.204–5; Rorlich; Salikhov and Khayrutdinov; Nogmanov 2005 (the latter two with quotes from original sources); also Zahidullin, pp.60–61; Ishakov, pp.76ff; Giliazov 1997, *passim*.

31   Gmelin 1751, vol.1, pp.73–74.

32   Abdullin, p.127; Georgi 1780–83, vol.2, p.26.

33   Ibneeva, pp.115–18; Salikhov and Khayrutdinov, pp.17–19.

34 Salikhov and Khayrutdinov, pp.19–20.
35 Khalit, pp.81–83; Georgi 1780–83, vol.2, p.50, for a general description of the mosques.
36 Ibneeva, p.116; Salikhov and Khayrutdinov, pp.19–20; Abdullin, pp.126–27.
37 Georgi 1780–83, vol.1, p.19.
38 My thanks to Alexander Morrison for pointing this out.
39 Giljazov 1997, pp.21–23; Ishakov, pp.76–77; Khayrutdinov 1997, p.132.
40 Khayrutdinov 1997, pp.134–43.
41 Abdullin, pp.120–21; Khayrutdinov 1997, pp.33–35.
42 Abdullin, p.146.
43 The heavily painted faces of Tatar women are corroborated by nineteenth-century accounts: Fukhs 1817 (repr. 2005), pp.155ff; Turnerelli, p.316.
44 Gilmanov, p.59.
45 Georgi 1780–83, vol.2, pp.26–27 (see p.28 for village produce).
46 Ibid., p.25.
47 Ibid., pp.24, 50. An 'abyss' may have been a lettered person.
48 Zahidullin, p.61.
49 Georgi 1780–83, vol.2, pp.23–24.
50 Ibid., p.24.
51 Ibid., p.22.
52 Gmelin 1751, vol.1, p.71; Abdullin, p.139; Zahidullin, pp.58–59.
53 Abdullin, pp.140–41.
54 *Azbuka Tatarskovo Iazyka*, Moscow 1778.
55 Bell, pp.19–20.
56 Ibid., pp.23–24.
57 Bruce, p.234.
58 Parkinson, p.111.
59 Minorsky, pp.287–88.
60 Khodarkosvsky 2002, pp.126ff; Vásáry, pp.85–86.
61 Georgi 1780–83, vol.2, pp.74–75.
62 Ibid., pp.72–73.
63 Tooke 1799, vol.2, p.75.
64 Perry 1716, pp.87–89.
65 Ibid., pp.89–90.
66 Hanway, vol.1, pp.110–11.
67 Ibid., pp.108–9.
68 I owe this detailed breakdown of the Tatars around Astrakhan to Victor Victorin. See also Gmelin 1770–74, vol.2, pp.84ff; Georgi 1780–83, vol.2, pp.80ff. There were an estimated 9000–10,000 semi-nomadic Karagah-Nogais and about 1000–2000 Turkmen in the Astrakhan region.
69 Pallas 1812, pp.172–75.
70 Cf. Olearius 1967, pp.328–30.
71 Gmelin 1770–74, vol.2, p.123.
72 Ibid., tab.43; see also ibid., pp.84ff.
73 Georgi 1780–83, vol.4, p.379.
74 Gmelin 1770–74, vol.2, p.107.
75 Ibid., p.86.
76 Georgi 1780–83, vol.4, pp.378–79; Gmelin 1770–74, vol.2, pp.103–4.

77   I owe this information to Victor Victorin.

78   Gmelin 1770–74, vol.2, p.104.

79   Ibid., p.123.

80   Georgi 1780–83, vol.2, p.87.

81   Ibid., p.82.

82   Georgi 1780–83, vol.2, p.81; see also Gmelin 1751, vol.1, p.84.

83   Georgi 1780–83, vol.2, p.87; Gmelin specifies Sunni (1751, vol.1, p.129).

84   I owe this information to Victor Victorin.

85   Bruce, pp.247–49.

86   Bell, p.38.

87   Bell, p.43.

88   Cook, vol.1, p.260.

89   Hanway, vol.1, p.129.

90   Cook, vol.1, p.270.

91   Cook, vol.1, pp.318–20.

92   Cook, vol.2, p.120.

93   Hanway, vol.1, p.128.

94   Parkinson, p.173.

95   Perry 1993, p.855.

96   Ibid.

97   Pallas 1812, pp.261, 275. For the history of Iran from the period of Karim Khan Zand, see ibid., pp.261–76; Kazemadeh, pp.326–27.

98   See Georgi 1780–83, vol.2, pp.159–60 for the Persian community in Astrakhan and elsewhere in Russia.

99   Ibid., p.159.

100 Ibid., pp.159, 161; Tooke 1799, vol.2, p.115.

101 Ibid., pp.161–62.

102 Hanway, vol.1, p.335, reflected that the 'neglect of their moral duties' prepared the Persians for the 'ruin' in which they were involved (late Nader Shah period). He also commended them for hospitality, neatness, cleanliness, resignation (to their despotic government), but remarked that they were accustomed to cruelty (pp.330–31). See also Hanway, vol.1, chs 25–51, *passim*; Teissier 2004 and 2009.

103 Georgi 1780–83, vol.2, p.159.

104 Cook, vol.1, pp.306, 307.

105 Hanway, vol.1, p.102.

106 Cook, vol.1, pp.342–343.

107 Ibid., pp.307–10.

108 Ibid., pp.368–69.

109 Parkinson, pp.163–64.

110 Ibid., p.169.

111 Ibid., p.170.

112 Ibid., p.164.

113 Ibid., p.167.

114 Dale, p.102; for a critical review of this work, see Subrahmanyan, pp.390–91.

115 Dale, p.117.

116 Multan was at a crossroads of connections between India, Afghanistan, Iran and the Arabian Sea (Dale, pp.102, 105). This census source needs to be checked, as Subrahmayan argues that Dale's data are outdated (p.390).

117   Tooke 1799, vol.2, p.115.

118   Pallas 1799–1801, vol.1, p.254.

119   Teissier 2004, pp.253–59.

120   Mitter, pp.48ff.

121   Pallas 1793–94, pp.196–201.

122   Ibid., p.196.

123   Bell, p.39.

124   Bruce, pp.252–53.

125   Ibid., p.254.

126   Hanway, vol.1, p.128.

127   Parkinson, p.164.

128   Ibid., p.169.

129   Ibid., p.172.

130   Ibid., p.172.

131   Ibid., pp.174–75.

132   Herzig 2008, pp.6–8.

133   Curtin, pp.182–92; Herzig 1991 (unpublished D.Phil thesis, Oxford), pp.120–43; Herzig 2008, p.6; Georgi 1780–83, pp.425–26, 430–31.

134   Herzig 1991, p.143; Khachikian, p.101.

135   Georgi 1780–83, vol.3, p.425.

136   Herzig 2008, p.9.

137   Gmelin 1770–74, vol.2, p.147; Georgi 1780–83, vol.4, pp.425–26; Tooke 1799, vol.2, p.115. The Rostov on Don settlement, with its own bishop, had about 13,000 inhabitants.

138   Georgi 1780–83, vol.4, p.426.

139   Herzig 1991, p.143; Herzig 2008, p.7.

140   Gmelin 1770–74, vol.2, p.146.

141   Ibid., p.431.

142   Gmelin 1770–74, vol.2, p.146; Georgi 1780–83, vol.4, p.431; Herzig 2008, p.10.

143   Herzig 1991, pp.184–92 and *passim*; Herzig 2008, p.10.

144   Gmelin 1770–74, vol.2, p.146; Georgi 1780–83, vol.2, p.430.

145   Gmelin 1770–74, vol.2, pl.8, p.59.

146   Georgi 1780–83, vol.4, p.432.

147   Ibid., p.432.

148   Kahan, pp.89–90; Tooke 1799, vol.3, pp.509–10.

149   Ter-Sarkisiants, p.89. There was also an Armenian printing press in St Petersburg (1780). This was in a long tradition of Armenian presses, the first of which was established in Venice in 1512 (ibid.).

150   Georgi 1780–83, vol.2, pp.428–29, 436–37.

151   Gmelin 1770–74, vol.2, p.153.

152   Georgi 1780–83, vol.4, pp.429–30, 442–33.

153   Ibid., pp.428, 432.

154   E.g. Klaproth 1834, p.13, no.13 (Georgian exiles in Russia); Lockhart 1958, pp.256–58.

155   Georgi 1780–83, p.431.

156   Hanway, vol.1, p.120.

157   Cook, vol.1, p.289.

158   Ibid., p.290.

159 Ibid., p.255–56.
160 Ibid., pp.296–97.
161 Parkinson, pp.172–73.
162 Ibid., p.165.
163 Ibid., p.173.
164 Ibid., p.164.
165 Ibid., p.167.
166 Ibid., p.170.

4 Peoples: Kalmyks

Introduction

Kalmyk was the name given in Turkic and Russian sources to breakaway groups of Oirat or western Mongols (Torgut, Khosut, Derbet, Olöt) who gradually moved westwards from Jungaria, initially under the Torguts, during the seventeenth century. The Kalmyks referred to themselves as Oirats, Olöts or by their other tribal names.[1] They had been driven in search of new pastures by the east Mongols and the Kazakhs, eventually coming to the northern Caspian steppes, both sides of the lower Volga and on to the Don. Indirect contact between Muscovy and the Oirats had been established as early as the sixteenth century over trading rights in Siberia.[2] By the early seventeenth century contacts became direct and focused on the realities of this westward advance, including the mutual rewards of trade (Kalmyk livestock, hides and goods from the east, in exchange for small luxuries, cloth, metalwork, and eventually tobacco and alcohol[3]) as well as expectations of *yasak* (tribute) from the Russians, Kalmyk plunder of Russian settlements and devastation of Nogay tribes.

The first written agreement between the Kalmyk chief Kho-Urlück of the Torgut and the Russians, made in 1655, set the pattern for a string of such 'oaths'.[4] The Russians had seen the potential of military co-operation with the Kalmyks. Expectations of allegiance, subjection and military assistance were the terms for Russian protection against Kazakhs and other enemies. The rewards were booty, trade and freedom of movement for the Kalmyks and their herds.[5] The Russians also expected eventual conversion and sedentarisation. The Oirats had turned from Shamanism to Buddhism in the mid-seventeenth century, although elements of Shamanism persisted.[6] The question of conversion remained a strong bone of contention.

The Kalmyks on the whole refused to acknowledge that they were Russian subjects and maintained close relations with Tibet and Jungaria, despite Russian opposition. They achieved concessions from the Russians, but only when the need for Kalmyk military force was urgent or when strong leaders united them. The shifting, divisive policies of the Russians towards the Kalmyks resulted in the impoverishment of the ordinary people and erosion of Kalmyk freedoms, which ultimately led to an exodus back to Jungaria. Civil war among the Kalmyks in times of succession did not help their cause, nor did the animosity between tribes and harshness of some of their leaders. Khodarkovsky has argued that the confrontation between Kalmyk nomadic society and sedentary Russian, state-organised society could only result in failure.[7] The travellers witnessed key episodes in this history, from the Kalmyks' comparatively strong position at the beginning of the century to the fate of those who remained at its end.

The role of Kalmyk military forces, which usually joined Cossack ones, in Peter the Great's army against the Swedes, Persians and Turks is indicated by Perry, Bell and Bruce. The Kalmyk leader Ayuki, a strong Buddhist, had used relations with Moscow to achieve his own ends and took several oaths of allegiance in the process.[8] By the end of the seventeenth century he had become very wealthy, and by 1708 he was officially known as khan.[9] Bell described the historic encounter between Peter the Great and Ayuki at Saratov in 1722. The Tsar courted Ayuki in return for troops, and Ayuki was then strong enough to dictate the numbers he was prepared to send. Despite evidence of Kalmyk strength and wealth in the early eighteenth century, however, the Kalmyks' situation remained very much one of obligation. Though Bell considered the Kalmyks friendly, the possibility of Kalmyk raids was ever-present.

In a description of the succession crisis that erupted before Ayuki's death in 1724, between Dosang (the Russian favourite) and Ayuki's choice, his grandson Donduk-Ombo, supported by his uncle Cheren-Donduk, Bruce conveyed the often futile machinations of the Russians in such affairs, which nevertheless weakened Kalmyk unity. By this time pro- and anti-Russian factions had developed among the Kalmyks. Russians inevitably backed their own candidates, who were often the weaker party (in this case Dosang). Ayuki's death also precipitated the movements of some Derbets and Torguts to the Don.[10]

Cheren-Donduk became viceroy from 1732 to 1735,[11] with Donduk-Ombo, who was initially popular with the Kalmyks, reluctantly instituted as khan by the Russians in 1735–6.[12] Again this arrangement was fuelled by Russian military needs in the Kuban, Azov and Crimea against the Ottomans. As stated by Cook, Donduk-Ombo proved a strong but severe leader,[13] who also managed to extract concessions from the Russians over the removal of opponents and the return of fugitives, as well as substantial rewards.[14] The 1740s were a difficult time for the Kalmyks, however, with V.N. Tatischev, the governor of Astrakhan responsible for Kalmyk affairs, further subverting Kalmyk customs by enforcing Russian punitive law and restricting fishing and roaming rights.[15] Both Cook and Hanway stressed the robberies and occasional savagery of the Kalmyks on the the Volga and its the delta at this time, usually towards travellers. Hanway acknowledged the 'miserable poverty' of the Kalmyks and witnessed their children offered for sale. The Russians did not discourage this practice, as both Kalmyk children and adults were seen as valuable chattel.[16] By 1744 a third of the Kalmyk population was estimated to be impoverished.[17]

Another crisis followed Donduk-Ombo's death in 1741, when factions developed between Donduk-Ombo's Circassian wife, Jan, and her son Randel (Donduk-Ombo's choice), Ajuki's son (Galdan-Danjin) and the

Russian favourite, Donduk-Dashi (one of Ayuki's grandsons). Cook noted how Donduk-Dashi had been 'much caressed' by the Russians in order to make him compliant, but he concentrated on the fate of Donduk-Ombo's wife, with which Tatischev was directly involved.[18] He highlighted the fact that Jan, like other other Kalmyk nobles and chiefs, had at times transacted with the Ottomans and even Persians in order to secure protection.[19] Cook visited the imprisoned, ailing princess prior to her exile, uncharacteristically making this final part of her story in Moscow sound like a fairy tale. In the event, Donduk-Dashi became viceroy in 1741, and the family converted in 1744, and became the Princes Dondukov. Donduk-Dashi was succeeded by his son Ubashi in 1761,[20] by which time the *uluses* – units attached to noble chiefs (*tayishi*s) or lamas – were greatly depleted.[21]

In the 1760s changes were made to the Kalmyk constitution, which diluted the khan's power, and aggressive colonisation from Samara to Tsaritsyn further curtailed Kalmyk pastures.[22] Driven away from the Volga to barren steppes, the people became even more destitute. Meanwhile, the Tsaritsyn and Dnieper defence lines had restricted Kalmyk movements. The Kalmyks reacted by repeatedly petitioning Astrakhan and St Petersburg and occasionally raiding. By the late 1760s, encouraged by their clergy and fugitives from Jungaria, Ubashi started to take measures to leave.[23] This idea had already been mooted in the 1720s and 1740s.[24] The majority having crossed to the east bank of the Volga, some 150,000 Kalmyks set out to Jungaria in January 1771.[25] The Russians, despite seeing this as an act of treason, were unable to stem the exodus.

The journey proved calamitous for the Kalmyks. They died from hunger, cold and depredations by the Kazakhs, or were taken as slaves.[26] Only about 50,000 reached Jungaria.[27] Once there, they fared no better under the Chinese than under the Russians. When Parkinson visited Astrakhan, he was told that a few Kalmyks were trickling back. It was also rumoured that Ubashi's son wanted Russia's 'protection' once more,[28] but the Chinese prevented it. In the 1830s this episode was turned into a melodramatic orientalist tale, *Revolt of the Tartars or Flight of the Kalmuck Khan*, by Thomas de Quincey.[29]

Approximately 13,000 Kalmyks had remained on the west bank,[30] some unable to cross at the appointed time, some because they wanted to stay. They now lost all independence: the titles of khan and viceroy were abolished, their movements were restricted to the west bank, unless permission was granted, and tribes were divided into administrative districts based on location (e.g. Astrakhan, Stravropol, Don), breaking traditional units. They were subordinated to government ministries, with compulsory military duties.[31] Kalmyks who joined the Pugachev rebellion of 1773 suffered further reprisals.[32] In 1798 the Don Kalmyks (Dörberts) were incorporated into Cossack military units and became known as the Buzava, alienating them further from their tribal origins.

Parkinson's observations on the subordinate, disaffected status of the Kalmyks in the 1790s were fuelled by conversations with Pallas, an authority on the Kalmyks,[33] who had a high opinion of them,[34] and by other well-informed officials. Georgi blamed the Kalmyk exodus on loss of pastures, the 'necessary' restrictions put upon the khan, and the 'prophecies of their priests' about enforced conversions.[35] Parkinson reported on the oppressions of the Kalmyks by their own priests. *Tayishi*s, such as Donduk-Ombo, had also taken advantage of their people[36] (Pallas and Georgi made the same points[37]). The Kalmyk numbers quoted by Parkinson are contemporary local estimates but are not dissimilar to those of modern researchers. A visit to Prince Tiumen (Sereb-Djab Tiumen of the Koshuts),[38] who had been eleven years old at the time of migration and was now a major in the Russian army who had distinguished himself in battle, shows the fate of a Kalmyk chief turned officer. Despite Tiumen's status of *tayishi*, of which he was very aware but which was ignored by the Russians, and his military rank, he had to ask permission for his small horde to cross the river.[39] He nevertheless assumed his Kalmyk princely protocol by walking out of his tent before his guests, which Parkinson attributed to bad manners learnt from the Russians.

The Kalmyks' Buddhist beliefs were a source of discrimination not only by Russians but also by Muslim Tatars and a major cause of their marginalisation. Buddhism was foreign to the travellers as well. Bell described them as 'downright heathens'; to Bruce they were simply pagan. Hanway, with his usual Christian proselytising, found the worship of amulets [40] and other images 'blind and horrid' and assumed the Dalai Lama to be 'their supreme deity'. Cook, who thought Buddhism 'the religion of the Chinese', was more objective. He observed that the Kalmyks actually worshipped only one god,[41] with music that is 'not disagreeable', and noted such details as how a spear is turned in the ground as a symbol of eternity (and prayer). Both Cook and Hanway objected strongly to the Kalmyk way of disposing of the dead by exposure, which led them to be eaten by dogs. Parkinson was the only traveller to have direct contact with Buddhism; he visited a lama (appointed by Tibet) and attended a Buddhist ceremony in a tent temple or *khurul*.

Parkinson mentioned the failed attempts to convert the Kalmyks around Sarepta. Conversion was a persistent issue between Kalmyks and Russians, and was repeatedly brought up in 'treaties'.[42] Russian policy nevertheless continued: in 1724 the Bible was translated into Kalmyk,[43] and in the 1730s it was decreed that if any poor Kalmyk fugitive chose to stay in a town, for example when looking for work, they should be converted. Between 1725 and 1731 only about 200 converts were made, but by 1735 poverty had driven the numbers up to around 2600.[44] Notables also converted, usually in the hope of a khanship (e.g. Ayuki's grandson Petr Taishin). With court patronage, they fared far better than poor Kalmyk converts who were abused by everyone. In 1739 Stravropol, near Saratov, was founded to sedentarise and integrate Kalmyks converts. By the 1770s there were some 14,000 supposedly Christian Kalmyks in Stavropol district,[45] and around 200 in the Astrakhan region in the 1790s.[46]

Both Pallas and Georgi were realistic about the failure of the Stavropol project. Despite the building of churches, schools and houses, the Kalmyks remained Buddhist at heart, preferring 'to nomadise' and not 'trouble themselves with corn'. Only officials lived in town.[47] As a loyal official observer, Georgi stated that Stavropol Kalmyks were less rude than their 'heathen' brothers; now that they had accepted 'the killing of cattle', he wrote, 'good hopes may be entertained of them for the second and third generation'.[48] There were also Muslim Kalmyks near Orenburg and Azov, and even working for Donduk-Ombo, who had been converted after mixed marriages or having been abducted as slaves.[49]

Whereas the travellers were able to observe present-day Kalmyks, their knowledge of the history of the Volga Kalmyks was rudimentary, with the exception of Bell. At the beginning of the century, the travellers had far fewer sources to draw on for the Kalmyks than, for example, for the Mongols of Siberia. Thus the Kalmyks were conjectured to be 'western Tartars', descendants of the ancient Scythians, dispersed tribes or different hordes. Bell's account, however, is surprisingly close both to that provided by Mongol written histories[50] and to Pallas's account, first published in 1776.[51] This suggests that Bell had access to Kalmyk historiography via an interpreter or someone familiar with such sources. Bruce borrowed his out-of-date account of Kalmyk history from a seventeenth-century Jesuit traveller to China.[52] Interestingly, the entry states that the Kalmyks derived their lineage from Timur rather than Ghengis Khan, as did the east Mongols.[53] No details are given on western Oirat oral traditions, religious scholarship or art. Parkinson mentioned religious books and paintings but did not elaborate.[54] It is known, however, that the Kalmyks had their own religious traditions as well as canonical Tibetan and Mongolian ones.[55]

The travellers' combined their historical commentary with observations on the Kalmyks' nomadic way of life, 'manners' and physical appearance (figs 11 and 12). Physical descriptions (e.g. flat nose, black eyes, short stature, bow legs) generally concur, although Hanway added drama by stating that Kalmyk faces were more fierce and savage than Chinese ones.[56] Observations on tents, food, livestock, dress and arms were also generally included. Such entries, characteristic of ethnographic writing in the eighteenth century, were designed not only to satisfy the curious but to scientifically distinguish between races. Pallas drew attention to the accurate depiction of Kalmyk physiognomy and to how strongly the Mongol 'form' survived, despite intermarriage.[57] The tone of such descriptions, whether by academicians or travellers, can be neutral or disparaging.

figs.11 and 12

Ranking the Kalmyks within an evolutionary scale was also an objective. Early travellers described the Kalmyk nomadic way of life as that of the 'First Ages of the World', like that of the 'patriarchs' or Moses. Bell idealistically associated it with liberty and a natural abhorrence of tyranny. The theme of liberty versus tyranny was one of the strongest of eighteenth-century discourses in Britain and is associated in this context with the Scythians. Pallas admired Kalmyk laws, as an example of the 'more policed states of Europe [i.e. Russia], who effect to call the free peoples of Asia barbarians'.[58] These ideas were voiced somewhat less emphatically after the French Revolution.

Observations on character varied. Perry and Bell were respectful: in their accounts the Kalmyks emerge as courageous and warlike, believers in virtue, honest, hospitable, respectful of their women, good servants, and so on. Bruce thought them possibly 'the happiest people on earth', who were nevertheless untrustworthy vagabonds. For Hanway and Cook, who encountered the Kalmyks at a time of increasing hardship, they were barbarous yet brave. Parkinson, who knew the Volga Kalmyks when controlled and partly Russianised, dwelt on the 'politeness' and 'propriety' of Prince Tiumen, observing his western-style furniture and cutlery supplied for guests. Such qualities almost elevated the prince to the rank of a civilised (i.e. European) gentleman, with whom Parkinson could sympathise. The ordinary Russian view, that Tiumen was a 'gentleman' but that the rest of the Kalmyks were *cochons* (pigs), was symptomatic. The academicians' judgements were more nuanced. Pallas, for example, found the character of the Kalmyks 'far better than travellers usually describe it'. They were affable, frank, hospitable and happy to render service. They were, however, also lazy, cunning and dirty.[59] Parkinson's conversations at Sarepta indicate that, for some Europeans living in Russia, the Kalmyks and other Tartars seemed 'to be better people than the Russians'.

The Kalmyk way of life

The Bogdoi, Yousbeck, and Bucharsky Tartars, more towards China, live in Houses, and continue Winter and Summer in the same place; but the Cullmick, and several Hordes of Western Tartars, who border more towards the Czar's Domonions, live in Tents, and move Northward and Southward, according to the Seasons of the Year, with their Flocks, their Herds, and their Wives and Families. They are generally of a swarthy Complexion, black Hair, low Noses, and broad Cheeks, with little or no Beard. I had Opportunity when I was Camishinka, to observe much of their Way of Life, which is like that which Moses relates in the first Ages of the World; they neither plow nor sow, but move from Place to Place for fresh Pasture, and take the Fruits of the Earth as they find them. They keep Time with the Fowls of the Air, and move back Southward in the Winter to the Borders of the Caspian Sea; some of them going into the Latitude of 3 or 4 and 40 Degrees North, where there is little or no Snow that continues upon the Ground; and in the Beginning of the Year, as soon as the Snow melts away, and the Spring appears in its Verdure, they move on sometimes to the Latitude of 2 or 3 and 50 Degrees North, and some sooner an some later spread the Countrey in Parties, from 8 or 10, to 15, or sometimes 20000 of them or more in a Body and pitch their Tents in Streets and Lanes in the same regular Manner as in a Town or Village, and every one knows their due Place and Order; so that I have seen the Cows stop at their own Tents, when they drive them home to milk them.

As they go backward and forward, they usually come on the East side of the Wolga and stay 2 or 3 Weeks or more in a Place over-against those Towns where the Russes inhabit, and barter their Horses, Sheep and Cattle, which they have in great abundance, with the Russians, for Corn and Meal, for Copper and Iron, Kettles, Knives, Scissers &c. and take also some Cloth and Linen of the Russes. In moving their Camp and their Tents from Place to Place, as has been mentioned, their Wives and their Children are drawn on covered Machines fixed on two large Wheels of about 8 Foot diameter, and the Breadth is in proportion to the Height; so that they can easily ford over small Rivers; in which, as well as their Tents, they live like as in Houses; and Persons of Distinction have several of these for their Baggage and Retinue. They are drawn by Dromedaries, which is a large Beast bigger than a Camel, with two Humps on the Back, which serves as a Saddle for Men to ride on (there being just room enough for the largest Man to sit between the two Humps;) they have a Pace which is swift, easie and smooth, and these Creatures carry the Tents and Baggage of such who have not the forementioned Machines for it; they are taught to kneel down and to receive their Burden, tho' they do it (usually) with a grumbling sort of a Noise which they make.

With the Hair of these Dromedaries, the Tartars weave in the Fields a narrow stuff the same as Camlet; and the Russes, who begin to leave off the Use of Caps, have in the present Czar's Time, learn'd to make Hats, and the use of the said Dromedaries Hair for that purpose.

The Cullmicks have by Treaty, a small annual Pension allowed them by the Czar, which is paid them as Astracan, in Corn, and in Cloth, for which they are obliged to assist the Czar in his Wars, when he shall command them; not only against the Turks and Tartars, but his other Enemies; and tho' undisciplined, are a robust and warlike People, supposed to be of those ancient Scythians, who were so long famed for their War against the Persians. They have lately been useful to the Czar in his War with the Swedes, of which I shall speak more hereafter, when I shall mention the Regulations made in the Czar's army.

The common Tents, in which the Cullmicks and other forementioned Tartars live and move, with their Camps, from Place to Place, are made of small Lettice-Work, round like a Pidgeon-House, which they set up without Poles, and which when they strike, folds together in narrow Pannels. They cover them over with Wylock, which is a very light sort of Stuff, matted together like Felt or Hat-Work, but more loose and above half an Inch thick, which serves to keep out the Cold as well as Rain, as it lies shelving to carry it off. They are made with a door to go in at, and a Hole at the Top to let out the Smoak, when they have occasion to make a Fire, which they make in the middle of the Tent; and when they go to sleep they lie round the Tent; the ordinary People on Beds, being a Piece of the Wylock abovementioned, only usually made double the Thickness of that with which the Tent is covered; and when the Door is shut too, and the Hole which is at the Top is covered, their Tent is as warm as a Stove: The same Tents are used also by Persons of Distinction; only I have seen one of the Aucoes (or Chiefs) have his Bed made of Persian Silk, and his Tent richly lined with the same.

When I was employed at Camishinka on making the intended Communication between the Wolga and the Don, we had all the Summer long some or other Hordes of these Tartars, who came and pitched their Tents on the opposite side of the Wolga. They often came over the River, as well as the Russes went to them, to trade. They came many of them to see my Work, and were very curious in observing our Engines and Methods that we used. I had by this Means Opportunity of being civil to them, and they invited me and my Assistants over to their Camp, and asked us very proper Questions in Discourse concerning our Countrey and Place that we came from, and have made us very welcome amongst them.[60]

...

The Czar's Army, besides his own People, is composed of several Regiments of Cossacks, commanded by their own Officers. They are all Light

Horse, and have been very useful in the Russ Wars against the Turks and Tartars, and in the present War against the Swedes, have been usually sent out with Parties of Russ Horse upon any Expedition, to raise Contributions, and to burn or plunder the Countrey. The Czar has always a Party of Cullmicks who are obliged to attend his Army, according to a Treaty of Alliance made with them. They are a robust, War-like People, who only want Discipline to make them Soldiers. They once occasion'd a considerable Victory, which the Czar obtained over a Party of Swedes near Plesco, soon after the Loss of the Battel of Narva.

The Dromedary, which I have before spoken of, which the Cullmicks use to draw and carry their Baggage on the East side of the River Wolga, is a Creature, that a Horse that has not seen them before, is extremely frighten'd at, and will startle and run from with very great Precipitation; and upon the Russes coming up with a Party of Swedes, which they march'd to attack, the Cullmicks, with several of these Dromedaries in the Front, were order'd in the Attack, who, when they came near, so affrighted the Swedish Horse, that they gave way and broke their Ranks, and the Russes fell in upon them and routed them. The Cossacks were usually reckon'd about 10000 Men and the Cullmicks about 6000 and the Czar's Army which he has in Pay at all Places, and on all Occasions, is in the whole about a hundred and twenty or thirty thousand Men.[61]

(Perry 1698–1701)

At Saratov

After dinner a party of us crossed the river to visit a great horse-market, held by the KALMUCK TARTARS, we saw about five or six hundred of these people assembled in a field, with a number of horses all running loose, except those on which the TARTARS were mounted. The buyers came from different parts of RUSSIA ... These TARTARS are strong made, stout men, their faces broad, noses flattish, and eyes small and black, but very quick. Their dress is very simple, consisting of a loose coat of sheep-skins, tied with a girdle, a small round cap, turned up with fur, having a tassel of red silk at the top, leather or linen drawers, and boots, their heads are all shaved, except a lock behind, which is plaited and hangs down their backs.

They are armed with bows and arrows, a sabre and lance, which they manage with great dexterity, acquired by constant practice from their infancy. They are men of courage and resolution but much afraid of cannon, which puts their horses in disorder. As they are almost always on horse-back, they are excellent riders.

The dress of the women differs little from that of the men, only their gowns are somewhat longer than the coats of the men, a little ornamented, and bordered with party-coloured cloth; they wear earrings, and their hair all plaited into locks. The better sort dress in silks in summer. It must be observed, for the honour of their women, that they are very honest and sincere, and few of them lewd; adultery is a crime scarce ever heard of. The TARTARS make very good and faithful servants; and the more mildly they are used the better they perform their duty; for their wandering unconfined manner of life naturally inspires them with sentiments of liberty, and aversion, and hatred to tyranny and oppression.

All their wealth is in their flocks; like those who lived in the early ages of the world, they have camels, horses, cows and sheep. The horses are of a good size for the saddle, and very hardy; as they run wild till they are sometimes six years old, they are generally headstrong; they are sold at this fair at five to fifteen or sixteen crowns, and the strong well shaped natural pacers much higher. They have few camels, but many dromedaries, who have two protuberances on their backs. Their cows are of a middle size. The sheep large, having broad tails like those in TURKEY, the wool is coarse, but the mutton very fine.

In the preceeding century a KALMUCK prince, named TOR-GOTT-CHORLUKE [Torgut Kho-Urlück] came from ALACK-ULLA [Ala-Tau] (which signifies the spotted mountains) a country situation between SIBERIA on the north, and INDIA on the south, to the borders of RUSSIA; and brought along with him about fifty thousand families, or tents, as they sometimes reckon. In his march west-ward to the VOLGA, he defeated EYBALL-UTZICK [?] a TARTAR prince, who lived in tents beyond the river ENBO [Emba]. Advancing forward, he met three other TARTAR chiefs, named KITTA-HAPTZAY [Kitai-Kipchak], MALEBASH [Mailebash] and ETZAN [Etissan or Yedissan] whom he also defeated. And at last settled to the east of the VOLGA, under the protection of the RUSSIANS. CHORLUKE [Cho-Urlük] had six sons; DANGTZINQ [Daichin] the oldest succeeded him in the government, or chan-ship.[62]

The present Chan, named AIJUKA [Ajuki] is the fourth from CHORLUKE [Kho-Urlück] and is much esteemed in the east for his sagacity and justice. I am informed that the reason why CHORLUKE left his own country, was a dispute about the succession to the chanship ...[63]

They have no money, except what they get from the RUSSIANS, and their other neighbours, in exchange for cattle; with this they buy meal sometimes, but mostly cloth, silk-stuffs, and other apparel for their women. They have no mechanics, except those who make arms. They avoid all labour as the greatest slavery; their only employment is tending their flocks, managing horses, and hunting. If they are angry with a person, they wish he may live in one place, and work like a RUSSIAN. Their language contains none of those horrid oaths common enough in tongues of more enlightened nations. They believe virtue leads to happiness, and vice to misery; for when desired to do what they think wrong, they reply, in a proverb, 'Though a knife be sharp it cannot cut its own handle'.

On long marches all their provisions consist of cheese, or rather dried curd, made up into little balls, which they drink, when pounded and mixt with water. If this kind of food fails they have always many spare horses, which they kill and eat. They broil or roast the flesh before the fire, on pieces of broken arrows, and never eat it raw, as is commonly believed, unless compelled by necessity. They have indeed large pieces of horse-flesh, smoked or dried in the sun, which they eat: but this cannot be called raw. I have tasted some of it, and thought it not amiss.

As to their religion I can say little; they are downright Heathens, and have many lamas or priets, who can read and write, and are distinguished by their yellow habits. Their high priest is called DELAY LAMA, and lives far to the eastward.[64]

(Bell, June 1716)

Bell en route to Darband, after his trip to China

At this place [Saratov] we came up with the Emperor, who had appointed an interview with the Ayuka-Chan [Ayuki] and his queen to dinner on board the galley ...

The Ayuka-Chan came on horseback, attended by two of the princes his sons, and escorted by a troop of about fifty of his officers and great men, all exceedingly well mounted. About twenty yards from the shore the king alighted from his horse, and was received by a privy-counsellor and an officer of the guards. When the emperor saw him advancing, he went on shore, saluted him, and, taking him by the hand, conducted him on board the galley; where he introduced him to the Empress, who was seated on the quarter-deck, under a very rich awning.

Soon after Ayuka-Chan was got on board the galley, the Queen arrived on the shore, in a covered wheel-machine, attended by one of the princesses her daughter, and two ladies ... also by a troop of horsemen. When she was alighted, the Emperor went on shore to receive her, and, conducting her on board, introduced her to the Empress.

The Ayuka-Chan is an old man, about seventy years of age, yet is hearty and cheerful. He is a prince of great wisdom, and prudent conduct, is much respected by all his neighbours for his sincerity and plain dealing. And I recollect, that, when I was at Pekin, the Emperor of CHINA made very honourable mention of him. By his long experience, he is very well acquainted with the state of affairs in the east.

The Queen was about fifty years old, of a decent and cheerful deportment; the ladies, her attendants, were young; the princess, in particular, hath a fine complexion; her hair, a jet-black, which was disposed in tresses round her shoulders; and she was, in the eyes of the Kalmucks, a complete

97

beauty. They were all richly dressed in long robes of PERSIAN brocade, with little round caps, on the upper part of their heads, bordered with sable-fur, according to the fashion of the country.

The Emperor intimated to the Ayuka-Chan, that he would be desirous of ten thousand of his troops to accompany him to PERSIA. The King of the KALMUCKS replied, that ten thousand were at the Emperor's service, but that he thought one half of that number would be more than sufficient to answer all his purposes; and immediately gave orders for five thousand to march directly to, join the Emperor at TERKY.

Both the Emperor and the Empress were highly pleased with their guests; and in the evening, dismissed them with suitable presents. The Empress gave the Queen a gold repeating-watch, set with diamonds, which seemed to take her fancy, besides some pieces of brocade, and other silks of value.

It is well worth remarking, that this treaty, between two mighty monarchs was begun, carried on, and concluded, in less space of time than is usually employed, by the plenipotentiaries of our western EUROPEAN monarchs, in taking dinner.[65]

(Bell, July 1722)

'The happiest people on the earth'

There is no doubt but the Russians are powerful enough to curb the insolence of these vagabonds, were it not for the consideration of a benefit arising from the traffic for their furs and horses, which they bring every year in great abundance to Astrachan; and also for the service they are of to the Russians in their wars with Turks and Crim-Tartars being accounted the most alert at pitching and removing their tents of any people in the world, which they are accustomed to by their constant incursions to some or other of the neighbouring countries. It is principally from this view that the Russians looked upon it as a piece of policy rather to allay their fierceness by some presents, which, however, by continuance of time, they now demand as an obligation, than to engage in a war against a multitude of vagabonds who have so little to lose ...

The Kalmucks, as well as the other nations of Great Tartary, are Pagans. As to their persons, they are of a low stature, and generally bow-legged, occasioned by their being so continually on horseback, or sitting with their legs below them ... [I]n the time of war, they cover their head and body with iron net-work, which they call a pantzer, the links of which are so close, it is proof against any kind of weapons except fire-arms, as a bullet will break it, and generally carries some broken pieces into the wound, which makes them stand in great awe of fire-arms. Their only weapons are the scimitar, lance, and bow and arrow; but they are coming into the use of fire-arms, which, in time, will make them more formidable …

They are, in their own way, the happiest people on the earth, being fatigued with no kind of labour, but diverting themselves with fishing and hunting; and I can conceive nothing preferable to their way of living in the summer: but in winter they are obliged to cross the river, and live on the bare plain of Astrachan, where their only firing is the dried dung of the cattle, and the cattle themselves starving on the scanty produce of a barren desart. Here they remain till the spring, when their former habitation, on the east side of the river, is overflowed for near a month to a vast extent by the melting of the snow, and their country appears one continued sea over-grown with trees: as soon as this subsides, they return with great joy, swimming their loaded camels and cattle over the river, where the intervening islands make their passage easiest. It is to be observed, that the Kalmucks, when they go upon any expeditions, have no regard either to bridges or boats; they no sooner come to a river, than in they plunge with their horses, and sliding from their backs hold fast by the manes till they get over, and then immediately mount again, and so proceed. But to return to our passage down the river.[66]

(Bruce, 1722)

Kalmyk children

In passing the left shore [of the Volga], we frequently visited the Kalmucks in their kibbits, or tents, which we always found pitched on the most delightful places I ever saw, their country being a large plain, full of wood and meadows; and we were much diverted with a number of their children of both sexes, running naked along the shore; and upon throwing bread into the water, they swam in crouds to take it up, there being none of them but can swim to admiration.[67]

(Bruce, 1722)

At Svyatoi-Krest, on the shores of the Caspian

[A]s the Cossaks and Kalmucks serve the emperor in his wars, no purchase no pay, having only bread allowed them while they continue in service, all the prisoners and booty they take is their own … the Kalmuck Tartars, were now [after the Daghestan expedition, see p.181] sent home to their own country through Circassia and the deserts of Astrachan, richly provided with slaves and cattle of all sorts …[68]

(Bruce, 1722)

A battle for Kalmyk succession, autumn 1723

There happened at this time, a great confusion among the Kalmuck Tartars, occasioned by the death of the cham's eldest son, who left five sons; the eldest of whom, with two others, were born of a concubine, and the two youngest of the best beloved wife: the eldest, whose name was Dasa [Dosang], claimed the right of succession, in consequence of his seniority, which was a good title, notwithstanding his mother was a concubine; the two youngest, born of the wife, and whose names were Dunduambu [Donduk-Ombo] and Batu, claimed in right of the marriage, and were favoured by the old cham, their grandfather, and by his second son, Shurundunduck [Cheren-Donduk] their uncle, who threatened prince Dasan with destruction to himself and his hord, or clan, which consisted of seven thousand men, if he offered to dispute the succession with prince Dunduambu. They were at that time prevented by the old cham, but he dying, prince Shurundunduck told his nephew, Dasan, that he was determined Dunduambu should succeed his grandfather in the sovereignty, and if he would not submit peaceably, he should be compelled to do it. But finding their threats had no effect upon the prince, they began to assemble and army of twenty thousand men, which obliged prince Dasan, with his two brothers, and his whole hord, to retire near to Astrachan, and he with his brothers came into the city, begging to protected against the usurpation of his younger brother, offering at the same time to submit his claim to the decision of his imperial majesty. Upon this the general and governor held a council, with the principal officers of both the army and garrison, in which it was resolved to send some troops for their protection; the governor intending to go himself to reconcile the contending parties, if possible.

This being the resolution of the council, governor Wolinski [A. Volynskii] desired me to go with him on this expedition, to which I answered that it was not my turn, but if he would procure and order from the general for my going, I would certainly go with great chearfulness; and accordingly, on the 20th of October [1723], I received an order to embark with four hundred men of our two battalions, one hundred dragoons, and four field-pieces, to proceed up the river to the place appointed for the rendezvous by prince Dasan; the governor proposing to follow immediately with some more troops, sent me before to satisfy the impatience of the prince.

On the 22th, we arrived at the desert of Beriket sixty wersts above Astrachan, where we pitched our tents, but it being intensely cold, Dasan provided us with sixty kibbets, which is the name of their tents, which are both warm and large, having a fire in the middle, and a hole at the top to let out the smoke ... Prince Dasan, with his hord, was encamped at two wersts distance from us, and sent us several cattle and sheep for provisions to our party: he sent also a jar of spirits distilled from mares milk, for the officers, which was as clear as water but strong, and of an agreeable flavour.

On the 23rd, we were reinforced by a detachment of two hundred men from our battalions, and three hundred and fifty Cossacks, which made us now a body of one thousand and fifty strong … being the senior officer, I took the command of the whole till the governor should arrive. On the arrival of this reinforcement, prince Dasan sent more cattle for their provision, and a sufficient number of kibbets for their accommodation. This evening we received intelligence that Shurundunduck, and his nephew, Dunduambu, were encamped with an army of twenty thousand strong, opposite to Zornayar, which being upwards of one hundred and fifty wersts from us, made us conjecture it would take some time before they could come up with us; but we soon found our mistake, for we were alarmed very early in the morning of the 24th by the breaking up of prince Dasan's camp, and seeing his people coming towards us in the utmost confusion. On this I drew up our men in all haste, and ordered the dragoons and Cossacks to mount and go to prince Dasan's assistance: we soon saw Shurundunduck's army advancing, which obliged Dasan and his people to take refuge in our rear, whom I persuaded to dismount such of his horsemen as had fire-arms, and to bring as many of his men as had bows and arrows, to fight on foot as we did, and I sent some officers and serjeants to draw them up in order: with these we formed a square towards the river, and secured their baggage and cattle in our rear. The enemy being advanced in the form of a crescent, and within gun-shot of us, made a halt to consult the mode of their attack. Dasan was in the utmost perplexity, and begged me to keep them at a distance with our great guns and fire-arms, assuring me if we did not, they would rush in upon us with a very sudden and furious attack, and throw us all into confusion.

On this emergency, I was very much at loss how to act, having no orders, and advised with the rest of the officers; when it was agreed to send and interpreter with a drum, to inform them of his majesty's troops being there for the protection of prince Dasan, who had entirely submitted the decision of his claim to his imperial majesty, and that it was expected they would do the same, being equally subject to the emperor; and as the governor of Astrachan was hourly expected, who might fall upon ways and means to reconcile their differences, they ought to wait his arrival. The messenger was sent, and brought back an answer: – That they knew very well Dasan had procured Russian troops to protect him from their just resentment; but as they were a free nation, they would do themselves justice, without submitting to the arbitration of any person whatever, and that they were determined to attack their brethren at all hazards, notwithstanding our troops, and if we interposed in their behalf, and should meet with any disaster, the blame would lay at our own doors. Having returned this answer they began to advance in a semicircle, intending to surround us, on which I ordered the field-pieces to be fired among them, and then loaded with grape-shot: all this time they avoided coming near our troops, but bent their whole force against their own countrymen, which obliged me to form a front against them, both to the right and left, and then began to play on them with grape-shot and small-arms, which made great havock amongst them, and their horses not being used to the thundering noise of fire-arms, became unmanageable and threw their whole body into the utmost confusion; on which our dragoons and Cossacks, seconded by prince Dasan's men, attacked them with such vigour, that they soon gave way on all sides and fled, while we plied them with the field-pieces as long as they were in reach.

We had two dragoons killed in this action, and seven wounded, and five Cossacks killed and seventeen wounded; five of our soldiers were wounded with barbed arrows; but of Dasan's men, there were three hundred and seventy-four killed, and upwards of five hundred wounded. Our dragoons and Cossacks returned from the pursuit with sixty-three prisoners, and Dasan's men took some hundreds; we could not ascertain the loss of the enemy in this short action, but it must have been very considerable. In the evening, when all was over, governor Wolinski arrived, and I acquainted him of the transactions of the day: he was much pleased with the message that had been sent to Dunduambu and Shurundunduck, and especially that we were not the aggressors in the action, nor had fired upon them till we were actually attacked. He said he would have come up sooner, but he did not imagine they would have made an attempt in defiance of our troops, but since they had done so, he would now consider them as rebels, and make an example of them as such. He then gave orders to hang all the prisoners, (who amounted to some hundreds), and Dasan's men executed the orders with great satisfaction. Among the prisoners was Dunduambu's greatest favourite and principal counsellor, whom Dasan put to the most cruel torture imaginable, and he had no sooner expired under the torment, than they divided his body in four, and stuck up the quarters on so many posts, and his head on another.

The governor, judging from what had happened, that a reconciliation would now be impracticable, advised prince Dasan, with his two brothers, to retire with their people under the Cannon of Krasnayar, where they would be safe from any attempt of their enemies, as it was impossible that our troops could remain any longer in the field in that advanced cold season, there being at this time a great fall of snow, which they immediately agreed to. We broke up our camp on the 25th, but we had scarce marched five wersts, when the enemy made their appearance in the same manner they had done the day before, and sent a messenger to the governor, to let him know they were sensible he intended to carry their enemy out of their reach, which they were resolved to prevent, let the consequence be what it would; nevertheless, if the governor could prevail on Dasan to agree to a partition of the sovereignty with Dunduambu, on reasonable terms, they were willing to hold a conference with him on that head. It was directly agreed that five chief men from each party should meet in the middle space between the two armies, where they conferred together above three hours, without being able to come to an agreement, and then they returned each to their own party. The enemy having observed that Dasan's party, during the conference, were transporting their wives, children, and cattle over a branch of the Wolga, now set upon Dasan's men with a most furious attack, and numbers were slain on each side before we could come up to prevent it, as the enemy still avoided coming near as much as possible; but upon our horse engaging them, and our firing with our cannon and small arms briskly upon them, they retired quite out of sight. Our dragoons return-ing from the pursuit, brought back twenty-five prisoners, who assured us, that Shurundunduck was retired towards Zornayar; on which the governor set out for Astrachan, leaving orders with me to see prince Dasan, and his Kalmucks, all over the river, and safe under the cannon of Krasnayar, where I arrived the 30th: but the prince finding his cattle could not subsist in so narrow a district, divided the hord, and distributed them among the numerous islands formed by the several branches of the Wolga, where they were to remain in full security till his majesty's pleasure was known. I set out on the 3rd of November, having prince Dasan, and his two brothers, under my convoy, and arrived at Astrachan that evening, where we found every necessary accommodation provided for their reception ...

The small-pox is much dreaded among the Kalmucks as the pest is amongst us: when any of them are seized with it, they immediately break up their camp and fly, leaving the sick in one of their worst kibbits with a killed sheep, part of which is roasted and part of which is raw, and a jar of water and some wood for fire; if they recover they follow the hord, which seldom happens, for they almost all die for want of attendance.[69]

(Bruce, 1723)

Around Tsaritsyn

In a deep valley, under the south side of this place [Tsaritsyn], is an encampment of KHALMUCK TARTARS, who are in friendship with the RUSSIANS so long as they awe them by their power; for these barbarians do not keep their faith more inviolably than some politer nations. The KHALMUCKS have the same sort of visage as the CHINESE, but more fierce and savage. These are dispersed tribes of those MUNGALIANS whom the CHINESE long since received as their conquerors. They are armed with bows and arrows, and feed on the flesh of horses, camels, dromedaries, and other animals, and eat the entrails of them, even when the beast dies of the foulest distemper. They throw their dead into open fields, to be devoured by dogs; of which many run wild, and some are kept for this purpose. If their bodies are thus devoured by any number exceeding six, they think honourably of the Rate of the deceased; otherwise he is a disgrace to his relations. I could not learn that they have any persuasion of the immortality of the soul; for the honour derived from the number of dogs which devour the body, rather seems to regard the reputation of the dead amongst the living, than any opinion concerning the happy or miserable Rate of the soul of the deceased.

They worship images, which generally consist of a small bit of wood about a palm in length; the upper part of it being rounded, is adorned with some rude marks to resemble human features; the figure being thus prepared is dressed up with a few rags. It is horrid to the imagination, that any creature bearing the form of human nature, should be sunk into such blindness, as to pay divine honours to so base a representation; though the difference of this and any other image-worship does not seem to be very great: their supreme deity is the DELLI LAMA. In fine weather and prosperous seasons, they caress these ragged deities, but treat them very ill when the contrary happens: and here it ought to be remarked, that the eye observes the externals of a religion, but to arrive at men's hearts is no vulgar task, especially where the ignorance of barbarous languages obstructs all familiar correspondency. The many violences committed by these barbarians, at length induced the RUSSIAN government to compel them to take up their habitations on the banks of the VOLGA, below ASTRACHAN, where they have a less field for robbery and murder, though here also they transgress ...

News was just then arrived, that the inspector of the customs, attended by four soldiers, in coming from ASTRACHAN, had been murdered by the KHALMUCKS ... FRENCH officers however assured me I might go down the VOLGA without danger, because the TARTARS of every denomination were kept in subjection to the RUSSIAN government; and that the murder of the inspector and his men, was a consequence of their rashness in attempting to steal some of the KHALMUCK'S children. I told them, that I was the more amazed at such an enterprize, as children two or three years old, had been offered me by the KHALMUCKS for two rubles a head. [70]

(Hanway, autumn 1743)

From Astrakhan to the Caspian

We left Astrachan under a convoy of the governor's barge with 12 grenadiers ... this old gentleman [Tatischev] had been greatly instrumental in bringing the TARTARS to a peaceable subjection to the RUSSIAN government: for this purpose he had taken all the large boats from the KHALMUCKS; so that here, as in other places, they were obliged to fish in small canoes ...

104

These people are miserably poor, subsisting on fish which they take in the VOLGA; they dry in the summer their winter's provision. They prefer to live on the banks, where flags and rushes are grown to a great height, these being some defence against the rigors of the cold season. There are seldom seen above 7 or 8 tents in one place, which contain 30 or 40 persons, who live in distinct families under one whom they chuse as their chief. Besides these, there are other KHALMUCKS, who travel to the south when winter comes on, and return northward in the heat of the summer.[71]

(Hanway, autumn 1743)

Kalmyk religion, marriage and burial customs

They [the Kalmyks] profess the religion of the Chinese, and pay worship to idols, but acknowledge, that they are only idols to express the great regard they have for some of their saints. They acknowledge only one God but keep holidays, and have no unbecoming way of worship. They praise God by vocal and instrumental music, having at such times books in their hands, the notes of which were wrote from the top to the bottom of the page. Their music consists of stringed instruments and cymbals, to which they beat time, and indeed it is by no means disagreeable. They have a spear about eight feet long, headed as other spears, broad, and double gilt: the neck of the head is encompassed by a ring, to which a leather thong is fastened of about a foot long, to the end of which a piece of lead or other metal is made fast. When they worship, one placeth the end of this spear on the ground, and, by an imperceptible motion of the hand, causeth the metal turn round, during the time of their worship. Upon enquiry, they informed me, that this rotation was an emblem of eternity.

They certainly believe in a future state, and have some singular rejoicing in the time of new moons, by building a small tower of earth, placing on it vessels filled with oil and other materials, which are set fire to, and exhibits light of different colours, round which they dance, gambol, and sing. They marry only one wife at once, nor must they know other women during their marriage-state. Their ceremony of marriage is reasonable, though not agreeable to the customs of any other country I know. It is this: A young pair, agreed betwixt themselves, retire, and live as man and wife for a year. If the young woman produceth a child in the space of one year, the marriage is completed and lawful; but if not, they either make another year's trial or part: Nor is the woman in the least rejected upon; she is greedily picked up for another trial by others, as if she were a young virgin.

Women, when married, are faithful to their husbands, for a contrary practice is punisheable with death, if the husband is so minded, and he is also executioner. An example of this I was once very sorry to see.

Some young men, belonging to my hospital, returning one evening home from the city, and having been overtaken with liquor, as they passed to the hospital by a few Kalmuck tents, they went in, and gave the woman liquor to intoxicate her. The husband not being present when they came there, gave them opportunities of using what liberties they pleased with the woman. In short, it was said, she was caught by her husband in the very act. He dismissed the guests without quarrelling with them, thereafter put his wife to death, and, next morning, I, with others, saw him dragging the dead body towards a bridge, from the middle of which he threw her into the river.

Their priests never marry, but then they have a right, by their law, to go into any man's wife for a night. The men are so far from resenting this, that they take a very great honour done to them. Their priests have no riches, for they are free to use any thing belonging to any of the Kalmucks, as their own property. They make pilgrimages to China [i.e. Tibet] for instructions and benedictions from their lama or high priest.

...

Their burials are very singular. I was told, that they bury, as we do, in the earth for a certain number of years; for an equal number, they throw then dead into the water, for another they burn the dead bodies; and lastly, at equal terms they expose the naked bodies on the ground, to be devoured by any animal, but they think, if their dogs eat them, it is a great sign of happiness in their after-state. I am very certain that they drew them out from their tents but a very short space, to be devoured by any beast or fowl, all the time I was at Astrachan, and that their dogs fed chiefly on them and fish, till I got a stop put to it ... [72]

(Cook, 1740s)

Wars and depredations

They [the Kalmyks] make continual wars or depredations upon their neighbours, but particularly against the Karacalpaaks, which obligeth the Russians to keep about three regiments of dragoons, and 4 or 5000 Cossacks; upon the banks of the Volga every summer, to prevent their passing that river. But generally it happens, that the Kalmucks have done the Karacalpaaks all the damage they could for the year, before the Russians can get to their stations, because the Kalmucks pass the river on the ice, and travel into the Karacalpaak country at the time when they are least on their guard, murder and destroy in great numbers, and carry many into captivity, together with their herds and numerous flocks of cattle.

The Karacalpaaks can pursue them no further than the Volga, because, by time they arrive upon the eastern banks, the Russians have formed their line, and deny them passage. The Karacalpaaks can only act against them in the winter season, when their formidable strength inhabit the desart on the borders of Circassia, 5 or 600 versts from the west side of the Volga, wherefore they kill and destroy all the poor Kalmucks which happen to fall in their way.

...

Their Prince always keeps strong guards of 20, 30, or even 40.000 warriors about his person. Their arms are scymitars, bows and arrows. They are the best bowmen, I believe, in the world, learning the bow from their infancy. They never submit or ask their lives, and seldom give quarter to an enemy, nor has the utmost Russian severity been able to curb this barbarous disposition ...

They are the most hardy of the whole human race I am told, that they catch any thing, and in a march, they would not go a mile out of their way to pass any river a mile broad. They plunge into the water and proceed with the greatest intrepidity.[73]

...

I used frequently, in a morning, to go in company with the Governor's eldest son, to shoot. One morning we went to a morass betwixt a rising ground and the Volga, on the banks of which many Kalmucks had formed a camp. As there was a great scarcity of water-fowl, we thought proper to separate, to no great distance however. I unknowingly approached a hollow place, where many dogs were making a breakfast on a dead Kalmuck. The dogs instantly attacked me; I fired my gun among them ...[74]

(Cook, 1740s)

A Kalmyk princess deceived

About the month of June [1740], the brave Kalmuck Prince Donduk Ambo died, it was said, of a fever. The Russian court now intended to appoint one named Donduk Daschee [Donduk-Dashi] Prince over the Kalmucks. They had kept him in Casan many years in a princely manner, had caressed him much, with a view to get him so far in the interest of Russia, as to persuade the Kalmucks to live in cities and villages on the banks of the Volga, and no more wander about the desart in tents.

Donduk Ambo's lady, a Circassian by birth, descended of one of the most illustrious families in Circassia, was of a different opinion. She had five children to Donduk Ambo, and even naturally wished that her children should succeed their father, and therefore at present summoned all the Kalmuck chiefs to attend at her tent. They frankly enough espoused her cause, and determined to keep near her person. It was said, at this time, that she had a body of at least 40,000 men, all warriors, who had been tried under the orders of the late Donduk Anbo. She encamped on the west side of the Volga, over against Astrachan, till the beginning of August, and then marched through the desart south to the borders of Circassia, where they wintered ...[75]

...

The Princess of the Kalmucks crossed the Volga, encamped in the desart on the west side, and fearing the Russians would make use of their regular forces to reduce her to obedience, retired sooner last year to the borders of Circassia, that she might either influence her relations to use their interest with the court of Russia in her favours, or if that could not be done to her liking, it was said she, with her faithful followers, were determined to put themselves under the protection of either of the Turk, as her husband had formerly done, or fly to Kouli Khan.

...

Early in the spring [of 1742], Mr Tatishoff sent great presents to the Princess of the Kalmucks, and wrote that the Empress had not only insured her and her children after her death, to rule over the Kalmucks, but had, to show what trust her Imperial Majesty put in her, appointed her general Governess over the whole kingdom of Astrachan, and had ordained him Tatishoff to receive, with most profound submission, and obey all orders which her Highness might think proper to honour him with, providing only they did not clash with the religion (which by the by Tatishoff cared as little for as the Kalmuck princess), and the fundamental laws of the Empire.

He sent several honourable officers to assure her, that all what he had wrote was true, and that in the great palace in the citadel was in order for her to live in, Peter the Great's palace in the county. The rich presents, the honourable deputation of officers sent to her, and the many letters, most of which he Tatishoff, forged, as if from the Empress, had at last the desired effect.

The deluded Princess even made haste to fall into the trap laid for her, by thinking that every thing said or wrote would be adhered to, with as much candor and honour as when Prince Golitzin governed the kingdom. She marched day and night till she arrived on the west bank of the Volga, over against the city. Mr Tatishoff lost no time in waiting upon her, and of throwing himself at her feet, assuring her that nothing could be more agreeable to him than to obey implicitly her high orders, begging to know, at same time, when her Highness would condescend to visit the metropolis, and there, in the presence of all principal officers, receive the insignia of her high office.

She either could not, or thought it needless to hide the pleasure it gave her to have such marks of the Empress's high esteem, as she thought conferred upon her; but told the Governor, that she would first consult with her elders or leading men, and send him an order to acquaint him with her pleasure, at a convenient time.

This farce continued six or seven weeks ...

At last, however, the Princess declared her intention of crossing the Volga, and receiving the investiture of the government. Great preparations were made; four thousand men lined the streets, forming a lane from the water-gate to the Governor's palace, the cannon were fired, bells rung, drums beat, and the musick played interchangeably: She walked from the river to the palace; for she neither would go in the Governor's coach, nor mount on horseback. She had a fine presence, and was truly a stately, comely, beautiful woman. Her eyes were large, black, and had a lustre which very few can equal; and she expressed much sweetness in her countenance. In a word, though she had seen forty years, she was one of the prettiest women I ever beheld. When she went into the great hall, followed by about forty of her own principal subjects, she was seated at the head of the table, with twenty Kalmucks on each side: The Governor sat at the foot of the table, and more than a hundred officers of the garrison stood the whole time of dinner.

After dinner, the Governor rose from the table, paid his respects to the Princess, and signified a desire to speak with her in the gallery looking to the Volga. Major Cherkassoff ... told me what passed there, for he interpreted betwixt her and the Governor ...

The Governor then made no secret to let her know, that she was his prisoner, and begged that she would not be alarmed nor terrified, because he assured her that no harm would happen either to her or her children; but that the Empire had pledged its honour that Donduk Dashee should be created Prince of the Kalmucks after the decease of her husband, that now it was to be put in execution. He observed to her, that if the Kalmucks who were in the great hall offered to rescue her, they would instantly be put to death. He said a great deal more: At last, when the Princess had dried up her tears, and first put him in mind of his many false promises alledging, that the Empress never could be guilty of such baseness, then she upbraided him, and assured him that though he might detain her, he never would get her children, for, said she, I have left directions with the elders on the other side not to deliver them up, even if she should be forced to send orders for that purpose, she then represented that the Kalmucks would desert the Russian protection to a man, but added, that if he would permit her to return, she would rather try what she could do to get the leading Kalmucks to submit to the Empress's pleasure.

She used many more arguments, but the most powerful were her tears, which flowed plentifully, and had that effect to make the old Governor join in chorus. The old man, weeping like a child, agreed that she should he allowed to return, if she would submit to he guarded by fire hundred soldiers under the command of his son ...

The Princess repassed the river, escorted by five hundred regular troops, a few irregular. I had heard nothing of them for several weeks, though we could see their camp daily from the walls of the city. At last, Major Tatishoff, the Governor's only son, sent a report to his father, acquainting him that the young children made their escape ... but that the Princess still was under custody, having seized her, just as she was going to take her horse at midnight ...

The regiment of dragoons, all the Cossack and Tartarian horse, were transported over the Volga. They scoured the desart every where for six days, to no purpose, after having rendered both men and horses almost useless with the great fatigue. The Princess would tell nothing, but smiled at their distress. The Governors eloquence for once cast away: He knew not what to do; his sleep left him: and his appetite failed. He durst not offer to use her cruelly, and indeed, if he had, the consequence might have proved fatal to her, which at that time she seemed very indifferent about.

At last he determined to leave the city, and encamp with her. He sent orders for two regiments of dragoons and four thousand Cossacks to march directly where he was; but whilst he lay opposite the city, a boat was intercepted bringing letters to the Princess, acquainting her that her children were in good health on the opposite side of the river, guarded by a respectable body of Kalmucks who determined lose every drop of their blood in their defence: but that they were farther up the river, at the distance of three hundred verts at least. Bad as these news were, the Governor was glad at this intelligence: and, to prevent, as much as possible, a junction between the Kalmucks on the east and west sides of the river, and also to prevent the children's getting to the west side, and then probably to Circassia. Tatishoff caused seize all their boats and stave them. After this he marched with his prisoner the Princess up the west side of the Volga, and permitted her to send and receive messages as often as she pleased, in company with some of his men: by which means he was well assured that a very great number of the most resolute Kalmucks had formed a strong camp, nor were to be forced by any regular troops: wherefore nothing remained but to try what policy, of which the Governor was great master, would do.

He permitted, as I said, any number of the Kalmucks to go from their Princess with messages to the Kalmuck army. Neither did he hinder any small number from their army to pay their respects to the Princess, only he obliged them to permit one or two of his interpreters to be present, that they might give him an account of whatever passed.[76]

...

About the last days of my abode in the camp [on the banks of the Volga] the governor desired that I would pay a visit to the Princess of the Kalmucks, who, he said, had long ago been complaining ... In company with the major, the governor's only son, I went to a very large tent, in form of a bee-hive, covered with felt, and lined with Persian silk. When I entered the tent, the Princess was lying on a down covered with silk; her face was from us ... She stretched out a well formed, fair skinned arm, I felt her pulse a long while, and asked her many questions ... I replied that a free serene air was the only remedy that I thought could remove the cause of her complaints ... She looked steadfastly at me ... with the beautifullest black eyes ... and suddenly turned about. I suspected she was weeping ...[77]

A cup of tea was brought ... The tea, I dare say, was good, but the Kalmucks put salt and butter into it; nevertheless I drank it, though extremely disagreeable ...

I surely never could pity any person more than this unfortunate princess, and had any way been in my power, she should not long have been prisoner, but all I could do was sympathize with her.[78]

...

I was informed, that the Princess of the Kalmucks and her children were treated with all politeness, and as illustrious personages, at Moscow: And that when the Empress arrived in that city, she deigned to pay them a visit, and was so fond of them that she gave them very great possessions to enable them to live in a princely manner. The Princess and her children took such a liking to the Empress, that they all were baptized, and the Empress stood god-mother.[79]

(Cook, June 1740–spring 1742)

Parkinson encounters Kalmyks near Sarepta

Several of brethren and particularly Christian Petrovitch, Conrad, the Surgeon etc. have told me that they look on the Tatars, the Calmucs, the Tchovaches and the Mordvans to be better people than the Russians.[80]

...

[Dr Pallas] had been on an excursion of ten days into the Oural Desert ... as far as Lake Kamysh ... There are a few Calmucks left in this desert, who however, would be glad to depart, but the Russians are unwilling they should because they regard them as disaffected; and they themselves are at a loss which way to [turn]. Their Brethren who made their escape and are settled on the Irtisch are laid under a necessity very disagreeable to them to quit their roving life and live in fixed habitations. The reason of their disaffection to the Russians is the oppressions and pillages they have suffered, particularly from the late Prince Potemkin and from General Paul. For that reason they fly away now (he was speaking I think when he said this of the Calmucks in the steppes of Kama) at the sight of a stranger: whereas formerly they were rejoiced at the sight and gladly went to meet him.

...

He [Dr Pallas] told us that there are about six principal hordes in this Desert between the Wolga and the Don; that the one encamped at present fifty Versts from Sarrepta is the largest consisting of 5,000 Kibitkas and perhaps 20,000 souls; that there are besides the great hordes, some straggling ones of less consideration, a hundred or two hundred in number.

In the evening we walked with the Mayor of the place, our good friend who had accompanied us everywhere, to the Calmuc Tents. We entered one of them, in the midst of which a fire was burning with a pan of milk over it, and we tasted their sour Milk or Koumiss. But this was from the cow; the Mare Koumiss, he told us, was thinner, more wholesome and more agreeable to the palate. [The pan] as soon as it was boiled was to be poured into the leather bag where by mixing with the sour milk already there it soon became the same. Before the Dish was handed to us, the Calmuc woman stirred it well about with a kind of Mill. This [Koumiss] and meal mixed up with the same constitutes the whole luxury of their Table. Yet our friend assured us that a rich Calmuc imagines no people in the world live so well, and are in general so well off, as themselves.

Two Priests, visitors from the great Horde who had come upon business to Sarrepta, were sitting at the foot of one of the Tents in which they proposed they [should] pass the night. There were four tents on this spot in all; and the People by whom they were inhabited were employed to look after the Cattle. There are several [Kalmyks] who when they have no property quit their horde for a time and even let themselves to do menial services or to work as labourers. They are the best people to entrust with the Care of Cattle.

When a stranger is known and recommended to them they treat him with great attention and take pains to satisfy his curiosity; but otherwise they take but little notice of him. The women do all the labourers' work. Except the woodwork they have all the trouble of fitting up the Tent. When they are under no apprehension of rain they frequently sleep in the open Air.[81]

...

The Calmucs hang up in the wind a piece of cloth with a prayer written upon it and when the wind shakes it about they think the efficacy as great as if they had uttered it themselves. We saw a piece of cloth of this kind to-day at one of the Calmuc Tents. They even [have] Mills which answer the same purpose. Their religion prohibits them from washing any of their utensils, perhaps on a principle of saving their water ... The Calmuc Priests [are] rich and oppress the People.

He shewed us a Moss which in an emergency the People eat. There is also another of a dark colour. The taste like that of Morelles ...

Old Brandt gave us his company while we were at dinner and Dr Sedler called upon us before the cloth was removed. He told us several curious things of the Calmucs and their language ... By way of paying him a great compliment a Calmuc chief told him that his (the Doctor's) wife was his (the chief's) sister. If you ask whether a child is a boy and it is a girl, they reply that it is a 'blunt boy'.[82]

(Parkinson, June 1793)

Guests of the Kalmyk prince Tiumen

[25 June 1793] We arrived at Sereglatske and having determined to visit Prince Tiumen who was with his horde near our route six or seven versts forward, we determined to stop here till break of day (damned bore, what the Devil is there to see).

[26 June] We actually set off at break of day as we had proposed, understanding that the Prince was up always early, and arrived at the Camp, which consisted of about 120 tents, soon after … His tents were three in number in the centre of the Camp and were distinguishable by their whiteness. We halted at some distance from [them] and sent John in quest of him with our letters. He requested us to wait a little while till his tent was ready for our reception; which it was not just then owing to his having had company to pass the night with him. In fact, however, I believe that the Princesses, viz. his wife and daughters, were asleep in it; for we saw two ladies presently after passing from this tent to another in a great hurry and dressing themselves as they went. He received us with great politeness. The tent . . . being open at the top and a little all round underneath was very cool and pleasant. A Carpet of white clean felt was spread all over the ground except a round space in the middle over which stood a Semi-globular Vessel covered with a Mat whereon lay a ladle. This was for their Koumiss. A Sopha, which I suspect had served for one of the beds (the other was on the floor), three Camp Chairs and two Carpets, on one [of] which his chair was placed and ours were intended to be [on] the other, composed the furniture.

After conversing for some time, we were served out of a wooden vessel, in the form almost of a short boot, with a dish of tea prepared in the Calmuc way, that is with tea, water, butter and salt. Our dishes were also of wood and by way of signifying that they were prohibited from washing their Utensils, a handful of shavings were brought in along with them to rub and clean the inside. This kind of tea, he assured us, was wholesome and I was so far from finding it unpalatable that I begged for a second dish. Before the Tea was brought in, his son had entered very neatly dressed and took his seat on a carpet which was spread for him on one side. He also partook of our fare, smoked his pipe as his father did (it was extraordinary that the Prince never once invited us to smoke) and seemed to be treated with much distinction. We observed that the Servants in handing anything to the Prince were very cautious not to set their foot on his Carpet. We were afterwards served with tea in our own way, with lemon juice to supply the place of Milk.

Upon begging leave, when we had sat for some time, to walk about the Camp, he conducted us to their places of worship, which consisted of four tents standing by themselves, where everything had evidently been prepared for our reception. In every one of these there was a kind of altar on which, beside some tinsel ornaments, were placed in several small pewter cups offerings of water barley, barley mixed with beans, cheese made of sour milk and sugar. At the back of the altar were either their religious books covered with a carpet (at least this was the case in one) or a Cabinet, the doors of which being open exhibited a variety of idols each in his niche sitting squat and often decorated with a string of Pearls. These Cabinets reminded me of the pictures over altars in Roman Catholic Churches which are often shut up in this manner with folding doors. On each side of the altar were hung the holy pictures containing a great number of extravagant figures, and dangling like so many colours. The faces in these were all in the Chinese style, as indeed those of the Calmucs are. It was remarkable that there was a glory round each of the heads. Some of these paintings, or rather tapestries, come from Tibet but in general they are manufactured at home.

The Prince and his son on entering each tent as a mark of reverence touched some or all of the holy pictures with their head[s]. We were shewn in one the Drums and trumpets which they make use of sometimes in their service; and also the Standard with a figure of the God of Battles and a long inscription upon it in Tangut, which they take with them when they go to war. The Prince took this very standard with him I understand when he served in the Cuban. Each of these tents is superintended by a certain number of Priests, who I suspect sleep and live in them.

When we had satisfied our curiosity here he invited us to visit the tent of the Lama. He used to be appointed by the Lama of Thibet. But of late it has been usual on account of the length and danger of the journey for the old Lama to fix before his death without sending to Thibet on some person properly qualified for his successor. Formerly also Pilgrimages were usual to that country but of late they have been discontinued, he said, for the same reason.

We found him sitting in the posture of his God which he did not alter in the smallest degree by way of return to our bows. Carpets were laid for us and we sat down crosslegged in the eastern fashion. What shall I offer you, he said; we seemed inclined to decline everything but upon the Prince's saying that their religion required us to take something, we accepted of some Koumiss or Mare's milk which was handed to us in a neat bason out of a wooden Vessel in the form of a short Churn that was standing by the Altar. It was thin, acid but by no means disagreeable having as Dr Pallas observed rather a vinous taste and resembling that, particularly white wine Whey. He enquired about our religion whether it was the same with that of the Germans; and about our language, whether that of our religion and of common life were the same, and about the size of our country. It was news to him that Great Britain was an island ... He conversed with great composure and when we were coming away wished us a safe return to our native country and to the presence of our Sovereign.

We bowed very respectfully on parting but he did not on this occasion or any other make the smallest movement in return.

The Lama seldom stirs out except to ride about once a week and walk in their processions. The Calmucs in general by being continually on horseback and at other times sitting generally in their manner, become feeble to such a degree that many of them can scarcely bear to be on their feet for an hour together. The Prince I think mentioned this. NB Their way is to give Names to their Children according to circumstances. For instance [said the Prince] if my wife had happened to be delivered of a son at this time, perhaps I should have given him the name of one of you in honour of this visit. The Prince told us that their Custom is to reckon the age of a Person from the time of his Mother's being with Child.

I shall now mention the arrangement of the Lama's Apartment and his dress. At his back was placed a thick roll of black leather which we took for his bed, and behind that a kind of sopha: before [this] was a little low form like what the Priests had before them when we saw them at divine service. On his right hand a little advanced stood an altar with the usual offerings upon [it], particularly several small conical lumps of sugar wrapped in paper, and in a cup on a stand by itself a dish of Calmuc tea, which he had probably presented this morning, as the primitie of his breakfast. Close by the Altar I observed the little Churn already mentioned and two boots like what had contained our Calmuc tea. On his left opposite to the Altar stood a pile of Boxes containing I suppose the holy things. Several Utensils of different kinds were scattered about the room, which however on the whole was very neat.

His dress consisted of a Calmuc Cap, a red outer Garment, an under one of yellow (B[ootle] calls it a Petticoat) and a shirt under that. What he had on his legs we could not see because they were hid.

The Prince before we went to the Lama had invited us to dine; and upon our expressing a wish to dress and wash ourselves first, had ordered a tent to be erected near our Kibitkas for that purpose to which we now retired. I forgot to mention that on rising from my awkward posture on the Carpet in the Lama's tent I had entirely lost the use of my limbs and could hardly scramble out.

The dinner was already serving up when we returned. A table was laid in the Tent on the Spot where the Koumiss had stood, the top of the tent was covered [?] down, the sides were opened all round in order to let thro' a current of air, and a canopy was raised over the Sopha. While we were at dinner, several spiders dropped upon us from the top of the Tent. Our dinner was in the Russian style, being preceded by a savoury collation and followed by Tea instead of Coffee. Caviare, dried fish, cheese made of cows milk, cheese made of sour milk such as we had seen on the altars, twisted white bread, butter, Eau de vie and a Medicine to mix with it composed the collation. Minced meat or rather soup, something between both, the fat of Mutton cut in slices, some slices of fat beef; pigskin filled with rice tasting strong[ly] of Garlic, Curry and Roast Mutton with lemon composed our dinner. The art of making the minced Meat or Soup above mentioned consists in boiling it very gently. The ingredients besides the Mutton are only water and salt. It was richly sprinkled with little pieces of fat. It was curious to meet with Rhine wine, English beer and English knives and forks in a Calmuc tent. Besides the Rhine wine and the English Beer he treated us with some wine that came out of his own Garden.

He did the honours of his table with great politeness and propriety and we were never at a loss for conversation. To account for which I must mention that our interpreter John was present all the while and even sat down with us to dinner. I forgot to mention that an old Musician played during our whole dinner time on an Instrument somewhat resembling a guittar and accompanied his playing with the Voice. One of his tunes was exactly a French one Bootle [knew], which was curious after what Pallas had remarked in general of their Music. Most of the songs were Love Songs, the ditties of despairing lovers. He [the Prince] told us that the Calmucs in their national meals sit on carpets and are helped according to Seniority.

When word was brought us that divine service was ready we rose from table and hastened to the consecrated tents; in one of which we found thirteen Priests forming two rows, six on one side and seven on the other, chanting in a low hoarse voice accompanied with the most ridiculous gruntings. They likewise twirled their hands round one another and snapped their fingers in a curious manner. But they presently took into their hands a bell and a sort of short staple [?], after which a tinkling of their bells in Chorus supplied the place of the latter of these operations. The Psalm or hymn or verse seemed continually to come to an end; there was then a pause, and a new beginning was made always by one particular Priest. When we had attended about three quarters of an hour the Prince inquired whether our curiosity was satisfied; observing at the same time that it would last an hour longer, and without any variation. We of course found ourselves disposed not to stay any longer. The Dress of the Priests was a cap turned up with five wings and having [a] shaft or spire in the middle of black twisted round with string in several places, an outer garment like a pair of stays, an under one not coming much below it, and a third somewhat in the form of a petticoat. There were little low benches before them and they all preserved the most unmoveable gravity of countenance and did not once turn their gaze towards us ... I understand that there are four services in a day, one in the morning, two in the middle of the day and one in the evening.

We now ordered our Kibitkas and returned with the Prince to his tent where we again drank tea. In the meantime he entertained us with a sight of two of their sacred Volumes, one in the Tangut the other in the Mongol language, by an exhibition of four dromedaries, and lastly of the Calmuc way of wrestling. The two combatants were perfectly naked except about the loins. Their contest resembled the old Palaestra: the object being, one to throw the other down.

Those Volumes I understand from him contain a history of God Almighty's gracious dispensations to their nation. I understood also that there are a great many of them. The Calmucs all ran to kiss them as soon as they saw them before they were brought in to us. They resembled in shape a book of accounts. The Mongol language was written in the same manner as the Calmuc and is I imagine the same. The Tangut was written from left to right like ours. But the letters very much resembled the Hebrew. This I understand to be the language of their religion and totally different from that of common life: as different, to use the Prince's expression, as Russian from Greek …

We agreed in thinking the behaviour of this Calmuc perfectly polite: yet he always went out of his tent before us, a piece of etiquette which I have since imagined he may have learnt from her Majesty's representatives the Governors and Governors general.

The Prince's horde consists he told us of about 3,000 families or Kibitkis. He had about 120 with him at present in this spot which his ancestors had been in the habit of frequenting for a century past. He proposed to remain here a fortnight, then to remove to his island in which he passes another fortnight; and from thence to the other side of the Wolga. For this purpose however, as we were informed by the Brigadier, he is obliged to obtain permission of the Governor, though he dissembled that to us, and insinuated that the Calmucs were all at full liberty to cross the river. Yet I remember that he seemed to be rather chagrined by the Question. The rest of his horde are dispersed all over the Steppe; but they are obliged to procure leave to go from him. Many individuals are possessed of a thousand horses and other cattle in proportion. Not more than four or five of these can be accommodated, he said, in the same place. He asserted also that the number of Calmuc families was 50,000, that there are 22,000 on this side towards the Wolga and 10,000 in the neighbourhood of Tcherkask. Yet the Brigadier, who pretends to be well informed, asserts that the whole number is not more than 15,000 or 20,000. He also maintains in opposition to Pallas and Vesilef that there are no Calmucs in the Steppe of Ural; and that the number of families who made their escape did not amount to more than 40 or 50,000. Yet he calculated that they amounted to 400,000 souls.

He says that the only people there [in the Ural Steppe] are a few Tartars. His account of the Calmucs who made their escape out of Russia is that the greatest part of them were destroyed by the Kirghese, owing to the want of fodder for their horses, and that no more than twenty thousand escaped with their lives. The Prince's account was the same except that they had received no intelligence of those who had escaped with their lives and did not know where they were. Now as it seems to be well understood that they are settled in the Irtish in the Chinese Territories, I imagined that this ignorance of his was pretended. He was but eleven at the time of this secession. Some of his horde was in the number, he said, of the seceders. I thought that he spoke of this event with evident marks of concern. This Horde is called the horde of Chachioutoch [corrupted form of Khoshut?][83] and the Prince's name is as he gave it himself after we had written ours by his desire 'Wladell i Knes [Sovereign and Prince] Premier Major Tiumen'. He seemed to make a great point of his title of Premier Major. I could not help remarking the Piety with which the Prince spoke of every future enterprise and future intention: adding also if it pleased God to prolong his life, by leave of Providence and so on.[84]

(Parkinson, 1793)

'A small party at the Governor's'

We dined a small party at the Governor's of which [one] was Prince Tiumen, who did not seem to be treated with much distinction but considered as a premier Major and nothing more ... There is a reserve and gravity in his deportment which I could fancy denotes dissatisfaction.

The Governor told me that ... Tiumen has the manners and sentiments of a Gentleman but the rest are 'cochons'.[85]

(Parkinson, July 1793)

ENDNOTES

1   Pallas 1788–93, vol.1, p.495, n.1.
2   Khodarkovsky 1992, p.74. I am much indebted to this book for the history of the Kalmyks until 1771.
3   Ibid., p.27.
4   Ibid., pp.90–92.
5   Ibid., pp.92ff.
6   Pallas 1788–93, vol.1, pp.569–70; Georgi 1780–83, vol.4, p.58.
7   Khodarkovsky 1992, p.3.
8   Ibid., pp.100ff.
9   Ibid., p.144.
10   Georgi 1780–83, vol.4, p.9; Pallas 1776, pp.24–96 (with genealogical tables) and Georgi (derived but abbreviated from Pallas) sketch Kalmyk history by 'stem' or tribe (Georgi 1780–83, pp.6–14).
11   Khodarkovsky 1992, pp.170–80, 196–201.
12   Ibid., pp.201–5.
13   Ibid., p.212.
14   Ibid., p.205.
15   Ibid., pp.216–17.
16   Ibid., p.206.
17   Ibid., p.221.
18   Ibid., p.214.
19   Ibid., e.g. pp.139, 146 and *passim*.
20   Ibid., pp.213–24.
21   Ibid., p.224.
22   Ibid., pp.225, 230.
23   Ibid., pp.224–31.
24   Ibid., pp.177, 217.
25   They went variously via Central Asia, the rivers Jaik and Emba, Lake Balkash and the River Ili.
26   Khodarkovsky 1992, p.234; *Ocherki istorii kalmytskoi ASSR*, p.218ff.
27   Khodarkovsky 1992, p.232.
28   *Ocherki istorii kalmytskoi ASSR*, p.219.
29   First published in *Blackwoods Magazine* in 1837; ed. W.E. Simonds, 1899.
30   Khodarkovsky 1992, p.232, n.88.
31   *Ocherki istorii kalmytskoi ASSR*, pp.226–29; Khodarkovsky 1992, pp.234–35.
32   *Ocherki istorii kalmytskoi ASSR*, pp.221–25.
33   For other eighteenth-century Russian academicians' sources on the Kalmyks, see *Ocherki istorii kalmytskoi ASSR*, p.4. Academician G.F. Müller had a particular interest in the eastern Kalmyks, and intended to write a proper history of them (Müller 1762, pp.123–53, 273–79; pp.291ff. are partly based on the journal of Ivan Unkovski, who had been an envoy to Jungaria in 1722–24 [*Sammlung Russicher Geschichte*, vol.1.]); Black, p.42. For those able to read Dutch, see Witsen.
34   Pallas 1776 and 1788–93, vol.1, p.499. Pallas found the character of the Kalmyks 'far better than travellers usually describe it' – affable, frank, jolly, hospitable, happy to render service. Their bad qualities were that they are dirty, lazy and cunning.
35   Georgi 1780–83, vol.4, pp.11–12.
36   Khodarkovsky 1992, p.212.

37 Pallas 1788–93, vol.1, p.555; Georgi 1780–83, vol.4, p.17.

38 This Prince Tiumen was presumably the same who built the Khoshutovsky Buddhist Temple *c.* 100 km north of Astrakhan (Tyumenevka, now Rechnoye village) in 1818 to commemorate the Kalmyk cavalry's participation in the Napoleonic war of 1812. See *Ocherki istorii kalmytskoi ASSR*, pp.248–57. For another western traveller's visit to Prince Tiumen, see Potocki, pp.61–75, who says that Tiumen was respected for being of the blood of Genghiz Khan.

39 According to Pallas 1799–1801, vol.1, Tiumen had 892 tents following him.

40 For amulets such as described by Hanway and given to the Kalmyks by their priests, see Pallas 1788–93, vol.1, p.559.

41 This is also concession made to Hinduism by certain eighteenth-century European observers, see Teissier 2004.

42 *Ocherki istorii kalmytskoi ASSR*, pp.203–6; Khodarkovsky 1992, pp.106–7.

43 Khodarkovsky 1992, p.177.

44 Ibid., pp.205–06.

45 Georgi 1780–83, vol.4, p.121

46 Pallas 1799–1801, vol.1, p.117.

47 Pallas 1788–93, vol.1, pp.175–77; Georgi 1780–83, vol.4, p.121ff.

48 Georgi 1780–83, vol.4, p.123.

49 Khodarkovsky 1992, p.39; Georgi 1780–83, vol.4, p.125.

50 Halkovic; cf. HKK, pp.41–42. Bell's entry owes nothing to Ebulgazi Bahadur Khan (1729–30), the principal contemporary source in the west on the Kalmyks.

51 Pallas 1776, vol.1, p.56; see also Pentii Aalto in the *International Journal of Central Asian Studies* 1 (1996), n.p.

52 P. Avril, *Voyages...* (1692) in Jean, p.144. For other Jesuit travels and entries on Tatary, see e.g. Astley, vol.1, pp.392ff (mostly derived from Father Gerbillon). By the time Bruce was in Russia, Ochirtu Tsetsen-Khan had long been defeated.

53 Otchirtu Tsetsen-Khan was a Khoshut, once a rival of Ayuki, who was defeated in 1677 by the Jungarians. The Oirats were not directly descended from Ghenghis, although the Khoshuts claimed descent from his brother. Timur was a Turk, not descended from Chenghiz although he claimed it. When Timur is mentioned in this entry, it may have referred to the Chenghiz line.

54 Pallas has a very long passage on Kalmyk Buddhism, which includes details on idols, painted images, holy books (Pallas 1788–93, vol.1, pp.533–74) and Kalmyk laws (pp.528–33). See Georgi for Kalmyk songs and the legend of Ghessur Khan (Georgi 1780–83, vol.4, pp.61–120), and on the history of the Kalmyks (ibid., pp.181–85).

55 Kara, pp.137ff; see the references to Pallas and Georgi directly above.

56 By the 1740s Chinoiserie was still in vogue in Britain, and the Chinese were not yet demonised as they were to be at the end of the century; see Teissier 2004.

57 Pallas 1799–1801, vol.1, pp.117–18.

58 Ibid., p.528.

59 Ibid., p.499.

60 Perry 1716, pp.83–87.

61 Ibid., pp.276–77.

62 Bell confuses the names of tribes with the names of 'Chiefs'.

63 This must have been a local term, see Hanway, vol.1, p.347.

64 Bell, pp.29–34.

65 Ibid., pp.317–19.
66 Bruce, pp.240–43.
67 Ibid., p.244.
68 Ibid., p.295; Lockhart 1958, p.188. Sultan Mahmud attacked with Usmi Ahmad Khan.
69 Bruce, pp.327–35.
70 Hanway, vol.1, pp.100–02.
71 Ibid., pp.138–39.
72 Cook, vol.1, pp.257–59.
73 Ibid., pp.259–61.
74 Ibid., pp.301–02.
75 Ibid., p.303.
76 Cook, vol.2, pp.66–72.
77 Ibid., p.77.
78 Ibid., pp.77–80.
79 Ibid., p.85.
80 Parkinson, pp.142, 144.
81 Ibid., p.145.
82 Ibid., p.147.
83 *Ocherki istorii kalmytskoi ASSR*, p.226; Pallas 1772 writes Choshot; Pallas 1799–1801, vol.1, pp.116–17 for the numbers of tents associated with particular chiefs.
84 Parkinson, pp.154–60.
85 Ibid., pp.178–79.

ANTIQUARIAN AND HISTORICAL ACCOUNTS

Introduction

The travellers featured in the previous chapters were not antiquarians, but most had connections with the British antiquarian and scientific world. Perry, Bell, Cook and Hanway all had contacts with the Royal Society; Bell mentioned collecting for Hans Sloane while in Siberia, and both Cook and Hanway were potentially involved with the Royal Society over Tatishchev's history.[1] The Oxford don Parkinson had connections through his tutoring and touring. These travellers would have been aware of institutional collections in London or St Petersburg,[2] and, as befitting eighteenth-century middle-class professionals,[3] they also collected for themselves.

Although only Parkinson visited an archaeological site – Bulgar, one of Kazan's late eighteenth-century tourist sights – the others were aware of the history of the regions they traversed, either from previous travellers or from contemporary accounts. They alluded to most aspects of the middle Volga's 'Tartar' historical past, including the two Mongol-period Sarays; Bulgar, a centre of the Bulgar and later Golden Horde state; the khanates of Kazan and Astrakhan and their annexation by Russia; and a landscape that evoked the ancient Scythians and the legendary Timur. The earliest actual remains mentioned are those of 'Old' Saray (Selitrennoe), on the left bank of the Akhtuba upstream from Astrakhan, and 'New Saray' (Tsarevo), also on the Akhtuba, about 115 km to the north.

Old Saray was founded by Chinghiz Khan's grandson Batu around the mid-thirteenth century, after the successful Mongol campaigns of the 1220s onwards to conquer the Russian principalities, the Bolgar state and the steppes of eastern Europe. The Golden Horde was the name given in Russian sources from the sixteenth century onwards to the Mongol khanate, also known as the Ulus Jochi,[4] which controlled the western Mongol empire from the mid-thirteenth century until its fragmentation in the first half of the fifteenth, and the emergence of new khanates, such as those of Kazan and Astrakhan.

Old Saray was ethnically diverse, with many markets and separate merchant quarters accommodating different peoples.[5] It was also religiously diverse, with Christian Byzantine, Russian, Catholic and Muslim communities, but it became increasingly Muslim after Khan Özbek converted in the fourteenth century.[6] The site, which was newly built, and has only been partially excavated, runs for several kilometres along the

Akhtuba. It encompasses a palace, houses, underground living space and stores, bath-houses, a medresa,[7] large ceramic and glass-making workshops, reservoirs, villas on the outskirts and tombs.[8]

Cook did not describe Old Saray but merely refered to it as 'an antient city', which was plundered for bricks and treasure. His mention of precious stones is confirmed by excavations showing artisans' workshops for processing semiprecious stones.[9] A good eighteenth-century account was given by Pallas, who visited in the 1770s and referred to it as an ancient site lived in by Nogay Tatars.[10] He described buildings revealed (and damaged) by saltpetre works, which had 'magnificent' high, regular walls, façades and pillars in the 'Gothic style', with floral and foliate stucco work, varnished tiles and mosaics.[11] He added that time, weather and destruction, including boatloads of bricks taken to Astrakhan, had greatly diminished the remains, and that much looted material ended up in the hands of those whose only interest was 'sordid gain'.[12]

The new capital, New Saray or the Tsarevo site, was built during the 1330s. Although smaller than Old Saray, it had similar streets, a square, villas, houses and dug-outs, reservoirs, tombs and workshops. It was fortified after it became involved in the internal disputes of the Golden Horde but was sacked by Timur in 1395.[13] Georgi visited the site guided by a Tatar, whose information shows how alive local historiography was. Georgi described the remains of tombs, a palace and a villa, or 'the palace of the queen'. He also gave the site a historical context: it was 'thought to have been the residence of Achmet, King of Grand Tartary, or the capital of the Golden Horde'.[14] His informant had evidently conflated the history of Golden Horde Saray with that of a city of the later Astrakhan khanate.[15] New Saray was also mentioned, less comprehensively, by Pallas. He wrote of remains of walls, streets and foundations, piles of bricks and traces of excavation, with no possibility of discerning a city plan.[16] Georgi attributed the city's final destruction in the mid-fifteenth century to the Russians and the Nogays, not to Timur.[17] Further historic sites up towards the Yaik were also mentioned by Georgi's Tatar guide, including such Golden Horde towns as Vodyanskoe (Beljamen) and Ukek near Saratov, and villages along the Volga.[18] Some were sacked by Timur, and revived, others declined definitively.

It is clear from Gibbon,[19] from Tooke's introduction to Georgi's *Russia*, Georgi himself and other scholars,[20] and geographical compendia[21] that enough original travel accounts or translations of Arabic and Persian texts were available in the west for the history of the Mongols in Russia to be broadly known at the time. Academicians in Russia would also have drawn on Russian chronicles. The Mongol origins of Saray, for example, were known in the west, as was its approximate location[22] and its name (with that of 'Tartary', see Introduction). This had acquired a certain literary cachet since the publication of thirteenth-century travellers' accounts, such as those of William of Rubruck and Marco Polo, and the spurious fourteenth-century *Travels* of Sir John Mandeville.[23] A reference to Saray is found in Chaucer's *Canterbury Tales:*[24] the *Squire's Tale* begins: 'At Saray in the land of Tartary,/ There lived a king who warred continually/ With Russia ... This noble king was known as Cambuscan' (Chengis Khan?).[25]

Although the travellers do not demonstrate a detailed knowledge of the region's history, their accounts are valuable because they testify to its historiography in popular imagination, both local and western. Perry and Bruce were inaccurate about the Tsarevo site: Perry linked it to a 'Scythian king'; Bruce, following Olearius,[26] linked its construction (not its destruction) to Timur. The Scythians were considered in the west to be the precursors of the Tartars and Mongols, both in terms of geographical distribution and customs.[27] It was to this tradition that Perry referred, rather than to the actual Cimmerian, Sauromatian or Sarmatian presence in the region.[28] Timur, the last great Asiatic khan and empire-builder, was a significant anti-hero in the west [29] (not least for the accounts of his exploits in India, echoed by Nader Shah's), but he was also extremely important regionally, as, to a lesser extent, was Alexander the Great.[30] The extent to which Timur, rather than previous Mongols, such as Batu, and even Chenghiz Khan, resonated in the Tartar landscape is shown by Bell's and Bruce's comments (both echoing Olearius)[31] on the environs of Simbirsk (Ulyanovsk). The area around Simbirsk and Undory (Bruce's Ureneskora) does have Golden Horde remains,[32] but the 'camps and entrenchments' Bell referred to at Simbirsk were built by Moscow in seventeenth century as part of the defences from the Volga to the Oka.[33] Bell also mentioned the 'burial mound' of Mamai,[34] a breakaway emir of the Golden Horde who was defeated by Grand Prince Dimitri at Kulikovo (beyond the Don) in 1380. He was murdered in Kaffa (Crimea) and did not die, as local legend had it, in the Middle Volga.[35] Such a memorial would have been one of several tombs and shrines of Tatar saints, sheyks or military leaders in the Middle Volga.[36]

The site of Bulgar, mentioned by Bruce and visited by Parkinson, was perhaps the most significant in the Middle Volga at the time, both archaeologically and in terms of Muslim Tatar historiography. It was an important centre in the pre-Mongol period, as part of the Volga Bulgar state, and in the period of the Golden Horde. The state of Bulgar emerged around the confluence of the Volga and the Kama in the tenth century as the result of Turkic Bolgar tribes who arrived in the Middle Volga in waves in the eighth and ninth centuries from the Kuban and the Caucasus, and who interacted with the local Finno-Ugrian population.[37] It consisted of several tribal centres, of which Bulgar was one.[38] These centres were dependent on the Khazars[39] until the end of the tenth century. They had a mixed population, which was originally semi-nomadic but by the later tenth century had become settled farming and manufacturing communities, whose wealth was based on trade.[40] Bulgar on the Volga was well placed to take advantage of this. It had colonies of foreign merchants and traded to the north, Central Asia and the Arab khalifates. Islam was adopted by the Bulgarians during the tenth century,[41] and Bulgar flourished until the Mongol invasions. It was destroyed but later revived and was absorbed, with the rest of the state, into the Golden Horde.[42] With the disintegration of the Golden Horde, Bulgar's importance was gradually usurped by Kazan. Russian raids contributed to its collapse in the early fifteenth century.

Ancien Batimens a Bolgars   fig.13

The site described by Parkinson and illustrated by Pallas (fig.13) dates to the Golden Horde period (second half of the thirteenth century–fourteenth century). Bulgar and its funerary inscriptions in Arabic and Armenian (mostly twelfth- to fourteenth-century) attracted much attention in the eighteenth century. The site was recorded, for example, by Deacon Mikhailov in 1712;[43] Müller described how Peter the Great, on his way to the Persian campaign of 1722, asked for copies of the inscriptions to be made and for brickwork to be repaired.[44] Catherine II, who visited in 1767 on her tour of the Volga and Kazan and categorically requested its preservation, gave the most impetus to the documentation of Bulgar.[45] Lepekhin, for example, from his travels of 1767 or 1768, gave details of its inscriptions,[46] while Pallas illustrated its monuments, some of which he compared to those of Kasimov and Tashkent, and coins,[47] and Georgi noted its 'splendid monuments'.[48]

Bulgar's history would have been known to the academicians, who nevertheless did not dwell on it. Pallas simply treated it as a worthy ancient site but noted how Tatars came there to buy souvenirs, especially coins. This detail, confirmed by Parkinson, who mentioned Tatars coming to pay 'their devotions', highlights the cultural and ideological significance of Bulgar for the Middle Volga Tatars. This was despite, or perhaps stimulated by, the presence there of a Russian church and monastery, the conversion of a mausoleum into a chapel, the destruction of parts of the site in the 1730s and 1740s, and the reuse of Tatar material for building.[49] There had also been a previous Christian presence, as attested by a fourteenth-century Armenian church and cemetery and medieval Russian Orthodox crosses.[50]

The prestige of Bulgar and Timur was not only part of popular and local oral and chronicle traditions but was deliberately developed in eighteenth-century Volga-Ural historiographies, culminating in the late eighteenth-century *Tawarikh-i Bulghariyya*.[51] Bulgar was promoted as the centre of the region's first Muslim state. Timur was shown as an ideal Islamic ruler, whose destruction of Bulgar was justified by its rulers' failure in their religious duties. Chinghiz Khan, by contrast, was depicted as an infidel. According to A.J. Frank, such historiography, which had a strong Central Asian, Sufi-inspired element,[52] was an attempt to create a single, Bulgar-based Islamic identity for the Volga-Ural Tatar communities. This would have included the militant Bashkirs, whose natural preferences were for nomadic, Chingisid traditions in contrast to the more sedentary identities of some Volga Tatars. This historiography, in Frank's view, gained impetus from the Orenburg Spiritual Assembly established in 1788 to regulate Muslim hierarchy and the supervision of mosque communities and schools in Russia.[53]

Bulgar was also key to a wider debate, which continues today, on the origins of the Volga and Kazan Tatars. Were they descendants of the Golden Horde (Ulus Jochi) or of the pre-Mongol Turkic Bulgars?[54] As noted by Georgi, the eighteenth-century Kazan Tatars acknowledged the complexity of their origins. Such attitudes would have been nuanced by dynastic or family affiliation, education and other factors. Tatar preoccupation with the past was never in doubt, however. In Georgi's words, 'It is not only the great that boast of their genealogies, even the meanest people ... warm their imagination with raptures on the ancient splendour of the Tartarian empire, and often break out in wishes and ardent longings for the restablishment of their former power.'[55] As evidence, he pointed to the Bashkir rebellions. In the nineteenth century the influential Kazan intellectual Shihabeddin Märcani deliberately created a national Islamic, Tartar history for Kazan, linking both the Volga Bulgars and the Golden Horde to Kazan identity.[56]

The early travellers Bell and Bruce gave succinct accounts of the khanate histories of Kazan and Astrakhan and their conquest by the Russians. Bell stressed the strategic importance of these conquests, and Bruce the military aspect; both noted the fate of the Kazan khanate's rulers. The later merchant travellers preferred to dwell on Kazan's importance as a shipyard and trading centre. For Parkinson the past histories of Kazan and Astrakhan seemed irrelevant to his diary.[57] There was no mention of remains from the khanates' past, although, according to Georgi, parts of a monument of the 'ancient Tatarian kingdom' could be seen in the fortress of Kazan, as well as by the Kazanka, and in the environs of Astrakhan.[58] On his way to Kazan, Bell mentioned the 'oratory' at Kasimov (Qasim) near the River Oka. The ruins at Kasimov were considered 'very beautiful' and, like the site of Bulgar, 'worthy of preservation'.[59]

Kazan was the ancient northern border fortress of the Bulgar state, dating from the eleventh or twelfth century.[60] A legend attributing Kazan's founding to the conqueror of the Bulgar state, Batu, is unsupported, although a Mongol link to the city is possible; coin evidence shows that Kazan was known before the mid-fifteenth century as Bulgar al-Jedid (New Bulgar).[61] In the fourteenth and fifteenth centuries Kazan became increasingly important, and became a principality (possibly of Middle Volga Bulgar origin),[62] before being taken over by a khan of the Golden Horde, Ulu Muhammed (the granson of Tokhtamysh) around 1437.[63] This was the beginning of the Kazan khanate. Its territory stretched from beyond Ufa in the north-east to below Saratov in the south; it shared its western border with the Kasimov and Crimean khanates.[64] From the start, the khanate veered between independence and conflict with Muscovy. This led to Muscovy's direct interference in Kazan's disputes of succession, first from the line of Ulu Muhammed, then from outside (Kasimov, Crimea).[65]

In the fifteenth century Muscovy was still weak enough to need an alliance with the Crimean khanate against Poland and the Great Horde (the remaining nomadic kernel of the Golden Horde between the Don and the Yaik), and to strengthen relations with the Ottomans. Crimea saw itself as the heir to the Golden Horde; its claim to Kazan's throne was initially supported by Muscovy. When the alliance with Crimea broke down, a contest ensued between the two for control of Kazan. Kasimov was the centre of a vassal khanate created by Ivan III in the mid-fifteenth century for Qasim, a rebel son of the khan of Kazan. It was effectively controlled by Moscow and used in its struggles against Kazan and the Golden Horde.[66] By the sixteenth century Muscovy had become the greatest military power in the region, and its designs on Kazan consolidated. In 1552, after Kazan's third rejection of Muscovy's unpopular puppet ruler Shah Ali, whom it replaced with a khan from Astrakhan, Yadyger Muhammed, Ivan IV took the city.[67]

This conquest was a great prize: Kazan had long-established trade routes to the east and south, as well as forests, agriculture and fishing. It was also a great symbolic moment: it proclaimed Muscovy's strength, the triumph of orthodoxy over the infidel, and the development of empire. Ivan declared himself Tsar of Kazan (and later Astrakhan). Bell and Bruce glossed over the fate of Kazan's princes, but it is true that Yadyger Khan was taken to Moscow, converted and given an estate.[68] Becoming Christian and swearing allegiance to Muscovy was to become a safe bet when dealing with the tsars. For the khanate's population the effect was drastic. The Muslim urban elite were dispossessed, land rights were reassigned to Russian church and noblemen, and Russian peasants settled among a mixed rural population of Tatars, Chuvash, Cheremis and Mordvin. Christianity was at first brutally enforced.[69] Tatars were forbidden to carry weapons and were driven from the city, with only a few allowed to settle in a suburb.[70] With time this policy became more pragmatic.[71] The fall of Kazan did not, however, put an end to local rebellion, which lasted throughout the later sixteenth century and beyond.

Astrakhan (formerly Xacitarxan, Hadji-Tarkhan) was a Golden Horde centre that, like Saray, was destroyed by Timur.[72] It later revived, and the khanate (1466–1556) was founded by a dynasty of Noghay princes (Qasim I) after the break-up of the Golden Horde.[73] This khanate extended from the Kuban steppe to the Caspian and to below Saratov;[74] it was weaker than Kazan and always subject to rival Crimean, Noghay and Muscovite interference.[75] The conquest of Astrakhan (and ideally Crimea) was, after Kazan, the logical next step for Ivan. After a siege by Muscovy, aided by the Noghays, khan Yaghmurchi fled, and a vassal of Moscow, Dervish Ali, was installed. In 1556, when the khan's loyalty turned, the khanate was annexed.[76] In 1558 the city was rebuilt by the Russians, some 11 km from its original place downstream on the left bank of the Volga.[77] The name Astrakhan originally had various forms and theories as to its origin. Bruce's account derived from Olearius' conjecture, which, even at the time, Georgi thought unfounded.[78] More importantly, as Bell noted, while Astrakhan's annexation secured Russian control of the area, it did not deter the threat from Persia, the Ottomans and Crimea.

Kasimov

The sixteenth [October 1715] we came to KASSIMOVA, formerly the residence of a TARTAR Prince, but the family is now converted to CHRISTIANITY, and retains only the old name of KASSIMOVSKY CZAREVITZ. The place is at present inconsiderable. There are still here a few MAHOMETAN TARTARS who are allowed the free exercise of their religion, and have a small oratory. I accompanied our interpreter to visit one of them, an old acquaintance of his. He was a very decent man; we saw a horse newly killed, which they intended to eat. They prefer this kind of food to beef, and invited us to share their repast, which we declined, pretending we had not the time.[79]

(Bell, 1715)

Ivan IV takes Kazan

CAZAN was anciently the capital of a part of TARTARY, and the seat of government, where the royal family resided. It was taken from the TARTARS by Czar IVAN VASILOVIZ, in the year fifteen hundred and fifty two, in consequence whereof an extensive country to the southward, easily fell into his hands. The conquered princes were converted to Christianity, and had lands assigned them in their own country, where the family still subsists.[80]

(Bell, 1715)

The fate of the kings of Kazan

The kings of Casan, in former times, maintained very bloody wars with the Russians, and frequently laid them into contribution, bringing commonly an army of sixty thousand men into the field; but they were at last subdued by Ivan Basilowitz, in the year 1552, and the royal family brought prisoners to Moscow, where their posterity still remain, the chief whereof is called the Cazanski czarowitz to this day.[81]

(Bruce, 1722)

At Simbirsk

[T]he 9th [June 1716 we passed] SINBIRSKY, pretty large, and the capital of a province of that name ... SINBIRSKY is defended by a castle. Near this place are evident marks of camps and entrenchments, which I was told were the works of the great TARTAR general, called TIMYRAK_SACK, or LAME TIMYR, or TAMERLANE, who came to this place with a great army; but being informed of an insurrection in his own country SAMER-KANT, now BUCHARIA, returned home.

The 10th we put off from SINBIRSKY with the wind contrary ... We passed two hills, one of them exhibiting a very beautiful prospect, the other containing mines of sulphur as clear as amber. We passed also a mound of sand, of considerable bigness, in the middle of a plain, where they say was buried a famous TARTAR prince called MAMAY.[82]

(Bell, June 1716)

Bulgar and Undory

About sixty wrests below Casan, the river Kama falls into the Wolga on the left side ... and at [sixty] wrests distant from thence, on the right side of the river, stands the town of Tetus ... twenty-five wrests below that on the opposite side, the river Utka falls in, which rises next to the city of Bulgar, the capital of the Tartarian kingdom of that name. Some wrests lower is an island called Staritza ... and not far below that, stands the ruins of a considerable city among the Tartars, called Ureneskora, destroyed by Tamerlane; it is most delightfully situated and famous to this day for the sepulchre of one of their saints, to whom they pay great devotion.

A good many wrests below this, on the right side are likewise to be seen the ruins of two other great cities, not far distant from each other; pleasantly situated near the banks of the river: the first was called Simberska, the second Arbuchim; they were likewise destroyed by Tamerlane.[83]

(Bruce, June 1722)

The ruins of Bulgar

We dined at the Governor's, Prince Baratiew's [S.M. Baratiev]; and in the afternoon about five o'clock set off for Bolghari, an old Tartar town, in the way to Simbirsk about 114 Versts distant from Casan. As the Governor had furnished us with an Ensign and a soldier who went before to order horses, we got on very fast and arrived at the end of our journey at seven in the morning … The ruins of Bolghari consist of two towers and seven or eight other ruins scattered over a tract of ground about six Versts in circumference which is surrounded by a ditch. We visited every one of these ruins with all possible attention and ascended both the towers, one of which could not be less than 100 feet high; as the others might be seventy or seventy-five. Near the latter are thrown about a great number of sepulchral stones with Arabic and Armenian Inscriptions, which we could not see at this time owing to their being covered with snow. The Tartars, we are told, still come every year in the summer as a sort of Pilgrimage in parties of ten or fifteen or fifty to pay their devotions on the spot where the tower stands. They come in Kibitkis and remain there encamped for two or three days. We made our progress through these ruins attended by a crowd of peasants, I counted at one time twenty. When we came back to the cottage where we took up our abode the greatest part of the village were ready to receive us; and what seemed curious, the Men and the women apart. They bowed most respectfully as we passed by. The crowd also attended to see us off did the same, standing all of them with their hats off.[84]

(Parkinson, 1793)

'The ancient Residence of a Scythian king'

About 40 Russ Miles below the formention'd town of Czaritsa, which Word in the Russ Language signifies Queen, in the Latitude of 48 Degrees and 20 Minutes, there is to be seen the Ruins of a large City, call'd Czaroff Gorod, in a very pleasant Situation, and which is said to have been the ancient Residence of a Scythian king.[85]

(Perry, 1698–1705)

Near Kamishinka

About forty miles from this [around Kamishinka] and at a small distance from the river-side, are to be seen the ruins of a great city, formerly called Czarefgorod, built, as is related, by Tamerland: its palace and walls were all of brick, and have served the city of Astrachan with materials, these many years, for building their walls, churches, and monasteries.[86]

(Bruce, June 1722)

The site of Old Saray

North from Astrakhan, about a distance of seven miles, the Russians dig up a kind of earth, in a place on the west bank of the Volga, called sal litri, a corruption of sal nitri ... and make as good salt petre as can be made anywhere. They say, that this has been an antient city. I doubt not the truth of this, because brick has been found frequently under ground, and money also, some of which both silver and gold, I have seen, and am in possession of some at present, though the characters are not, I believe legible. The men frequently find precious stones in digging this earth. Whether they have been lost accidentally in former ages, or are natural minerals, I shall not dispute; but I am certain, that some of them are quite rough, and of little value till they are polished.[87]

...

At the distance of about twenty versts from it [Astrakhan], our horses being much fatigued, we were obliged to halt ... The Colonel told me, that, since my departure from Astrachan, a few merchants travelling this way halted for refreshments at that place, and, when they were taking their dinner, part of the cliff fell down, and with it, an earthen jar full of old Tartar coin, some of which he had seen, both gold and silver.[88]

(Cook, 1740s)

Ivan IV takes Astrakhan

This place was taken from the TARTARS, in the year 1554, by the warlike Czar Ivan Vasiliovitz; whereby all his conquests on the Volga were secured, and the way prepared for farther extending the RUSSIAN dominion, to the south and east; which hath been successfully attempted since his time.[89]

(Bell, 1716)

The Russians fortify Astrakhan

Czar Iwan Basilowitz, having conquered the kingdom of Casan, in the year 1552, turned his arms against the Nagayan Tartars, and took Astrachan, their capital, by assault, in the year 1554; and to secure his conquest he surrounded the city with a strong wall. Czar Michael Fedrowitz, besides strengthening the city with some new fortifications, built that part of it called Strelitza-Gorod, or the city of soldiers, as the military had their quarters assigned them there ...

Astrachan, their principal city, they relate to have been built by a Tartar king, whose name being Astra, gave his city that of Astra-chan, or kin.[90]

(Bruce, July 1722)

ENDNOTES

1 Bell, p.166; Cook, vol.2, p.469; Hanway, vol.1, pp.117–19. Cook also knew indirectly the famous physician and collector Dr Mead (Cook, vol.1, p.9).

2 E.g. Bell p.167; Tooke 1799, p.48.

3 See for example MacGregor 1994, 2007; Teissier 2004.

4 That is, descended from Jochi (Chinzghiz Khan's eldest son).

5 Allsen, p.42; for trade see Fedorov-Davidov 2001, pp.200, 213ff.

6 Allsen, p.42.

7 Ibid. For mosques at the Voyanskoye and Zaporozhye sites, see Fedorov-Davidov 2001, pp.57–58.

8 Fedorov-Davidov 2001, pp.19–22 and *passim*.

9 Ibid., p.21.

10 Pallas 1788–93, vol. 5, p.157.

11 Ibid., pp.157–60.

12 Ibid., pp.159–60.

13 Fedorov-Davidov 2001, pp.22–25; Olearius 1967, p.318, mentions the site.

14 Georgi 1780–83, vol.4, pp.294–95. Georgi probably refers here to one of the later Ahmads (Ahmad, son of Timur, *c.*1465, or his sons of the White Horde); see Bosworth, p. 253.

15 I thank Leonard Nedashkovsky for this clarification.

16 Pallas 1788–93, vol.5, pp.330–31. The city is in fact better preserved in plan than Old Saray; Fedorov-Davidov 2001, pp.23–24.

17 Georgi 1780–83, vol.4, p.295; Allsen, p.43.

18 Fedorov-Davidov 2001, pp.25–27.

19 Gibbon, vol.3, ch.64, pp.802–4. Gibbon's notes give the best range of available sources in the west during the eighteenth century.

20 E.g. Ebulgazi Bahadur Khan.

21 E.g. Hakluyt, vol.1 (used by Gibbon); Harris, vol.1, bk 4 (Rubruck, Jenkinson etc); *A New General Collection* ... (London 1745–47), vol.4, bk 3 (Carpini, Rubruck, Marco Polo etc.).

22 Gibbon, vol.3, ch.64, p.804 (Serai); Ebulgazi Bahadur Khan, p.786 (Sharisaraizik).

23 For Rubruck, see Jackson and Morgan, pp.255, 257, 259; Marco Polo, see Latham,

p.34; Mandeville, see Moseley, p.161. Carpini does not name Sarai but met Batu and mentioned his 'going along the Volga'; Dawson, p.56.

24 Allsen, p.43.

25 Chaucer, trans. Wright 1985, pp.344ff, 426 (notes). It is thought that the source of the tale was Sir John Mandeville.

26 Olearius 1967, p.318.

27 E.g. Gibbon 1995, vol.1, pp.1031–35; Petis, p.4.

28 I thank Leonard Nedashkovsky for this information. See also, for example, *Tesori della Steppa di Astrakhan* 2005; Christian, *passim*.

29 E.g. Jean du Bec, *The Historie of the Great Emperor Tamerlan* ... (1597, 1750); Samuel Clarke, *The Life of Tamerlane the Great* ... (1664); Niccolao Manucci, *The General History of the Mogol Empire from Its Foundation by Tamerlane* (from F.F. Catrou, 1709). In the late eighteenth century the spurious *Institutes, Political and Military* ... *by the Great Timour* ... (see White) were a politically motivated promotion driven by British India (see Teissier 2009). For Gibbon, Timur was 'rather the scourge than the benefactor of mankind' (Gibbon 1995, vol.3, p.852); for White, Timur was illustrious, perhaps over-ambitious, but he had acted according to the times and governed with wisdom, justice and benevolence (White, pp.iii–v), thereby sanctioning the British in India. Timur was also prominent in the British theatrical canon, for example Christopher Marlowe's *Tamburlaine the Great* (1590), Christopher Saunders's *Tamerlane the Great* (1681) and plays by Nicholas Rowe (1720) and John Dryden (1767), and in *Bell's British Theatre* (1797). For Alexander on the Volga–Ural Muslims, see Frank 2000.

30 I thank Alexander Morrison for the latter reflection. See also Frank 2000.

31 Olearius 1967, pp.307–8, 311.

32 I am grateful to Leonard Nedashkovsky for this information.

33 Khodarkovsky 2002, p.132; Pallas 1788–93, vol.1, pp.125ff.

34 Olearius's Mamaon (see Olearius 1967, p.311).

35 For the battle see, e.g., Ostrovski, pp.155–56; Martin, pp.214–15. There is still a 'Mamaev' kurgan in Volgograd, commemorating the Battle of Stalingrad.

36 Olearius, ed. Baron 1967, pp. 307, 316; Frank 1998, pp.50ff, 85ff.

37 Hrbek, pp.1304–8; Christian, *passim*.

38 Others, for example, were Bilyar, Suvar, Nikolsko-Baranskoye. Bilyar eventually superseded Bulgar. Many sites of this period remain to be identified and excavated.

39 The Khazars were a nomadic people of mixed Turkic, Finnic and other descent, who inhabited the south Russian steppes. They unified in the sixth century and came to dominate the western Eurasian steppes from the seventh century to the tenth. They became an international power but were tempered by the rise of Islam. In the eighth or ninth century Khazar kings and some of the elites converted to Judaism. The 'empire' collapsed in the mid-tenth century, chiefly due to the rise of Muscovy and Bulgaria (Christian, pp. 282–98; Barthold and Golden, pp.1172–81).

40 Hrbek, p.1306; Christian, p.296.

41 Frye; Canard (for Ibn Fadlan's account); Rorlich 1986.

42 Hrbek, p.1308; Rorlich; *Ocherki Istorii SSSR*, pp.424–25.

43 Khlebnikova, p.33.

44 Black, Buse and Moessner, p.68 (doc.4 from 'Istoriia Akademi Nauk G.-F. Millera 1725–1743', St Petersburg 1890), pp.252–54.

45 Ibneeva, pp.123–24.

46 Lepekhin, vol.1, pp.167ff (Russian edn. 1795, pp.266ff).

47   Pallas 1788–93, vol.1, pp.188–95; vol.6, pls 8, 9.
48   Georgi 1780–83, vol.2, pp.12–13 (he also mentions Bilyar).
49   Fechner, p.25; Smirnov, pp.12, 17 (fig.6), 18 (fig.7); Ibneva, p.124.
50   I thank Leonard Nedashkovsky for this information.
51   Frank 1998, pp.47ff; see also Frank 2001.
52   Frank 1998, pp.50ff, 67ff, 72–76, 82ff, 85ff; Frank 2001, pp.151ff.
53   Frank 1998, pp.34–39; 80, 85; Crews, *passim*.
54   For a brief introduction and bibliography of this subject, see Rorlich, pp.6–9.
55   Georgi 1780–83, vol.2, p.16.
56   Schamiloglu; for Tatar verse, see also Matthews and Bukhavaen.
57   Parkinson did not get round to editing or publishing his diary; had he done so, he
      might have included more historical detail.
58   Georgi 1780–83, vol.2, p.13. The date of these remains cannot now be established.
59   Pallas 1788–93, vol.1, pp.39–44; see also Tooke 1799, vol.2, p.48.
60   My thanks to Leonard Nedashkovsky for this information; see also *Istoriia Kazani*,
      1988, vol.1, pp.1–20; Rorlich, pp.22ff.
61   My thanks to Leonard Nedashkovsky for this information.
62   Rorlich, p.19; Bosworth, p.259.
63   *Istoriia Kazani* 1988, pp.21–25; Khudiakov, pp.17-49.
64   See Khodarkovsky 2002, map 3; Khudiakov, p.4 (map).
65   Bosworth, p.259; *Istoriia Kazani* 1988, vol.1, pp.22–44.
66   Bennigsen 1978, pp.723–24.
67   *Istoriia Kazani* 1988, pp.51–76; Martin, pp.325–26; Khodarkovsky 2002, pp.106–
      7; Stevens, pp.106–7.
68   Khodarkovsky 2004, pp.99, 109.
69   For the early Christianisation of Kazan, see Zahidullin, pp.39–57. For the early mixed
      Tatar and Chuvash military servitors (*pomeshchiki*) in the area, see Romaniello, pp.61–77.
70   Barthold and Bennigsen, p.849; Rorlich, pp.37–41; Kappeler 2001, p.29.
71   Kappeler 2001, p.29.
72   Spuler 1960, pp.721–22; Martin, pp.203, 313 (with bibliography).
73   Bosworth, p.258; Spuler 1960, pp.721–22; *Ocherki Istorii SSSR*, pp.440–42.
74   See Khodarkovsky 2002, map 3; Khudiakov, p.4 (map).
75   Martin, pp.354–55.
76   Spuler 1960, p.722; Bosworth, p.258; Khodarkovsky 2002, pp.110ff.
77   Spuler 1960, p.722; my thanks to Leonard Nedashkovsky for confirming this.
78   Olearius, ed. Baron 1967, p.325; Georgi 1780–83, vol.4, p.343.
79   Bell, pp.15–16.
80   Ibid., p.20.
81   Bruce, pp.233–34.
82   Bell, p.27.
83   Bruce, pp.234–35.
84   Parkinson, p.111.
85   Perry 1716, p.92.
86   Bruce, p.243.
87   Cook, vol.1, pp.280–81.
88   Cook, vol.2, p.45.
89   Bell, p.35.
90   Bruce, pp.246–47.

PART II: THE CASPIAN

6 SCIENCE, TRADE AND NAVIGATION

Introduction

Some scientific questions posed by the Caspian Sea and its extreme environmental conditions have already been touched on in travellers' accounts of Astrakhan and the Volga. Bell and Hanway[1] continued existing traditions of commenting on the Caspian, as they had done with the Volga.[2] Recurring themes were the variation in the Caspian's water levels, its salinity, evaporation, size and depth, and its fish and other wildlife. Bell continued Perry's focus on evaporation and the link with the Royal Society through Halley's paper on the evaporation of the Mediterranean in the *Philosophical Transactions* of 1687.[3]

Mapping, for practical rather than political reasons, was another aspect of the study of the Caspian. Hanway published a map of soundings of the Caspian coast by Captain Woodroofe in the 1740s (finished 1745), both for the benefit of British merchants and as a result of Nader Shah's demands (see p.245). This was a significant achievement, given the poor quality of previous maps. Hanway also published a coasting pilot of the sea, extracted from Woodroofe's journal,[4] and referred to a map by the Dutch Captain Carl Van Verden, made at the time of Peter the Great's interest in the Caspian, which coincided with his invasion of Daghestan and northern Persia, in which Bruce was involved as engineer and mapmaker (see pp.181, 183, 222). Most travellers were amazed by the variety of wildlife on the Caspian's islands and shores near Astrakhan. Bruce's comments comparison of flocks of flamingos to a marching regiment is particularly apt for a military man.[5]

The Caspian fisheries, extending from the south and east of Astrakhan to the River Yaik (Ural), became a vast resource for the Russian crown and were almost more renowned than the Volga ones. The fisheries were hugely profitable, despite being taxed; Pallas estimated that 1,760,390 roubles were brought in annually by large sturgeon fishing alone.[6] They were criticised by Western observers, however, as they were seen to benefit the merchants, nobles and the crown, who owned and ran them, at the expense of those working on them, who were considered to be in a state of vassalage.[7] Parkinson mentioned a fishery owned by a merchant company, which charged 2000 roubles for membership. Pallas described fifty-six merchant ships owned by Astrakhan merchants during the 1790s.[8] The fisheries also had their own legends, such as that of the poor, illiterate Tikon Demidoff, who became rich by establishing fisheries around Astrakhan with Peter the Great's support. By the time Cook was in Astrakhan, one of the Demi-doffs had ships of 200 tonnes trading to Persia (he does not specify in what) and 'was esteemed one of the richest merchants in Astrachan'.[9] Fishing was relentless in spring, autumn and winter; the different kinds of fish traps (*utschiugii*)[10] impressed all observers. 'Scarcely anywhere in the world is there such a variety of contrivances and machines, some of them truly sensible and ingenious, for the capture of fish … particularly in the confines of Astrakhan,' remarked Tooke.[11] The fisheries were operated from stations (*vatagii*) owned by contractors and run by up to 120 men, with their own vessels, accommodation and facilities for salting, storing and pickling fish. Smaller fishing huts also operated along the Caspian.[12]

Bell conveyed the otherworldly, unknown feel of the lower Volga basin and of the Caspian beyond; he and his party anchored at a fishery on his way to Persia in 1716. Parkinson, on the other hand, was unaffected by such Gothic atmosphere on his visit to an *utschuig*. Apart from a few factual details, he concentrated on the pleasures of the trip, from which he was briefly but unpleasantly distracted by the smell of a fish cave. He commented on the place's flatness and reedbeds, which reminded him, perhaps disappointingly for potential readers, of Holland. He also referred to a convert Tatar wedding (he does not say which group) performed by the governor of Astrakhan on the return trip.

In terms of navigation and trade, travellers' accounts address three main subjects: Caspian trade (with particular reference to Astrakhan), Russian and other merchant shipping on the Caspian, and the frustration of British merchants in their efforts to trade with Persia. The entries mostly date from the late 1730s to the early 1740s, although they refer to earlier shipping and trade on the Caspian. In 1716 Bell noted, 'The navigation of the Caspian belongs solely to the Russians; the PERSIANS and other borderers having nothing but fishing boats.'[13]

The 'considerable' Astrakhan fleet in Peter the Great's reign, mentioned by Woodroofe, was not itemised but presumably included both merchant vessels and warships. The Caspian fleet, even in its heyday under Peter, probably never achieved the cachet of those of Azov or of the Baltic.[14] After his death, supporting the fleets was no longer considered viable, and the admiralties went into decline.[15] By Elton and Cook's time the emphasis of the 'fleet' was already on merchant and transport ships. By the end of the eighteenth century Pallas's figures show that the admiralty had only two frigates and two caloupes, and that most vessels were trading or fishing ones.[16] In 1793 Parkinson was informed 'that the Russians had three frigates and four other small armed Vessels in the Caspian'.[17]

As the academicians, Tooke and others observed, the Caspian's international commerce and its links westwards to the Black Sea were 'of a very ancient date'.[18] Accounts of this trade can be traced back through European medieval and Classical, as well as Muslim, sources. For the Russians, after the conquest of Kazan and Astrakhan, the Caspian became an extension of the Volga trading route. It opened the southern route to Persia and India and subsequently became part of the northern transit route to the west. Silk from Iran was always the main commodity for the west; with English trade, this was essentially in exchange for woollen cloth. The Armenian diaspora had long been involved in the Levant trade with Iran.[19] In the seventeenth century, after bilateral trade between Russia and Iran developed from the late sixteenth century onwards, the Armenians of New Julfa (the Armenian quarter of Isfahan), who benefited from political neutrality and contacts with the Christian world, effectively gained control of the transit trade through Russia to Iran.[20]

Although Russia and Persia were the dominant powers to the north and south of the Caspian respectively, with occasional occupation by the Ottomans in the south and west, they did not have an untroubled monopoly of the Caspian's main ports in the eighteenth century, as will be seen. A brief overview of these ports from contemporary sources[21] is given here to provide a background to the Caspian trade and some of the travellers' experiences. The major Russian ports on the Caspian (except for the brief Russian possession of Darband and Baku in the 1720s) were guriev on the River Yaik (Ural) and Kizliar on the north-west coast. The latter was especially important, not only as an intermediary between Astrakhan and Persia, but for the Terek and Caucasus markets. The Persian ports on the west coast (from north to south) were Darband, which, despite its shallow harbour, was used by Russians for trade with Daghestani Tatars; the small port of Niazabad, which was a centre for distributing European goods to Shamakhie (the capital of Shirvan) and Shirvan; and Baku, which was the region's principal port. Baku was pivotal to the silk trade with Shamakhie as well as trading in naphtha (crude oil), saffron, cotton and rock salt. Shirvan had thrived because of the silk industry in the early eighteenth century, but it became progressively impoverished because of conflict and tariffs imposed by local khans, such as Fath Ali Khan in the 1760s and 1770s.[22] Russian consuls were traditionally based in Baku[23] and it had had thriving communities of foreign (Russian, Greek, Armenian and Indian) merchants. By the end of the century only Armenians and Indians were left. This was partly due to the diminishing quality of silk from Shirvan.

Another major centre, particularly favoured by the Persians, was Enzeli, north of the great mart of Resht, the capital of Gilan. Enzeli was another example of the complexity of the Caspian ports. In the later eighteenth century it had a shared jurisdiction: Old Enzeli was controlled by Persia, and had Persian and Persian-Armenian merchants, whereas New Enzeli had a Russian garrison and a consul, with Russian and Russian-Armenian merchants. Resht was another pivotal centre, with Russian, Armenian, Crimean and Turkish merchants all involved in the trade in raw silk, fabrics, 'apothecaries' and European goods. By the 1780s Resht was considered one of the 'first commercial' towns of Asia, with silk prices rising considerably because of high demand. On the southern coast of the Caspian, in Mazanderan province, were the ports of Farabat and Medshetisar, frequented by Russians and Armenians and involved in the local silk trade (inferior to that of Gilan) as well as trading in rice and cotton via the capital, Balfrush. Again, by the later eighteenth century these ports were being impoverished by the demands of the local khans. The last major port on the south coast was Astarabad, which traded in produce similar to that of Mazanderan, but whose primary market was Kandahar. The main ports on the east coast were the Bay of Balkhan and Mangyshlak. The Bay of Balkhan was in the hands of Turkmens, who traded in rice, cotton and naphtha. Mangyshlak was the principal port of trade between Russians, Turkmen, Central Asians (Khivans, Bukharans, Kirghiz) and India (see Map 4).[24]

The extent and volume of international trade and the success of ports were very variable in this turbulent region. War and political unrest, such as during the Afghan and Russian invasions of the 1720s or of Nader Shah's campaigns of the 1730s–1740s clearly disrupted official trade with and within Persia. Trade which was not contraband was also subject to royal monopolies, such as caviar or rhubarb in Russia,[25] and silk under Nader Shah. It was vulnerable to the demands of local khans and, occasionally, sabotage between merchant groups. Piracy and robbery were perennial problems. In Gilan and Shirvan silk-worm disease was also a factor. Tooke and Coxe were realistic about the Caspian trade in general; it was less considerable than it was made out to be, but it had grown steadily from around 400,000 roubles in the 1760s to over 1 million in 1775 and later, under the comparative peace of the Zand dynasty (1750–94).[26] Coxe was optimistic about Russian–Iranian trade relations during the 1780s because of a proposed treaty with Ali Murad Khan Zand (whose reign, however, was short-lived, 1781–85) and the partial lifting of restrictions on Russian merchants.[27] Catherine's reign had an impressive foreign trade record, notably after the annexation of Crimea.[28] Pallas, however, writing on the Caspian trade, stated that the price of Russian imports from Persia (notably silk and madder) and even 'Bucharia' (cottons) was ruinous and far outweighed Russian exports. He urged the local development of silk and other manufactures.[29]

The entries by Woodroofe, Hanway and Cook focus on the Russo-British trade debacle over Persia, and of the effect of Nader Shah's advances in Daghestan and Central Asia (see pp.203–04 and 234–35) in the 1740s. The story of the hopes of direct British trade with Persia via Russia and the Caspian, which had started with the English Russia (or Muscovy) Company in 1555, the impetus it received through Captain John Elton's efforts from 1738 onwards, and its subsequent suspension by Empress Elizabeth because of Elton's collusion with Nader Shah are extensively described by Hanway[30] (see also pp.19 and 40). Hanway set out to trade woollen goods worth £5000 in Persia at the very time Elton and, by default, Woodroofe were fraternising with Nader Shah and the Russians were beginning to show their displeasure at this association (see p.40).[31] Finding no market for these goods in Ghilan, Hanway set out from Astarabad to Mashad, hoping to follow Elton's idea of establishing a new branch of trade there and onwards to India. In 1744 there was a rebellion in Astarabad, and Hanway was robbed of his goods. He was eventually partly compensated by Nader Shah and returned to Astrakhan in autumn 1744 with a cargo of raw silk.[32] Having experienced the disfavour of the Russians, he returned to St Petersburg via Moscow in early 1745.[33] He eventually realised, as had more experienced merchants before him, that, even without the Elton affair, such a direct trade route was too perilous. A limited silk trade to England resumed via St. Petersburg in 1749.[34]

Hanway's summary of the profits of the British Caspian export trade in woollen cloth and other European goods from 1742 to 1746 show the fluctuations in trade at this period: 170,000 crowns in 1742; 252,000 crowns in 1745; and 20,000 crowns in 1746 (the year Elizabeth suspended the British Caspian trade). The total amounted to £174,398. Imports of raw silk (which amounted to £93,375) also show fluctuations. Hanway was aware that these trade figures, which he concludes to have been profitable, despite plunder, might have been better, given the personnel and effort involved.[35] Almost a third of the merchants engaged in this trade had died by the 1740s.[36] In 1766 the commercial treaty with Britain was renewed, but protectionism was increased.[37] Later in the century British trade remained in abeyance on the Caspian but was very active in Crondstat and St Petersburg until the beginning of the Napoleonic wars.[38] Cook and Hanway itemised the commodities traded via Astrakhan. Hanway was more precise than Cook about the diminished trade with the Caspian and Central Asia because of the troubles in northern Persia in the 1740s.[39] Both mentioned the restrictions placed on Russian merchant vessels in times of war, the manner in which the government 'engrossed' or commandeered the trade in certain articles, such as rhubarb, and the jealousy of Russian merchants.

All the British merchants were disparaging about the quality of Russian merchant vessels and Russian sailors' poor navigational skills, the inconvenience of the position of Astrakhan and its shipyard, and Russian merchants' lack of interest in international trade. Moreover, Russian merchants had many state and bureaucratic restrictions to contend with,[40] which compounded their disadvantage vis à vis foreign merchants, notably the Armenians. Gmelin attributed the diminution of the Russian Caspian trade in the 1740s primarily to the Armenians. He blamed them for over-supplying the market, not honouring contracts and defrauding 'clumsy' Russian merchants. He also blamed both the British, for their 'designs' on Persian trade, and Nader Shah.[41] Although Gmelin's (and many academician's) feelings towards the Armenians were either ambivalent or hostile, both Woodroofe and Hanway detected what now seems predictable Armenian displeasure at British initiatives.[42]

'The water is excessively salt'

The CASPIAN sea is of an oblong irregular figure, about one hundred and fifty leagues in length, from north to south, and forty or fifty leagues broad. The water is excessively salt, except where it is sweetened by the VOLGA, which is at least to the distance of ten leagues from the influx of that river ... It contains an abundance of fish; but no shell-fish, except a kind of cockle, the shells of which are very pretty. In some places there is a great depth of water. The PERSIANS observe that of late the sea has retired considerably from the shore; which they reckon ominous, presaging some calamity to the kingdom. It has no tides but such as are caused by the wind; and, notwithstanding the great quantities of water daily received, it continues nearly about the same height. Dr HALLEY has demonstrated, that, exhalation in so hot a climate, is sufficient to account for this phenomenon, without having recourse to subterraneous passages.[43]

(Bell, 1716)

Birds of the Caspian

[Islands of the Caspian] feed a vast number of cattle in the summer; and as they are all surrounded by vast quantities of thick tall reeds, the great number of wild fowl, especially sea-fowl, is past description; upon firing of a gun, they rise in the air like a cloud, when numbers of them may be killed with great ease; a greater variety is not to be seen any where in the known world. Besides swans and common wild geese, there is large kind called by the Russians *baba*, or crop-geese, and by other pelicans; their bills being a foot and a half long, and two inches broad, are forked at the ends; some of these fowls, from the head to the feet, are above seven feet in length; under their bills they have a shrivelled skin hanging, resembling a bag ... this bag they make use of to hold the fish that they catch ... There is another kind called spoon-geese; their beaks are long and round ... this fowl, when it puts its beak in the water, makes a most hideous noise ... by some called red geese, by others flamingos, are in great flocks on the

Caspian shores; they walk after their leader in a very regular order, and at a distance appear not unlike a regiment of soldiers following their commander; their legs are very long, of a scarlet red, and they have very long necks, the plumage of various colours, but their heads are like scarlet; it is in every respect a most beautiful bird ... As for wild ducks, their variety is incredible, and to describe their different kinds almost impossible. I cannot, however, pass over two of the without notice ... the one is called the scarlet duck ... it is very large, and delicious eating, the other is the yellow-duck, whose feathers are entirely of that colour; these are also very large and fat and most excellent eating ...[45]

(Bruce, 1722)

'This place had an aspect of horror'

On the 5th of August [1716] we quitted ASTRACHAN in five vessels, three of them flat-bottomed, and of about an hundred and fifty tuns burden, with three masts and ten guns each; the other·two common barques. We sailed from Astrachan about noon; and at night came to an anchor at a fishery, called UTTZUGG. Both the banks are now flat; to the westward barren sands, and to the east marshy tall reeds abounding with vermine; so that we neither eat nor slept in quiet, notwithstanding all the precautions we could use. I must confess this place had an aspect of horror, especially when it is considered, that, besides the wild and dismal appearance of the banks, we were carried down a mighty river into a great gulf, in many places of dangerous navigation, and whose shores are inhabited by inhospitable and barbarous nations; for such I reckon all of them except the RUSSIANS and PERSIANS.

Next morning, at break of day, we got under sail, and about ten entered the CASPIAN sea; into which the river discharges itself by seven or eight large channels, and many lesser ones; two only of these channels are navigable by ships of any burden. At night we cast anchor near four hillocks of dry sand, cast up by the sea, called TZETEREY BUGORY ... all which distance we had not above six or seven feet water ... so that the passage is extremely dangerous in hard gales of wind.

The 7th early, we again set sail with a gentle breeze ... which soon drove us out of sight of land ... About noon the wind shifted to the south, which obliged us to come to an anchor, where we lay for near three weeks in calms and contrary winds.

All this time we did not see a single ship, besides our own, except one Russ vessel that came from GUILAN in PERSIA, with some ARMENIAN merchants ...[46]

(Bell, 1716)

Fortunes built on fisheries

In this place [Bosmakov] also are large fisheries, to which the neighbourhood of the saltworks is of great advantage. These extend even to the sea, reaching south eastward as far as YAEIK, and also 100 miles above ZARITZEN. From these fisheries all the country is supplied as far as St PETERSBURG: the vessels are loaded with salt fish, and sent away in the spring; but as fresh fish keeps good as long as it is frozen, the winter is no sooner set in, than it is transported by land as far as MOSCO and St PETERSBURG.[47]

The first establisher of these fisheries was TIKON DEMEDOFF a carrier, who settled there about 50 years ago; his whole fortune then consisted in two horses, but through his industry and abilities he became the greatest merchant in that country. The crown, which before his time was a stranger to those advantages, has of late years, besides the salt, engrossed some of the fisheries also.[48]

(Hanway, 1743)

Parkinson tours the Astrakhan fisheries

Before dinner we called on Sovolofski and De Ligne, two officers of the Guards, at the house of the former who is married to a daughter of General Beketof and received an income of 50 or 60,000 roubles from his Fishery. He told me that he possessed 200 Versts of coast on the Caspian Sea near Kislar to which he had transported about 200 Peasants who however did not enjoy their health, being very subject to the Scurvy and to inflammatory as well as intermittent fevers.[49]

The whole number of fishing and transport Vessels belonging to this place were he said 200. He had five of his own.[50]

The O[ver] Commandant assured us that grants of Fisheries had been made to several Russian Nobles on condition that they people the Country adjoining. He mentioned particularly the Names of Satlikoff and Besborodko. Saltikoff's estate lies in an Island in the Caspian Sea which belongs properly to Persia. He derives a revenue of 1,500 roubles a year from it. Others enjoy a much greater revenue. Yet not one single Peasant have they planted in these lands agreeably to the conditions of the Grant. The O[ver] Commandant has sent an account of all this. The Fisheries are carried on by People sent from Astracan who are able if industrious to earn a great deal of money. I imagine that it does not answer to plant Colonies in these parts. Sovolofski had settled two hundred Peasants on his estate; but they had been a great many of them carried off. The 20,000 colonists settled on the line, the Vice-Governor told me, had been reduced to 10 [10,000?].[51]

The Governor's carriage was ready for us this morning [5 July] at half past three in order to go in a party down the river to an Utschug thirty versts off and see the Astracan Fishery. This Utschug belongs to a company consisting of all the Merchants in Astracan, i.e. of all those who register themselves as such to the amount of 2,000. Their right of fishing extended formerly over all the several [branches] of the river between the capital Town and the Sea; but the town has curtailed them from time to time by grants to private Persons ... Yet notwithstanding these retrenchments, the fishery in question is capable (as Nikita K. told me) of producing a profit of 100,000 roubles.

Our party was the Dr., M. Agathi, an Italian Architect ... the Governor, ourselves, two or three Russian Officers and two or three Persons belonging to the Governor. The flotilla consisted of three boats, all rowed by Tartars, some converted and others not. Our navigation was for some time down the Wolga in all breadth and Majesty, but afterwards, for the greatest part of the way, down one of the numerous Arms into which it divides itself ... The flatness of the country and the border of reeds which we had on each hand after we quitted the Wolga reminded me exceedingly of Holland. As the wind was favourable we were generally able to use sails and arrived in Utschug in good time.

Having regaled ourselves with a glass of brandy and some excellent fresh Caviare, we walked out to see the houses in which they deposit their barrels of Caviare, and the Cave in which they lay up their fish. The cold was so great and the Stink so horrible that I could not bear to stay long. It is encompassed as the Cave we saw before with Ice, and filled with Piles of salted fish.

On our return dinner was ready and having all of us taken a nap after it, which our jollity rendered very necessary, we reimbarked in order to go back; hoping to see some of the fish taken in the way, in which owing to the stormy weather we were disappointed ... At setting out the wind was against us, presently after which there fell a dead calm; a little before we reached however the end of our voyage a favourable breeze struck up and we were able to use sails, but with so light a Vessel, such unskilful sailors and so much canvas, not I believe without danger.

We landed at one spot and walked a considerable way till we came to a Tartar encampment where the Governor married a couple, where I ate some excellent Macaroni Soup and where they invited us to have some Koumis. The evening was uncommonly fine, the setting sun and the objects on the bank of the river were charmingly reflected by the water and our Tartars, especially as we passed by the Encampments in sight of the young Girls, sang merrily. We landed in the Tartar Suburb and were conveyed home from thence six in a carriage. I was glad to get home in any way, being excessively sleepy and tired.[52]

(Parkinson, July 1793)

Shipping at Astrakhan

[Astrakhan] stands 100 Versts ... from the Bar, at the principal Entrance of the Volga. This is very inconvenient, because those Ships or Vessels that are fit for the Caspian, are not adapted for mounting the stream of the Volga to Astracan, and which they are frequently longer about than in making their Voyage or Passage cross the Caspian, besides the Delays they are subject to, both in going and coming, from the Guard-Ship at the entrance of the Volga. Whereas had Astracan been actually a sea-port on the Caspian, all these and many more Inconveniences had been avoided. There does not appear to be above 20 or 25 Vessels which cross the Caspian, that belong to the Russ Merchants of Astracan; there are some of them a Sort of Fly-boats; the rest are Smacks or Hoys, the former about 250 Tons burthen, the latter 100 to 150 Tons. Whilst the Crown of Russia kept the province of Gilan in its possession, the Russians of Astracan employed their Vessels themselves, chiefly in carrying Provisions of all Kinds to supply the Russian Army; but now their Vessels are mostly freighted by the Armenians, for whom they carry Goods and Passengers to and from Astracan to Derbent, Backu and Resht; also in carrying Nephta* (*an oil used in Lamps etc which issues out of some mountains near Astracan and Backu) and Passengers from Backu to Reshd, for the Persians; likewise Provisions for the Russians Garrison, and others at Turky [Terki]. The Russ merchants at Astracan, of whom there are many very rich, don't concern themselves much with foreign Trade, which is in a manner wholly in the Hands of the Armenians and Indians, but confine themselves to the Fisheries on the Caspian and Volga, in which they find great profit ...

The Russian Fleet, which belongs to the Government, is chiefly laid up at Astracan, where there is an Admiralty ... But there is another Ship-Yard (just within the Bar, at the Entrance into the Volga out of the Caspian, 90 Versts below Astracan) it is named Jerkee [Yerkie]. Here are fitted out and laid up all the Vessels of the Crown that annually cross the Caspian, and it is a convenient Place to sit or careen at; the worst at his Place is, that when it blows hard at S.E. and E.S.E. the Island of Jerkee is liable to be laid wholly under Water, without the Bar. Thirty Versts below is a sandy Island, named Cheterybuger; on this Island lay the principal Guard-ship. This is a tolerable good Road ... Here it is that all Vessels coming from Gilan, Backu and Derbent, perform their Quarantine, but the Passengers commonly have Leave to perform theirs on the Shoar on the Island. Thus far the Command of the Astracan Admiralty seems to extend (though the Sovereignty of all the Caspian was claimed by Peter the Great, when he was at Astracan, on his Expedition to Persia).[53]

(Elton and Graeme, in Spilman, 1739–40)

'Heght boats'

The Astrachan merchants alone are allowed to have ships on the Caspian sea, and they generally have betwixt twenty and thirty for sea service, which they call heght boats. These vessels carry, one with another, one hundred tuns, but are built very flat like the Holland ships, and therefore are only fit for the coast: because they cannot sail, like the British, near the wind.[54]

(Cook, 1740s)

'A sea very little known'

PETER the GREAT had a considerable fleet of vessels on the CASPIAN, which are long since perished. The largest they had then, was of about 180 tuns, of a circular form, which when loaded, they were obliged to strap with hausers, to prevent her falling to pieces. This, with several others, was built in the admiralty yard at CASAN. The merchants now float down timber to ASTRACHAN, where for want of a proper yard and mechanics, they build in the old RUSSIAN form, long flat bottomed vessels with square sails, and the top sails to bawl down upon the deck: with such ships, by the help of good ground they navigate the CASPIAN. Their cordage is exceeding strong, as are likewise their anchors made in the antient form, notwithstanding they are very ill shaped. On the contrary, the modern ones made by the famous DEMEDOFFS in SIBERIA, the patentees of the iron works, tho' better proportioned are not so strong. Their canvas is chiefly made at YARISLAW and MOSCO, and is generally very good.

The RUSSIAN merchants and pilots were ready to give Mr ELTON the best information they could in regard to the navigation of the Caspian but as their skill extended little further than coasting, and a superficial knowledge of the soundings along shore, he could reap but little advantage from their experience. They rather discouraged us by their apprehensions of rocks and shoals, which they pretend are very thick in different parts of this sea, but chiefly between APSHERON and BALKHAN. It might indeed be said that we were venturing into a sea very little known, where commerce had never made any considerable progress; the natives of those inhospitable shores, except the RUSSIANS, having hardly employed their imperfect navigation to any other purpose than to surprize and plunder their unguarded neighbours.[55]

(Captain Woodroofe, in Hanway, 1742)

Hanway's map

I have introduced a chart of the Caspian sea, with which Captain WOODROOFE presented me on his return from thence. This chart I esteem very correct, and an improvement of that which Peter the Great ordered to be made by VANVORDEN, with regard to the soundings, and also the coast, as well as the eastern parts of the sea, where WOODROOFE was sent by the King of PERSIA to make the most minute observations ... If we should ever navigate the CASPIAN again, they may be serviceable to traders, or if they prove of any use to the RUSSIANS, I shall receive an additional pleasure.[44]

(Hanway, 1750s)

Export controls

I may certainly affirm that the produce of Persia, Armenia, Georgia, India, Buchar, and Chiva, are imported by the Caspian sea from all these countries, such as silks, satins, velvets, brocades, cotton cloaths of all denominations, jewels, some drugs, copper and many other things, together with Persian wines, and variety of fruits and sweet meats, confections, etc. From Russia they transport to Persia and other nations named above, but very few goods: because many articles of the produce of Russia are prohibited to be exported to these nations, though they are allowed to be exported to the different nations of Europe. Thus, iron, hemp, pitch, tar, gun-powder, salt-petre, sulphur, flint-stones and everything fit for ship-building and war, are reckoned contraband to be exported to any port in Persia. Meal only by the immediate permission of the Court, is exported: Cloaths of different sorts, woolen manufacturies, fish, salt and a few other things are also permitted to be exported; the Armenians are allowed indeed to transport European goods of all sorts, except warlike and naval stores, but they must sell none in Russia, and must buy them with the produce of raw silks of the Persian growth, or jewels.[56]

(Cook, 1740s)

Hanway observes trade on the Caspian

The commerce of ASTRACHAN is very considerable, though much diminished by the troubles in PERSIA, and the frequent revolts and insolent behaviour of the TARTARS. Not long ago they traded to KHIEVA and BOKHARA, but at present their commerce is confined to the EMPRESS'S dominions and PERSIA. The inhabitants had about 38 vessels, from 60 to 100 lasts (of two tuns ENGLISH) for the PERSIAN trade, of which some belong to the government and mount a few small pieces of cannon. They are commanded by a midshipman under a commodore who is generally only a lieutenant in rank, and these under the admiralty. This office is generally stocked with all naval stores, as well for the use of the vessels belonging to the EMPRESS, as to supply the merchants.

The trading ships carry provisions to the frontier towns of TERKIE and KISLAR, situated on the CASPIAN sea, and likewise merchandize to the several parts of PERSIA, at certain stated rates. They are also occasionally employed by the PERSIANS, to carry provisions from GHILAN to BAKU, DERBEND, and other places; but the RUSSIAN government observing that their merchant ships were employed in the transport of provisions towards their own frontier, for the use of the PERSIAN army, thought proper to take them into their service; and from that time they sent only a few vessels to PERSIA, under the authority of the imperial flag, that they might be priviledged from any arrests or exactions on the part of the PERSIANS. But since NADIR'S death, and the abandoning of the enterprize of building PERSIAN ships in the EUROPEAN manner, the RUSSIAN vessels have been again restored to the merchants.

Their foreign trade consists in red leather, linens, woollen cloths, and EUROPEAN manufactures, which they export to PERSIA, the greatest part for the account of the ARMENIANS; in return they import several manufactures of PERSIA, particularly those of CASHAN, as silk sashes intermixed with gold, for the consumption of the POLANDERS; wrought silks and fluffs mixed with cotton; rice, cotton, a small quantity of drugs, and especially raw silk. They also bring rhubarb, but as the government has engrossed this article, private persons are forbid to deal in it under penalty of death. From KHIEVA they formerly brought gold, lamb skins, cotton, and other commodities; but this trade is now discontinued as I have already observed.[57]

(Hanway, Astrakhan 1743)

Repercussions of the Elton Affair

The governor of Astrachan [V.N. Tatischev] being alarmed at ELTON'S proceedings, and finding that this new trade began to grow offensive to his court, thought proper to put captain WOODROOFE'S ship under the same restrictions as those of the RUSSIAN merchants. In order to prevent jealousy, and comply with the RUSSIAN regulations we had already given an account in ASTRACHAN of all the ship's stores ... but it was now demanded of me to give an account of those stores to the consul in GHILAN, and likewise a written obligation, that no BRITISH seamen should go into the SHAH'S service, or give any instructions to his subjects. By this means we should be liable to be arrested at the pleasure of a RUSSIAN consul, though out of the RUSSIAN dominions ... as things were thus circumstanced ... I resolved to sign it ...

I had no conception how we could carry on a trade under such conditions. It was indeed our duty as merchants, to support a good understanding with the RUSSIANS in PERSIA, as far as consistent with the freedom essential to the support of our own interest; but beyond this was in effect to give up our commerce. The RUSSIANS about ten years before had evacuated GHILAN, and as they were the only navigators of the CASPIAN, their merchants were jealous of our enjoying any privileges independent of the RUSSIAN jurisdiction: besides, they had acquired great influence in GHILAN during the confused state of affairs under NADIR'S usurpation; so that upon the whole it appeared very plain to me, that the BRITISH CASPIAN trade in general was against the inclinations of the RUSSIANS.[58]

(Hanway, Astrakhan 1743)

'Your trade cannot last long'

When I left England in 1743, I remember that Mr RICHARD LOCKWOOD, a TURKEY merchant, discoursed with me to this effect: 'Either you will teach the RUSSIANS how to trade, and then become an object of their jealousy, if you have success in this enterprise; or you will be plundered in Persia; and in either case your trade cannot last long.' Experience has taught us, that his observation was just, and in some measure prophetical.[59]

The Parliament, by an act of 1749, now permits us to import raw silk from St PETERSBURG for our woolen manufactures: and I hope some advantage will accrue from it to this nation. Some time must pass before affairs in PERSIA will be sufficiently restored to allow of any considerable export of raw silk from thence; however this is abundantly made up to us by the supplies we receive from other countries.[60]

(Hanway, 1750s)

ENDNOTES

1   Hanway, vol.1, pp.155–57.
2   E.g. Olearius 1669, pp.141–44; le Bruyn 1759, pp.197–98; Ebulgazi Bahadur Khan, vol.2, pp.748–53; Georgi 1780–83, vol.4, pp.319–29; Coxe 1787, pp.389–90; Tooke 1799, vol.1, pp.232–41.
3   Perry 1716, p.106 (reference to the *Philosophical Transactions* of 1687, nos 189, 212).
4   Hanway, vol.1, pp.392ff.
5   See also Cook, vol.1, pp.161ff, 267ff, 280ff, for his descriptions of the environs of Astrakhan.
6   Pallas 1812, vol.1, p.219. See p.215 for examples of ownership, from the archbishop to collectives, including merchants.
7   Tooke 1799, vol.3, p.157; Hanway, vol.1, p.103.
8   Pallas 1812, pp.232–33; see also Kahan, p.295.
9   Cook, vol.1, p.250.
10 The Tatar word for dam.

11 Tooke 1799, vol.3, p.153. For an illustration of these traps (*saboikii* and *pereboikii*), see Gmelin 1770–74, vol.2, tabs 35–38 (for simpler methods see tab.39, 40).

12 Tooke 1799, vol.3, pp.143–44; Gmelin 1770–74, vol.2, tabs 42, 46, for the distribution of *vatagii* around Astrakhan.

13 Bell, p.57.

14 Phillips, *passim*.

15 Hughes, pp.80–83.

16 Pallas 1812, vol.1, pp.232–33.

17 Parkinson, p.169.

18 Tooke 1799, p.572; see also Coxe 1787, pp.380–84.

19 Curtin, pp.183–86.

20 Curtin, pp.186–92; Ferrier, pp.459, 472–73; Herzig 1991, pp.120, 131–32, 141–44.

21 Gärber; Gmelin 2007, *passim*; Soimonov 1765, *passim* (paraphrased by Tooke 1799, vol.3, pp.584–87); Coxe 1987, pp.390–400; Tooke 1799, vol.3, pp.573–77.

22 Coxe 1787, pp.394–95; Gmelin 2007, pp.33–34.

23 Mamedova, *passim*.

24 Gmelin 2007, p.283.

25 Kahan, p.187ff.

26 Coxe 1787, pp.400–1; Tooke 1799, vol.3, p.572.

27 Coxe 1787, p.400n.; Kahan, pp.215–28; de Madariaga, pp.471–74; see Gmelin 2007, pp.322ff for his proposals for improving the Caspian trade.

28 Tooke 1799, vol.3, pp.582–84; de Madariaga, pp.474–75.

29 Pallas 1812, vol.1, pp.221–32.

30 Hanway, vol.1, pp.1–8, 13–82; vol.2, pp.70–99, 102–5.

31 Hanway, vol.1, pp.163–64.

32 Ibid., pp.165–72, 189–207.

33 Hanway, vol.2, pp.11–13.

34 Hanway, vol.1, pp.viii–x.

35 Hanway, vol.2, p.101.

36 Hanway, vol.1, p.220.

37 de Madariaga, pp.373–74. See Cross, pp.46–89 for the commercial treaties between Russia and Britain in the eighteenth century, and the principal figures and families of the Russian factory in St Petersburg.

38 Tooke 1799, vol.3, pp.618, 642–45.

39 See Hanway, vol.2, pp.23–32, for an account of Persian trade between 1743 and 1745.

40 Kahan, pp.295–98; de Madaraiga, p.473.

41 Gmelin 2007, pp.317–18.

42 Hanway, vol.1, pp.150, 212; vol.2, pp.83, 35.

43 Bell, pp.57–58.

44 Bruce, pp.258–60.

45 Bell, pp.47–49.

46 Hanway, vol.1, pp.124–25.

47 Ibid., p.125.

48 Parkinson, p.169.

49 Ibid.

50 Ibid., p.171.

51 Ibid., pp.175–77.

52 Spilman, pp.10–12.

53   Cook, vol.1, p.290.
54   Hanway, vol.1, pp.115–16.
55   Hanway, vol.1, p.x.
56   Cook, vol.1, pp.289–90.
57   Hanway, vol.1, pp.126–27.
58   Hanway, vol.1, pp.158–59.
59   Ibid., pp.viii–ix.
60   Ibid., p.x.

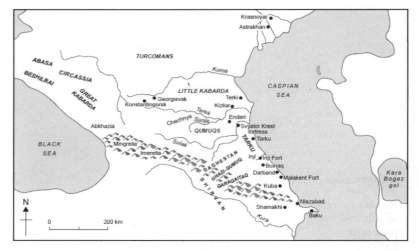

Map 3. The Caucacus

PART III: THE NORTH-EAST

CAUCASUS

7 EAST CIRCASSIA

Introduction

Russia's narrative of encroachment on the Caucasus was essentially one of solicited protectionism – of Christians, allies and trade routes. It was presented as a reclaiming of Christianity, and a response to Ottoman, Crimean and Persian hostility in the region. But it was also a story of aggression, coercion, displacement and colonisation, of bribery and reward for adopting Christianity. It was marked throughout by clashes of political aims and a mutual misunderstanding of social structures[1] and of the role of religion.

From the first diplomatic contacts between Muscovy and Lesser Kabarda (eastern Terek, between the Terek and Sunja rivers) after the taking of Astrakhan, Muscovy had promoted its own faction among the Kabardian princes. Ivan IV married a Circassian princess in 1561, and the Muscovite state assumed the role of patron. While some families converted to Christianity and became Russianised, most Circassian feudal princes, who were clan chiefs, considered themselves independent and entered into allegiances with the Crimea and the Ottomans when it suited them.[2] A fort built on the Terek at the influx of the River Sunja in 1567 to protect the interests of Ivan IV's father-in-law, Temriuk, became one of the earliest Russian military outposts in the region.[3] The settlement on the eastern Terek of mostly free Cossacks during the seventeenth century facilitated Muscovy's intrusion, as the settlers not only displaced local peoples and the *status quo* but were sometimes on the Russian payroll and used as guides or mercenaries.[4]

Bruce and Cook's entries cover Russian presence and expansion in the north-east Caucasus in the early and mid-eighteenth century, centered on Endirei and the fortress towns of Terki and Kizliar. Parkinson's entry focuses on the area around Georgievsk on the Mozdok line, in central north Caucasus between the rivers Terek and Kuma, in the late eighteenth century. Travellers referred to these areas as Circassia, an umbrella term used at the time to denote the tribes of west (Adyghe) and east (Kabardian) Circassia, which encompassed the southern bank of the River Kuban and Lesser and Greater Kabarda (western Terek, between the Mulka and Terek rivers). The Circassian tribes were considered by eighteenth-century observers to be the leading Caucasus tribes, having as their own subjects many smaller mountain tribes. In general descriptions they served as a blueprint for other mountain peoples of the Caucasus.[5]

Cook's eyewitness account is invaluable, as western sources for the Caucasus at this time are rare. Olearius and, to a lesser extent, Chardin[6] remained the key sources for western Europeans on parts of the Caucasus in the early eighteenth century. The notes on the populations, economy and religion of the Terek, Sulak and Aksai river regions (as well as Daghestan and Shirvan) made by Major (later Colonel) Johann Gustav Gärber, who took part in the 1723 campaign in Daghestan and north Persia, remain a valuable Russian source for the early eighteenth century.[7] Later in the century the academicians Güldenstadt (travelled 1771–72) and Pallas (travelled 1793–94), who were sent on missions and helped to investigate the north Caucasus further, provided important accounts.[8] Other travellers, such as Jacob Reineggs (travelled 1780s), Marschall Bieberstein (in the region c. 1796), Jean Potocki (travelled 1797–98) and Julius Klaproth (travelled 1807–8), also described these areas, while George Ellis, Georgi and Tooke gave general overviews of the 'Caucasian' peoples. Published official Russian records are referred to in the notes.

Villages, towns and forts

Endirei

Bruce, who took part in Peter the Great's Persian campaign of 1722, gave an account, before the main march south, of the 'destruction' of the Turkic Kumyk village and 'district' of Endirei (Russian Andreeva) between the rivers Aksai and Sulak, in present day Chechnya. Gärber described a large, inaccessible village between mountains and thick forests, which at the time of the Russian attack was independent, ruled by one Ay-Demir and nominally Sunni. Gärber attributed the village's origin to fugitive Russians and Cossacks who mingled with the local population.[9] This was possibly apocryphal, although the mingling of peoples in this area was a feature of early settlement here.[10] What is telling about Bruce's account are the numbers of troops sent in (possibly exaggerated) and the triumphalism with which he recounted the 'laying waste' of the province and the deportation of local people to Astrakhan. The total destruction of Endirei is confirmed in contemporary sources. Gärber also stated that the village was rebuilt after Ay-Demir swore allegiance to Russia.[11] This area had traditionally belonged to the shamkalate of Tarku. In the 1770s Endirei was under Kumyk princes (Temir and Jachsai Elda) from the family of the *shamkhal* (title of hereditary ruler) of Tarku, then supposedly under Russian 'protection'.[12] Although 'Mahomedan', it also had a mixed Georgian and Armenian population and was known as a centre for fugitives [13] and for 'Muslim learning'.[14]

Terki

Terki or Terskii Gorod had been founded in 1588,[15] as a fort at the mouth of the Terek. It was originally peopled by troops from Astrakhan, serving Cossacks, newly baptised Circassians, 'mountaineers' and fugitives, and became a focus for defence. Bruce's entry is almost entirely compiled from Olearius, who visited in 1638,[16] and is thus out of date. Olearius's account is significant for its discussion of the religious and governing policies of the Russians at the time. As with Kazan, non-Christians were at first not allowed within the citadel area. The naval officer and cartographer F.I. Soimonov, who was in the region at the same time as Bruce, confirmed that Terek Circassians and Cossacks lived on the perimeter of the fort.[17] By the early eighteenth century Terki was Russia's most southerly fort in the area and the key to its entry into the Caucasus. Since it was insalubrious and under threat, however, its population was moved to the fortress of Svyatoi Krest, built in 1722–23. Gärber referred only to (Terek) Cossacks as living in one of Terki's districts.[18] This period coincided with the reduction of Cossack freedoms (see below). [19]

A feature of this earlier period of Russian settlement, from the late sixteenth century to the more formal settlement programme of the late 1760s onwards, was the abandonment and relocation of forts due to unhealthy conditions, local uprisings and raids.[20] These opportunistically and sporadically built forts impacted greatly on local politics and economies. Not only did they take land and resources, to the extent that rivers were diverted and dammed,[21] but they became trading as well as defensive centres and attracted fugitives and small settlements of mixed communities on their outskirts.[22] The question of fugitives from Kabarda, who were baptised as a condition of protection, particularly vexed Kabardian princes.[23] Gärber's survey of regional divisions demonstrated the variability of the Kabardas' allegiance to Russia. Some mixed-religion Circassians of the Terek Plain, for example, were subject to Russia, chased off raiding parties and settled voluntarily near forts, under their own princes. The inhabitants of the mountains of Lesser Kabarda, however, although they were nominally Russian subjects and paid no taxes, remained warlike. In the upper reaches of Greater Kabarda, between the mountains of Georgia, Ossetia and Imeretia, their own princes (notably one named Islam) held sway even though they too were supposedly under Russian sovereignty.[24]

Kizliar

In 1735 Kizliar repaced Terki as the region's main Russian garrison and was the first fort to become a permanent town. It was still being built when Cook visited on his way to Shirvan. He wrote of a poor, dirty, characteristically mixed city of mostly non-Russians, including Circassians and Cossacks. By the 1770s the picture was very different. A description and map of Kizliar by Güldenstadt shows a well-laid-out town, divided into distinct parts, with two rivers: the Terek to the south and the smaller Kislarka to the north-west.[25] The pentagonal citadel, which was being built to the north-west of the town in Cook's time, was now finished and divided from the rest of the town by the Kislarka. In it were official buildings such as the governor's and officers' houses, the treasury, artillery and engineering bureaus. To the east, numerous different nations were grouped in their own districts, enclosed by an earthen wall. The Muslim quarter was the furthest east and included the Cherkassian neighbourhood under Prince Bekovitch-Cherkassky, a Kazan Tatar neighbourhood, a Persian (*Desik Aul*) merchant quarter and an Indian quarter. Such a diversity of peoples, with Russians in a minority, was characteristic of these frontier fortress towns.[26]

There were Armenian, and Georgian churches, a mosque (four were recorded at the turn of the century),[27] a school for newly converted Ossettians, law courts and markets. Beyond the enclosure to the north there was a market garden area, vines and mulberry plantations, where Armenians and Georgians also lived. The town was being further developed to the north and north-west.[28] Cook estimated 6–7000 inhabitants – possibly an overestimation, as in the 1770s the population was just over 4000.[29] Most Armenians, Persians, Georgians and, possibly, Indians were involved in the silk trade between Persia and Russia. The Persians were transients who brought the silk in, but the business side was run under an Armenian name.[30] At the end of the eighteenth century here the Armenians outnumbered the Russians three to one and were at the centre of regional north Caucasus trade.[31] The only trade Cook mentioned was the one in madder with Persia; he speculated on the possibility of profitable winemaking in the region. This became a reality, and despite attacks, Kizliar became a prosperous trading town and centre of wine, brandy and silk production with a growing population. It was the largest town in the north Caucasus until the growth of Stravropol in the nineteenth century.[32] Cook was there at a time when Russian mapping and knowledge of the Kabardas was becoming more professional.[33] He was curious about the naphtha (crude oil) wells beyond the Terek, in Chechen country outside the 'Russian dominions', and he conveyed how immediate the threat from 'wild Tartars' was perceived to be in the region. Official investigations of these natural resources, with a view to development, were continued by Güldenstadt and Pallas.[34]

Cook's entry on Kizliar coincided with the expansion of Cossack settlements on the Terek. Cook named a number of Greben Cossack villages on the north bank. The first known settlement on this side of the river by free Cossacks dated back to the mid-sixteenth century.[35] The history of the Greben Cossacks, as opposed to Cossacks officially settled by the Russian state or the Terek Cossacks,[36] was one of gradual weakening and unwilling, partial subordination to Russia. Having gradually moved northwards for reasons of security and economy in the seventeenth century, they were officially subordinated to Russian authority in 1720 and 1721, when Don Cossacks were also being relocated to the Sulak and Agrakhan rivers to become the Agrakhan host (large company of Cossacks).[37] Both the Greben and relocated Don Cossacks were severely depleted in battle and by disease at the time.[38] From the 1720s to the 1770s official Cossack settlement began to form a proper military line along the Terek and to symbolise permanent Russian presence in the north Caucasus. Mozdok, another permanent fort was built in 1763 on land ceded by a Christianised Circassian prince,[39] and in 1765 the Mozdok regiment was formed.[40] Barrett has written of the effect of these permanent settlements on local populations and environment, such as deforestation and disease, while also stressing the ambivalence, fluidity ('the middle ground')[41] and ethnic diversity of these regions.[42] The settlement and resettlement of Cossacks, as well as addition to regiments, was a prominent feature of Russia's advance in the north Caucasus, and created much discontent. Cook, who had much time for Cossacks,[43] conveyed the frustration of the Greben Cossacks, who were poor and considered themselves abused by the Russian state and the governor of Kizliar, V.A. Obolenski. The duties of these official Cossack hosts ranged from guard duties to agricultural and other manual labour.[44]

By 1770 the Russian presence in the north Caucasus was growing but still comparatively limited. Following the Russo-Turkish war of 1769–70, however, the Kabardas were ceded to Russia. This was confirmed by the khanate of Crimea in 1772 and by the Ottomans at the treaty of Küçük-Kainadji (1774). The Kuban was now the official boundary between Russia and Turkey. Georgia, which had requested Russian protection since the 1770s, officially came under Russian suzerainty at the Treaty of Georgievsk in 1783,[45] the same year Crimea was annexed. Thus, from the late 1770s to the mid-1780s, Russian encroachment and consolidation in the north Caucasus became inevitable and more aggressive. New forts and *stanitsas* (Cossack villages), such as Georgievsk, Ekaterinograd, Vladikavkaz and Stavropol, were built in a line that was to stretch from Mozdok to Azov by the end of the century and that brought extensive colonization.

Kabardian resistance to the Mozdok line had been brewing during the 1770s. This movement, which Russian sources attributed to Ottoman influence, sent deputies in 1772 to Chechnya, Endirei, Axai, Tarku and elsewhere to 'excite insurrections' against the Russians.[46] Conflict dragged on until 1779, when the Kabardians were defeated and acknowledged Russia once more.[47] Resistance to Russian expansion finally became an organised movement in the early 1780s. It was built on fertile ground, to which the creation of the viceroyalty of the Caucasus under Pavel Potemkin in 1785–86 contributed. This included a settlement and administrative programme for the region, the establishment of schools for 'Asiatics' and prospecting for natural resources.[48]

The resistance movement was spearheaded by a Chechen, Sheikh Ushurma or Mansur, whose origins and training are obscure. His possible Naqshbandi and Sufi affiliations are still debated.[49] Klaproth, following the Russian line, blamed the Ottomans for their influence on Sheikh Mansur and for the spread of the 'the religion of Mohammed' in the Caucasus.[50] Islam had been introduced early (around the eighth century) in the north Caucasus.[51] It was partly successful in Daghestan from the twelfth century onwards,[52] but further north and west its influence was more superficial and sporadic, and its role varied in different regions.[53] It was not yet a unifying force between peoples whose loyalties were to the clan and tribe, whose interests were so changeable, and whose local religious practices (Christian, Muslim and animist) varied even within one group.[54] In the 1790s, for example, the Abkhazian nobles were Muslim, whereas their people were as yet unconverted.[55] The resistance movement was initially successful, but its ideology ultimately proved unworkable, although it did much to raise awareness of Islam in the region.

In 1785 Mansur proclaimed a Holy War (*ghazawat*) against the 'infidel' Russians.[56] The proclamation urged the people of the north Caucasus to unify by adopting *sharia* law and dropping local customs. Mansur first ambushed and killed the Russian troops who had destroyed his village then went on the offensive against Kizliar and other forts of the Caucasus line. He was joined by Chechens, north and central Daghestanis and some Kabardian tribes, with the Abkhazians and Adyghes waiting in the wings.[57] The added disaffection of ordinary people and peasants to the growing power of local chieftains may have contributed to the movement.[58] Mansur's military successes were partial however, and his troops were finally routed by Colonel Nagel in autumn 1785. The Kabardas submitted to the Russians once more.[59] Mansur retreated to his base in Chechnya and continued his raids, but by 1786 the movement had begun to dissolve. In 1787 he moved west, encouraged by the Turkish governor of the Ottoman fortress of Anapa on the north coast of the Black Sea, as war between Russia and Turkey was imminent. There are conflicting views about Turkish attitudes to Mansur and the revolt, and about the war that broke out in 1787. Russian maintained that it was a Turkish 'plot'; in fact Mansur had approached the Turks first.[60] The fortress of Anapa finally fell in 1791, and Mansur was captured. He died at Schliesselburg fortress in 1794.[61]

The taking of Anapa under General Ivan Gudovich was recorded by Parkinson: 'Two thirds of the garrison at Anapa consisting of 25,000 men were killed. Goudovitch coolly observed that there were literally ruisseaux de sang.'[62] He made no mention of Mansur, although Pallas, who was in the Caucasus at a similar time,[63] mentioned 'the pretended new prophet' in the context of the Chechens, who were 'his most active supporters' and the most 'turbulent' and 'worst neighbours' of the Causasus line.[64] Islam was not identified as a factor in political instability in the north Caucasus by academicians or travellers of the time, except for Reineggs, who wrote of 'duty to creed' and 'fanaticism' in the context of the revolts of the 1770s.[65] Any rebellion was associated, rather, with Turkish intrigue and the nature of the tribesmen. For the time being, Mansur's resistance movement and its ideology were treated by the Russians as an aberration, which could be quelled by force, and not as a real or potential threat.

In 1792 a new policy of apparent appeasement was presented to the Kabardians. Some Kabardian legal practices concerning minor offences were accepted, subject to a non-Kabardian structure and a frontier law court at Mozdok with salaried Kabardian assistant judges. Although judges were appointed, the scheme was unpopular and hostilities continued.[66] Despite punitive actions, Russia's control of the Kabarda's internal affairs remained weak.[67] In 1796 a campaign against Daghestan and Iran removed the immediate military focus from the north Caucasus until the 1820s, with the 'pacification' and 'extirpation' policies of Nicholas I and General A.P. Ermolov towards 'the mountain peoples'.[68]

Fort Georgievsk

Fort Georgievsk was founded in 1777 on a steep verge of the River Podkuma and remained a very basic place. Parkinson arrived at a comparatively stable, if tense, time on the North Caucasus line, which was then commanded by General Gudovich. Travelling under Russian protection and as a guest of governors, Parkinson enjoyed what the forts offered in terms of society and diversions. Pallas described Georgievsk's redoubt and parapet fortifications but observed that, except for the governor's residence, there was scarcely any 'decent habitation'.[69] The location was also reputed to be extremely unhealthy[70] – a fact not mentioned by Parkinson. Although conditions at Georgievsk were almost as basic when Klaproth visited in 1807, it had nevertheless become the seat of government and regional capital in 1802.[71]

The visit to the forts of Georgievsk and Constantingorsk by Parkinson and his party included sightings of mountains (Elbrus, Beshtau), excursions to hot baths, mineral springs (to what was to become Kislovodsk spa),[72] Circassian villages and other locations, including the supposed fortress of Burg-ussan, which was in fact a natural outcrop.[73] They also enjoyed evenings of folk dancing and other entertainments. Parkinson, perhaps due to the shortness of his visit, as well as to Pallas's absence and the mindset of the military Russians he encountered, was cursory in his observations. He described the landscape in such routine terms as 'gay and delightful' or 'precipitous', and his account is even less evocative than those of the academicians and other contemporary travellers to the north Caucasus, such as Potocki.[74] The contrast with the heightened 'oriental' exoticism of Caucasus-based British tales of the second half of the eighteenth century is marked.[75]

Parkinson hardly addressed the landscape's ancient history. He noted only 'Tartar' burial places, in contrast to Pallas, who mentioned sepulchral hills, 'Circassian' burial monuments and 'Tartarian houses of worship' from the Golden Horde site of Madshar, which he compared to the monuments on the Achtuba.[76] Other late eighteenth-century travellers, such as Pallas, Reineggs, Potocki and Klaproth, frequently referred to descriptions of the region by classical authors, including Herodotus, Strabo and Pliny.[77] Such historical geography was not an empty display of learning; rather, it helped to disentangle origins and make the region more approachable. At the same time, classical writers' view of the region as partly savage or alien ultimately justified subjugation. While the 'Tatar' past was not ignored, Christian remains[78] served to validate Russian claims to the region.

Parkinson's remarks nevertheless transmit much of the local atmosphere. He ridiculed the military showmanship ('parade') of Russian governors, while revealing the underlying tensions and the necessity of substantial Cossack escorts to protect his party from the Circassians' 'aptness to revolt', including the possibility that they had poisoned wells in order to prevent a fortress being built at the 'Eaux Aigres' (Kislovodsk). Parkinson's account also conveys the variety of Caucasian and Turkic peoples in the area: Circassians, 'Abbaizas' (Abazes, Abkhazians), Georgians, Armenians, Turkish girl captives from Anapa, 'Turcomen' and Nogays.

Peoples and customs

The Circassians (figs.14 and 15) to whom Parkinson and Cook referred were groups of Lesser Kabarda, who were nominally vassals of Russia.

figs.14 and 15

They had a history of being 'unsafe and turbulent', according to Pallas.[79] If united with the Kabardians beyond the Kuban, they had the potential to 'bring a considerable body of men', who might be dangerous to 'neighbouring powers'. This was unlikely to happen, Pallas concluded, because of the number of princes and their internecine quarrels.[80] The 'Abbaizas' (Abkhaz) mentioned by Parkinson on a tour around Constantingorsk were nominally subject to the Kabardians and Russians, and lived near Constantingorsk, by the rivers Kuma and Podkuma. Other Abkhaz lived beyond the Kuban, outside Russian control. Some, such as the Beshilbai of Great 'Abassa' (Abkhazia), were so warlike that it was thought they could not be subdued even if the Russians were sent against them.[81] The 'Bassars' mentioned by Parkinson do not appear in accounts by Güldenstadt, Pallas and others. The name may have been misspelt or be a variant of Abassa.[82]

Parkinson wrote of the cancellation of a visit to a Nogay prince. The presence of displaced nomadic Nogays in the north Caucasus was a reminder of the perpetual tension between Russia, Crimea and the Ottomans over the River Kuban and the migration (often enforced) of these peoples back and forth across it. The group living by the Kuma and Podkuma was either one that survived dispersal after they left the Crimea in 1783 or part of the Mangut tribe (under Prince Mursak-girei) who were brought to the Kuma in 1790, of which there remained fifty-seven nobles and 18,000 subjects governed from Constantingorsk. The remainder of the tribe had fled to the opposite side of the Kuban, where they were persecuted by the 'mountainous nations'.[83] Parkinson also mentioned an audience given to Turcoman Tatars at Georgievsk. Also known as 'Trukhmenes' in eighteenth-century sources,[84] these were Turkic nomads who inhabited the steppe behind Kizliar, between the Terek and Kuma rivers. They were Muslims who had been driven west over the Yaik by the Kalmyks. They had first been subject to the Mongols and eventually became Russian subjects. Pallas wrote that, compared to the 'poor and uncivilized' but independent Turkmen on the east coast of the Caspian, these were 'rich', 'gay and comely', under 'the present constitution'.[85]

Colonies

Parkinson witnessed a phenomenon that was gradually altering the economic and political landscape of the Caucasus, and which went in tandem with the growing forts: the development of Russian and European colonies. Such colonisation had been Russian policy since the early 1780s (formalised in 1786),[86] designed to supply food for the troops and to 'people the frontier'.[87] Russian colonies, 'from several parts of the Empire', were owned either by the aristocracy or the military and were intended to be Christian.[88] Pollock has argued that the peoples of Caucasia, whom Russia could not afford to ignore, played their own varied and important roles in determining Russian colonisation of the Caucasus.[89]Initially the experiment had been unsuccessful: by 1793 most of the villages established after 1786 had lost between a third and half of their inhabitants from disease, desertion and raids. The settlements also attracted disaffected people, such as gypsies and disbanded soldiers.[90] Parkinson's guide, General Gudovich, pointed out the fruitless deforestation and taking of local resources by people who did not settle. Despite the success of some colonies, the general felt it was not worth bringing his own peasants to the area.

Among the Caucasian groups divided in their own 'districts', who were not mentioned by Parkinson but mentioned by Güldenstadt, Pallas, Georgi and others, were the Ossetians, Ingushetians, Chechens, Svanettians and Kabardes (outside the boundaries of Russia), and the Turkic Kumyks. Armenians have been discussed in the context of trade in the region. Georgians, whom Parkinson encountered only in passing, were extensively described by Reineggs, Güldensdatdt and Klaproth.[91] Travellers' comments on the social structure, religion, physical appearance and nature of the Circassians ranges from comparatively detailed (e.g. Bruce) to very brief (e.g. Parkinson). Both Bruce and Cook conveyed the complex interplay between the Kabardian nobles and the Russian empire in terms of governance and religion. Published Russian records cast light on the incessant stream of Kabardian complaints about, for example: fugitives and the building of forts; on Russian decrees, instructions and requests for information on the region and its rulers; and on the region's relations with Turkey, the Crimea, Kalmyks and others throughout the eighteenth century.[92]

While vassals or under 'Russian protection', princes ruled their own subjects. Because Kabardian social structure did not allow one absolute prince above others, nor absolute rule over the nobles, fidelity was ensured by the princes' 'liberal and benevolent conduct'[93] and the sharing of spoils from raids. The Russians exploited this situation by frequent gift-giving, which could lead to Christianisation.[94] Parkinson said little about Circassian social structure, besides mentioning (as had Cook) the princes' lack of personal property and being dismissive about the 'usdens' (*uzden*s, i.e. free men or nobles). In fact the Circassians had a complex, stratified social structure, consisting of princes, nobles, vassals and slaves taken in conflict. Princes could demand tribute at will; they were not landowners but possessed arms, horses and slaves. The *uzden*s were obliged to render service to the prince and keep the people in order but could be involved in decision-making. According to Pallas, the chief occupations of these two classes were military excursions, hunting, raiding and carousing. Vassals were considered hereditary property and, with the slaves, did all the agricultural, forestry and domestic work.[95]

An account of marriage customs is given by Cook (from hearsay), while Parkinson provides first-hand observations of the conventions of the nobility, including the education of boys away from the family home, in other noble households, until a certain age. Parkinson also described how a married princess he visited lived in separate lodgings from her husband. His observations tally with Pallas's,[96] and this custom is also hinted at by Bruce (following Olearius), who further suggests that it might lead to a lapse in the wifely virtue. Neither Cook nor Parkinson mentioned the customary laws of hospitality and revenge of the Caucasus, which Pallas described as 'sacred'.[97]

The attempt at Christianisation and the 'paganism' of the Circassians is stressed in the Bruce/Olearius passage. Gärber's contemporary notes show the medley of religious beliefs in the Kabardas in the 1720s. The Circassians of Lesser Kabarda were variously Sunni Muslim or Christian (or nominally so), while continuing to follow their own traditions. Those living in the mountains of Upper/Greater Kabarda had anciently been Christian but had recently been converted to Islam.[98] Cook wrote in the 1740s that they 'professed' to be Muslims; in the 1790s Pallas called the Adighe and other formerly Christian Circassians 'ignorant' nominal Muslims, but added that the few priests (mullahs) among them, who wore deep red turbans,[99] were 'highly respected'.[100] He did not say where mullahs received their training, but this observation hints at an emerging Naqshbandi (a major Sufi mystical order) tradition of venerating teachers.[101] Pallas managed to be both politically correct and insulting to the Russian state by asserting, in the face of reality, that 'a small degree of zeal would have been sufficient to convert them to Christianity'.[102] Cook wrote that the Russians did not encroach on Circassian religious affairs – in other words that, unlike with the Tatars and other peoples of the Middle Volga, there was no institutionalised drive to Christianise Circassians at the time, but rather an ongoing process of enticement and rewards.[103] It was different with the Ossetians, who were said to be lapsed Christians, to have requested

Russian protection against the Chechens and Kabardians, and to be ripe for conversion.[104] In 1745 proselytisation began, and in 1752 the Ossetian Committee for the Propagation of Christianity was instituted. Between 1746 and 1764 the commission baptised more than 2000 people, but a religious school founded at Mozdok for 'the mountaineers' floundered because of bad management.[105]

Despite missionaries, including some from Sarepta,[106] schools and churches, and the protection given by forts, antagonism to 'infidel' Russians and continuing conflict prevented Christianity from making significant headway among the stronger nominally Muslim or semi-Muslim groups of the region. From the 1770s onwards, Catherine II's official policy of toleration and absorption of Muslims into the state, which was partially successful in the Middle Volga and the Urals, could not be properly applied or bear fruit locally among peoples who were politically unsubdued and whose commitment to Islam was still piecemeal, if growing. For any small group threatened by others (such as the Ossetians or the Ingushetians) and who approached the Russians for protection, Christianisation would have been part of the package.[107] The aim of Christianising the Caucasus was not abandoned, and in 1793 a Georgian archimandrite was commissioned to promote Christianity from Mozdok.[108]

In contrast to academicians' accounts,[109] the complexity of the Circassian and other Caucasian languages was barely addressed by the British travellers. All travellers, however, agreed on the subject of Circassian female physical beauty, already an established theme in western travel literature at the time of Olearius and Chardin.[110] Cook spiced up his description of one of Prince Bekovitch-Cherkassky's daughters with an element of voyeurism. It has been suggested that during the nineteenth century, when the subject of Circassian female beauty titillated the west, an element of homoeroticism also crept into western descriptions of Circassian males,[111] whom eighteenth-century sources reported to be strong, martial and handsome.[112] In general, however, the travellers showed little admiration of other qualities ascribed to Circassians. Parkinson repeated the commonplaces that they were 'addicted to robbery', 'stealing and pilfering' and 'apt to revolt'. Pallas, on a state mission and duty bound to be partisan, was nevertheless contradictory in his comments on the Circassians: while they apparently hated and resented Russia, and were turbulent, predatory and warlike, they were also heroic, brave, free, clean and handsome.[113] He was uncharacteristically blunt when writing of other Caucasians. Those who were then pro-Russian, such as the Ingushetians, who would make useful and loyal subjects, he described as honest and brave,[114] whereas the Ossetians and Chechens, who 'infested' roads, were hostile, lawless and predatory.[115]

Russian revenge on the people of Endirei

General Waterang [Veterani] had been dispatched some time ago, through the great desart of Astrachan, with an army of 7,000 dragoons, and 10,000 Cossacks, attended by 20,000 Kalmuck Tartars, with a very large train of camels to carry their provisions and water; and with orders to attack and destroy the province of Andreof, to revenge the many ravaging incursions made by them on the subjects of Russia: the general was shortly after followed by 10,000 Cossacks and 20,000 Kalmuck Tartars more, to augment his army, and enable him to complete the destruction of that province.[116]

While we were here [Terki] his majesty received accounts from general Waterang, with the agreeable news that he had defeated and cut to pieces a body of five thousand men, of the province of Andreof, and that he had burnt and destroyed their capital city, laid the whole province waste and carried off all the inhabitants that he could meet with, old and young of both sexes, amounting to many thousands; and sent them to Astrachan under the escort of five thousand Cossacks, and fifteen thousand Kalmucks; and had besides given liberty to several thousand Russian slaves of both sexes, who were then on their way to Terki, to be transported from thence by sea to Astrachan. For this signal success, we had orders to fire three vollies, from all our guns and small arms.[117]

(Bruce, 1722)

Terki and eastern Circassia

[The capital of Circassian Tartary] is the most southern boundary of his majesty's present dominions: this city is strongly fortified, and stands on an island formed by the rivers Terki [Terek] and Bustrow and is garrisoned by two thousand regulars and one thousand Cossacks, who are all horsemen; the native Circassians are not permitted to live near the city, but inhabit the country at some distance to it …[118]

Terki, the principal city, is seated in a very spacious plain, very swampy towards the sea-side, in 43 deg. 23 min. north latitude: it is about three wersts in compass, well fortified with ramparts and bastions in the modern style, well stored with cannon, and has always a considerable garrison in it, under the command of a governor. The Circassian prince who resides here, is allowed five hundred Russians for his guard, but none of his own subjects are permitted to dwell within any part of the fortifications. Ever since the reduction of those parts to the obedience of Russia, they have put in all places of strength, not only Russian garrisons and governors, but magistrates, and priests for the exercise of the Christian religion; yet the Circassian Tartars are governed by their own princes, lords, and judges, but these administer justice in the same way as the emperor, and in matters of importance, not without reference of the Russian governors, being all obliged to take an oath of allegiance to his imperial majesty.[119]

(Bruce, 1722)

Circassian appearance, language and religion

The apparel of the men of Circassia is much the same with that of the Nagayans, only their caps is something larger and their cloaks, being likewise of coarse cloth or sheep skins, are fastened only at the neck with a string, as they are not large enough to cover the whole body, they turn them around according to the wind and weather.

The men here are much better favoured than those of Nagaya, and the women extremely well shaped, with exceeding fine features, smooth clear complexions, and beautiful black eyes, which with their black hair hanging in two tresses, one on each side of the face, give them a most lovely appearance; they wear a black coif on their heads, covered with a fine white cloth tied under the chin: during the summer they all wear only a smok of divers colours, and that open so low before, that one may see below their navels; this with their beautiful faces always uncovered, (contrary to the custom of most of the other provinces in these parts), their good humour and lively freedom in conversation, altogether render them very desirable: notwithstanding they have the reputation of being very chaste, though they seldom want opportunity; for it is an established point of good manners among them, as soon as any person comes in to speak to the wife, the husband goes out of the house: but whether this continency of their's proceeds from their own generosity, to recompense their husbands for the confidence they put in them, or has its foundation only in fame, I pretend not to determine.[120]

...

Their language they have in common with the other neighbouring Tartars, although the chief people among them are also not ignorant of the Russian; their religion is Paganism, for notwithstanding they use circumcision among them, they have neither priest, alcoran or mosque, like other Mahometans. Everybody here offers his own sacrifice at pleasure, for which, however they have certain days established rather by custom, than any positive command: their most solemn sacrifice is offered at the death of their nearest friends, upon which occasion both men and women meet in the field to be present at the offering, which is an he-goat; and having killed, they slay it, and stretch the skin with the head and horns on, upon a cross at the top of a long pole, placed commonly in a quickset hedge, (to keep the cattle from it) and near the place of sacrifice is offered by boiling and rotating the flesh, which they afterwards eat. When the feast is over, the men rise, and having paid their adoration to the skin, and muttered over some certain prayers, the women withdraw, and the men conclude the ceremony with drinking a great quantity of aqua vitae, and this generally ends in a quarrel before they part.[121]

(Bruce, 1722)

Circassia in the 1740s

Circassia, according to the accounts I have got, is, that the country lying between Asoph [Azov], the Palus Maeotis on the west, the high hills of Caucasus inhabited by the Georgians and Daghestan Tartars on the south, the Caspian sea on the east, and the desarts of Astrachan ... on the south, confine it. The western half of this country is under the protection of the Turks, the eastern half under the protection of the Russians, and a part of the south is claimed by the Persians.[122]

(Cook, 1746-47)

Kizliar

The Russians have built a city called Kizlaar about sixty versts from the Caspian sea, and when I was there, were finishing a strong citadel of earth, in which a garrison of 500 regular troops are kept, and about two or or three thousand Cossacks. The Russians have also given liberty to the Cossaks to build towns on the banks of the river Terek ... The city Kizlaar is in latitude forty four degrees, and consequently the climate cannot be very bad; because it is well watered by rivers, is a plain level country, and the city is built almost in the middle of what properly belongs to the Russians.[123]

Kizlaar ... is a new city, and consequently not completed; it may contain six or seven thousand inhabitants, besides the garrison, and other people belonging to the army, consisting of Russians, Cossacks and natives of the country. The streets are not paved, and consequently very deep and dirty; the houses mean, and very ill built of timber: In short, it is a poor dirty city, the streets are so very deep in rainy weather, that horses have stuck fast in the mud: There are only two shop-keepers here.

Lately was built upon the north-west of the town, a fortification or citadel of earth, in form of a pentagon, surrounded with a very deep and broad ditch, palisadoed round about; and to the west of that are casarms for the garrison, which consists of five hundred men from the garrison of Astrachan; besides which, commonly three or four regiments of regular troops are cantoned here; and three, four or five thousand Cossacks, not inhabitants of the country, and some Circassians, commanded by their own chief Bekovitch.

The Russians formerly built a fortification by the sea, which they called Sulack; but, it being very unhealthy, they deserted it, and caused the inhabitants to retire to this place. There are eight or nine Cossack villages very neat, situated west of Kizlaar, upon the banks of the Terek. These Cossacks are called Grebinski Cossachi: They inhabit a very rich country, abounding with everything which nature can produce.

The people of Kizlaar carry on a good trade with the Persians for a root which grows naturally here, fit for a beautiful red colour; being the winter season I saw none of it, but imagined it was rubia tictorum [madder]. Very many reeds grow here; the finest capers in the world, and a great variety of very useful herbs: Vines grow wild in the woods; the grapes are small, but they produce good wine, and if they were cultivated, would be of great advantage to the proprietor.[124]

(Cook, 1746–47)

Cossack villages

The Russian villages (beginning at Kizliar from east to west Barazdinskaya, Dubofskaya, Karklakingskaya, Kurdjukoff, Staro Gladkoi, Nova Gladkoi, Sedrin, Tscherslonoi, Bragetskoi) are all situated on the north-side of the Terek river, but Bragutskoi (not under Russian protection) is on the south-side. The inhabitants of all these villages are chiefly Cossacks, and are reckoned more warlike than the Don Cossacks ... They told me, that their courage is much kept under by great oppression from the commandant of Kizlaar, their governor [V.A. Obolenski] who did not bear a good name ... I desired to know from the Cossacks, What was the reason that they were obliged to find horses for passengers (though in her Majesty's service) without payment, as they do through all Russia? They answered, That that was but a trifle to what they were otherways burdened with; that no officer paid for horses; and added, that they were the most miserable slaves belonging to the Russian empire; because they were impotent, poor, and at too great a distance from the court, and had none to represent their grievances.

Our dragoons, and their horses, were cantoned in these villages. I persuaded three of the officers, with a few of their men, to go with me to the wells ... not in the Russian dominions. [Bragetskoi] is situated six miles to the wells ... This well vomited up boiling water, which smelled strongly of naphta, into a bason ... near which were seven smaller springs of the same kind of water ...[125]

At Kizlaar, I was surprised to find, that when I had drawn the corks of naphta water ... the water was quite sweet ...[126]

(Cook, 1746–47)

Circassian government and religion

Those under Russian protection are governed by their own princes, the chief of which is called Bekovitch ... (the son of Brigadier Bekovich, who was murdered by the Buchareans on the east side of the Caspian) [see pp.215–19]... He is a major general of irregulars in the Russian army: But he never was ordered to leave Circassia, where it is thought he can be of the greatest service to the empire.

There are other Circassian princes under the Russian government, quite independent of one another. But none so much honoured as he is. Tho' the Circassians honour their princes much, yet they cannot absolutely command them to any piece of service, unless they are so inclined themselves; wherefore it is always necessary to get a majority on their side, and the prince is obliged to divide all the spoils, every one in the expedition having the right to share, and if the prince at any time, gets presents from the Empress [Elizabeth], which they do frequently, every one of his subjects expects either a part; if divisable, or something equivalent of it otherwise. They under Russia are so far subject to the Russians that they swear to be subject to the general laws for the good of Russia and themselves. But the Russians never offer to encroach on their religious affairs.

They profess the Mahometan religion, and have, like the Turks, a plurality of wives and as many concubines as they please.[127]

(Cook, 1746–47)

Circassian appearance and customs

The Circassians are comely, beautiful, well made people, both men and women; they are generally of large size, and are very good soldiers; their arms are bows, arrows and scimitars, but they shoot well with a single ball out of rifled pieces; their principal people only are in possession of fire arms.[128]

...

I was told that they have one very singular custom ... when the Khan's lady is in labour, the first Circassian man who gets notice of it, placeth himself at the door of the harem, or house where the women are kept ... (like the Turks). When he had once taken his station, no other Circassian dares to deprive him of it. When the woman is delivered, some old servant woman is sent to the gate to declare to the Circassians that the Khan's wife is delivered either of a son or daughter, or both; if a son, the child being richly dressed, is brought to the gate and delivered to the Circassian [noble, not the father] whose right it is by their law, he carries the infant to his house, provides a nurse for him, and educates him as his own child, until he acquires the age of nine or ten years, then he is restored to his parents, at which time they have great rejoycings. The reason they act in this manner, is, that the child may be brought up hardily, and become a buggateer or hero; which qualification is very necessary among them, and without which he will be very little esteemed.[129]

. . .

[Y]ou see that they pay great regard to their chiefs, and honour ancient houses much. A noble family will not let their daughters go to the common people, or those under the rank of their own family. I never heard that they have any other ceremony of marriage than a simple contract between the parents or the childrens tutors, and the young pair are permitted to visit and see one another in the presence of the parents: If, after the bridegroom has made two or three visits, they are satisfied with one another, the affair is concluded, and she is carried home to his house in a close painted wagon in company of her women who are to live with her.[130]

In Circassia no other dowry is given with their daughters than a few suits of rich cloaths, ornamented with jewels, and a few women: But the bride-groom is obliged to produce on the wedding-day such a number of horses, dromedaries, cows etc. as was agreed upon. If they have no such number of their own, they make incursions upon their neighbours and carry off as many as they stand in need of, or lose their lives in the attempt.[131]

. . .

The Circassians wore *togae* or long gowns: Their hair is cut short, so that at a distance, when uncovered, one would be apt to think that they wore small caps; they are all shaved, except their whiskers. When they are mounted on horseback, they have a sabre fixed to the saddle under their left thigh, and another hanging at their left side. This they do, lest one should happen to be broken in engagement.[132]

(Cook, 1746–47)

Cook visits Princess Bekovitch

One evening as Major Berezin and I were returning from hunting, passing Prince Bekovitch's harem, we saw his daughter, a lady of about sixteen years of age, walking in the garden. She saw not us, which gave us an opportunity of seeing one of the beautifullest of the whole creation.

In the evening we told the ambassador, who, though old, admired beauties, and as she was a relation of the Golitzins, obtained liberty from her father to pay her a visit. None were present but the Major and me: She was very richly dressed; at this interview she presented a glass of arrack to the prince, and after a short while retired. This young lady might have had her equals; but it was the opinion of us all that none could surpass her in beauty.[133]

(Cook, 1746–47)

From the Caucasus line of forts, 1793

We arrived at Georgiew [Fort Georgievsk] early in the morning and found a lodging prepared for us, though only consisting of a single room, was the best the place afforded and the same as was given to people of the first consequence ... Not long after we were waited on by a Lietenant Col. on the part of the Governor-General [I. Gudovich] ... to invite us to dinner ... [After dinner and a rest] we sallied forth with all the parade of an Eastern prince in view of his enemy, with an escort of between twenty and thirty Cossacks, with two carriages and half a score horses for those who chose to ride when we arrived on open ground ... We paraded up and down the Steppe in hopes of seeing Mountains of Snow and particularly Elburus [Elbrus], which at last we had the pleasure of doing ... This extraordinary mountain rises like an immense pyramidical Mass and towers above all the rest ... A notion prevails that Noah's Ark rested upon it, and as it is forked, caused the gap between the forks ... the Baschtagh [Beshtau] was the most striking and conspicuous object in the gay and delightful landscape, which was also enlivened by a little encampment at the back of the Kuma, whose course ... is marked by a tract of woodland abounding with all sorts of game. The rest of the country is Stepp, here and there dotted with haystacks, sprinkled as usual with barrows, and in a few places cultivated a little: the[y] produce Oats, Grütze [crushed oats], Barley, Melons and Cucumbers.[134]

...

There is a great deal of parade in the Governor's whole style of living and particularly of military parade. He evidently affects the Character and reputation of a soldier, besides which the idea of being constantly on these frontiers in a state of war, give a colour and apology for all this ...[135]

I never saw military subservience carried to such a length as in the presence of the Governor General ...[136]

(Parkinson, July 1793)

A sightseeing expedition

We set out today ... to see the Mountains of Bestovie or the five Mountains [Beshtau] ... We changed horses at a redoubt ... a few versts from Constantinogrost [Constantingorsk] ...We proceeded from hence [a reservoir] on horse back by one of the most perilous roads I ever passed to several natural reservoirs ... where we found bathing Circassians of both sexes. [The ride had been] over smooth uneven rocks by the side of Precipices where a slip must have been fatal ...

Had the Atmosphere been clear we should have commanded a fine view of the mountains ... At the foot of the mountains we saw and afterwards [went] through a couple of Circassian villages ... The materials of their houses were the same as those of the Russian Villages, Mud for the walls and reeds or straw for the roof. Another thing which struck me in this ride were the Tartar burial places, which are for the most part on an eminence, often on one of those which in ancient times had been raised as a funeral Monument, and which being of a square form and composed of white stones contrasts very agreeably often with the verdant lawn on which they stand. The heat of the day was excessive and we rode very fast.[137]

We were received at the fortress [Constantingorsk] with all the honours of war ... Amongst other attendants when we arrived were four or five Circassian Princes. It was our intention [in the afternoon] to have visited a Prince of the Nogai Tartars; but as his brother had died on this day a twelvemonth before, it was kept as a day of mourning and he could not receive us. These Nogai Tartars fled from the Crimea to M. Caucasus, from whence they have ventured back into these plains and fixed their habitations.[138]

On our way to the Tartar village through the Circassian, I exchanged hands with the Circassian Prince ... and went into his house. A carpet being spread on the Ground near this tree [to which guests attach their horses] ... persons sat down and had water poured in their hands with which they dipped their face and stroked their whiskers to shew us the way of receiving their guests. In the house, which consisted of a single room and was open at the top, there was a wooden Divan about a foot high at one end and this constituted all the furniture ...

When we returned to this village we stopped there again ... we contented ourselves with begging leave to be introduced to the Princess, who lives apart in a house by herself. The husband did not accompany us, it being contrary to their ideas of Propriety for the husband to visit his wife in the day. When he steals to her even in the night it is with the utmost privacy. She received us standing on her divan without moving in the least in answer to the bows which we made on entering. Carpets were spread [for] us and we sat down crosslegged as she also did; and in a short time we were served out of a sort of kettle with a bason full of Maxomi, a very strong fermented liquor obtained from meal, said to be very wholesome and which I did not find disagreeable. The Princess had with her, standing by her, a little child belonging to some other prince whom she had taken to bring up. It is a singular custom of these People not to educate their own children; but to do it one for the other. Two or three dirty women attended as Domestics and one sat down I think on the same divan. About the tent and peeping in at the door we observed several young Girls, whose faces were very beautiful and confirmed the notions commonly entertained of Circassian Beauty.

I was told that when the old women of the Village dine with the Princess, which I believe they do every day, they must all be satisfied before she is permitted to eat a Morsel: for the purpose of shewing that they are all equal.[139]

(Parkinson, July 1793)

'Addicted to robbery'

The Circassians are so addicted to robbery that I heard a story of them stealing in the night a present of horses, or some such present, which they had made to a friend on the preceding day ...[140]

The Princes have no property of their own but can demand whatever they please. The Usdens live wholly a life of pleasure and idleness and are many of them in their way very rich. [141]

The dress of the Circassians is a cap in the form of a Melon cut in two, a loose Asiatic robe fastened round with a girdle to which they hang their knives, trowsers down to the ankles; and red slippers nicely fitted to their feet. The Princes and Usdens [Uzden] wear Sabres, Pistols and coats of Mail.[142]

(Parkinson, July 1793)

An expedition to 'Eaus Aigres'

The General, M. Verofkin [Commandant of Constantingorsk] ... two Georgian Princes, ourselves and one of the young officers who had conducted us to the hot baths, set off this morning [23rd July) on an excursion thirty two Versts farther towards the Mountains, in order to visit the Eaus Aigres [Kislovodsk], where we found Lt. Col. Manseroff and his lady, L. Col. Liwoff and his lady with her mother residing on account of their health. We were accompanied by a guard of a hundred Dragoons partly for security and partly out of respect for us and the General. The Circassians are so apt to revolt and can be relied on so little that the company had a guard of thirty men. In this expedition we presently quitted the plains and entered a hilly country ... We stopped on the way to visit a subterranean passage or Cavern ... which they pretended had formerly served as a resort or asylum of Banditti, and which the Circassians assert is fifty Versts in length ...

The company received us in the most obliging manner; we dined ... [in] a tent built like a house which he [Lt. Col. Manserof] had transported hither in two Kibitkis; and in the evening we took an airing to a Bassar [?] village ... During dinner as well as after our tent was surrounded by Circassians, Bassars and Abbaizas [Abkhazes] of all descriptions, Princes, Usdens and Peasants leaning on their staffs and observing with great attention everything that passed. They danced at the request of the company several Circassian dances, the greatest excellence of whereof consists of poising themselves on the toes.[143]

I observed a great deal of Indian Wheat in the neighbourhood of this village. The waters of this Spring raised a sort of sand or gravel ... it sinks however immediately to the bottom; the water sparkles and has a brisk champagne tatste which it loses in some degree if not immediately drunk. They prescribe it for all kinds of obstructions ... It generally goes off in urine and after clearing the body afterwards fortifies it. The people of this country have long had a confidence in its medicinal virtues, but they are capable of spoiling it for fear the Russians should be induced to create a fortress there, because this would retrench their liberty by taking from them the power of stealing and pilfering, their most favourite occupation.

Considering the remoteness of the Spot, I never was in a place where I enjoyed less privacy.

We stayed here to today on purpose to go and see the ruin of an ancient fortress [Bursang] supposed to have belonged to the Huns when they were in possession of the country ... it was never once mentioned till it was too late ...[144]

[On return to Constantingorsk] Our dinner ... was as agreeable as it had been before ... A servant who was with the Georgian Princes, as also an Armenian gentleman who played on the 'Balilaka', entertained us with several Georgian dances; as did afterwards up stairs a little Turkish Girl taken at Anapa and kept by the Prince Arbilianoff. Another young Girl, who had been taken at the same place and was kept by Verofkin, made also part of the same company. Being desperately wounded himself with a sabre in the right hand, the young girl was brought to him by his officers. She was then fourteen or fifteen. He has a child by her and she is become a Christian.[145]

[Prince G. Arbilianoff] gave Bootle[146] a very curious Circassian staff and also a Turkish dagger taken at Anapa. He gave me one ... called a Kingall, from Korasan, calculated for quick defence. [He] presented Bootle also with a dagger of the Mountains made at Tiflis: as he did each of us ... with a pair of Georgian slippers ...[147]

(Parkinson, July 1793)

Problems of Russian colonies

We could see from [the hill] some large villages which gave the General occasion to say that in the hands of Individuals the Colonies did not prosper. If a grant of land was made to an Individual he was apt to take the fish and cut down the wood without making any establishment. They had a class of people in Russia, a sort of Yeomanry, between the Peasant and the Gentleman, who succeeded much better because they settled on the spot and addicted themselves to husbandry. There were some Colonies I think of this kind which were very prosperous. He had villages where there was not land enough for his Peasants. Yet it was not worth his while to transport them hither ...

[W]e betook ourselves to our beds in the Kibitkis ... the Court as usual and the Tops of the houses were crowded with people sleeping in the open Air. There were thirty one degrees of heat today in the shade.[148]

(Parkinson, July 1793)

ENDNOTES

1 Khodarkovsky 1999, p.400.
2 Atkin 1988, pp.145–47; Bennigsen-Broxup, p.2; Lemercier-Quelquejay, pp.37–40.
3 Khodarkovsky 1999, p.395; Barrett 1999, p.9.
4 Lemercier-Quelquejay, p.40; Barrett 1999, pp.20–22.
5 E.g. Georgi 1780–83, pp.98–99; Ellis, pp.18–33.
6 Chardin writes on the Black Sea region, Georgia, Mingrelia, Imretia and mentions the 'Cherks' and other Caucasian tribes (e.g. Chardin, pp.76–77, 82ff, 106ff, 186ff.
7 Published in 1728 (Gärber).
8 See Pollock, pp.30–70 for an analysis of academicians in the Caucasus at this period.
9 Gärber, pp.69–71.
10 Barrett 1999, p.18. A story that this village was founded by a Cossack named Andrei is almost certainly apocryphal (ibid., p.15).
11 Gärber, p.70; Soimonov 1763, pp.80–81.
12 Gärber, p.70; Güldenstadt, pp.172–73.
13 Reineggs and von Bieberstein, vol.2, pp.61–62; see also Gmelin 2007, p.302.
14 Klaproth 2005, p.317.
15 Barrett 1999, p.19.
16 Olearius 1669, pp.135–36, 308–9.
17 Soimonov 1763, p.72.
18 Gärber, p.61; Barrett 1999, p.32.
19 Barrett 1995, p.591.
20 Barrett 1995, p.590.
21 For example, the Sulak in the Stavropol district in the building of Svyatoi Krest fortress (Gärber, pp.63–64).
22 Barrett 1995, pp.582–89.
23 *Kabardino-Russkie Otnoschenia* 1957, vol.2, e.g. nos 175, 177, 193; Barrett 1995, *passim*.
24 Gärber, pp.68–69.
25 Güldenstadt 1787, vol.1, pl.iii; from the citadel to the walls, excluding the developments outside, the town measured *c.*1000 'faden' across and *c.*300 lengthwise (1 faden = 1.8 m).
26 Barrett 1995, p.591; Klaproth 2005, p.305 writes of the multiple languages spoken by traders at Mozdok.
27 Barrett 1999, p.34.
28 Güldenstadt 1787, Vol.1, pp.180–81, and key to the plan, pp.xvi-xvii.
29 Barrett 1999, p.34.
30 Güldenstadt 1787, vol.1, p.181.
31 Barrett 1999, p.34.
32 Ibid., pp.33–34.
33 *Kabardino-Russkie Otnoschenia* 1957, vol.2, 1744 map of the Kabardas by S. Chichagov; see also nos 52, 93, 131.
34 Güldenstadt 1787, vol.1, pp.198–217; Pallas 1812, e.g. pp.348–49, 351–52. 359
35 Barrett 1999, p.13.
36 The origins of the Terek Cossacks are unclear, but they were among the first to be associated with Terskii Gorod and to serve the Russian state (Barrett 1999, pp.18, 21).
37 Barrett 1999, pp.31–32.
38 Ibid., p.33.

39 *Kabardino-Russkie Otnoschenia* 1957, vol.2, nos 151, 164. Klaproth 2005, p.202.

40 Barrett 1999, p.38.

41 I thank Alexander Morrison for this observation. See Barrett 1999, p.7; for a contrary view, see Khordarkovsky 1999, p.405.

42 Barrett 1999, *passim*; Khordarkovsky 1999, *passim*.

43 Cook, vol.2, pp.171–73.

44 Barrett 1999, p.37.

45 Mineral prospecting had taken place in Georgia, into which a new road was built in 1782 (Klaproth 2005, pp.210–11).

46 *Kabardino-Russkie Otnoschenia* 1957, vol.2, no.229; Klaproth 2005, pp.204–5.

47 Klaproth 2005, pp.204–10.

48 Bartlett 1979, p.120; Klaproth 2005, p.214.

49 Bennigsen 1964, pp.175 ff (this remains the seminal article); Zelkina 1996; Zelkina 2000, pp.250–51; Knysh, pp.920–22.

50 Klaproth 2005, pp.212, 316–17.

51 For a recent overview of this subject, see Zelkina 2000, pp.26–30.

52 Ibid., p.28.

53 Zelkina 1996, p.243.

54 Zelkina 2000, pp.34–39.

55 Pallas 1812, p.383.

56 Bennigsen 1964, pp.159ff.

57 Ibid., pp.188–89.

58 Ibid., p.171.

59 For example they were expected to provide, for a salary, men for service. The Ingushes and Ossetians were also expected to provide men to protect the roads. Klaproth 2005, pp.214–15.

60 Klaproth 2005, pp.212–13, 316–17; Bennigsen 1964, pp.180–84.

61 For a summary, see Bobrovnikov, pp.204–5.

62 Parkinson, p.183.

63 There is no indication from Parkinson that they travelled together here, although some of the same places were visited by both.

64 Pallas 1812, p.439. For Reineggs and von Bieberstein on Mansur (including his 'melancholic and sullen disposition') see vol 1, pp.284–87; Klaproth 2005, p.212.

65 Reineggs and Bieberstein, vol.1, p.283.

66 Pallas 1812, pp.371–72; Atkin 1988, pp.163–64.

67 Atkin 1988, p.164.

68 Words used by Nicholas I in 1829: Kappeler 2001, p.183.

69 Pallas 1812, pp.337–39.

70 E.g. Pallas 1812, p.340; Klaproth 2005, p.167.

71 Pallas 1812, p.337; Klaproth 2005, p.167; Barrett 1999, p.75.

72 Parkinson, n.186.

73 Pallas 1812, pp.345–46.

74 Pallas uses such terms as 'magnificent' 'majestic' 'beautiful valleys' 'lofty and colossal' (1812, pp.335, 340); Potocki writes of 'menacing' or 'monstrous' rocks', 'beautiful valleys', 'agreeable tableaux'(1980, pp.147, 153, 155).

75 E.g. Duff; Moser.

76 Pallas 1812, pls xi–xiv, pp.327–32, 336, 376–77; for Madshar see also Klaproth 2005, pp.224ff. He lists previous records of Madshar, including one by Gärber.

Georgi mentions Madshar in his general survey of 'Tartar' ruins of the empire (Georgi 1780–83, vol.2, pp.11–12).

77   E.g. Reineggs and von Bieberstein, *passim*; Pallas 1812, pp.84, 390, 392, 437; Klaproth 2005, pp.279, 293.

78   E.g. Klaproth 1834, pp.177–88 (plates in Güldenstadt 1787).

79   Pallas 1812, pp.390–95.

80   Ibid., pp.403–4; for the tribes beyond the Kuban see pp.412–19; see also Klaproth, pp.134–37.

81   Pallas 1812 pp.383–84; Klaproth, pp.130–34.

82   He is unlikely to be referring to the Bassians, a mixed tribe who lived in Great Kabarda beyond the Malka (Pallas 1812, pp.427–28).

83   Pallas 1812, pp.421–22; Güldenstadt 1834, pp.173–75.

84   Georgi 1780–83, vol.2, pp.93–96; Güldenstadt 1834, p.176; Pallas 1812, pp.298–300.

85   Pallas 1812, p.298.

86   Bartlett, pp.120–22. For an overview of Catherine II's settlement policies, focusing on New Russia, Crimea and Bessarabia, see Brandes, pp.19–47.

87   Pallas 1812, p.319.

88   Khordarkovsky 1999, pp.425–26.

89   Pollock, pp.381–82 and *passim*. See also Breyfogle, Schrader and Sunderland, p.2.

90   Pallas ed. 1812, pp.319-324; Bartlett 1979, pp.122-124; Khordarkovsky 1999, *passim*.

91   See also Chardin.

92   *Kabardino-Russkie Otnoschenia* 1957, vol.1 (sixteenth and seventeenth centuries); vol.2 (eighteenth century).

93   Pallas 1812, p.403.

94   *Kabardino-Russkie Otnoschenia* 1957, vol.2, nos 90, 91, 151, 182.

95   On Circassian social structure, see Pallas 1812, pp.401–3. Klaproth 2005, pp.314–15.

96   Marriage, as courtship, was regulated by social class (Pallas 1812, pp.397, 403, 405, 406–7).

97   Pallas 1812, p.404.

98   Gärber, pp.68–69.

99   Red headgear is traditionally associated with the Kizilbash Sufi group (Savory, p.243), but this seems unlikely here.

100 Pallas 1812, p.401.

101 Algar, pp.933–37; Nizami, pp.937–39; Zelkina 2000, pp.67, 101ff (in the Caucasus).

102 Pallas 1812, p.401.

103 E.g. Klaproth 2005, p.202.

104 Ibid., p.201.

105 Ibid., p.209.

106 Ibid., pp.415–21.

107 Ibid., p.205; Pallas 1812 p.438.

108 Klaproth 2005, p.208.

109 Güldenstadt is the most thorough. In vol. 2 (1791), pp.189–246, he assembles vocabularies, arranged by district, of many of the Caucasian peoples, including Daghestanis. See also Pallas 1812, e.g. pp.440–41. Etymology and parallels with 'known' tongues, with a view to tracing origins, were the issue. Other travellers,

such as Reineggs, also briefly addressed language (e.g. Reineggs and von Bieber-stein, vol.1, pp.239–41).

110 Olearius 1669, pp.137, 310, writes of 'well shaped', 'handsome', 'lustrous' women. Chardin (e.g. pp.84, 190–91) is at pains to stress the beauty and desirability of Mingrelian and Georgian women, as well as their 'wickedness' and lasciviousness. The origins of this theme may originally have been developed in conection with Georgian women sold by the Circassians across the Middle East. I thank Alexander Morrison for this last observation.

111 King, p.134.

112 Pallas 1812, p.398, writes of men's 'slender loins' and 'Herculaean structure'.

113 Ibid., pp.398–421 and *passim*.

114 Ibid., pp.436, 438.

115 Ibid., pp.431, 438–39.

116 Bruce, pp.257–58.

117 Ibid., pp.262–63.

118 Ibid., p.260.

119 Ibid., p.263.

120 Ibid., pp.263–64.

121 Ibid., pp.264–65.

122 Cook, vol.2, p.242.

123 Ibid., p.243.

124 Ibid., pp.251–53.

125 Ibid., p.254.

126 Ibid., p.257.

127 Ibid., p.244.

128 Ibid., pp.243–44.

129 Ibid., pp.244–45.

130 Ibid.

131 Ibid., p.246.

132 Ibid., p.251.

133 Ibid., pp.250–51.

134 Parkinson, pp.180–81.

135 Ibid., p.181.

136 Ibid., p.183.

137 Ibid., pp.183–84.

138 Ibid., p.184.

139 Ibid., pp.184–85.

140 Ibid., p.184.

141 Ibid., p.185.

142 Ibid.

143 Ibid., p.186.

144 Ibid., pp.187–88.

145 Ibid., p.188.

146 E. Wilbraham-Bootle, Parkinson's tutee.

147 Parkinson, p.189.

148 Parkinson, pp.191–92.

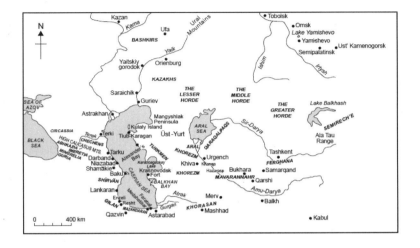

Map 4. The Caspian and Central Asia

8 DAGHESTAN, SHIRVAN AND GHILAN

Introduction

Russian campaigns in Daghestan, 1722

The second Afghan invasion of Persia in 1722 by the chief of the Ghalzai Afghans, Mir Mahmud, and the ensuing collapse of the Safavids provided the perfect opportunity for Peter the Great to extend his control over the Caspian and its trade, and to pre-empt Ottoman moves in the region. Peter the Great had already sent an embassy to Persia in 1715 under Artemi Petrovich Volynski,[1] in which John Bell had participated.[2] Its chief objectives were to conclude a commercial treaty, promote the raw silk trade through Russia rather than through the Levant Company, and to gather information on the Caspian and its rivers, with a view to Indian trade. These official objectives were longstanding Russian ones, but an interest in Persia with a future invasion or intervention in mind also appears to have been contemplated.[3] The treaty was concluded in 1717, even though the failure of the Safavid state and general rebellion were foreseen.[4]

Bruce participated in the first campaign as an officer and engineer. His account, with those of, for example, the officer Feodor Ivanovich Soimonov and the Russian consul at Resht, Semeon Avramov,[5] are major sources for the history of the 1722 invasion. Bell, who was also present, presumably as physician, gives a less comprehensive but more benign account of the campaign.[6] As these campaigns have been much written about,[7] only key extracts from both travellers' accounts are included here, balanced with their observations on peoples and places. Much of the sequence of events as recounted by Bruce has been left as it was written, to give a sense of the author's voice and of an eighteenth-century travel narrative.

Bruce's accounts of the campaigns are corroborated by other contemporary sources. It begins by giving the ostensible reasons for the first invasion: panic in Shamakhie, which had been taken over in an uprising of the major Daghestani clans (Qaitaq, Qaraqaitaq, Ghazi Qumuq and another Lezgi chiefdom) and the resulting murder and plunder of Russian merchants.[8] There was nothing new about either the ill treatment of Russian merchants or the conflict between Christians and Muslims in the region, or the changing allegiances of Caucasian tribes. In the early eighteenth century, however, local tension between Sunni (Daghestanis, Afghans) and Shi'ia (Persian) Muslims also came to a head.[9]

The army, comprising about 99–100,000 men, and a fleet of about 274 vessels[10] set out in the heat of summer. Having passed through Terki, the army entered 'Asia' in early September. Bruce showed the precariousness of travelling through Daghestan and the independence and volatility of local tribal chiefs as the army marched deeper into the region. Bruce and Bell's description of Daghestan's political structure and its 'independent principalities' (which for them represented most of the Caucasus, including the Kabardas) is very general but broadly accurate and already known from Olearius.[11] Northern Daghestan was divided into several feuding clan- and family-based khanates, the principal ones at the time being the shamkhalate of Tarku, the small principality of Utemish and the areas controlled by the Usmi of the Qaitaq and Qaraqaitaq, above and to the east of Darband. Further east and to the south were the Ghazi-Qumuqs and Lezgis. They considered themselves absolute owners of their land, but sided militarily with each other, and with the great powers, either Russia or Persia, when it suited them.[12]

After a friendly but ultimately equivocal reception by Adil Giray, the *Shamkhal* (hereditary ruler) of Tarku (and not of all Daghestan, as stated by Bruce), who had taken an oath of allegiance to Peter in 1719,[13] the march continued to Old Buinaq. Peter had issued manifestoes warning of the Russian advance and intended to commandeer the resources of Daghestan. He sent a summons to Mahmud of Utemish and Akhmad Khan, Usmi of the Qaitaq and Qaraqaitaq, requesting supplies. Having received savage proof of defiance from the khans, as well as facing an army of tribesmen, the Russian army pursued the enemy into Utemish, massacred the population and destroyed villages. Peter then ordered forts to be built at the River Inji and at Malakent, as he was to at the River Sulak (Svyatoi Krest) on his return march,[14] to 'keep these people in awe'.

In contrast Darband, under its deputy governor Imam Quli Beg, surrendered willingly, giving an apparently joyful welcome to the troops. Quli Beg's privileges were confirmed by the Russians and he became major-general of the troops.[15] Further pleas of assistance against the Afghans from Baku and Caucasus Christians were also greatly encouraging to the campaign. Peter's plans were thwarted, however, by the destruction of the fleet's stores in a storm (mentioned by Bell but not by Bruce)[16] and the warnings of a Turkish envoy sent by the Grand Vizier, Damad Ibrahim, not to advance into Shirvan. Whether a decision by the Russians, had their troops been re-supplied, to advance further would have led to outright war is debatable. The Turks had been approached as protectors by Lezgi and Shirvani leaders, and had taken Shamakhie under their protection in 1722, making Da'ud Beg governor of Shirvan.[17]

On his return march Peter found that the forts at Malakent and Inji had been attacked by rebel Persians, Usmi Ahmad Khan and Mahmud of Utemish respectively.[18] A brutal punitive force was sent to deal with them. Peter then demonstrated the Russian strategy of peopling annexable areas with Russians, this time making use of rescued Russian and other Orthodox Christian slaves, who were 'left to inhabit' Svyatoi Krest. This fort, designed by Bruce, was garrisoned with 18,000 infantry and Cossacks under the command of a general.[19] Revolts and reprisals in this area were to continue, including a revolt by the once-friendly Shamkhal Adil Giray, who had been antagonised by the construction of Svyatoi Krest.[20] The revolt was quelled in 1725, Adil Giray was taken captive by the Russians and the shamkhalte abolished,[21] to be revived by Nader Shah in 1734.

The second Russian campaign, which started in November 1722, was precipitated by pleas from the inhabitants of Resht for Russian protection to counterbalance the taking of Shamakhie by the Turks, and for further support for Tahmasp. This campaign resulted in the taking of Resht and Baku in 1723.[22] Bruce did not participate this time, as he was on a mission to survey the Caspian in 1723 (see p.222), but he referred to the taking of Baku and the general situation in Shirvan and Gilan at the time in his survey, from which extracts are included here.[23] Extreme force was used in Baku, where the governor and inhabitants had changed their minds about the Russian 'protection' they had requested. When Baku surrendered, some officials previously appointed by the shah were confirmed in their positions by the Russians,[24] although the desire to evict both Turks and Russians from the area continued. A local plot between the deputy governor (*naip*) of Baku and Hadji Daud, governor of Shirvan, in which a certain Devla Guli Bek was implicated, was foiled. Conspirators were executed or exiled, leaving the town much depleted except for Armenian and Indian merchants.[25] Gilan and Mazanderan provinces had a tradition of independent local clans and dynasties. They had been incorporated into the Safavid state in the sixteenth century, but their resistance to central authority remained. They regularly rebelled and were subject to outside interference by Turks and Russians, and tribal dominance by, for example, the Qajars in Mazanderan.[26] Turkmen raids were also a feature of centres such as Astarabad.[27] The disintegration of the Safavid state fuelled further rebellion, and local governors looked to their own interests.[28]

Bruce skated over the protracted negotiations that officially ceded Gilan, Mazanderan and Astarabad to Russia in 1723. Tahmasp II's envoy, Ismail Bey, who had brokered the treaty with Russia to the displeasure of the shah, ended his days in exile in Astrakhan (see pp.69–70). The Turks were left in control of Shamakhie and part of Shirvan, with the dividing line between Russian and Turkish gains at the confluence of the Kura and Aras rivers.[29] By 1725 the Turks had also occupied Georgia, Armenia and parts of Azerbaijan.[30] Russia relinquished her claims in 1732 and 1735, since the occupation was too costly in terms of logistics, human lives and the rise of Nader Shah.[31] It was not until the reign of Catherine II that Russia again became actively expansionist in this part of the Caucasus and west Caspian.[32] Bruce did not disguise the heavy toll of the 1722 campaigns on the Russian army and its officers. He specifically mentioned the commissioning of more suitable 'ships of burthen' and galleys for future Caspian expeditions under Peter the Great (compare Woodroofe's comments on the Caspian 'fleet' pp.146).

Peoples and places, 1722–23

Bruce and Bell's accounts give only basic information on the towns of Daghestan, Shirvan and Ghilan in 1722; as a soldier and engineer, Bruce focused mainly on fortifications. The notes on Daghestan and Shirvan made by Major (later Colonel) Johann Gustav Gärber, who took part in the 1723 campaign and was later a member of the Russo-Turkish border commission,[33] are also very informative. The records of Soimonov, edited by Academician Müller in 1763, are less telling in this respect.[34] Hanway and Cook's accounts include passages on their experiences in Daghestan and north Persia, but as these areas were part of Persia in the 1740s, they are outside the scope of this book. Daghestan, Shirvan and Gilan were later described by Academician Gmelin,[35] who travelled to Persia in the 1770s and died a hostage in Daghestan in 1774, by Reineggs and, briefly, by Bieberstein, who was in the area in 1796.[36] Some of their observations are included here, as they amplify Bruce and Bell's comments and contribute to a sense of place and history.

Daghestan

Tarku was the capital of the Shamkal of the lowland Turkic Qumuq tribe bordering the Caspian. They were descendents of one of the region's three major feudal principalities (the Qazi Qumuq) of the fifteenth and sixteenth centuries.[37] In the early eighteenth century the territory of the Shamkal stretched from below Kizliar and the border with Circassia to the Buinaq Mountains to the south, where Utemish and the Qaitaq and Qaraqaitaq tribes held sway (not as far as Darband, as Bruce affirmed), north and east of Darband.[38] Tarku was a rich agricultural province that had been nominally under Persian rule until its involvement with Russia. Gärber noted how crucial the principality had been to Persia during its conflicts between Shirvan and Daghestan, and in representing Persian interests in the region. Although receiving a stipend from the shah for these favours, the Shamkal had never given revenue to Persia. It was characteristically Sunni, and its inhabitants spoke a mixture of Turkish, local Tatar (Azeri) and Arabic ('Arap').[39]

Bell and Bruce conveyed the atmosphere of Tarku by each describing a social visit. Bell described the Russian emperor's visit to Adil Giray, while Bruce related a visit by himself and other officers to a private house, where he focused his observations on the women. As already noted, the mention of 'ethnic' or 'foreign' women's beauty, or lack of beauty, was a standard component of eighteenth-century travelogues. Bruce's anecdote brings in two themes that became prominent in nineteenth-century Russian Romanticism and the Caucasus: that of captivity (whether of hostages or of women) and the beauty of Caucasian women.[40] In western European sources these two themes were already established in the eighteenth century, as was the spectacular Caucasian landscape. Bruce's awareness of the literary allure of the subject can be seen in the touch of drama he added to it: the ladies' utterance, when told of the freedom of western women, 'Oh happy, happy country', would not have been out of place in an eighteenth-century British theatre.

Gmelin's observations are somewhat contrary. He noted that Daghestani women (probably depending on their class) were not necessarily secluded but were harshly treated.[41] Bell, while remarking on the looks of Adil Giray's wife and daughter, comments on the emperor's pleasure at the 'romantic situation' of Tarku. At this period a compliant Caucasus could be appreciated for its landscape, but it is doubtful whether Peter the Great would have used the term 'romantic', which became current in the later eighteenth century in Russia[42] and was not used by academicians. Here Bell interpreted the Tsar's feelings, without irony, with a term that was used in England as early as the seventeenth century in relation to the beauty and fertility of a landscape.[43] Bruce's comments on the Caspian range, which 'hide their head in the clouds', and Mount Ararat (confused with Mount Elbrus, which cannot be seen from the Caspian plain and only from the top of Elbrus), were in keeping with most travellers' accounts of the region,[44] but he was also pragmatic, pointing out the mountains' usefulness to mariners.

Peoples

Both Bruce and Bell commented on the manners, religion, dress and physical appearance of the Daghestanis (for Bruce represented by Tarku). Bell was characteristically balanced, referring in passing to Daghestani valour, unruliness, rashness, independence and honour in hospitality. Bruce's assessment, on the other hand is highly derogatory: they are mischievous, barbarous, savage. These labels accord with those of Classical writers such as Herodotus, earlier western travellers in the Caucasus such as Chardin, Olearius,[45] and later academicians.[46] Whereas Gärber described the Daghestanis as brave and fast on horses (as did Cook in the 1740s) and did not dwell on moral character,[47] Gmelin was scathing, describing the people of Daghestan as malicious, rapacious, debauched, cowardly, lethargic, ignorant and lax in their religion. He concluded that it was impossible that 'such unrestrained conditions' should exist so close to the Russian Empire.[48] Whereas Bruce's observations seem almost stereotypical, Gmelin's appear heartfelt, both personally and on behalf of an empire that could not subdue this part of the Caspian.

Issues of religion and language were addressed perfunctorily by the travellers. They observed, for example, that people of this part of the Caucasus were overwhelmingly Sunni Muslim, but with some Shia and Christian Armenians, and spoke a mixture of Turkish, a dialect of Arabic, or Persian. Conversion to Islam in the region had in fact been gradual and piecemeal. Introduced in the seventh or eighth centuries, Islam became widespread, although sometimes only superficially, only from the sixteenth century onwards.[49] Before the Arab conquest, Christianity had been introduced into Daghestan from neighbouring Armenia, Georgia and Albania in the fourth and fifth centuries, and aspects of Christianity survived, together with local pre-Christian religions, into the eighteenth century. In his survey of the 'Tartars' of the Terek and Daghestan, Gärber described them as Sunni (until Persian Shia influence appeared in Shirvan) but gave no hint of the real intricacies of religion in these mountain areas, which also included partial adherence to Islam and Christianity as well as animism, Christian orthodoxy (Armenians) and Judaism. In the coastal towns, mixed populations belonged to several denominations. The complexities of the region's language and religion were more comprehensively addressed by Güldenstadt later in the century.[50]

Darband

Bruce, with Gärber, Gmelin and other travellers, distinguished the different parts of the town of Darband, which was laid out lengthwise and noted for its fortifications and steep walls.[51] Bruce's description tallies with most of Gärber's.[52] The main citadel and garrison, with the khan's residence (parts of which, according to Gmelin resembled 'subterranean holes'), were in the upper town.[53] The deputy governor (*naip*) and most of the population lived in the middle part, where there were many mosques and caravanserais.[54] The lowest part of the town, once inhabited, was largely abandoned by the early eighteenth century. Bruce (with Olearius) and Gärber referred to Greeks and Turks who had once lived in Darband.[55]

Even if the troubles in the 1720s drove non-Muslims away, the population had habitually been mixed, whether because of trade or occupation. Languages spoken there were Farsi (Persian) by the educated classes, and Azeri Turkish.[56] The official religion was Shiism. Bruce borrowed from Olearius a reference to Jews, who were reported to trade in stolen children and other captives.[57] Such 'mountain' Jews (known as Tat or Dagh Čufut), some of whom came from Persia and others possibly of Khazar descent, had intermarried locally but still, according to Gärber, were persecuted everywhere in the region and involved in the most menial work.[58] Writing in the 1770s, Gmelin mentioned a mixed population of about 4000 in Darband, of which some 100 Armenians occupied the upper (and to a lesser extent the lower) parts of the town, with Persians, Turkic Tartars and Indians. The Armenians presumably lived in the upper part of the town because they were both powerful and had to be watched.[59] Gärber, in his general description of Armenians in the region, wrote of their ill treatment in the 1720s and the minor exodus this provoked.[60] Both Armenians and Jews had to pay approximately double the tax of Muslims.[61] Most Armenians were said to have left the region during Nader Shah's time (see pp.77–8).[62] Bell, Gärber and Gmelin mentioned Darband's agricultural richness, yet by the time Gmelin was there, the city, which was then under the absolute control of Fath Ali Khan of Kuba, was impoverished from the khan's taxes and fairly derelict.[63] Its international trade was also poor, partly because of its difficult harbour, although local trade in silks and cottons from Gilan and Shamakhie, in exchange for thin mountain cloth and saffron, was successful. [64]

All observers mentioned the antiquity of Darband and its walls. As both Bruce and Bell commented, legend affirmed that the city was built by Alexander the Great. Alexander's association with the defences of the Dariel Pass (which was then confused with the Darband Pass) against the Scythians and the Amazons derives from the Greek Alexander Romance of the second century BC.[65] It is found in Persian and Arabic histories, medieval eastern and western poetry and accounts by early travellers, such as Rubruck, Marco Polo, Christopher Burroughs, Jenkinson and Olearius.[66] The Sassanians were said to have built on Alexander's foundations in Darband. Thus the legend of Alexander as a protector in the region both preceded and survived the spread of Islam and was still current in the eighteenth century.[67]

The travellers did not generally refer to local oral or written khanate historiographies or traditions. Reineggs was exceptional in quoting from the 'Derbendic History' (i.e. the *Darband-nama*), a history of Daghestan and Darband from the Qubad Sassanian period to the twelfth century. Copies were presented to Soimonov and Peter the Great.[68] A contemporary translation was made by a Kazan Tatar, who was chief translator to the Russian army.[69] Bieberstein mentioned the 'historians of the East' and quoted from d'Herbelot's *Bibliotèque Orientale*.[70] British travellers had either no awareness of these sources, even through interpreters, or had no interest in them. Local traditions relating to Darband burials were mentioned by Gmelin.[71] Gärber and most travellers noted the many old gravestones belonging to different denominations (Persian, Armenian, Tatar and other undecipherable ones) around Darband, which pointed to the town's antiquity and diversity.[72]

187

Astarabad and Resht

Although Bruce's descriptions of towns in his 1723 survey of the Caspian are characteristically brief, even inaccurate, they convey the rich economic life of Mazanderan and the disarray and economic hardship in Gilan brought about by the events of 1722–23. In their descriptions of Astarabad, Bruce and Soimonov recorded only the town's fortifications (Bruce), houses with tiled roofs and extensive surrounding woodland.[73] They ignored the town's monumental architecture, including buildings from the time of Shah Abbas. Resht, according to Bruce, was fortified like Astarabad; by contrast, Soimonov and Gmelin (and Olearius) stressed that it was unfortified and merited the designation of town only because of its position as the centre of the Gilan silk trade.[74] Soimonov was slightly more forthcoming than Bruce, noting Resht's houses with tiled roofs and the Russian merchants' caravanserai, built on the edge of town and resembling a 'castle'.[75]

Bruce's mistake about Resht is perplexing, particularly his statement that the Russians had to build their own defences there. He may have confused Resht with another town, as he was writing up his memoirs; or the fortifications he referred to may have been those of the caravanserai or the commander's, and later governor's or khan's, palace (as described by Gmelin). Bruce said nothing about the thick forest in which Resht was situated and which the Russians partially cleared during their occupation.[76] Gmelin was particularly detailed on Resht, mentioning its eight town quarters, including a Jewish one, the impressive khan's residence containing 'dyed foreign carpets like the Gobelins of Paris', nine mosques and several caravanserais.[77] A redoubt built by the Russians on the Qazvin road still remained in Gmelin's time, though neither the citadel nor the caravanserai survived.[78]

Baku and Svyatoi Krest

Bruce arrived in Baku (fig.16) shortly after it had been taken. His description of the town's defences, towers and famous harbour are broadly corroborated by other travellers. Gmelin again gave a far better idea of the feel of the town. He observed the 'beautiful' buildings of the upper town, including the medieval and later royal palace, a 'noble pile of buildings' (much damaged by the Russians, according to Cook),[79] mosques, the khan's seafront residence, and a newly constructed (c.1770s) palace in the 'Oriental-European' style outside the city, the caravanserai and shops, ordinary flat-roofed houses, and a remaining Russian redoubt.[80] Baku was a multi-ethnic, mercantile town of Persians, Tartars, Armenians, Indians and possibly Jews, and mixed-race inhabitants, where Turkish and Persian were spoken. The town was nominally Shiite and the countryside Sunni, according to Gärber.[81]

fig.16

Bruce and other travellers mention Astarabad as a place of trade, noted for the excellence of its silk and fruits. It was widely acknowledged that Gilan produced the best Persian silk for export, although this trade was much disrupted by the 'troubles', according to Bruce. He showed how

the Russians benefited from this by exchanging surplus silk for provisions in Astrakhan. The 'silk manufactory' he mentioned must have been one of those established by Peter the Great in the early eighteenth century, with French and Italian expertise as well as what could be learnt in Gilan. Early silk manufacturing in Russia (from imported silk) was located in and around Moscow, and Moscow remained a major centre of the industry in the eighteenth century.[82] In 1725 there were about nine silk plants, which produced low-quality, simple goods such as shawls, kerchiefs and ribbons.[83] Luxury items remained imported. Domestically produced silk generally failed in Russia until the 1790s (see Pallas's comments on pp.24 and139).

The second valuable commodity Bruce wrote about was the 'nepht' (naphtha or crude oil) found in wells and springs around Bishbarmak (Barmach) Mountain and Baku. Peter the Great was aware of the value of this oil, which, with salt, was a commodity Baku traded with Iran and Russia. Bruce mentioned buying naphtha; Soimonov reported that all officers and soldiers were given 'portions' of it, and that the Russian crown derived an annual revenue from it.[84] The oil was of two types: white or yellow, and black. It had many uses: in warfare, for lime burning, as fuel, as a religious symbol for Zoroastrians, and in medicine. The white kind burned more rapidly than the black and was less pungent. When distilled it was used in medicine. The black variety was used as fuel and much traded. Both were transported in leather bags or earthen and glass vessels.[85] Bruce made another error in locating Bishbarmak between Resht and Baku, before the River Kura, whereas the mountain lies north of Baku. Naphtha was probably available for sale wherever there were wells along this coastline and, given the renown of the mountain (mentioned by most travellers),[86] locals may have claimed that other peaks were actually Bishbarmak. Bruce may have wished to assert that he had seen the famous mountain or had simply misremembered its location.

Bruce's last proper stop on his survey before returning to Astrakhan was at the fortress of Svyatoi Krest.[87] Gärber wrote that the citadel and 'town' were inhabited by serving peoples, and that the outskirts were teeming with Armenians, Georgians, Chechens and 'mountain' traders.[88] Despite Bruce's optimism, the fortress with its strong garrison was abandoned by the Russians in 1735 for Kizliar (see below).

A punitive expedition and Bruce's first sight of the Caucasus

[T]he emperor made preparations for an expedition to take satisfaction for the injuries he had received from the rebel Persians, bordering on the Caspian sea. Mr Wolinsky [A.P. Volinsky], whom his majesty had sent as ambassador to Myr Maghmut [Mir Mahmud], the usurper, was just returned from Persia, with a very unsatisfactory answer. The people about mount Caucasus, on the west side of the Caspian, had taken Schamachie, in the province of Shirvan, and put three hundred Russian merchants to the sword ... and seized their effects to the amount of above a million rubles: the Russian caravan from China, had been treated in the same manner by the Usbeck Tartars, who were in alliance with the usurper; and the inhabitants of Androfska [Andreov], near the borders of Russia, had made frequent inroads on the Russian territories, and pillaged, burnt, and destroyed, every thing they met with, and carried off a great number of people, of both sexes, into slavery. Mr Wolinsky, who had been sent to demand satisfaction for these insults, returning without being able to obtain the least satisfaction, determined the emperor to seek redress by force of arms ... [see p.165] While this was in agitation, there arrived three successive expresses from Chach Hussein, the dethroned monarch of Persia, imploring his majesty's aid and assistance against the usurper, on conditions too advantageous for so wise a prince to neglect, and which hastened forward the expedition.[89]

On the 20th [July 1722] we weighed from the mouth of the Wolga, under the command of the great admiral Apraxin; their majesties, the emperor and empress, having sailed before us for Terki, the capital of Circassian Tartary ...[see p.155, 165][90]

[T]he fleet sailed [from Terki] in the morning of the 27th, with a very favourable breeze, and passed the island of Trenzini, and soon after we saw land on both sides of us, occasioned by a peninsula which formed a large bay, upwards of forty wrests long, and here we had the first view of the high mountains of Caucasus, which seem to hide their heads in the clouds. The mountains of Taurus and Arrarat, are so contiguous to the Caucasus, that they appear like a continuation of the same mountain, which crosses all Asia, from Andreof or Mongrelia, to the Indies. Mount Arrarat is one vast rock, exceeding even Caucasus itself in height ... It is said to be the same one which the ark rested after the Deluge. The Armenians ... believe there are still some fragments of that ark on this mountain ... Those high mountains are of great use to mariners in these parts of the Caspian, as most of them have very little knowledge of the compass; the different appearances they make toward the sea, serve as an instruction to the pilots in determining whereabouts they are.[91]

(Bruce, July 1722)

A meeting with Adil Giray of Tarku

We ... began our first march in Asia: the heat was so intolerable, that numbers of our men dropt down by the way ... On the 5th [August] we marched ten wrests up the river [Sulak], to a place intended to ferry over our army; on our march we were met by the shafkal [shamkhal] or prince, of Tarku, the chief of the Daghestan Tartars, who was attended by a very grand retinue, and welcomed his imperial majesty into the Daghestan territories, and offered his assistance to the utmost of his power; his subjects, at the same, brought us all manner of refreshments. On the 6th ... [having crossed the river and formed a camp] evening the governor of Gorski, and the governor of Axay, two Daghestan princes, came to wait upon his majesty: the first brought him a present of three fine Persian horses, with rich furniture, and six hundred wagons for the baggage, each drawn by two oxen, besides fifty fat oxen to kill for the army: the latter presented his majesty with six fine Persian horses ... and one hundred oxen for the army ...[92]

(Bruce, August 1722)

The government of Tarku

On the 12th [August 1722], we reached the city of Tarku; the shafkal [shamkhal Adil Giray] met the emperor half-way, and conducted him to the city; it stands on the side of a hill, quite open, without any walls, and our army encamped on a spacious plain below the town. Being now arrived at the capital of Daghestan Tartary, I shall endeavour to give some description of the province and city, from the best information I could obtain. Their territory reaches from the river Bustow, their boundary with Circassia, all along mount Caucasus, as far as Derbent, and they are neither subject to the Turk not the Persian, but are in general governed by the shafkal, who is their supreme head: his office is not hereditary but elective. The whole country of Daghestan is divided into small districts or lordships, each under the jurisdiction of its proper lord, or myrza, who, though hereditary, is nevertheless not absolute, but his authority is controlled by that of some of the chiefs among them. All these petty lords acknowledge one whom they call shaskal as supreme head, to whom they pay their respect, but not passive obedience.[93]

(Bruce, August 1722)

'The sovereignty of Daggestan'

The country [Daghestan] is divided into several free independent principalities, as KABERDA [Kabarda], SHAFFKAL, USSMEY [Schamkal and Usmi are titles] and many others, who are at first elected by the people; and though that office is sometimes known to continue in the family of the person elected for several generations, yet it hath frequently happened, that, either through male-administration, or in consequence of wars among those different states, a chieftain with his family have been deposed, or banished, and another appointed in his place. It hath been known that the Sophy of PERSIA hath placed and displaced some of those princes among the DAGGESTANS, who lye the most contiguous to PERSIA. Both the Sophy and the OTTOMAN PORTE lay claim to the sovereignty of DAGGESTAN; but, of late years, those people, trusting to their own valour and the natural strength of the country, pay little regard to these mighty monarchs, who sometimes threaten them, at other times court their friendship.[94]

(Bell, 1722)

Dress in Daghestan

Their habit is a long close coat, commonly of a dark grey, or black, coarse cloth, over which they wear a cloak of the same stuff; and in winter, of sheep skins: they wear a square cap of a great many pieces sewed together; their shoes are for the most part made of horses hides, sewed together only at the instep; the poorest man among them is provided with a coat of mail, head-piece, and bucket, besides a scimitar, javelin, bow and arrows.[95]

(Bruce, 1722)

Observations on religion and physique

The religion of the Daggestans is generally MAHOMETAN; some follow the sect of OSMAN, others that of HALY. Some of those people are CHRISTIANS of the eastern or GREEK church. Their language for the most part, is TURKISH, or rather a dialect of the ARABIC, though many of them speak also the PERSIAN language.

The men are for the most part, well made, many of them are employed in the service of the Sophy, and frequently raised to high stations … As to their women, they are esteemed to be the most beautiful of any in ASIA, as well for features and complexion, as also for fine shape; on which account many of these poor girls are purchased, at high rates, or stolen away, for the use of the seraglios at ISPAHAN, CONSTANTINOPLE, and other eastern courts.[96]

(Bell, 1722)

'Mischievous, barbarous, and savage'

These people are generally very mischievous, barbarous, and savage, living for the most part by robbery and plunder; a great part of their livelihood is for men to steal children, not sparing even those of their nearest relations, whom they sell to the neighbouring Persians … They are called Dagestans, from the word Dag, which signifies in their language, a mountain, and are from thence called mountaineers; they pretend to be the descendants of the Amazons …[97]

(Bruce, 1722)

Hospitality admired

One article I cannot omit concerning their hospitality, which is, if their greatest enemy comes under their roof for protection, the landlord, of what condition soever, is obliged to keep him safe, from all manner of harm or violence, during his abode with him, and even to conduct him safely, through his territories, to a place of security.[98]

(Bell, 1722)

Tarku's houses and women

The city [of Tarku] … contains above three thousand houses, and is very full of inhabitants; the houses are all two stories high, platformed on top, standing close to one another: the women walk upon them in the cool of the evenings, as the men do in the streets. Every house has a garden stored

193

with all kinds of delicious fruits, and all well supplied with fine springs of water: as for their women, they are incomparably beautiful. Both in feature and shape, with a fair, clear complexion, accompanied with lovely black eyes and hair; but as the men are very jealous, they are always locked up, so that it is no easy matter to get a sight of them; and I believe we should not have seen any of them if it had not happened ... by accident.[99]

(Bruce, 1722)

Fit for a prince

This place [Tarku] is pleasantly situated in a hollow between two high hills, rising, like an amphitheatre, to within a small distance of the top; having a full view of the CASPIAN sea. The Prince's house is the uppermost, and overlooks the whole town; it consists of several apartments, with a spacious hall, after the PERSIAN manner, having a terrass and small garden adjoining.[100]

(Bell, 1722)

Society in Tarku

Next morning, the Aldiggerey [Adil Giray] came and waited on their Majesties, and invited them to dinner; which was accepted of.

Towards noon, the Princess, spouse to the Adilggerey, came and paid her respects to the Empress ... This lady came in the equipage of the country, that is, in a covered wagon, drawn by a yoke of oxen, with a few footmen to attend her, and escorted by a small party of horse. The lady, though somewhat advanced in years, had still the remains of a handsome person. She had along with her, in the wagon, a young lady, her daughter, who was so pretty that she would have been deemed a beauty in any part of EUROPE. When they entered the Empress's tent, her Majesty stood up to receive them; they then took off their veils, and behaved with great decency. They were richly dressed after the PERSIAN fashion. After they had drank a dish of coffee, they took their leave, and returned to the town.

Soon after their departure, the Emperor and Empress went to the town to dine. The emperor went on horseback, the Empress in her coach, attended by some of the court-ladies, and escorted by a battalion of the guards. The street was so narrow, and, near the palace, so steep, that the coach and six horses could not proceed quite to the palace; which, when her Majesty perceived, she alighted from her coach, and walked the rest of the way on foot. The Emperor was much pleased with the romantic situation of the place. In the evening they returned to the camp.[101]

(Bell, 1722)

Behind the scenes in a Tarku household

We had the liberty to go into the city to buy necessaries ... and being in town one day with several officers, well escorted, we saw one of the principal inhabitants going into his house, when we made bold to throng in with him ... much against his inclination ... [but] being informed by our interpreter, that we were officers of rank ... he at last reluctantly consented, and led us into his apartments; the floors were all covered with very fine Persian tapestry, without any other kind of ornament, excepting some fine mattresses, and silk quilts, upon which they lie at night; they have neither chairs nor tables, but all sit or lie on the floor: instead of glass in the windows, they have blinds, very curiously checkered of plaited reed, through which they can see what passes in the street without being seen within; the walls and ceilings are all white, without any ornament. After this he led us into a square court, divided in the middle by a high wall, which separated his own apartments from those of the women; having shewed us also his garden, very well stored with all kinds of fruit, he invited us to sit down with him on a sofa under a piazza, and entertained us with coffee, fruits and sweet-meats; when captain Brunie ... shewed him a very pretty shaving-glass he carried in his pocket, and observing he was much pleased with it, the captain made him a present of it, which seemed to ingratiate us with him ... we begged the favour of him to let us see his women in their dress, only at a distance; to which ... he at last consented ... [he] went himself to their apartments to order them to get ready ... he then went in again, and brought out four of his wives, and eight of his concubines, and placed them all in a row that we might have full view of them, in which posture he left them standing ... the ladies, however, seemingly displeased to be gazed at, at such a distance, advanced with one accord, and seated themselves upon a sofa opposite to us, at which forwardness our host seemed not at all pleased, and they, not regarding him in the least, examined our dress very narrowly, and put many questions to us, by our interpreter, especially relating to the customs and dress of our women, and how many women were allowed in our country to each man; on being informed that no man was allowed to have more than one wife, and that women had the same liberty as the men to walk abroad and visit their neighbours; they clapped their hands, and cried out with emotion, 'O! happy, happy country!'. Our host not being at all pleased at their conduct, ordered them immediately to their apartments, and they obeyed with much reluctance. They were all most lovely creatures, but the concubines excelled the wives in beauty: the reason is obvious, for they are married to their wives by proxy, and the others taken from choice.[102]

(Bruce, 1722)

Politics and resistance

His Majesty's manifestos having been published, not only throughout Daghestan, but also Derbent, Backu, and Schamachie; letters were received from Derbent, on the 15th [August 1722], with assurances, that the manifestoes were received with great joy there, and that they would, with the utmost pleasure, put themselves under the emperor's protection whenever he arrived there with his army.[103]

This day [17 August] we passed the river Manas ... and the river Boinak [Buinak] and encamped for the night at Old Boinack, having marched thirty wrests, and come through large fields of cotton and saffron ... From this place his majesty dispatched three Cossacks, with a guide, to sultan Udenich [Mahmud of Utemish] who lived at some distance among the mountains, requiring him to send a deputation in order to a conference, and desiring him to supply the army with beasts of burden, to transport our baggage to Derbent.

On the 18th we marched twenty-five wrests, and encamped on the banks of the river Nitzi [Inji] where the guide returned to us, with sultan Udenich's answer, having his nose and both ears cut off, and informed his majesty that they had, in his presence, put the three Cossacks to death, in a most cruel and barbarous manner: the sultan bade him tell the emperor, that whoever of his people fell into his hands they should be treated in the same manner, and as to the desired conference, they were ready to hold it with their scymitars in their hands.

On the 19th, the Tartars appeared on the side of the hill, about twelve thousand strong, to put their threats into execution ... a great slaughter ensued, and the Tartars fled ... leaving behind them six and seven hundred men dead on the spot, and forty were taken prisoners; among whom there were some persons of distinction, and their Mahometan priest, who had been one of their principal leaders, and not only advised but perpetrated with his own hands, that horrid cruel murder of the three Cossacks, cutting open their breasts while they were yet alive, and taking out their hearts, and whose bodies were afterwards found stuck upon stakes near the sultan's palace ... our dragoons ... pursued the enemy to the very gates, which they also entered, putting every one they met to the sword, amounting to upwards of three thousand men; for they had sent away their women and children to the mountains ... besides the slain, the sultan's residence and six other villages were burnt and entirely destroyed.[104]

Lord admiral Apraxin, who commanded the army in chief, had been examining some of the prisoners, and asking them why they had put our innocent messengers to so cruel a death, they replied that it was done by their sultan's orders at the instigation of the priest: the priest being thereupon interrogated, very boldly answered, that he would have done the same to every one of our people ... to revenge the treatment of the Tartars of Andreof [Andreov] had received from us … besides they were a free nation, and would subject themselves to no prince on earth. [105]

The emperor, with a view to keep these people in awe, ordered a fort to be erected on the river Nitzi, under the direction of baron Renne, lieutenant of the guards, as engineer, and all the Kalmuck Tartars, some with Cossacks, were left to cover and protect the works.[106]

(Bruce, 1722)

The city of Darband

The 23rd [August 1722], we continued our route through … delightful vineyards … to Derbent. His majesty was met half way by the governor and principal citizens, who presented him with the keys of their city, offering, at the same time, to admit their troops into the citadel, to garrison it for the protection of their city, which had defended itself against the arms of the usurper Maghmud [Mahmud, son of Mir Wais, chief of the Ghalzai Afghans]: this generous offer met a very gracious reception. We marched through the city… under a triple salvo of their artillery, and encamped on the south side of the town, being now entered for the first time into Persia. We could now see Mount Ararat from our camp, rearing his summit far above the rest of the Caucasus. The emperor now appointed a governor and three thousand men to garrison the castle, to whom the inhabitants, with much joy, gave the immediate possession of …

The city of Derbent, in the province of Shirvan … is situated on the shore of the Caspian; the walls are carried into ten feet deep of water, to prevent one's passing that way; its length from east to west, is nearly five wrests, but its breadth is not proportionable. It is not only the frontier of Persia, lying on its utmost confines on this side, but may with great propriety be called the gate of it, reaching from the mountain into the sea. The city is divided into three distinct quarters; the castle situated at the top of the mountain, had always a strong Persian garrison. The second, and principal, reaches from the foot of the mountain to the lower town, which makes the third, and reaches the sea-side. This last, which was formerly inhabited by Greeks, is not now much frequented, being for the most part converted into gardens, since the place was regained from the Turks. The whole city is enclosed with a very strong wall, so broad that a wagon may drive along the top of it without the least inconvenience, and flanked with square towers at proper distances. The walls are built with large square stones, which appear like a heap of sea shells cemented together, yet are hard and durable as marble, and when polished look extremely beautiful. The houses are built and furnished in the same manner as those of Tarku; the inhabitants are all Mahometans, except some Jews, whose chief business is trading in stolen children, brought to market here by the neighbouring Tartars of Daghestan; or some Turkish or Russian captives, which they pick up on some of their excursions, which the Jews carry farther into Persia, and dispose of.[107]

The natives in general are of opinion, that the city of Derbent was built by Alexander the Great, and that the long wall [on the mountains above the sea] ... reached to the Euxine [Black Sea], was built by his order, to prevent the incursions of the Scythians into Persia.[108]

(Bruce, 1722)

Darband and environs

The situation [of Darband] is very pleasant, rising gradually from the sea to the top of the hill, commanding a very extensive prospect, especially towards the south-east. About thirty miles due south stands one of the highest mountains in PERSIA, called SHACH-DAGH [Shah Daghi] which is always covered with snow. To the eastward of the town are many large vineyards ... of which they make a considerable quantity of both white and red wine, of strength sufficient to preserve it round the year, and longer if required. The people of substance there keep their wine in jars, buried under ground, by which method it will keep good for years.

They have also fruitful plains in the neighbourhood; and, at some distance, is a large forest of walnut-trees, oaks, etc. As this place is a frontier of great importance, the Sophy of PERSIA always appoints a person of distinction for its governor.[109]

(Bell, 1722)

Malakent Fort

Thirteen store ships having arrived at the mouth of the river Millukenti [Malakent] with provisions, from Astrachan, for the army, we marched thither [on the 24th August] and found them at anchor. Here his majesty proposed to make a harbour for his ships on the Caspian, as there was no other place near Derbent fit for that purpose, and I received orders to erect a fort to cover it: the dragoons were immediately set to work to provide fascines and palisades, and the infantry to break the ground.[110]

Two messengers now arrived in our camp; the one from the city of Schamachie, and the other from Baku, imploring his majesty's assistance against Myr Maghmud, the usurper; and very soon after came three messengers, viz. from the Armenians, Melitener, and the Georgians, who all of them of the communion of the Greek church; praying the emperor to send some of his troops to enable them to defend themselves against the usurper, as they were fully determined to persevere in their allegiance to their rightful sophi ...[111]

(Bruce, 1722)

The Ottoman threat

Our army was in readiness to set forward the next day, when, to our great surprise, a Turkish ambassador arrived from Schamachie, informing the emperor that they had taken possession of that city, and that it was by orders of the grand signor his master, that he came to signify to his majesty, the umbrage taken by the Porte at the progress he had made in those parts; and likewise to desire him to withdraw his forces; and if the emperor should refuse, to declare war against Russia. Upon weighing this matter duly, his majesty did not think it proper to proceed, as he did not chose, at this juncture to have any rupture with the Turks ... he therefore immediately resolved to return back ... the provinces which had so earnestly sought our assistance, were afterwards obliged to put themselves under the protection of the Turks.

All these troubles and disorders at this time in Persia were occasioned by the indolence and sloth of Shah Hussein [Shah Sultan Hussein] ...[112]

(Bruce, 1722)

Return to Daghestan

[A]n express arrived from Derbent, which informed his majesty that a body of 10,000 rebel Persians had attacked our fort at the river Millukenti that the enemy were obliged with the loss of 600 men; and that the other fort, at the river Nitzi, had been surprised and taken by sultan Udinach, who had quartered all the garrison, and crucified the officers ... The emperor now lost no time in dispatching a body of light horse ... 10,000 Cossacks and 15,000 Kalmuck Tartars, who went with such expedition, that they came upon them living in the utmost security; put several thousands of their men to the sword, the two sultans Udinach [Mahmud of Utemish] and Maghmut [Usmi Ahmad Khan] very narrowly escaped, leaving their women, children and cattle, a prey to the vanquishers, besides their slaves, the whole amounting to several thousand of both sexes. Among the slaves were four hundred and thirty-seven Russians, of both sexes, who were now left to inhabit the new city of Swetago-Krest; the emperor allowed the captors two rubles a head for the Russians ... When the remaining prisoners were offered for sale, there were found among them upwards of two hundred Georgian slaves, all Christians of the Greek church; for these an agreement was made with the captors at ten rubles a head ... and they were likewise left to people the new town.[113]

We lost on this destructive expedition, above one third of our whole army, not in battle, but by sickness and fatigue.[114]

(Bruce, 1722)

Bruce on campaign, October 1722

[A]n express arrived from Resht ... desiring his majesty to send them a sufficient number of ... troops to defend them against the usurper Myr-Maghmut, and offering to put their strong city into our possession ... at the time of their landing [1000 men], the usurper being near the town ... the inhabitants were afraid to admit our troops into the town ... on receiving intelligence of this general Lawasof [V.Y. Levashov] was sent with four thousand more men to join them, and ... the inhabitants admitted them into the city ... and we remained in full possession of the province, without the least disturbance from the usurper.[115]

It may be proper to observe here, that the jealousy which the march of our army into those parts, had excited in the Turks, and the umbrage they had taken at it, was afterwards adjusted by our ambassador at Constantinople, where it was mutually agreed that the Turks should keep Shamachie; that Armenia, Melitener[116] and Georgia, should remain under their protection; and that the emperor, if he chose it, might subdue all the provinces bordering on the Caspian sea.[117]

His majesty being now determined to make all his conquests in future by sea, without running the risque of ruining an army with marching again by land, gave immediate orders to build a sufficient number of ships of burthen, and finding our former gallies too small for any distant expedition, gave likewise orders to build number of double gallies of forty oars, to contain above three hundred men each ... He left General Matuskin [Matyushkin] here to command the army ...[118]

We left all our gallies here, and proceeded in open boats up the ... Wolga, so that instead of enjoying any rest in this place, we were again put to intolerable hardships; and we who had the honour of being the body guards of this indefatigable monarch, underwent greater fatigues, harder duty, and severer punishment for neglect of it, upon all occasions, than any of the rest of his army.[119]

(Bruce, October 1722)

At Astarabad

The city of Astrabat [Astarabad, modern Gorgan] stands on the river Nare [Gurgan?] ... Astrabat is fortified with high and thick walls, flanked with towers, and is a place of great trade. This makes the southern extremity of the Caspian sea, and lies in 36 deg. 50 min. north lat. This province, with the neighbouring provinces of Terebat [Tabarsaran], Massanderan [Mazandaran] and Gilan, produce abundance of raw silk, coffee, saffron, and cotton; their silk is esteemed the best in all Persia, and by it they carry on a great trade to different parts, especially to Russia, where a silk manufactory is established at Moscow. This country abounds with the most delicious fruits of all kinds, especially their grapes, which are surprisingly large. In coasting the country from hence we made very particular enquiries of the inhabitants concerning some whirlpools, laid down near this shore in some old maps, but we could neither hear nor discover the least appearance of any such thing. In passing the provinces of Terebat and Massanderan, we saw a most delightful country, abounding with plantations of mulberry trees, and watered by a great number of rivers, whose banks were full of houses, and wherever we landed the people shewed us the utmost civility, furnishing us most cheerfully with whatever we wanted at an extraordinary cheap rate (see note 120).

(Bruce, 1723)

The Gulf of Sinsili [Insily] and Resht

On the 18th [July 1723] arrived at the gulf of Sinsili ... we went through this gulf in four fathom water ... to the city of Resht, the capital of the province of Gilan ... the city is square, and fortified in the same manner as Astrabat, with strong walls and towers.

General Leewatof [V.Y. Levashef] was now governor, with a garrison of 5.000 men: they were employed at this time in building a citadel of five bastions to command both the town and harbour ...

Provisions were both scarce and dear at present, as the rebels had plundered and laid waste the whole country as far as Baku, and what they had, both for the support of the inhabitants and garrison, they were supplied with from Astrachan. The raw silk, of which the inhabitants had great quantities on their hands, for want of sale during the troubles, they sent to Astrachan in the transports which had brought the troops to Resht, and they had provisions in return for their silk.[120]

[After two weeks] we set out again northward ...we arrived at the river Linkeran [Lankaran] on the 4th of August. Not far from this river stands the famous mountain Barmach [Bishbarmak], remarkable for the oil called naphta, which issues from it in thirty different pits ... the oil is of two kinds, brown and white: the brown is of a strong disagreeable smell ... it is used for burning in lamps, in dressing of leather ...; the white ... has a pleasant smell, is the most valuable, and is used as an infallible remedy in strains and bruises ... I bought several jars of each kind, and carried with me to Astrachan, where it proved to be a very desirable commodity.[121]

(Bruce, 1723)

At Baku

On the 18th [August 1723], we arrived at the river Cyrus, or Kur [Kura] which is joined by the river Araxis [Aras] and is the most considerable river on the western coast of the Caspian ... We proceeded for the city of Baku, where we arrived the next day, just after General Matushkin [M.A. Matyushkin] [had started] his return to Astrachan. Baku had surrendered after a short bombardment, and brigadier Knez [Prince] Baratinsky was left governor of the city, with a garrison of four thousand men. Baku ... is very strongly fortified with three walls within each other, each with towers, and which forms three distinct divisions of the city; the innermost standing on the highest ground, by way of a citadel, commands the rest: it is mounted with a number of brass cannon. The governor with his garrison, took possession of this part; the outer wall is well supplied with iron cannon, the gates were strongly guarded ... At small distances from the city, stand three high watch-towers, built on eminences, from which they can discover the approach of any enemy by sea or land, at a great distance. At the south end of the city, there is a large bay formed by a peninsula ... and forms a very spacious commodious harbour, where ships can load and unload close to the gates of the city, in four and a half fathom water, safe from all winds except the south ... this harbour is, without dispute, one of the most commodious for trade, in all the Caspian; especially with Schamachie [Shamakhie] which is reputed to be the largest and most populous city in those parts, and is only three days journey from hence. At Schamachie there are factories from all the eastern nations, which occasions that city to be much resorted to from all parts.[122]

(Bruce, 1723)

Svyatoi Krest fortress, Daghestan

[2 September 1723] We proceeded ... along the coast ... to the river Sulack; and I went the same evening, in the twelve-oared boat, fifteen wrests up the river to the fortress of Swetago Krest, or Holy Cross, where I found the fortifications surprisingly advanced, and wooden houses built on both sides of the river in regular streets, agreeable to the plan, and so numerous that the whole army were now lodged in them. The wooden bridge was also finished, with two draw bridges ... so that easy communication was opened between both sides of the river. The troops here were in good health and high spirits, and kept up a weekly correspondence with the garrisons of Derbent and Terki in Circassia; neither of which had been molested by the Daghestan Tartars since we left them … This fort promises fair to be an effectual check upon the irruptions of the Daghestans into the Russian territories, in which they used to do much mischief, and carry off a number of inhabitants into slavery.[123]

(Bruce, 1723)

Daghestan in the 1740s

Nader Shah reunited much of Iran during his rise to power and rule (*c*.1727–47), as well as regaining Shamakhie and territories relinquished by Russia. His attempts to subdue Daghestan, however, were more protracted. Nader waged several campaigns in the area (1734, 1735 and 1741–43), at first with both the Ottomans and Daghestanis and finally in revenge for his brother's killing by the Lezgis in 1738. Khans who submitted, such as the former schamkal of Tarku, were restored to their offices. With others, such as the Qaraqaitaqs, who persisted in resisting, the policy was similar to the Russian one: burning of villages, resettlement, building of forts.[124]

Nader partially blamed the Russians for his difficulties in Daghestan. He intended to march north to Kizliar in 1742 but was forced to return south in early 1743 because of Ottoman agitation and to prepare for a new campaign against the Turks. Daghestan was thus left partially unsubdued.[125] Cook's entry (from his own publication and from a diary in Hanway) shows how Nader's advances in Daghestan frightened the Russians, who expected war. It also shows how Nader's poorly rationed, exhausted troops suffered in the intractable Daghestani terrain in snow and driving rain,[126] and records the characteristic (no doubt temporary) offer of allegiance to Russia from Daghestani chiefs in the face of Nader's advance. A petition to General Tarakanov to this effect, listing seven chiefs and their troops (supposedly more than 66.000 men), of which the Usmi Ahmed Khan and the 'tribe of Aparz' constituted the biggest forces, is given in Hanway's survey of Persian history.[127] Cook, who was by Enzili when Nader was murdered in 1747 in a conspiracy,[128] and Hanway[129] are valuable sources for the history of Nader Shah and the rebellious atmosphere in Gilan, Mazanderan and Shirvan in the 1740s, although this history falls outside the scope of this book. [130]

Cook's comments on Daghestan and Daghestanis in general are sweeping and, as he acknowledged, derived from Olearius. He did attempt, however, to clarify broad differences between the northern and south-eastern Daghestanis (Lezgis). Cook also differs from earlier commentators in his description of these 'Tartars'. To him, although guilty of 'rapine', they were 'well made' and 'the bravest people in the world', who did not 'violate the laws of hospitality'. In this context it was Nader Shah who was the 'barbarian'.

Cook noted the early Christian presence in the region and the Daghestanis' laxness as 'Mahommedans'. The latter, with regard to the Lezgis, was confirmed by Gmelin.[131] The crosses Cook referred to are Georgian and Armenian ones.[132] Cook also commented on Daghestani trade, with particular reference to the circulation of 'false' (counterfeit) Persian money, in which the Armenians colluded. Persia was habitually short of ready money, for reasons that ranged from royal hoarding to an outward flow of money to the holy places, which resulted in pressure on reliable currency. Money was also regularly debased.[133] In Gilan and Mazanderan the situation was still more complicated, since each khan struck his own coins and fixed their value. In 1779 in Shirvan, according to Gmelin, there was nothing but 'adulterated' money, which was easily counterfeited and could result in great loss to traders.[134]

After the death of Nader Shah, the political balance of Daghestan, Shirvan and Ghilan changed with the rise of the khanate of Kuba under Fath Ali Khan. The Qaitaq and Qaraqaitaq (under an Usmi), and the schamkalate of Buinaq survived, albeit sometimes divided between warring family members,[135] but were kept in check by Fath Ali Khan, who also dominated Shirvan and parts of Ghilan. His gains gradually receded after his death in 1789. Güldenstadt, Gmelin, Ellis (from Pallas and Güldenstadt), Reineggs and Bieberstein list Daghestani districts, family numbers and their respective overlords at this period.[136] The schamkalate of Tarku veered between subjection to Russia and attempted independence. In 1796 Catherine II launched a campaign against Persia in the wake of Persia's attack on Georgia, under Agha Mohammed Khan Qajar, in 1795. The Russians' ambitious aim was to subdue Daghestan en route. The campaign was predictably only partially successful; some khanates offered (temporary) submission, and local supporters were installed in Darband and Shirvan. The Russians left in 1797 after the Emperor Paul curtailed the mission. Despite withdrawal, the Russians persisted in their policy to acquire the west coast of the Caspian under General P. Tsitsianov in the early 1800s.[137]

'The troublesome Daghestans'

The summer was not far advanced, when Lieutenant-general Tarakanoff was dispatched with three regiments to Kizlaar, to accept of a proposed friendship and fidelity from any of the Circassian, Georgian, and the rest of the Daghestan Tartar chiefs, and also to observe the motions of Kouli Khan [Nader Shah], upon whose honour little trust was to be put …

The Georgian prince, general of artillery accompanied by many of his natives, arrived in Astrachan ... [and waited] in expectation that war would soon be declared against the Persians. Indeed with us every thing looked very much that way. In Astrachan, amongst the great, every thing was transacted with such secrecy, that nothing from them was to be known ... but amongst the officers ... it was said, that a very considerable army of regulars were on their march for Astrachan.[138]

I doubt not that such reports, and the troublesome Daghestans, who, at different times, cut off the flower of Kouli Khan's army, hindered that barbarian from falling upon the city of Kizlaar, and borders of Russia; for he advanced as far as Targu [Tarku], where his army, starving, having very scanty allowance of provisions, was by day and night, almost constantly assaulted by small bodies of these brave highlanders; and at last, in no small confusion, with the loss of the greatest part of his artillery, was obliged to retire to a castle he had built, as a bridle upon Usmei [Usmi], a Dagestan potent prince ...[139]

(Cook, c.1742)

Daghestanis and Lezgis

The Tartars from the borders of Astrachan to Derbent, are all Mahometans, of the sect of the Turks; but some things make me believe, that a majority of them had formerly professed the Christian religion. They have meetings at certain times of the year, where they divert themselves, without being able to account for the cause, any other way than that their ancestors did so before them, but these times correspond exactly with the times appointed by the Greek church for their festivities: Add to this, that I was assured there were at this day very many crosses of stone erected in this hilly country, and that the natives kept their annual meetings at or near these crosses, where they yet remain ...[140]

The difference between the Daghestan and Lesgee Tartars, I think is not clear in authors; I therefore desire my readers to remember, that I call the Daghestan Tartars, those who inhabit the hills between Derbent, and Circassia; and I call those who inhabit the hills south, and south-east of Derbent, all the way to the banks of Cura, Lesgee Tartars.[141]

(Cook, 1747)

Lezgis in the 1740s

As the neighbourhood of this city [Darband] is the country of the LESGEE TARTARS; before we depart from hence, it is necessary we should say something concerning them, and the more as they are well known to be some of the bravest people in the world. Their country extends south from the near the latitude of about 40 leagues, and 25 westward. They are under several chiefs (SCHEMKALLS), who, in case of danger to their common liberty, unite their forces. Some few have been occasionally subjected to the PERSIANS; but the CARACAITA [Qara-Qeytaq] (a species of LESGEES so called) and their neighbours to the north and west of PERSIAN dominions, it does not appear, at any period of time, that they have ever submitted. Indeed their situation is such, with regard to the natural bulwarks of their mountains, that so long as they retain their virtue, they can hardly be enslaved: their chief is called OUSMAI [Usmi – a title]. Olearius gives an account of the humourous manner of their chusing the SCHEMKALL. This is done by a priest throwing a golden apple in a ring, round which the candidates are seated, and the person whom it stops at, becomes their sovereign; but as they live under a kind of republican government, the distinction paid him is not very considerable.

These people are able to bring 30 or 40 thousand men into the field. The residence of the OUSMAI is about 30 ENGLISH miles north-west of DERBEND. They have had frequent wars with the PERSIANS, and lastly with NADIR SHAH, who, with 15,000 men, pursued a large body of them into the hills; but was at length glad to retreat, after sustaining a very considerable loss. Several PERSIANS, who were taken prisoners on that occasion, were cruelly maimed in their noses, ears, or eyes and sent to NADIR with messages of defiance.

These people are often guilty of rapine, not only in the low-lands, and in large bodies, but also in flying parties, pillaging the ARMENIANS and GEORGIANS, whose trade brings them between BAKU and DERBEND; otherwise they are often obliged to pay a heavy contribution for a safe convoy. These TARTARS are however remarkable in this, that if any stranger travelling in their country, or on the borders of it, seeks their protection, and chuses a guide from among them, let him meet never so strong a party, it is enough if the guide declares that the stranger is his guest; for they are hardly known to violate the laws of hospitality ...(see note 142)

(Edited diary of Cook, 1746, in Hanway)

The Lezgis' appearance and religion

In their persons they [the Lezgis] are well made, of good stature, and extremely active: their countenance is swarthy, their features regular, and their eyes black, full of life.

Their dress resembles the GREEK or ARABIAN manner, many of them wearing the same kind of drawers reaching down to their ankles. Their caps are not so lofty as those of the PERSIANS, neither do all of them wear their beards, some preferring whiskers only.

They live after the manner of the PERSIANS, professing the MAHOMMEDAN religion; but at the same time they talk very lightly of the pretended miracles of MAHOMMED; adding, that he was a very artful man, and whether he has any particular interest with the ALMIGHTY, will be best known hereafter. That they once professed the CHRISTIAN religion, seems to be in the highest degree probable. A FRENCH missionary (a JESUIT, with whom I was particularly acquainted in GHILAN, and from whom I received the greatest part of this account), who resided some time in their country, affirms, that he found among them several books relating to CHRISTIANITY. The same is confirmed by the expedition which NADIR SHAH made, when, among other spoils, he brought away divers books, some of which he had the curiosity to order to be translated; and from thence it appeared that they had been CHRISTIANS. The PERSIANS will hardly be persuaded that they do not continue as such, seeing that they drink wine without reserve, and marry but one woman (according to the missionary's account, others say that a plurality is allowed ...) (see note142).

(Edited diary of Cook, 1746, in Hanway)

The Lezgis' farming and manufacturing

Their [the Lezgis'] vallies are exceeding fertile, producing plenty of wheat, oats, and barley, with abundance of sheep, whilst their hills are covered with vines, from which they make very good wine, and have great plenty of it. Their country is for the most part very pleasant. They are ingenious in several manufactures of wool and camels hair; and none of the neighbouring nations equal them in making fire-arms, which they sell to the PERSIANS. The ARMENIANS bring them dyed calicoes, and other manufactures of PERSIA, also rings, knives, and ear-rings made in EUROPE, in return of which they receive madder (a root which dyes red); also fire-arms, and coarse woollen manufactures; together with false PERSIAN money; for as the coin of this empire is made small and thick, it is counterfeited exactly with very little silver. It is said the ARMENIANS accept of this counterfeit for a quarter of it's current value; however this may be, it is certain there are great quantities of this money in PERSIA, not only silver, but gold also. These TARTARS trade likewise with the RUSSIANS with their madder, taking in exchange, shoes, boots, and cloathing of dressed sheep-skins.[142]

(Edited diary of Cook, 1746, in Hanway)

Endnotes

1   Governor of Astrakhan, 1719–25.

2   Bell, pp.36–142.

3   Lockhart 1958, pp.103–4,176; Mamedova, pp.12–14, 108.

4   Lockhart 1958, pp.125–26.

5   Mamedova, *passim*; see also the references in Lockhart 1958.

6   Bell, vol.2, pp.323–72.

7   E.g. Baddeley; Lockhart 1958 (this remains the best and most fundamental source in English); Atkin 1988; Hughes; Khodarkovsky 1999 and Barrett 1995 (for the background). For the eighteenth century, see also e.g. Gordon; Hanway, vol.2.

8   Mamedova, p.19, points out that the amounts reported to have been taken vary.

9   Lockhart 1958, p.7.

10 The precise numbers are unclear. Soimonov 1763, p.65, gives 106,000 men, including 5000 sailors, but see Lockhart 1958, p.179.

11 Olearius 1669, p.302.

12 Barthold and Bennigsen 1965, pp.85–88; Atkin 1988, pp.142–43; Bennigsen-Broxup, p.22.

13 Lockhart 1958, p.176.

14 Ibid., p.183.

15 Gärber, p.85.

16 Bell, vol.2, p.389.

17 Lockhart 1958, pp.216–17.

18 Ibid., p.188.

19 Bruce, p.294.

20 Lockhart 1958, pp.355–56.

21 Gärber, p.71.

22 Lockhart 1958, pp.242–46.

23 See also Gordon, pp.266–67.

24 Gärber, p.98.

25 Ibid.

26 Vasmer and Bosworth, pp.938–39; Spuler 1965, pp.1111–12; Nikitine and Bosworth, p.450. See also Ebulgazi Bahadur Khan, pp.731–37.

27 Vasmer and Bosworth, p.939; Ebulgazi Bahadur Khan, pp.736–37 (he calls the raiders Uzbeks).

28 Axworthy, p.63.

29 Lockhart 1958, p.231 ff; Lockhart 1938, pp.58–59.

30 Lockhart 1958, p.266.

31 Avery, p.84ff; Perry 1993, p.854; Hughes, p.59.

32 Atkin 1988, pp.153–67. For Russian archival material of this period see Tikhonov, Simonovitch, Dreniakin, Serebrov and Butkov in Kosneva and Khachaeva 1958.

33 Gärber.

34 Soimonov 1763.

35 Gmelin 2007; Pollock, *passim*.

36 Reineggs and Bieberstein, vol. 2.

37 Barthold and Bennigsen 1965, pp.86–87.

38 Gärber, p.71. Gärber, pp.70–83, gives a breakdown of these districts (and their rulers), configured around local rivers (e.g. Buinak), and the upper or lower reaches of mountains.

39   Ibid., pp.71–72.
40   Layton; King, *passim*.
41   Gmelin 2007, p.306.
42   McLaughlin, p.419.
43   Immerwahr, pp.20–21.
44   E.g. Chardin, pp.138–39; Olearius 1669, p.139. Parkinson, p.181, identifies Mt Elbrus as Mt Ararat. See also Ebulgazi Bahadur Khan, p.690.
45   Olearius 1669, pp.303–4; Chardin, pp.156–58 (Georgia), pp.90ff (Mingrelia); Ebulgazi Bahadur Khan, vol.2, p.615.
46   Güldenstadt, p.156, refers to the Lezgis as even more crude, intractable and predatory than other Caucasians. Bieberstein (Reineggs and Bieberstein, vol.2, pp.111, 112) describes the tribes as 'rude, wild, crude, uncivilized, unfriendly'.
47   Gärber, p.71.
48   Gmelin 2007, pp.304–5.
49   Barthold and Benningsen 1965, p.86.
50   Güldenstadt, pp.512–27 has Qazi-Qumuq, Lezgian etc. vocabularies. As with other north Caucasus languages, the aim here was to find linguistic affinities and origins. See also Ellis, pp.58–59, for a 'specimen of the Abkhaz language'.
51   E.g. Olearius 1669, pp.299–300; le Bruyn 1759 (travelled 1703), pp.196–97; Gmelin 2007, pp.7–9.
52   Gärber, pp.86–87.
53   Gmelin 2007, p.8.
54   Ibid., p.9.
55   Olearius 1669, pp.299–300.
56   Gärber, p.85. I thank Alexander Morrison for clarifying this.
57   Olearius 1669, p.300.
58   Gärber, pp.1178–118. For the Jews of Resht, see Gmelin 2007, pp.169–70.
59   Gmelin (2007, p.19) writes that the Armenians in Darband were 'always near' (i.e. complicit with) the khan.
60   Gärber, p.116.
61   Ibid., pp.116–17.
62   Herzig 1991, p.143.
63   Gmelin 2007, pp.11, 13–14.
64   Ibid., pp.10–11.
65   Runni, pp.130–63. For Alexander the Great and the Volga–Ural Mountains, see Frank 2000.
66   See the references in Runni.
67   Reineggs and Bieberstein, vol.1, p.128.
68   Storey, p.423.
69   Ibid., p.424.
70   Reineggs and Bieberstein, vol.1, pp.129–35; vol.2, e.g. p.101. See also Sixsaidov, pp.297–315, with references. D'Herbelot's *Bibliothèque* ... (completed by Antoine Galland) was published in Paris in 1697, with subsequent editions in 1777–79 (The Hague), and 1781–83 (Paris).
71   Gmelin 2007, p.13.
72   Gärber, p.87; Gmelin 2007, pp.7–8; see also Reineggs and Bieberstein, vol.1, p.130.
73   Soimonov 1763, pp.225–26.
74   Olearius 1669, p.291; Ebulgazi Bahadur Khan, pp.734–35; Hanway, vol.1, p.280;

Soimonov 1763, pp.188–89; Gmelin 2007, p.221;
75 Soimonov 1763, p.118.
76 Hanway, vol.1, p.280.
77 Gmelin 2007, pp.221–22. See also Cook, vol.2, pp.333–34; Hanway, vol.1, pp.280–81.
78 Gmelin 2007, p.228.
79 Cook, vol.2, p.305.
80 Gmelin 2007, p.32.
81 Gärber, p.98; Gmelin 2007, p.32.
82 Hughes, p.152 n.143.
83 Kahan, pp.89–91.
84 Soimonov 1763, p.174.
85 Gmelin 2007, p.28ff.; Hanway, vol.1, pp.383–84; Cook, vol.2, p.303.
86 E.g. Olearius 1669, p.152; Bell, pp.55–56; Cook, vol.2, p.296 (Cook tried to follow Olearius's route); Gmelin 2007, p.22ff (with illustration).
87 Bruce, p.294.
88 Gärber, pp.63–64.
89 Bruce, pp.227–28.
90 Ibid., p.260.
91 Ibid., pp.265–66.
92 Ibid., pp.266–68.
93 Ibid., pp.269–70.
94 Bell 1764, vol.2, pp.392–93.
95 Bruce, pp.270–71.
96 Bell 1764, vol.2, p.394.
97 Bruce, p.270.
98 Bell, vol.2, pp.344–45.
99 Bruce, p.274.
100 Bell, vol.2, p.382.
101 Ibid., pp.382–83.
102 Bruce, pp.271–73.
103 Ibid., p.274.
104 Ibid., pp.275–77.
105 Ibid., pp.279–80.
106 Ibid., p.281.
107 Ibid., pp.281–83.
108 Ibid., p.284.
109 Bell 1764, vol.2, pp.390–91.
110 Bruce, p.286.
111 Ibid., p.288.
112 Ibid., p.289.
113 Ibid., pp.294–96.
114 Ibid., p.300.
115 Ibid., pp.300–1.
116 The name 'Melitener' does not correspond to any modern region.
117 Bruce, p.301.
118 Ibid.
119 Ibid., pp.301–2.
120 Ibid., pp.318–19.

121 Ibid., pp.320–21.
122 Ibid., pp.321–22.
123 Ibid., pp.322–23.
124 Jones 1799, pp.343–48.
125 Lockhart 1938, pp.84, 211, 238ff, 245; Perry 1993, pp.854–55; Avery, pp.44, 48; Axworthy, *passim.* Jones 1799, p.358, states that when Nader Shah left Daghestan, all had been subdued.
126 Jones 1799, p.350.
127 Hanway, vol.2, p.534.
128 Cook, vol.2, pp.337, 339 (see also pp.258–350, 358–410).
129 Hanway, vol.1, pp.169–73, 186–328.
130 Another foreign source for this period, not consulted by me, is Lerch, pp.365–476.
131 Gmelin 2007, p.305.
132 Gasanov, pp.81–82.
133 Ferrier, p.464.
134 Gmelin 2007, p.78.
135 E.g. Reineggs and Bieberstein, vol.2, p.307.
136 See notes above and bibliography for works cited by all these authors. For Reineggs see Reineggs and Bieberstein, vol.1; for Bieberstein see vol.2.
137 Atkin 1988, pp.165–66, 170ff.
138 Cook, vol.2, p.87–88.
139 Ibid., pp.88–89.
140 Ibid., p.281.
141 Ibid., pp.372–73.
142 Hanway, vol.1, pp.372–75.

Part IV: Central Asia

9 Travels in 'Independent Tartary'

Introduction

The parts of Central Asia or 'Independent Tartary' (as it was then known in European sources) mentioned in the travellers' entries in this chapter are the east coast of the Caspian (Turkmen territory) and the cities of Khiva and Bukhara to the south and south-east of the Aral Sea. Parts of Kazakhstan are mentioned in passing. Other parts of Central Asia, such as Samarqand (part of the Bukharan emirate at this period) and the rest of Mavarannahr, or east of the Sir Darya (e.g. Tashkent, Khoqand), and south-east Khorezm, are not mentioned at all by the travellers. The reasons for this will become apparent.

The entries cover two significant periods of the region's history: the early eighteenth century, including the attempted invasion of the east coast of the Caspian and Khiva by Russia; and the mid-eighteenth century, shortly before and during the Persian invasion under Nader Shah, when British merchants were investigating potential trade with Khiva and Bukhara. As yet, most of the region, except for Kazakh lands and small parts of the Caspian coast (Mangyshlak), was untampered-with by Russia.

The regions the travellers described were complex, with a rich steppe and urban cultural and trading heritage. They were characterised by tribal (Kazakh, Uzbek, Turkmen) and dynastic (Khiva, Bukhara, Khoqand) rivalries and alliances, and clashes between nomads, the military and urban centres, which had classes based on different ethnic groups, such as the political and military class of Turkic Uzbeks, sedentary commoners known as Sarts[1], and captive Persian, Russian and other slaves. The eighteenth century is generally considered to have been a difficult time for independent Central Asia. The growth of rival Uzbek tribal forces (Manghits, Qongrats) fragmented and destabilized the rule of urban centres. There was aggression from outside (Russia, Persia, Jungaria), Kazakhs moving into Mavarannahr and seizing Bukhara in 1727–28,[2] and gradual Russian encroachment on the Kazakhs. Yet it was also a time of economic development in Khoqand and Tashkent, of new trade routes, of the development of a new courtly ritual in Bukhara related to tribal and Islamic aspirations (from the mid-century onwards), and of literary activity in the late part of the century.[3]

In contrast to academicians' observations on the Kazakhs, contemporary observers' records of Central Asia were far more eclectic than for some other regions covered by this anthology. They highlight the value of travel accounts as sources, whether as plain narratives or as deliberate intelligence. Information on Turkmen or the Uzbeks of Khiva and Bukhara was largely derived from the reports of merchants, diplomatic envoys, military personnel, prospectors, surveyors, adventurers, Tatar spies and the like who returned safely from the region, sometimes after a long time.[4] Envoys and merchants, such as Florio Beneveni and Danila Rukavin, or others reporting to Russia usually had information-gathering instructions.[5] These were not always possible to obey, however, as they depended on the situation on the ground, which was often volatile. Thus what might be politically relevant one year might not be the next; information was sometimes out of date and, as shown in published accounts, fairly general and even repetitive. Information from official Central Asian envoys or merchants was tenuous.

Except for Gmelin's description of Mangyshlak and 'Astarabad' Turkmen, and Pallas's account of trade to the 'Kirghiz' and 'Bukharas' via Orenburg, academicians' accounts (Müller, Georgi) were second-hand, although Müller had direct contact with archivists and administrators in Orenburg.[6] Relevant eastern sources known to non-orientalists in the west at the time were those found in Barthélemy d'Herbelot's *Bibliothèque Orientale* (several editions 1697–1799) and Abu'l Gazi (or Ebulgazi) Bahadur Khan's (Khan of Khorezm, 1643–63) *Shajare-i Turk* (known in English as *A General History of the Turks*), which was translated and edited in German, French and English (the last 1729–30).[7] Local manuscript histories and other works in Chaghatay or Persian began to be known in Russia and Europe only in the nineteenth century, after the Russian conquest.[8]

Contacts between Muscovy and Khiva and Bukhara began in the fifteenth century but became regular in the sixteenth century, with the initiative at the time being Central Asian. Despite regarding itself as superior to Muscovy, these states hoped that Muscovy's growing military might be used to their advantage. The primary aim of these contacts from the beginning was to safeguard trade and merchants, but they gradually entailed requests for protection from Kazakhs, Kalmyks, Turkmen or rival factions.[9] In 1675–76 there was even a request from the Khivan Khan Anusha to build a fort at Mangyshlak.[10] The language of this 'diplomacy' stressed friendship and trust, with the occasional calculated deference on the Central Asian side and contempt and sometimes flattery on the Russian side.[11] The reality was less decorous, involving Cossack raids in Khorezm,[12] the mutual detention of envoys, the keeping of Russian slaves (notably in Khivan territory, occasionally released from Bukhara), raids on caravans from Russia, the exploitation of customs dues, and a Russian readiness to exploit internal weaknesses (including the occasional acceptance of a high-ranking refugee at Kasimov as possible leverage).[13] Relations became increasingly focused on trade routes leading to India and on Central Asian resources.

By the early eighteenth century Russian–Central Asian relations were well-rehearsed but fraught with the cultural and political misunderstandings familiar from Russia's early dealings with steppe peoples. So far there had not been outright offensives. This changed with Peter the Great. The tsar was motivated by ambitions to open and partially control trade to India, by confused reports of gold in 'Little Bucharia' (Khorezm, Mavarannahr, Ferghana) and the possibility of reopening a channel from the Amu-Darya to the Caspian[14] (substantiated by the Khivan ambassador Ashur Biy, in Russia c.1713–14).[15] He was also swayed by his decision to take at face value the verbal promise by Khan Shah Niyaz in 1700 (via his envoy Dostek Bek Bahadur) that he would become a Russian subject[16] and the encouragement of such officers as Bekovitch-Cherkassky. Peter initiated activity from the west and the north: he ordered surveys and reports on the east coast of the Caspian, which led to the expedition of 1717 and, simultaneously, the building of forts on the northern frontier and along the Irtish.[17]

Although Shah Niyaz's declaration of readiness to become a subject was made much of in Russia,[18] it was actually a form of flattery and a bargaining tool to extract redress over various grievances, such as the abuse of customs dues, and to broaden trade.[19] Peter the Great's tone when responding to him had been crushingly superior, already taking for granted his subjection.[20] Niyaz's successors, however, such as Yadigar, who briefly became khan in 1712 and had a different diplomatic approach, did not raise the issue of subjection when addressing the tsar.[21] Ambassadors, meanwhile, continued to travel to St Petersburg.

Prince Cherkassky's expedition

In 1714 and 1715 Prince Cherkassky, a converted Kabardian noble who had married a Russian Princess Galitsin,[22] was ordered to prospect and chart the east coast of the Caspian and to travel inland to investigate the course of the Amu-Darya. Travelling inland from Tiub-Karagan and Mangyshlak, he came across a dry riverbed going west, blocked by dams, which was assumed to be a branch of the Amu-Darya (or possibly the Uzboy, a dry channel believed by the Russians to be the 'original' bed of the Amu-Darya). The aim was to unblock any dams and revive this supposedly old branch of the Amu-Darya as a route to the Caspian. In autumn 1716 preparations for the expedition started in earnest: forts began to be built at Tiub-Karagan and Krasni-vod, with a third either at Alexander Bay or slightly inland.[23] Conditions were extremely difficult, due to lack of water and building materials, the onset of winter and attacks from local tribes.[24] Despite this, Cherkassky remained optimistic.

Peter's instructions of 1716 to him were clear: besides investigating the Amu-Darya's course (and making it flow into the Caspian) and routes to India, Cherkassky was to build a fort for 1000 men at the old (supposed) mouth of the Amu-Darya and secretly to build another fortress at the site of the dam, to persuade the Khivan khan to become a faithful subject, and to try to gain the Bukharan khan's support.[25] Peter was apparently confident that a show of strength and gifts would make the khan compliant. In his imperious message to Shir Ghazi of 1716, advising him of Cherkassky's imminent visit, Peter stressed friendship and that Cherkassky was being sent on a matter of mutual interest;[26] he said nothing of troops or forts.

By March 1717 a large expeditionary force numbering 3000–4500[27] (including dragoons, infantry and cavalry, Cossacks, engineers, interpreters, and Russian, Tatar Armenian and Khivan merchants) had left by land and sea for Guriev. Camels carried water, provisions, building materials and gifts. They advanced towards the Emba and the Üst-Yurt plateau, sending messages of peace and exchanging gifts with the Khivan khan's ambassador. They then advanced further into Khorezm to the vicinity of a river or ravine called Kara Gymbet[28] or beyond, where their camp was surrounded and repeatedly attacked by a coalition of Uzbek, Turkmen, Kazakh and probably Aral tribes.[29] A new ambassador arrived, who assured them that the khan knew nothing of this. Meanwhile, the Khivan khan had apparently received a message from the Kalmyks that the Russians meant war.[30]

After further assurances of peace from both sides, Cherkassky was persuaded to come closer to Khiva and see the khan himself. They exchanged gifts, and Cherkassky, against his officers' advice, was persuaded to split his troops for lodging in five different places (presumably five of the main Khivan fortress towns). There they were massacred. Left with just 200 soldiers, Cherkassky was ambushed near the khan's tent, beheaded and flayed. His head, stuffed with straw, was apparently sent to the khan of Bukhara as a gift. The soldiers were also killed, although the khan freed some Muslim Tatars, Circassians and Kalmyks, and a few escaped.[31] The fortresses that had not been abandoned or whose garrison had not been driven out were dismantled after Cherkassky's defeat became known.[32]

The Khivan khan's move had been tactically brilliant. His explanation was that the Russians were supposed to come in friendship but they came with an army, had built forts on the Caspian and intended to do so on Khivan territory.[33] Peter's gamble had not paid off because, despite years of parley, there was a fundamental misunderstanding of Khivan independence and 'diplomacy', and of their disdain for Russians and certainly for a Circassian-turned-Christian-Orthodox. There were no direct military reprisals for this, although a new Khivan ambassador from Shir Ghazi, who arrived in St Petersburg in 1721, was imprisoned,[34] and there were plots to ferment things locally. In 1728 Russia encouraged the Aral Tatars to invade Khiva and murder the shah. In the event the shah was murdered locally, and the Aral Tatars retreated. Fear of repercussions was still felt in Orenburg in the 1750s.[35] Russia also attempted to influence Khiva via its Kazakh or Karakalpak elected khans, to no real result. Trade continued, despite the usual problems over envoys, merchants and pillaging. Bell presented the story from the Russian standpoint, one of gross treachery on the part of the khan and gullibility on Cherkassky's part. In contemporary Russian sources the story came to symbolise Khivan barbarity for many years afterwards.

Peter's attempt to gain information on India and to prepare for the main expedition was not one-sided. Piotr Davidov was to reach Bukhara via Persia,[36] and another officer, the Tatar nobleman Muhammed Tevkelev, had been appointed to travel to India via Persia.[37] These missions came to nothing, due to problems encountered in Persia. The encirclement of the south-east also continued with the attempt under Colonel Ivan Bukholz to build a fortress at Lake Yamish and along the Irtish. This was unsuccessful, but it resulted in the construction of a fortress at Omsk in 1716. Others were built at Semipalatinsk in 1718 and at Ust-Kamengorsk in 1720. Orenburg, which became pivotal to Russia's eastern trade and to contact with the Kazakhs and Central Asia, was founded in 1735.[38]

Bekovitch-Cherkassky's ill-fated expedition

The people of CHIVA, a territory ... eastward from the CASPIAN sea, having several times robbed and plundered some caravans of RUSSIAN merchants going to BUCHARIA, his Czarish Majesty determined to send a small body of regular troops and some Cossacks to defend satisfaction for such outrages committed in times of peace. For this purpose Mr Beckvitz, a captain of the guards, who was appointed to command this expedition, repaired to ASTRACHAN, in summer 1716, in order to make all the necessary preparations against next spring. Having accordingly embarked his men, provisions, and ammunition, at the proper season, he steered his course along the CASPIAN sea, and landed at a place called KRASNA-VODA, i.e. red water, as near to CHIVA, as he conveniently could. This place was barren, and uninhabited. Having therefore moored his transports, he erected a small fort to secure his retreat, in case of accidents.

In the meantime he sent a friendly message to the Chan of CHIVA, to notify his arrival, and to desire he would furnish him with provisions and quarters for his men; for which he offered to pay ready money. The crafty TARTAR returned for answer, that he might come to KHIVA with the greatest safety, where all his demands should be granted. At the same time, sent him a present of fruits and fresh provisions, and guides to conduct him on the road, accompanied with the highest expressions of respect to his Czarish Majesty. Mr BECKVITZ, having left about three hundred men in the fort, to guard the camp and provisions, proceeded with the rest, and a few field pieces, towards CHIVA.

In three or four days he arrived in the neighbourhood of the town, where he was met by several of the chiefs, who came with compliments from the Chan, and to settle matters relative to the cantonment of the soldiers. This particular was difficult to adjust.

Mr BECKVITZ insisted, that all his men should be quartered in the town, and nothing but infatuation could have influenced him to alter so prudent a resolution. But the TARTARS started many objections against putting it in execution, and pretended that the Chan and themselves were willing to agree to it; but that the people were averse, and jealous of having so many armed men lodged within their walls. And therefore they proposed, as a means of quieting the minds of the people, that he should separate his men, in order to be quartered more conveniently in the adjacent villages, that himself should have lodgings in the town, with a sufficient guard to attend him. This motion was strongly opposed by all the officers, who looked on it as a stratagem laid for their dest[r]uction. And such in reality it proved in the end.

Mr BECKVITZ, deluded by false promises, at last consented to canton his men. No sooner were they divided into small parties than they were enclosed, and attacked by great numbers of TARTARS; and most of them either killed or taken prisoners, who were afterwards sold for slaves. A few of them taking the alarm stood to their arms, and made a brave defence for some time, endeavouring chiefly to regain their camp and ships; but having a barren desart to pass, and the TARTAR horse harassing them day and night, they were at last obliged to submit to fatal necessity. The imprudence of the general was the sole cause of all these misfortunes; for, being in no want of provisions or ammunition, had he only kept his men together, the whole combined power of these TARTARS could not have prevented his regaining the camp and shipping.

The camp was next attacked by the TARTARS. But they were repulsed by the garrison, which, having now intelligence of what had passed at CHIVA, demolished the fort, reimbarked the men and stores, and set sail for ASTRACHAN. The season was now too far advanced to gain that port: this circumstance, together with the hard gales of contrary wind, obliged them to put into NIEZABATT [Niazabad] in order to pass the winter. Here they were hospitably received by the PERSIANS; and the presence of the ambassador at SHAMACHY, contributed greatly to the relief of these poor unfortunate people.

Unhappy BECKVITZ himself, happened to be taken prisoner. He was sent for the Chan's tent, on some pretence of business, where they first struck off his head; then after venting their barbarous rage on his dead body, they flayed it, and, having stuffed the skin with straw, placed it, a miserable spectacle, on one of the city gates.

This unfortunate gentleman was the son of a petty prince, or chief of a tribe in TZERKESSIA, and had been sent to RUSSIA in his infancy, as a hostage for his father's fidelity.[39]

(Bell, Niazabad 1718)

The Kazakhs

The Kazakh steppe, which in the eighteenth century stretched east of the River Ural to around Lake Balqash, was of great strategic importance to Russia. Russian Kazakh diplomatic relations began in the late sixteenth century and were prompted, like so many of Muscovy's early contacts with her indigenous neighbours, by the conquest of Kazan and Astrakhan, and by Russia's advance into Siberia. Co-operation over trade and the protection of routes and forts were central to Russian interest in the Kazakhs, and tensions between the Oirats and the Kazakhs or the Kazakhs and Bukhara came to be exploited.[40] From the late sixteenth or early seventeenth centuries the Kazakhs had been divided into three hordes (*zhüz*): the Lesser or *Kshi* (north of the Aral and the Caspian), the Middle or *Orta* (on the central steppe) and the Greater or *Uli* (Semirech'e). This classification referred to seniority rather than to size.[41] In the seventeenth and eighteenth centuries the Kazakhs were repeatedly attacked and forced westwards by the Jungars or Oirats, their traditional enemies, and in the eighteenth by the Bashkirs from the north-west.[42]

Peter the Great strove to manipulate the Kazakhs of the Lesser Horde, who were particularly vulnerable because of their proximity to the growing Russian orbit,[43] into oaths of allegiance through gifts and promises of protection. The first nominal pledge of allegiance to Russia, never popular among the Kazakhs, was given in 1731 by Abulkhayir and a few of his nobles, although it is far from clear that Abulkhayir spoke for his people. Khodarkovsky has written in detail about these relations, concluding that what the Russians interpreted as submission, the Kazakhs thought of as alliances.[44] In the 1770s Georgi described the Lesser and Middle Hordes as being dependent and vassal to the empire, while not depending on its laws or paying tribute. He constructed a picture of relations that might seem mutually advantageous (including 'largesses' to the khan and his people) but which the Kazakhs did not take seriously.[45] As with Russia's other efforts to expand its empire into nomadic or tribal lands, negotiations meant different things to each party. On the Kazakh side there was pragmatism and necessity; on the Russian, expectations of subjection and lack of commitment to native demands.

Russian policy consisted in divisive support for different ruling Kazakh factions, and veered from aggression to appeasement. Confused policies either supported the khans or the people, and attempted to replace the position of khan with a single provincial administration over divided hordes with their own courts.[46] The ultimate aim was that the Kazakhs should 'settle' (i.e. turn to sedentary agriculture). Russian policies simultaneously included hemming in Kazakh lands by forts and colonies, restricting pastures, and prohibition to cross the River Yaik (Ural).[47] They achieved little except uneasy agreements and hostility among the Kazakhs to pro-Russian factions. But they eventually wore some of the Kazakhs down. In 1801 Bukey Khan crossed the River Yaik with his horde and settled in the empire. By 1822 the title of khan was abolished, and the identity of the hordes was gradually dissolved by Russian bureaucracy. By 1860 the Greater Horde had officially come under Russian rule.[48]

ENDNOTES

1   These could be Persian-speaking Tajiks, or Turkic-speaking, or bilingual.
2   Holzwarth, pp.127–28 and *passim*.
3   Levi 1999 and 2007; Morrison, pp.11–12; Sela, pp.38–71, 102–7.
4   Kügelgen, for travellers to Bukhara; *Istoria uzbekskoi SSR*, vol.1, pp.435–44 and *passim*; vol.2, p.56.
5   E.g. to Bekovitch-Cherkassky. *Russko-turmenskiie otnoshenia*, doc.5; to Beneveni, pp.136–37; to Bukholz, Müller 1760, vol.4, pp.210–12.
6   Black, pp.122, 143.
7   Literally 'The Genealogical Tree of the Turks', completed in 1665 by Ebulgazi Bahadur Khan's son.
8   Bregel 1988, pp.2–3.
9   *Materiali po istorii uzbekskoi, tadzhikskoi i turkmenskoi SSR*, pt 3, nos 1–114; *Istoria uzbekskoi SSR*, pp.435–40; Allworth 1994, pp.39–44.
10   As reported in *Istoria uzbekskoi SSR*, vol.1, p.439.
11   Allworth 1994(a), pp.86–87, n.10.
12   Allworth 1994(a), p.8.
13   *Istoria uzbekskoi SSR*, p.439; Howorth, p.896.
14   Müller 1760, vol.4, pp.187–89.
15   Allworth 1994(a), p.90–93.
16   *Materiali po istorii*, doc.116; Allworth 1994(a), p.43.
17   Müller 1760, vol.4, p.209ff; *Istoria uzbekskoi SSR*, p.441.
18   It was even announced in the Moscow journal of 1703. Kühlewein, p.538.
19   *Materiali po istorii*, doc.116; see also docs 115, 117 relating to complaints.
20   *Materiali po istorii*, doc.118.
21   Bregel 2007, pp.48–49; Allworth 1994, p.44.

22 Müller 1760, vol.4, p.201; 1762, vol.7, p.160.

23 *Istoria uzbekskoi SSR* states that the third fort was inland, but see Rukavin, p.20; *Russko-turkmenskie otnoshenia*, doc.21; Müller 1762, vol.7, pp.169–70.

24 E.g. partly described in *Russko-turkmenskie otnoshenia*, doc.21.

25 Ibid., doc.5.

26 Ibid., doc.6.

27 The numbers given for this expedition vary. Rukavin, p.21, has 3200. *Russko-turkmenskie otnoshenia*, doc.24, has 6240 plus 110 miscellaneous merchants, interpreters etc., but this probably includes the total numbers for the expeditions of 1714–17. Müller 1762, vol.7, pp.165–66, 174, has more than 4000. Modern accounts also vary, e.g. Allworth 1990, p.95 (6600) and 1994, p.9 (3500).

28 The expedition's route is difficult to reconstruct because of differences in names of places and river beds. Kniazhetskaya, p.44, for example, mentions that the attack took place around a River Akkyl (after Kara Gymbet), whereas the *Russko-turkmenskie otnoshenia*, doc.13, mentions only Kara Gymbet. Müller 1762, vol.7, p.176, thought that the assault took place near Urgench, because there was fresh water there.

29 *Russko-turkmenskie otnoshenia*, doc.13.

30 Ibid.

31 There are many references for this story. The basic ones comprise: published eighteenth-century archival material (e.g. *Russko-turkmenskie otnoshenia*, docs 7, 9, 11, 13, 21, 24, 25); Müller 1760, vol.4, pp.201–6; vol.7, pp.156–85; Rukavin, pp.20–23. Contemporary sources include Kniazhetskaya, pp.11–50; *Istoria uzbekskoi SSR*, vol.1, pp.440–41; Allworth 1990 and 1994 (with references).

32 *Russko-turkmenskie otnoshenia*, doc. 21.

33 Ibid., doc.13; di Cosmo, pp.76–78, 95ff (to Beneveni).

34 Allworth 1990, pp.96–97.

35 Rukavin, pp.23–25.

36 *Russko-turkmenskieoOtnoshenia*, doc.21; Kniazhetskaya, p.35.

37 Müller 1762, vol.7, p.175; Kniazhetskaya, pp.40–41.

38 Müller 1760, vol.4, pp.210–15; Allworth 1994, pp.9–10.

39 Bell, pp.146–50; see also Hanway, vol.1, pp.188–89 for an account of the story.

40 Khodarkovsky 2002, pp.147–49.

41 Bregel 2003, p.76.

42 Ibid., p.58; Khodarkovsky 2002, p.153.

43 Ibid., pp.150–52.

44 A diary written in German by the Prussian–British adventurer John Castle (*Journal von der AO 1736 aus Orenburg zu dem Abul Geier Chan ... 1741*), which recounts his trip to Khan Abulkhayir, is outside the scope of this anthology. I intend to publish an edited translation of this work. See also *Kazakhsko-russkie otnoshenia*; Erofieva; Frank 2003.

45 Georgi 1780–83, vol.2, pp.251–54.

46 Khodarkovsky 2002, p.179.

47 Ibid, pp.178–79.

48 Ibid., pp.182–83.

10 Mapping and charting the Caspian

Peter the Great's interest in the Caspian as an entry to the east is demonstrated by the number of surveys and maps he commissioned from *c*.1714[1] onwards and around the time of his invasion of north Persia (e.g. those of Carl van Verden , 1719–21, and F.I. Soimonov, 1724–27).[2] Bruce was also commissioned to map the Caspian in 1723. He stated that the map or chart and copies were presented to his superiors and the emperor.[3] As this map was not published in his memoirs, however, and is so far untraced, it remains unclear whether the chart was incorporated into other maps (possibly Soimonov's?) or ever published. Soimonov became an expert on the Caspian; he published a navigational atlas of it in 1731.[4]

These early maps are striking for their lack of detail for the Caspian's eastern shore and the confusion over the names and locations of its rivers from the Emba southward.[5] In the early eighteenth century, Russian cartography was still weak, although actively encouraged by Peter the Great with the practical and theoretical assistance of Europeans, such as A. Farquharson.[6] Thus several eighteenth-century western maps of the Caspian were part compilations of previous ones.[7]

Bruce implied that he was the principal surveyor, but gave no information on the instruments or earlier maps he used. He did, however, describe his mission in some detail:

> I got very unexpected orders to go all around the Caspian Sea, to survey and sound it, and to lay down, in a chart, all the islands, rivers, creeks, and bays, with the different soundings, and for this service had one of the strongest new built gallies, of forty oars, carrying two eighteen pounders in her prow, twenty four swivels, and three hundred men … two sub-engineers were appointed for my assistants.[8]

Bruce named three major rivers after the Emba (Oxus, Daria and Ossa), which do not correspond to those on other maps.[9] This was not necessarily a sign of incompetence, but may record genuine onomastic variety, depending on who was supplying the names. Time of year and changing natural conditions were also factors where the flow of rivers was considered. A significant discrepancy, however, arises over Bruce's placement of what he calls the Oxus (Amu Darya, Gihun), which he showed flowing into the Caspian between the gulfs of Alexander and Karabuga. No other map shows this river (or any other) here, and only Herman Moll's map, complemented and published by John Perry in 1716, shows a river called the Amu Darya flowing into the Caspian. The consensus was that, if a branch of the river had once flowed into the Caspian, it had flowed into the gulfs of Karabuga or Balkhan but was long since silted up.[10]

Bruce or his informants probably mistook another river (later silted up) for the Oxus, not realising that the Oxus was synonymous then with the 'Daria' (i.e. the Amu Darya). He placed 'the famous river Daria' below Carabuga, probably in Balkhan Bay. This is closer to the speculated location of the dried-up Amu Darya and to Krasnovodsk, one of the places associated with Prince Bekovich-Cherkassky's expedition of 1717 (see Ch.9). Whether this river was actually a flowing tributary of the Amu Darya or another river, such as de Lisle's Tadzien (Uzboy), is unclear. It is clear, however, that there was excitement about the Amu Darya and a desire to gratify the tsar. Bruce reported that Peter was indeed very pleased to know of a 'famous river' in this location, where a fort could be built to guard against the Uzbeks.[11] The river appears to have been too far north for the modern Atrek and Kurgan, either of which would then correspond to Bruce's Ossa or Orxantes. Potential confusion also arises over Mangyshlak. The port of that name was known to be on the Caspian's north-east coast, although there was another centre called Mangyshlak in the south, mentioned by Bruce.[12] Uncertainty in the west over the names of these rivers continued into the later eighteenth century.[13]

Despite its puzzling cartographic details, Bruce's survey gave the location of Turkmen and other tribes, and conveyed the anxious but also pleasurable atmosphere of a voyage down the coast.

Bruce's survey of the Caspian, 1723

On the 26th [April 1723], we arrived in the river Jaick [Ural] the mouth of which is one hundred fathoms broad, and eighteen feet deep; we went to the town of Jaick, which stands about one mile up the river, and is well fortified, has a strong garrison of Russians and Cossacks, to keep the Kalmuck and Nagayan (an Uzbek horde) Tartars in awe, and to prevent them from attacking each other, as they live in perpetual enmity. The Nagayans inhabit all the country from Astrachan to the Jaick, all along the seacoast, two hundred and fifty-five wersts in extent; and the Kalmucks posses that vast tract of land, from Saratof and the great desert of Beriket, and that tract to the south of the Jaick, all along the shore to the river Yembo [Emba] which is ninety-three wersts from this place. We stayed only one day at Jaick, and provided ourselves with fresh meat and water. Being informed by the governor that there was a large gulf to the eastward of this place, to the river Yembo, but too shallow to admit our galley, I sent one of the engineers with two of the boats, to go round and survey it, and join us again on the opposite point, for which we proceeded immediately, and sailing south, we anchored on the 30th, between the island of Kulala, and the point of the main, in six fathom water, in view of the mountains of Karagan, and from hence we had a clean and deep shore. At this place begin the territories of Turkistan, of the Turkumanian Tartars. During our stay here, waiting the return of the engineer, we laid in plenty of wood and water, and diverted ourselves with fowling and fishing ... Our engineer, with the boats, joined us again on the 10th of May, who reported that ... he found only from five to eight feet of water; that the whole shore was so covered with reed that they could only land at the mouth of the river Yembo ...

We left the island of Kulala on the 11th [May], on our way to the gulf of Iskander, where we arrived on the 20th. All along this coast there is a great depth of water, so that we could land with our galley on any part of it. A great number of small rivers fall into the sea from the mountains, but we could not learn their names, although I attempted to get information by sending the twelve oared boat, with an officer and twenty-four men, and an interpreter to speak with the people on shore: but they no sooner came near enough, than the Tartars let fly a volley of arrows at our people, who returned the salute with a discharge of their musketry, and we fired one of our great guns from the galley at them, which made them retire towards the mountains in great haste. They always appeared in great parties, on horseback, well armed, and we saw several of their hords, or camps, at a distance, which they move at pleasure, and wander from place to place, for those Tartars have no settled abode: they continued to attend us every day in great parties to watch our motions, out of the reach of our guns, and they disappeared entirely on our arrival in the gulf of Iskander, which is one hundred and eighty-four wersts from the Isle of Kulala. In this gulf ... we found ... exceeding good anchorage; it would be one of the finest harbours in the world, as both sides of the entrance are extremely well calculated to erect forts upon, for its defence. It lies in 43 deg. 20 min. north ...

We left the gulf on the 26th [May], the proceeding along the shore two days in good depth of water; we arrived in the river Oxus, being ninety wersts from the gulf. This river is both large and rapid, and is about a musket-shot broad at its entrance. Here we found a few unarmed Tartars, who sold us some sheep, and informed us that several hords of Turkumanian Tartars were encamped on the banks of the river, a little way above, and that Usbeck Tartars encamped on the other side, this river dividing the two nations. We had hitherto seen nothing but fine weather, intermixt with calms and light breezes; but this night we had a dreadful storm of wind, attended with rain, thunder, and lightning, which obliged us to run the galley half a werst up the river for shelter, where we anchored in the middle of the stream, not daring to venture on either side for fear of the Tartars, having Turkumanians on the north, and the Usbecks on the south, hovering at a distance. The storm lasted till next day at noon, when we left the Oxus, and sailing along-shore in deep water, with a clean bottom, attended by parties of the Usbeck Tartars, who observed our motions at a distance from the sides of the mountains ...

The 2nd of June, we arrived at the gulf of Carabuga one hundred and five wersts from the river Oxus; the inlet of the gulf is about two wersts broad, and at one werst within is an island, where we landed with our galley, and encamped the people to refresh themselves on the shore, and get our vessel cleaned: from hence I dispatched the two assistants, in the largest boats, to survey the gulf; directing them to proceed along the opposite sides till they should meet, then return to the island: in the mean time, I sounded all around the inlet, and had from five to six fathom water; I could observe no current here either in or out. The gulf, from north to south, is seventy-five wersts, and fifty from east to west, deep water, a clean bottom, and the shore steep, all around the gulf; it is surrounded with high mountains; two large rivers (the Morga and Herat) fall into it from the east; the entrance is formed by two narrow necks of land, and might be easily secured and fortified; and this island, which is two miles in circumference, would serve for a protection to the shipping. ...

[W]e took our departure from Carabuga on the 22nd and coasted along shore from six days, in very hot weather without the smallest breeze of wind, which made it intolerable for the poor soldiers, who were obliged to row all the way, and anchoring every night, we had continual flashes of lighting, and these sometimes accompanied with dreadful loud claps of thunder, which are very frequent in this country during the summer. We were every day attended along the shore by numerous parties of the Usbeck Tartars, who seemed very jealous of our intentions, which obliged us, as often as we wanted to send ashore for fresh water, to fire our great guns at them, which kept them at a distance, by which means we supplied ourselves.

One hundred and forty wersts southward from Carabuga, we entered the mouth of the famous river Daria on the 28th; it lies 39 deg. 15 min. north latitude. It is here where the gold sand is washed down from the mines in the mountains, and here where the unfortunate prince Alexander Bekewitz, a few years ago, with an army of 3,000 men, were treacherously massacred by the Usbeck Tartars ... I now saw the place where the fort had been erected, on a narrow neck of land, opposite to the mouth of the river and which forms a spacious harbour capable of containing a number of ships of burthen, as there is from three to four fathom water close to the shore, on a clean bottom with good anchorage; so that it was a great pity the prince suffered himself to be over-reached by these treacherous Tartars. If this port had been maintained, which might have been done without any manner of danger, it would, in process of time, have been a most glorious acquisition towards enriching the Russian nation. I intended to have gone some way up this River; but as the Tartars had taken the alarm at our appearance here, and were already come from their camp in for-midable bodies, I was obliged to lay aside the design and leave the place; and passing two bays and three islands called Goat Islands, we came to an anchor at one of the islands for the night, where we landed, saw a number of goats, and killed five of them.

The next day being the 29th, we arrived at Minkislack on the north-side of the river Ossa, or Orxantes, sixty wersts from Daria. This river divides the Usbeck Tartary from Persia, is both large and deep, and ships may ride at anchor here in great safety. Here we were glad to find people dwelling in houses, for we were not seen a house from the time we left Astrachan, except at Jaick. We found the people of Minkislack both civil and kind: they live after the Persian manner, whose subjects they are, and we got all sorts of refreshments at a very cheap rate, and were afterwards no more honoured with an escort of Tartars. From Minkislack we proceeded along a clean shore, in deep water ... where abundance of small rivulets fall in to the sea, and the country, abounding with villages, is overgrown with a great variety of fruit trees.

The 4th of July, we arrived at the inlet of the gulf of Astrabat [Astrabad] one hundred and fifty wersts from Minkislack: we entered and anchored within the gulph ... [14]

(Bruce, 1723)

Return to Astrakhan via the island of Trenzeni

[We] reached, on the 17th, the extremity of the peninsula, which forms the gulf of Agrechan, and came to an anchor in the evening ... between ... the high land and the island of Trenzini opposite to the city of Terki in Circas-sia ... The island ... is the largest in the Caspian sea ... and now as all the coast from hence to Astrachan had been sounded on our former expedi-tion, I judged it needless to coast it again, so that we took our departure ... we arrived at the mouth of the river Wolga on the 24th of September, having been gone five months and six days ...[15]

I must acknowledge this was the most pleasant jaunt I ever had in my whole life ...[16]

(Bruce, 1723)

ENDNOTES

1   Kniazhetskay, pp.57–104, gives a major role to Bekovitch Cherkassky as map-maker of the Caspian and believes to have found his map (pp.76–77). See also *Russko-turkmenskie otnoschenia*, docs. 17, 18 about the difficulties experienced by officers in this work.

2   Shafranovskii, pp.101–4; Soimonov worked as Van Verden's assistant on the early 1720s map before becoming autonomous.

3   Bruce, pp.326, 346.

4   *Atlas i lotsiya kaspiyskogo morya* (ref. Postnikov 2000, p.81). This has not been seen by me. See also Soimonov 1763 and 1765 on the Caspian and its trade.

5   Van Verden's map of 1719–21 (*Atlas minor*, Thomas and John Bowles, London 1736; copy by H. Moll), which claimed to be an exact copy, merely shows the outline of the Caspian. It hints at rivers on the east coast but does not name them. Such omissions highlight how unknown the east coast was to both Russians and westerners. As with travellers' topographical knowledge, cartographers such as De Lisle relied on classical Arab, Muslim, Georgian and Armenian sources to comple-ment their knowledge of the Caspian (Allen, pp.137–50). Peter the Great presented Van Verden's 1720–21 map to the French Academy. This was used by de Lisle in his *Carte des Pays Voisins de la Mer Caspienne* (1723).

6   Appleby 2004(b); Appleby 2001, pp.191–204; Goldenberg and Postnikov; Post-nikov 2000, p.81.

7   Mapping the Caspian had a long history both in the east and the west, see Bran-caforte 2003, pp.154–68; Bagrow, pp.3–10; for the sources for Olearius's map of Persia and the Caspian, see Brancaforte, pp.163–83.

8   Bruce, p.311.

9   E.g. H. Moll with additions by J. Perry (1716) has two rivers flowing into the north-east Caspian: the Taumasse and the Oxus. De Lisle (1723) has four rivers on the east coast: the Agous into the Gulf of Alexander, the old course of the Oxus into Carabuga Bay, the Tadzien into Balkhan Bay, the Atrek and the Astrabat. A. Maas's map (1735; *Atlas universalis*, 1795, no.144) has the dried-up Oxus or Gihun into Balkhan Bay, followed by the Kurkan and Astrabat. Later maps pub-lished in Hanway (Hanway, vol.1: map of the 1745 Russian embassy, and Captain Woodroofe's survey) show the dried-up Oxus running into Balkan Bay.

10   Even Jenkinson knew this: see Hakluyt, p.81.

11   Bruce, p.346.

12   For example in A. Maas's map of 1735.

13   A map by S. Dunns of 1786 shows four (unnamed) rivers running into the Caspian from below Balkhan Bay (see Dunns); Coxe's map (1784) shows three rivers (unnamed, one the Kurgan) below Balkhan Bay.

14   Bruce, pp.311–18.

15   Bruce pp.323–24.

16   Ibid.

Introduction

Urban and nomadic Central Asia had extremely longstanding, interdependent trade links with India, Persia, Rus and later Muscovy (via Siberia and the khanates of Kazan and Astrakhan) and China.[1] A link with Britain, via the Muscovy Company, had been made with Anthony Jenkinson's mission to Bukhara of 1558–59, with the (abandoned) goal of finding a route to China.[2] In the eighteenth century trade routes between Central Asia and Russia were strengthened and developed through the established north Caspian port of Mangyshlak, via Samara to Guriev on the River Yaik (Ural), via Orenburg across the steppe to the Aral Sea, then to Tashkent, Bukhara and Khorezm, from Siberia (Ishim, Irtish) to the central Sir Darya, and from Omsk, the upper Irtish and Jungaria. As already discussed, Central Asia's links with India were a major factor that drove the Russians.[3] Bukhara, at the western end of the old Silk Route, remained the principal crossroads for this trade during the eighteenth century, despite difficulties, such as Nader Shah's invasion and tribal feuding, and the rise of Khoqand.[4]

Emboldened by Britain's treaty of commerce with Russia of 1734, the prospect of eastern trade with Persia via the Caspian (proposed by John Elton in 1738) and Elton's enthusiasm, two sets of British merchants (Elton with Graeme and Thompson with Hogg) decided to investigate the potential of trade with Central Asia in 1739–40. Before his commitment to Nader Shah (1741), Elton had been involved in the Orenburg expedition of 1735 and had mapped the River Yaik as well as the south-east frontiers of Russia. At that time, according to Hanway, he had encountered many nomads and merchants of the frontier caravan routes and ports,[5] resulting in 1740 in a formal proposal to the British minister at St Petersburg (Edward Finch). He proposed that British trade should be not only with Persia but also with the 'Bokharas and beyond', with the principal 'mart' being Mashad,[6] regarded by Nader Shah as his capital. Being close to Shirvan and Ghilan, Central Asian goods could then be exchanged for raw silk. These Britons would be the first since Anthony Jenkinson to risk a trade mission to Central Asia.[7]

Although Elton's plan was ambitious, Central Asia's transit trade was known to be rich. He appears to have aimed both to use and to sideline Russia. The British hoped to import various commodities from Central Asia and beyond, such as precious stones, musk and gold (no mention is made of cotton), in return for which they would export woollen products.[8] The inner Asian trade at Orenburg was extremely varied; it included cotton cloth, indigo and tiger skins form India; half-silk cloth, silver and gold coin, lapis lazuli (from Badakhshan), balas rubies, dried fruits, millet, rhubarb (from China), saltpetre, lamb and camel skins, camels and horses. Russian exports included sugar, pelts, skins, leather, sheets, utensils, needles, coral pieces and dyestuffs (cochineal). This trade was largely managed by Central Asians and other Tatars (e.g. from Kazan, Orenburg) to the detriment of Russian merchants, who were out of their depth. They were dependent on interpreters and guides, at the mercy of Russian and local bureaucracy, beset by problems arising en route and unable adequately to compete in local markets. Russia's disadvantage in this enterprise increased throughout the century; by its end, trade that was profitable to Central Asia was unprofitable to Russia.[9] Pallas, like modern scholars, attributed this decline to the growth of maritime trade but also to the poor quality of goods (particularly raw silks) from north India as opposed to those from the better 'manufactures' of the south coast.[10]

The dominance of Tatar merchants and the disadvantages of 'foreign' ones comes through in Thompson and Hogg's accounts. They described the high duty (5% in contrast to 2.5% for Muslims) paid in Khiva for their goods, presumably mostly wool, and how they could not sell enough to maintain themselves, let alone make a profit. Khiva suffered because its routes were less central and its commodities less varied.[11] Thompson had a different experience in Bukhara, where the duty on all imported goods was 1% and on exports 10%. Both merchants concluded that the effort was not worth it. Both were there during Nader Shah's reign, which did affect trade. Thompson attributed the mid-century decline in Bukharan trade to pillaging and war with Persia. British fabrics did reach Central Asia in the early nineteenth century via Russia and India.[12]

Journeys to Khiva and Bukhara

The travellers were about to encounter lands that were a great contrast to the comparative convenience of the Volga or centres within the Russian Empire. They would face desert, pillaging tribes and remote oasis towns with a reputation for savagery and frequent political upheavals. They would also be on constant alert over protection, which was in the hands of various Tatars and local guides, who themselves were under fear of attack, and could be frightened off or change sides. Merchants' accounts reveal that they were aware of some of the dangers and theoretically ready to face them. Once in Astrakhan, however, Elton and Graeme found they had to abort their mission to Bukhara. They were deterred by Armenian reports of the problems facing the raw silk trade in Persia under Nader Shah, but mainly by rumours of the Persian invasion. Poor shipping and the dangers of the steppe also contributed.

Given Elton's supposed knowledge of trade affairs, he and Graeme seem to have been opportunistic and unprepared, but perhaps they were also hampered by limited funds. They regretted having been unable to gain 'knowledge of a Country so little known to Europeans'. Thompson and Hogg, in contrast, decided to approach Khiva and Bukhara from the north. They conveyed the hazards of the journey, the volatile political situation and the territories of various Tatar groups. They knew that they had to wear local clothes (as had the envoy Beneveni on his way to Khiva in 1725)[13] and use local guides. They were accompanied by Kazakh ('Kirgeese') guides sent by Janibek Batyr, a clan chief of the Lesser Kazakh horde, with whom Russia was then on co-operative terms. They met up with his horde in the steppe 800 versts (530 miles) from Iaitsk (Urals'k) and travelled with them to the south-east of Orenburg. They then joined a caravan of Kazakhs and Turkmen for the journey to Aral and beyond.

Urgench, Khiva and Bukhara

The first Central Asian urban centre the merchants reached was Old (Konye) Urgench, formerly on the Oxus Delta. Urgench had been the capital of Khorezm until it was destroyed by the Mongols and then by Timur, under whom it partially revived. It had been known to travellers to Khorezm on the western caravan route (cf. Jenkinson). In the seventeenth century New Urgench was founded closer to Khiva, because of changes in river channels.[14] Thompson and Hogg described the place as ruined, except for what they took to be a mosque but was possibly a mausoleum. It is significant that this monument was still used as a place of worship and that the site itself was known to yield 'gold'. Old Urgench was mentioned by the editor of Ebulghazi Bahadur Khan's *History* as ruinous but still having a functioning bazaar.[15] The merchant Rukavin, travelling to Khiva in 1753, mentioned New Urgench, noting the city walls, two mosques, a khan's residence and a few stone houses (empty, due to a raid by the Kalmyk Khan Ayuki).[16]

Khiva

The travellers reached Khiva in September 1739. At the time Khorezm extended south of the Aral Sea along the Amu Darya and its tributaries skirting Lake Sariqamish and narrowing to around Dargan to the south east.[17] Although the site dated back to the third and fourth centuries and was mentioned in Arab sources from the tenth century onwards, Khiva did not become the capital of Khorezm until the sixteenth century.[18] With Urgench, Khanga, Fitnak and Hazarasp it was one of Khorezm's principal fortress towns,[19] but it never developed the cachet of Bukhara or Samarqand.

The merchants' comments on the town are brief. They mentioned the 'mean' caravanserai, three basic gates, a strong earth wall and a ditch. The houses were low, flat-roofed and of mud brick. Given that foreign merchants or envoys were kept in circumscribed lodgings, closely watched and usually in a state of anxiety, it is unsurprising that topographical and architectural observations were restricted and only partially correct. Dr Eversmann, who was part of an embassy to Bukhara in 1820, made it clear that his notes had to be written clandestinely – it was always dangerous to ask questions or take a walk, except on commercial business.[20] Beneveni, for example, returning to Russia via Khiva in 1725, after an embassy to Bukhara in 1721–25, filled his report with details of his dealings with Khan Shir Ghazi or his 'Minister' Dostum Biy (Döstum Arbab), the threats from Aral Tatars and rivalry with Bukhara. He mentioned only in passing the caravanserai, the 'city palace' with inner and outer courtyards under porticos, and the khan's 'country house'.[21] Equally, Rukavin (1753) mentioned only Khiva's city walls, which according to him were not very high.[22] There is a tendency in Russian reports to downplay the strength of Central Asian defences, and to gloat over Russian artillery, as Beneveni did with Shir-Ghazi.[23]

Although eighteenth-century Khiva was perhaps unimpressive to western eyes, there was building work going on (e.g. the Shir-Ghazi madrasa), and there were many older monuments, such as the Kuhna Ark, the Akh Shikh Baba tower, madrasas and mausoleums.[24] Surprisingly, the merchants said nothing of the bazaar or slave-market. This paucity of published information in the eighteenth century certainly helped portray Khiva as a desolate, and later demonised, backwater. An account by Captain Nikolai Muraviev of his stay in 1819–20[25] gives an idea of Khiva in the early nineteenth century. For him, the view of the town with its 'gold balls' (cupolas) and 'azure' tiles gleaming above the city walls, surrounded by the 'verdure' of gardens, was very agreeable.[26] He was also impressed by the superimposition of canals and handsome bridges. Although he was accommodated in a clean, well-furnished house (under guard), he was apparently less impressed by the khan's palace. The brick-built gateway was 'in good taste', but Muraviev was then led through three courts, which he described as dirty, sanded and clay-walled, until he reached a large fourth court with climbing plants, where the khan's tent stood.[27] Muraviev also mentioned the many gardens around Khiva, 'sprinkled' with the private forts of rich inhabitants.[28] It was not all so engaging however; he also mentioned some 3000 Russian and 30,000 Persian slaves in Khiva at the time.[29]

Bukhara

In contrast to Khiva, Bukhara was already renowned in the east as a trading, cultural and religious centre, but comparatively little known in the west, except by repute to orientalists. It was certainly known to merchants, from

Jenkinson's account, although not mentioned by Thompson, who arrived in Bukhara at the time of the Persian invasion. He described a city of 'stately buildings' of brick and stone, now fallen on hard times, with its bazaars mostly ruined and trade greatly diminished. Unlike Jenkinson, he did not mention Bukhara's different districts or elaborate on the bazaars, or on the nature or decoration of buildings, many of which Jenkinson had found sumptuous.[30]

Fuller descriptions of Bukhara were given by the envoy Florio Beneveni (in Bukhara 1721–25), the captive Philip Efremov (*c*.1774) and, in the early nineteenth century, Dr Eversmann (1820) and Alexander Burnes (1831–32). Beneveni described a town of some 15,000 inhabitants, which, except for the city walls with twelve gates, the khan's enclosed 'castle' on a mound, the mosques, madrasas and a high tower, seemed 'quite humble'.[31] Efremov noted the morning (Charsu) and afternoon market (at the Registan), two tiered madrasas, stone mosques on every street, the khan's private bath and the public baths.[32] The artillery, comprising cannon and mortar, were according to him never used and only for show.[33]

Eversmann better conveyed the city's wealth and atmosphere. It had very narrow streets, with the Registan being the only open space, and was intersected by canals and besieged by beggars. There were many 'towers' (minarets), from the highest of which transgressors were hurled, and apparently 360 mosques, and 285 schools with 300 teachers. A third of the city consisted of caravanserais and markets (including the famous jewellery and antiquities market) frequented by merchants from throughout Asia.[34] Eversmann mentioned its resident Jews and Indians. The Jews, who were 'much oppressed', had their own quarter and specialised in making wine and brandy, and dyeing silk and cotton. Some were traders and doctors.[35] According to Burnes, they numbered about 4,000 in the 1830s.[36] Settled Indian merchants kept to their caravanserai[37] and, according to Burnes, were circumscribed and discriminated against. They could not have their own temple, worship publicly or ride within the city walls. There were approximately 300 Indians in Burnes' day,[38] and a few Armenians.[39]

Most eighteenth-century accounts suggest that the climate for cultural or ethnographic investigations in Khiva and Bukhara was not ideal. British merchants were more interested in trade and, for observers reporting to Russia, practical information (e.g. height of city walls, size of army, etc.) was more relevant than information on historic buildings, written and oral culture or ethnography.[40] They appear to have been oblivious to or wary of Bukhara's reputation as a centre of Islamic scholarship, and religion was addressed only superficially. All eighteenth-century travellers mentioned mosques, but few gave details.[41] Thompson highlighted the difference between the Bukharan Sunnis and the Shi'a Persians,[42] and the extent to which Persians were disliked, even more than Christians. The Bukharan religious establishment was also home to several religious orders, of which the most important was the Sufi Naqshbandiyya.[43] Its ties with the Muslims of the Volga–Ural region or the Caucasus were not recorded, although known by administrators and academicians.[44]

Despite the merchants' professed desire to see Khiva and Bukhara, there is no romanticised orientalism or sense of wonder in their descriptions. Georgi mentioned the 'magnificence of eastern splendour' of the Khivan khan's court, but his tone implies mockery rather than romance. He wrote of Bukhara as being the only spacious and considerable city of Bucharia, and then generalised about brick- and wattle-built domestic architecture and the bad gildings on mosques and the khan's palace.[45] Any British eighteenth-century sense of romance with regard to Central Asia involved its past and was based on the view of certain orientalists, such as William Jones, of the 'rich and flourishing' history of the 'large and beautiful kingdom' of fourteenth-century (Timurid) Mavarannahr. By the eighteenth century the region was simply in the 'possession' of the 'warlike' Uzbeks.[46]

Unlike India, China, Turkey or Arabia, Central Asia had only a minor role in eighteenth-century literary orientalism.[47] In contrast to the Caucasus, the picturesqueness of Central Asia, juxtaposed with its renowned savagery, appears to have been noted by western observers only from the early nineteenth century onwards.[48] In the British case, close observation was politically motivated and connected to the training of officers serving in India, such as Alexander Burnes. Some of the change in viewpoint, however, is attributable to the development of British travel writing from India from the second half of the eighteenth century. This genre personalised adventure; it had many narratives including the exoticism, backwardness, difference and tyranny of a place that was being conquered.[49] All these resonate with early nineteenth-century British narratives of Central Asia.

Government

Knowledge of Central Asian government was minimal for travellers such as Bell. He reported that Khiva was governed by a khan 'elected by the people'. The merchants mentioned the absolutism of the khan of Khiva but believed him to be controlled by the religious establishment. In Bukhara the khan was portrayed as oppressive and luxurious.

Despite Khiva's bluster, its internal affairs in the eighteenth century were unsettled and the khan's position never secure. The khans, who were among the last of the Arabshahid dynasty,[50] were increasingly controlled by Uzbek military chiefs (*inaqs*) from the Qongrat tribe, and were murdered or deposed in fairly quick succession. To maintain the tradition that only a member of the Chingisid line could hold the title of khan, they were forced to choose khans from among the Kazakhs, Karakalpaks and Bukharans, which created particular tensions and weaknesses. The state was also continually threatened by Aral Tatars and Turkmen nomads, and involved in campaigns in Khorasan.[51]

Bukhara had been the seat of an Uzbek khan since the early sixteenth century and the capital of Transoxiana from 1561. The Old Shayba-nid state,[52] which had included Ferghana, Khorezm, Balkh and parts of Khorasan, was much reduced by the eighteenth century.[53] In 1711 'Ubay-dallah Khan was assassinated. His successor, Abu'l Fayz Khan (1711–47), was even weaker, and power shifted to the *ataliq*s (senior *amir*, first minister) of the Manghit tribe.[54] During his reign, Kazakh raids (1723–28) on the central region of Mavarannahr led to the abandonment of cities, loss of agriculture, migration and the diminution of Bukhara's central author-ity.[55] Beneveni, sent to Bukhara to broker an accord and trade agreement with Russia, conveyed the difficulty of the khan's position and the tension created by various Uzbek factions (1721–25).[56] The advent of Nader Shah was particularly momentous for the khanships of both Khiva and Bukhara.

Nader Shah

Having taken Balkh and defeated Uzbek forces under Nader Shah's instruc-tions, Nader Shah's son Riza Quli Mirza, governor of Khorasan, impul-sively advanced over the Oxus in 1737 and threatened to take Qarshi. He had been recalled by Nader Shah, partly because the small Persian army under Riza Quli Mirza's command was considered no match for potential joined tribal forces and the possible involvement of Russia. The Khivan Khan Ilbars II (1728–40), however, had been bullish about the Persians and gathered a large coalition of Turkmen tribes with a view to invading Khorasan, but he turned back, fearing a Kazakh attack. Partly as a desire to punish Ilbars, Nader Shah, now back from his Indian campaign, reached the Oxus in 1740. Abu'l Fayz Khan of Bukhara sent messages of submis-sion, which Nader Shah accepted. He spared Bukhara violence but had coins struck in his name, commandeered rations, fodder and horsemen from his supporter, the son of the *ataliq* Muhammed Rahim Biy, did some building work and annexed Bukharan territory south of the Oxus. He confirmed the khan in his nominal position and took two Bukharan prin-cesses as brides for his son and nephew. He also deployed men to subdue the Yüz tribe and to remove Timur's tombstone from Samarqand.

Now effectively controlling Bukhara, Nader Shah set off for Khorezm, where he anticipated resistance. The army crossed the Oxus and set out in the direction of the Khivan fortresses, repelling a large number of Turkmen and Uzbek forces. Ilbars took refuge in successive fortresses and was besieged by Nader Shah at Khanga. The khan was then executed with his attendants at the request of relatives of ambassadors who had been murdered by him. All towns except Khiva, which had been briefly taken by the Kazakh khan Abulkhayir with Russian support, surrendered. Khiva itself surrendered after three days. Nader Shah took an inventory of Khiva, again commandeered provisions and horsemen, freed Russian slaves and Khorasani prisoners and appointed a Chingisid (Tahir Beg), related to the Bukharan khan, as khan.[57] This appointment was short-lived: Tahir Beg was murdered as a result of a coalition of Aral and Urgench Turkmen and Bukharan Uzbeks[58] – evidence of the sense of autonomy of some of the tribal groups. Thus Nader Shah's invasion and its aftermath appear to have aroused both tribal power and resistance. In Khiva, according to Hanway, Nader Shah encountered Thompson and Hogg, who were given permission to trade in his 'dominions' and dismissed. According to the merchants, the Persian army still showed the spoils from the Indian campaign.[59]

Thompson left Bukhara, heading south-west to Persia, as the route via Khorezm was unsafe. He observed the harsh conditions in areas that had once been under Bukharan control, and whose villages were now deserted. The caravan also encountered further evidence of Nader's campaigning – Afghans who had been relocated after Kandahar was subdued.[60] Thompson described this area as Uzbek, essentially meaning non-Persian, although Woodroofe pointed out that there were Uzbek tribes did even in the Balkhan area, and on the south-eastern borders of Khorasan.

Nader Shah also hoped to pacify some of the Turkmen by using the resources of Balkhan Bay and erecting a fort there. He employed Elton and Woodroofe for the survey. The entries show the value of Nephtenoy (Chelekan) Island in terms of its oil (naphtha) and fresh water, although its Turkmen inhabitants subsisted on piracy. The harsh conditions in the rest of Balkhan Bay were not suitable for the shah's plans, and the enterprise came to nothing.

After Nader Shah's departure, his assassination in 1747 and the murder of Tahir Beg, rebellion festered in Khiva. There was a quick succession of nominal khans, some of whom held the title more than once (e.g. Yadigar II) and were even kept in seclusion.[61] Khiva's khans ruled on average eight years, observed Georgi, writing in the 1770s.[62] Russia tried to interfere by supporting her own Kazakh candidates (e.g. Ghaib, 1747–58). Ethnic clashes (notably Turkmen and Uzbek) dominated, and there was a famine in 1770. The Qongrat *inaq*s nevertheless reasserted their rule, and Khorezm maintained its reputation of being 'formidable in war'.[63] In 1804–6 the Qongrat dynasty was established under Eltuzer, followed by his brother Muhammed Rahim Khan.[64]

Bukhara's affairs fared better than Khorezm's after Nader Shah. Following the death of his appointee (Muhammad Hakim, the effective ruler), Bukhara was dominated by tribal feuding and sacked in 1745. Nader Shah sent troops, and another Uzbek chief (*ataliq* Muhammad Rahim) took charge. In 1756 he appointed himself khan and founded the Manghit dynasty.[65] This usurpation of the title and new dynastic order has been directly attributed to Nader Shah's patronage and militarism.[66] Legitimacy via the Chingisid line was at first maintained through marriage, but in 1785 Shah Murad took the title of *amir*, breaking the tradition and putting greater emphasis on Islamic rule.[67] Under Shah Murad (1785–99) greater consensus was achieved with the Uzbek tribes, and Merv was captured.[68] Georgi confirmed that the Bukharan khan had more authority than others in the region,[69] although Forster (*c*.1784) wrote that, compared to the glories of Chinghis and Timur, it was 'very limited'.[70]

Khiva and its Persian lambs

While we were at ASTRACHAN, an ambassador arrived there, from the Chan of CHIVA [Khiva], going to ST PETERSBURG. On his arrival he sent, according to the eastern custom, some small presents to our ambassador; they were brought by part of his retinue, and consisted of a hawking glove, a small knife, an embroidered purse, and some fruits.

CHIVA is a large territory, lying about two or three days journey eastward from the CASPIAN sea; bounded by PERSIA on the south, and BUCHARIA to the east. The capital, which bears the same name, is large and populous; and governed by a Chan, elected by the people. They are very troublesome and dangerous … And though CHIVA is well fortified its situation in so sandy and barren a desert is its best defence.[71]

At ASTRACHAN they have great quantities of lamb-skins, grey and black; some waved, others curled, all naturally, and very pretty, having a fine gloss, particularly the waved, which, at a small distance, appear like the richest watered tabby; they are much esteemed, and are much used for the lining of coats, and the turning up of caps in PERSIA, RUSSIA, and other parts. The best of these are brought from BUCHARIA, CHIVA, and the countries adjacent, and are taken out of the ewe's belly, after she hath been killed, or the lamb is killed immediately after it is lambed; for such a skin is equal in value to a sheep.

The KALMUCKS and other TARTARS, who inhabit the desert, in the neighbourhood of ASTRACHAN, have also lamb-skins, which are applied to the same purposes; but the wool of these being rougher, and more hairy, they are far inferior to those of BUCHARIA, or CHIVA, both in gloss and beauty, as also in the dressing, consequently in value; I have known one single lamb-skin of BUCHARIA sold for five or six shillings Sterling, when one of these would not yield two shillings.[72]

(Bell, Astrakhan 1716)

Traders' troubles at Khiva

All things being thus unhappily circumstanced made us determined to proceed directly from Astracan to Khiva, and thence to Bokhara, for which Place the Goods that we had with us were chiefly sorted and designed; in order to which we view'd a Vessel belonging to a Russ merchant, which was bound to a Landing-Place, where a ferry boat brings Goods of all Sorts proper for that country, on the East Side of the Caspian, from whence cross the Step (or Desert) in about ten Days we might arrive at Chiva, and so on to Bokhara, to which place two Russ Factors were going in this Vessel, and also several Chisinsky [Khivan] Tartars, who came in this same Vessel from the Port or Landing-Place last Year. But on more mature deliberation we were forced to lay aside this Design, tho' with much Regret, since our Curiosity made us eager to have seen Bakhar, and from thence to have return'd back thro' Persia: At the former we were sure to have sold our Goods for a considerable Profit, and at the same time have gained Knowledge of a Country so little known to Europeans, and on which we chiefly placed our Hopes. The chief Reasons that dissuaded us were, that the Vessel, on examining her, we found to be an old crazy flat-bottom Fishing Vessel, our companions to be only two or three mean Russians, and in crossing the Step to Chiva from the Place we land, the great Risque we run of being plunder'd and sold for Slaves. For though it should be true that the Khan, or Governor, does on Notice of this Vessel's Arrival at the landing-Place, send a small convoy to meet and protect the Carravan (for the Goods and Passengers this Vessel bring are call'd;) yet this is but a slender Security, as he may at the same time send a much stronger Party to plunder them. All the Tartars are known to be most subtil and artful at Stratagems, therefore one must be always on one's Guard, and cautious in dealing with them, for they won't fail to deceive you if any way they possibly can. But what prevail'd with us most to desist from this Expedition, was the Certainty we had of the Persians having fallen into that Country; so that had we arrived safe at Chiva and Bakhara, there was little Hopes of our Return by Way of Persia; and if so, then the principal End of our Journey would have been lost, and we should have gain'd no Information of the Silk Trade in the Province of Ghilan; to which Place we were forced again to turn our Eye, tho' we had but a sad and gloomy prospect in that Quarter. What supported us was, that the Armenians shipped off goods for Reshd, and so we now resolved to do, and to stand the same chance they did.[73]

(Elton and Graeme, in Spilman, Astrakhan 1739)

Setting out from St Petersburg

We set out from St PETERSBURG with a small quantity of goods, expecting to return by the end of the ensuing winter. Our intention was to learn, if any trade could be carried on amongst the TARTARS, particularly those of KHIEVA and BOKHARA.

The 12th of June [1740] we proceeded on our journey [from Samara] under a convoy, and traveling south-east in a beaten road through a desert 300 wersts, we arrived the 17th at YAIEK ... Here we changed our European for TARTAR habits, and providing ourselves with camels, horses, and other necessaries, we discharged our RUSSIAN attendants. It was not without the utmost difficulty that we persuaded some KHAL-MUCKS and TARTARS to engage in our service: the COSSACKS of the YAEIK absolutely refused, giving us many instances of the distress of their own people, who had been plundered and made slaves in attempting to go to KHIEVA; but we resolved to encounter all difficulties. A chief of the KIRGEESE [Kazakh] TARTARS had sent us two persons as guides; and we flattered ourselves that the authority of their chief, would be an inducement to their fidelity in our defence.

Finding other KIRGEESE, who were returning home from YAIEK with merchandize, we joined them, making in all about twenty persons on horseback; our goods were loaden on camels. The 26th of June we set out on our journey, and traveled due east about 60 wersts every day, through a desert without any road or path; the TARTARS directing their course by remarkable hills and rivulets, well known to them. We were obliged to keep watch day and night, knowing that when parties meet, the weakest, even if they are of the same HORDA (a tribe of TARTARS) are subject to many inconveniences, and if they are of different HORDAS, they kill those who are advanced in age, and make slaves of the young people.

On the 7th of July we perceived a party at a distance, and our companions pursued, and took three KHALMUCKS, with seven horses. This was esteemed a legal, and a valuable prize, and was attended with this further advantage, that we procured intelligence of the HORDA we were in quest of.

July the 11th, we fell in with a party of KIRGEESE, with whom most of our company remained; so that we were constrained to continue our journey with our two guides only. We proceeded north-east till the 16th, when we arrived near the HORDA of our friend, JEAN BEEK BATER [Janibek Batyr]: he made us the compliment of sending his son, with several other relations, to meet us, who conducted us the next day to his KABITKA (tent ... in use among the KHALMUKS). On reckoning our distance, we found it eight hundred wrests from the river YAEIK. This TARTAR-chief was sitting on a carpet in his tent: he arose and bid us welcome, and making us to sit down with him, he took a large dish of

KUMEESE (mare's milk, fermented), which he drank, and made us do the same. We gave him some small presents, which he divided among the company. Some days after we made him a more valuable present, telling him that our design in going to Khieva, was to fix and carry on a trade there; in which, if we succeeded, we should bring much larger cargoes; and then it would be more in our power to requite him for all his favours; in answer to which he assured us, that we might command all the service in his power, to forward our design: and insisted that we should continue with him till the extreme heat was abated, and refresh our cattle, which from hard travelling, were in very weak condition.

The KIRGEESE TARTARS possess a very extensive tract of land, having the BASHKEERT [Bashkir] TARTARS to the north, the black KHALMUKS, with the city of TASHCHUND [Tashkent] to the east, the KARAKULPACK TARTARS and the ARAL lake to the south, and the river YAEIK to the west. That part which borders on the RUSSIAN dominions, was under the authority of JEAN BEEK, whose name on all occasions was honoured with the title of BATER (the word means hero).

We proceeded north-east till the 16th, when we arrived near the HORDA of our friend, JEAN BEEK BATER ... 800 wersts from the river JAEIK ...

We remained with JEAN BEEK, and travelled in his company till the 8th of August, when we found ourselves in the latitude of 51 1/2, five days journey to the south-east of ORENBURG. The city is lately built by the RUSSIANS, as a barrier against the KIRGEESE and KARAKUL-PACK TARTARS, and likewise with a view of opening a trade with them for furrs, gold-dust, and rhubarb. Having received directions from JEAN BEEK, and taking one of his relations for our guide, we joined a caravan of KIRGEESE and TURKUMAN TARTARS, about sixty in number. With these we travelled south-west near 50 wersts a day for eight days: we met several parties, but received no harm from them; although several TUR-KUMANS joined us, who, after having been robbed of their effects, had with great difficulty escaped with their lives. [See note 75.]

(Thompson and Hogg, in Hanway, February–August 1740)

Reaching the Aral Sea

August 6th, we reached the ARAL lake, which is reckoned 22 days journey from ORENBURG, and 12 from the river YAEIK. We traveled south along a very high and rocky shore, where we were scarce able to get any water once in two days; and this was so bitter and salt, that necessity only obliged us to drink of it. The KARAKULPACKS inhabit the east shore of this lake, where the river SIRR [Sir Darya] falls into it, and the ARAL TARTARS the south shore, where it receives the great river AMO [Amu

Darya]. The latter use only small fishing boats, and never venture far from the shore. It is said that a person cannot conveniently ride round this lake in less than 35 days, being computed above 1000 ENGLISH miles. There are abundance of wild horses, assess, antelopes, and wolves; here also a very fierce creature, called JOLBART,[74] not unlike a tyger, which the TATARS say is of such prodigious strength as to carry off a horse.

September 3rd, we left the lake, and arrived at a valley full of brush-wood, and almost knee deep of stagnated water. We were informed that this was the channel of the river OXUS, which had run betwixt the ARAL lake and the CASPIAN sea; but was stopped up by the TATARS many ages since. [See note 75.]

(Thompson and Hogg, in Hanway, February–August 1740)

Onwards to Urgench and Khiva

The 5th [September], we came to the city JURGANTZ [Urgench], which appeared to have been a large place; but was now entirely in ruins, no other building remaining than a mosque. Here our company were very devout: they offered their prayers to heaven for their safe journey, and then went in search of gold, which they said, they had frequently found washed out by the rains from amongst the ruins of this city. We travelled on south-east till the 8th, when we arrived at some villages belonging to the TARTARS of KHIEVA. On the 9th, our company left us, and with our guide only we proceeded due west 9 hours, and reached the city of KHIEVA [Khiva], which is 17 days journey distant from the CASPIAN sea, and from ORENBURG 33, computing a day's journey to be 40 RUSSIAN wersts (27 ENGLISH miles).

We took our lodgings in a caravanserai, which was a very mean building. Here our goods and baggage were immediately searched and valued. For which we paid duty 5 per cent. We had the full liberty to sell them; but we could not dispose of a sufficient value to maintain ourselves and our cattle: for NADIR SHAH, who was then on his return from INDIA, was expected to make this place a visit; so that it was our misfortune to arrive when the state began to be in great confusion. The people were so infatuated as to think themselves a match for the PERSIANS; but when they heard that the SHAH was with them in person, they were greatly terrified.

A few days after our arrival, one of the KIRGEESE came to us by night from our guide, and informed us, that if we consulted our own safety, we must return immediately; that the company we had parted with on the 9th, had been plundered by the TURKUMANS, and several of them killed; that they durst not stay longer in these parts; but were resolved to make up their loss on the road by reprisals. Finding he made impression on us, he took his leave, promising to return in the spring, in company with our guide, if the country was in peace. KHIEVA lies in the latitude of 38 1/2, and is the residence of a KHAN. It is situated on a rising ground, has three gates, and is defended by a strong wall of earth, very thick, and much higher than the house: it has turrets at small distances, and a broad deep ditch full of water. The place is large, but the houses are low, the greatest part of them being built with mud; the roofs are flat, and covered with earth. It commands a pleasant prospect of the adjacent plains, which, by the industry of the inhabitants, are rendered very fertile.

The dominions of KHIVA are of so small extent, that a person may ride round them in three days; it has five walled cities, all within half a day's journey of each other. The KHAN is absolute, and entirely independent of any other power, except the MULLAH BASHI, or high-priest, by whom he is controled. The KIEVINSKI TARTARS differ very little from the KIRGEESE; but surpass them in cunning and treachery. Their manners are the same, only that the KIRGEESE live in tents, whilst the others inhabit cities and villages. Their only trade is with BOKHARA and PERSIA, whither they carry cattle, furrs, and hides, all which they have from the KIRGEESE and TURKUMEN TARTARS, who often prove very troublesome neighbours to them. The place itself produces little more than cotton, lamb-furrs, of a very mean quality; and small quantities of raw silk, some of which they manufacture.

The consumption of EUROPEAN cloth, and other commodities, is inconsiderable, as is the whole trade of this place; so that no profit can be expected any ways proportioned to the risque. The duty on all goods belonging to CHRISTIANS is 5 per cent. And to all others who are not of the MAHOMMEDAN faith: but on the goods of MAHOMMEDANS only 2 1/2 percent. The whole revenue arising to the KHAN does not amount to 100 ducats yearly. Their coin is ducats of gold, each weighing one MUSCAL, or 3 penny-weight ENGLISH; also TONGAS, a small piece of copper, of which 1500 are equal to a ducat. Their weights are the great BATMAN equal to 18lb RUSSIAN, and the lesser BATMAN 9 1/4, which they divide into halves, quarters, and smaller parts. Their measure is called GAZ, equal to 12 inches ENGLISH.[75]

(Thompson and Hogg in Hanway, 1740)

Hanway continues the story

These factors [traders] remained in KHIEVA till the 15th of December, the PERSIANS having in the interim taken possession of this place, the particulars of which I shall insert in the life of NADIR. The small quantity of goods which they had with them they sold to the PERSIANS; but not being able to recover the money, Mr HOGG was obliged to remain there, intending to return home by the same rout he came, whilst Mr

THOMPSON proceeded to BOKHARA, designing to return home through PERSIA, and over the CASPIAN sea. The TATARS whom Mr HOGG expected as a convoy, having been attacked by the TURKU-MANS, were driven back to their own country, except those who lost their lives in a skirmish. Hence it was not till the 6ᵗʰ of April that he left KHIEVA, and finding that the TURKUMANS were roving upon the western side of the ARAL lake, he passed the AMO, and traveling eastward to the country of the KHARAKHULPACKS, in fifteen days he crossed the river SIRR, which falls into that lake, and thence proceeding in search of JEAN BEEK, the chief of the KIRGEESE TARTARS, he was set upon by seventeen of them, and plundered, narrowly escaping with his life. He found means however to make his complaint to JEAN BEEK, who was gone upon an expedition against the BLACK KHALMUCKS, and obtained restitution of part of what he was robbed of, with a promise of the remainder, which was never fulfilled. It was as good fortune as he could expect to get safe to ORENBURG; and from thence in the next spring he arrived in St PETERSBURG, to the great satisfaction of his friends.[76]

(Hanway, 1740)

Mr Thompson in Bukhara

This [Bukhara] is a large and populous city, lying in the latitude 39 1/2 three days journey to the northward of the river AMO: it is the residence of the KHAN, who is entirely absolute, though his power extends very little beyond the city. The adjacent country is called TURKISTAN, and is governed by several BEEKS [biqs] or chiefs, who are wholly independent of each other, as well as of the KHAN of BOKHARA.

The town is situated on a rising ground, with a slender wall of earth, and a dry ditch: the houses are low, and mostly built of mud: but the caravanserais and the mosques, which are numerous, are all of brick: the BAZARS, or market-places, have been stately buildings, but are now the greatest part of them in ruins; these are generally built of brick and stone. Here is also a stately building of the same materials, appropriated for the education of the priests, who receive very considerable profits by their public discourses on the different points of their religion, which is the same as that of the TURKS. They differ from the PERSIANS, not only in regard to MAHOMMED'S successor, but in particular ceremonies: their hatred to the PERSIANS is much greater than to the CHRISTIANS, and they esteem themselves equally unclean by touching either of them; never omitting to wash themselves immediately after leaving their company.

The place is not esteemed unhealthy as to the air and soil; but the water is so very bad, that many of the inhabitants are confined several months in the summer by worms in their flesh, which they call RISHTAS:

some of these, when taken out of their bodies, prove to be above 40 inches long. There are also serpents and scorpions which infest their houses, and are very venomous; the sting of the scorpion causes great pain, and sometimes death: the most effectual remedy they find for the immediate cure of this distemper is to bruise the scorpion, and apply it to the wound.

The inhabitants of this city are more civilized and polite that those of KHIEVA; but are also cowardly, cruel, effeminate, and extremely perfidious. Great numbers of JEWS and ARABIANS frequent this place; through they are much oppressed, and often deprived of their whole possessions by the KHAN, or his attendants, who seize them at their pleasure; and notwithstanding they pay most heavy taxes, it is criminal in them to be rich.

The trade of BOKHARA is much declined from what it was formerly: their product is cotton, lamb-furrs, down, rice, and cattle; and they manufacture soap, cotton-yarn, and callicoe, which they carry to PERSIA, and receive in returns all sorts of manufactures of that country; such as velvet, silk, cloth, and sashes: woolen-cloth is also brought hither from PERSIA, as likewise shalloons [lightweight woollen twill], indigo, coral, and cochineal. They have rhubarb, musk and castorium, and many other valuable drugs from the BLACK KHALMUCKS [Oirats] and TASHCUND [Tashkent]. Formerly they received lapis-lazuli and other precious stones, from BIDDUKHSAN [Badakhshan] the capital of the country of that name, which is computed sixteen days journey from BOKHARA. But the late wars, and the frequent robberies on the roads make it difficult to procure any of these commodities; so that they are carried through another channel. The KHAN and his officers are possesses of very rich jewels; but never dispose of them, unless in cases of the greatest necessity, and even then they are jealous of them being carried out of the country.

They make very little consumption of EUROPEAN commodities: as to cloth, they use it mostly in caps; but no foreign commodity bears a price proportionable to the risque of bringing it to market …

The duty, on all imported goods, belonging either to natives or foreigners, is 1 per cent. And on goods exported 10 per cent. The revenue from this duty is reckoned 1000 ducats yearly in time of peace, which but seldom happens. The PERSIAN and TARTAR languages are both spoken here; but all their writings are in the PERSIAN tongue.[77]

(Thompson, in Hanway, 1741)

Mr Thomson's return

Mr Thompson continued at BOKHARA till May; when he received notice that the ARAL TARTARS had plundered all round KHIEVA; … As the Tartars had beset all the roads, and cut off several caravans coming from MESCHED, threatening even BOKHARA itself; Mr THOMPSON continued impatient till the end of July, having no prospect during that time of traveling with any security. Several people, who had escaped from KHIEVA gave an account that the OUSBEGS had recovered that place, and destroyed the PERSIAN KHAN with all his attendants. Upon this the communication with KHIEVA was prohibited, the PERSIANS intending them a second visit; for which purpose they had ordered provisions for a large body of men.

The road to PERSIA being now the only safe way of returning to RUSSIA, at length he joined some merchants …[78]

(Hanway,1741)

From Bukhara to Meshed

On the 8th of August we set out, and traveled east, passing through several OUSBEG villages till the 12th. After turning to the south, and traveling through deserts we came the 16th to the river AMO, and crossed it at KIRKIE, a fort belonging to the OUSBEGS, subject to PERSIA: here we paid a small duty, and proceeded south-east through deserts till the 21st, when we arrived at ANTHUY [Andkhuy] an OUSBEG city; computed, in the direct road, to be only three days journey from BOKHARA.

This country was then entirely subject to the PERSIANS, who carry on a great trade in cattle. Here we were detained ten days, waiting for a caravan, which was dispatched the 31st, when we set forward, and traveled west through narrow vallies bounded by high mountains: having passed several villages which were deserted by the OUSBEGS, we arrived the 6th of September at MARGIEHAK [Merochak] the first PERSIAN city on that side. This is a very strong place, surrounded by a double wall, and governed by a KHAN: it has a garrison of 500 men, and is defended by several pieces of cannon. In the summer it is very unhealthy, by reason of the very frequent pestilential winds, which often kill those who are exposed to them. To secure themselves against this inconveniency, the people hide themselves under ground, or falling flat on the earth, cover themselves with wet cloaths, till these winds blow over. The cattle which are most exposed, are generally destroyed by these winds, though they are but of a short continuance. During our stay here, which was only four days, most of the people in the caravan fell sick, and the great part of the cattle, which was the chief part of their merchandize, died.

On the 11th we traveled still west, through dry and sandy deserts, where we got only two pots of water during four days, and this was so bitter, and smelt so strongly of sulphur, that the cattle would hardly drink it. On the 15th, continuing our journey by a high ridge of rocks, and a small rivulet of salt water, we came at length into a beaten road. We passed through many villages, the greatest part of which were being chiefly AFGHANS, brought from the new conquered dominions. The country hereabouts is very dry, barren and mountainous.

September 22nd, we arrived at MESCHED, the capital of KHORASAN, and the favourite city of NADIR. It was at this time governed by his son RIZA KOULI MYRZA ...[79]

(Thompson, in Hanway, 1741)

Nader Shah employs Elton

[I]t seems that NADIR with his usual sagacity foresaw a rebellion from that side of TURKUMANIA, which induced him to employ his new servant ELTON; his intent being to send a fleet to BALKHAN with provisions, in order to build a fort and keep a garrison in that place, to awe the TURKUMAN TARTARS. This step could not but give great offence to the RUSSIANS, because their barrier would become so much the weaker, and the PERSIANS might the more easily invade RUSSIA on that side, which has always been considered as impracticable.[80]

(Hanway, 1743)

Surveying Balkhan Bay for Nader Shah

[14 Sept 1743] We weighed [anchor] and came in close under the east side of NAPHTONIA [Chelekan]. The coast is difficult of access, the land being very high; it extends itself six or eight leagues north and south, and contains about 36 families, who have 28 large boats with several wells of NAPHTA (so called by the Russians; the Persians call it Cherican) ... The harbour is on the east side of the island ... NAPHTONA has plenty of sheep, wild goats, camels and assess, with exceeding good water ... all the springs along this coast, except here, and on IDAK, are salt and brakish. The soil is fruitful ... There is an old mosque, to which the inhabitants come to worship. These people subsist entirely by piracy, making continual depradations on the neighbouring parts of PERSIA.[81]

September 17th
We continued sounding, and got up to a small island on the south side of the bay, called DAGADAW, where we anchored in two fathom of water.

The day following we went with the long-boat to survey the island ... our pilot carried us to two springs, where there were many tracks of camels and sheep. The water was brackish ... and yet the TURKUMANS and their cattle drink of it. I was informed, that it is now 100 years since the OXUS emptied itself into the upper end of this bay. As this river was often dried up in many places in the heat of the summer, the TURKUMANS imagined, that by stopping the mouth of it they could preserve it above.

But the contrary fell out, for the water having no passage to clear away the sand, which was constantly blown off the desert into this river, it is filled up, and scarce any vestiges of it are now remaining near the CASPIAN sea ...[82]

September 18th

As we continued sounding the bay, we found the water grew shallow ... When we arrived at the foot of the mountain [DARGAN] we saw 14 boats at anchor to the southward of DARGAN, where there is a wide bay that extends into the CASPIAN ... This day we weighed, and ran up into nine feet water, and moored the ship near the foot of the mountain.

Here captain Elton and NASEER AGA went in search of a convenient spot, on which they might build a fort. They had taken with them on shore the PERSIAN soldiers, a pilot, and four sailors, with arms and ammunition sufficient to make a defence against those Tartars, in case of attack ... we saw 14 boats steering to the westward ...

September 22nd

Upon our first approaching NAPHTONIA, the inhabitants imagined we were driven there by distress, for which reason they manned all their boats with design to cut us off. But observing that we beat the drum and fired the morning gun ... they concluded that we were sent by the SHAH to destroy them; upon which they made all haste back to save their families and cattle. The former they conveyed in boats to BALKHAN ... [the latter with slaves] they transported ... to DARGAN. [The latter perished from wild beasts and want of water] ... they [then] sailed ... southward, while the TURKUMANS and several OUSBEG TARTARS who frequent this neighbourhood, fled up into the mountain of BALKHAN.

These pirates were possessed of 17 boats more, which were then on a cruise on the coast of MAZANDERAN and ASTRABAD. 'Tis their custom to send only half of their boats out at a time ...

Captain Elton ... proceeded in his survey ... This prince [Nader Shah] had been informed, that there was plenty of fresh water in those parts; but upon examination it was found that the springs were overflowed with salt water ...The island of DAGADAW was judged the safest place for the garrison, as the magazines would be there most secure from any surprise by land on the part of the TARTARS. With regards to fresh water, Captain Elton proposed to provide a number of boats, and to bring it from NAPHTONIA ... as the navigation between the two islands is extremely safe.[83]

(Captain Woodroofe in Hanway, September 1743)

246

Dealing with pirates

To remedy this evil [depredations], NADIR SHAH some years since offered to forgive all that was past, and to receive them into his favour, if they [people of Naphtona] would come and settle about ASTRABAD bay, where they might have lands and sell their NAPHTA to the inhabitants of that quarter. This they accepted, and carried on a brisk trade for about two years, selling their NAPHTA to the PERSIANS, TURKUMANS, and roving OUSBEGS, and purchasing provisions to supply the inhabitants of the islands. But having had an opportunity of collecting a number of boats, they grew tired of this way of living, and returned to their trade of piracy; so that BALKHAN became a general rendezvous of robbers. NADIR SHAH being at the time engaged in his expedition against the MOGHOL, postponed the reduction of these people till his return. But upon enquiry he now found it attended with great difficulty, for the place is almost inaccessible by land, and the country so wild and barren, that none but those hardy people the TURKUMANS can live in it.[84]

(Captain Woodroofe, in Hanway, 1743)

ENDNOTES

1   Burton, *passim*.

2   Appleby 2004(a); Hanway, vol.1, pp.5–6; Hakluyt, pp.77–89.

3   Müller 1760, vol.4, pp.185–87; Levi 1999; Dale 2002.

4   Pallas 1788–93, vol.1, pp.532–37; Coxe 1784, vol.3 , pp.21–22; Georgi 1780–83, vol.2, pp.137–41; Bregel 2003, pp.68–69; Allworth 1994, pp.19–28; for Khoqand, see Levi 2007.

5   Hanway, vol.1, pp.15–16.

6   Ibid., pp.35–36.

7   These merchants are referred to as British 'agents' in Soviet sources (*Istoria Uzbekskoi SSR*, p.55).

8   Hanway, vol.1, pp.16, 38–39.

9   Allworth 1994(a), pp.25–28.

10 Pallas 1788–93, vol.1 pp.358–59. Georgi 1780–83, vol.2, pp. 139–40, mentions the difficulties encountered by Bukharan trade when traversing Kazakh lands.

11 Burton, p.17, speaks of seventeenth-century trade, but the same principle applied later.

12 Burnes 1973, vol.2, pp. 424–35.

13 Di Cosmo, p.92.

14 Bosworth 2004, pp.892–93; Bregel 2003, *passim* (Old and New Urgench), p.86 (monuments of Old Urgench).

15 Ebulgazi Bahadur, pp.438–40.

16 Rukavin, pp.30–31.

17 Bregel 2003, pp.58, 60, 66–67.

18 Ibid., p.84.

19 Others were Urgench, Khanga, Fitnak and Hazarasp. Rukavin, p.27, lists Anbiri (Ambar), Shabat (Shahabad), Keit (Qiyat or Kat), Chep (?), Azaris (Hazarasp) and Urgench. See Rukavin, pp.27–28, for the few inhabitants of the fortress towns that were used primarily in times of war (except for Khiva and Urgench).

20 *Russian Missions*, p.51. Burnes was expressly forbidden to use pen and ink when in Bukhara (Burnes, vol.1, p.270).

21 Di Cosmo, pp.76–79, 91–114.

22 Rukavin, p.27.

23 Beneveni, p.131 (poor Bukharan defenses, no artillery); Di Cosmo, p.102 (Shir-Ghazi).

24 Bregel 2003, p.85; Arapov, pp.87ff.

25 To negotiate trade via Krasnovodsk rather than Mangyshlak, see *Russian Missions*, pp.106–7.

26 Ibid., p.100. This description evokes those of visitors seeing the onion domes of Russian churches the first time (cf. Parkinson's approach to Kazan).

27 Ibid., pp.104–5; see Bregel 2003, p.67 for a map of nineteenth-century Khiva.

28 Ibid., pp.89, 100.

29 Ibid., p.94.

30 Hakluyt, p.85.

31 Beneveni, p.124.

32 Efremov, pp.66–69.

33 Ibid., pp.69–70.

34 *Russian Missions*, pp.37–40, 48; see Burnes, pp.274–75 for his description of the Registan and its peoples.

35 *Russian Missions*, p.42.

36 Burnes, p.275.

37 *Russian Missions*, p. 48; see also Dale 2002, pp.126, 132; Levi 1999, p.539.

38 Burnes, pp.285–86.

39 Ibid., p.275.

40 The captive Efremov, who had the time to observe, gives details on diet, women's dress and punishments, and even has a glossary of Russian–'Bucharian' (Efremov, pp.74–78, 85–86, 194–224.

41 I have not been able to check all eighteenth-century Russian travellers to Bukhara (or Khiva); see von Kügelen, pp.417–18, and notes for references. See Burnes, vol.2, pp.365–67, for example, on the influence of the religious establishment on the state.

42 Cf. Efremov, p.62.

43 Babadzanov, pp.385–413. The founder of the order, Bahauddin Naqshband, is buried near Bukhara.

44 Georgi 1780–83, vol.2, pp.131–32; Frank 2003, p.275 (Kazakhs trained in Bukhara); Frank 1996, *passim*; Azamatov, *passim*; Kemper, pp.18ff, 50ff, 81ff, 98ff, with references to Bukhara in the index. Crews, pp.31–32, 52, 55, 62, 96 and *passim*, highlights the role of Kabul in this network.

45 Crews, pp.132–33.

46 Jones 1773, pp.xxiii–ix.

47   This was expressed, for example, by references to princes or princesses of Samar-
      qand in Oriental tales. See Ballaster, pp.194 (Turandot), 303 (Moghul).

48   E.g. Burnes, p.268, was 'lost in amazement at the novel scene'. Vambéry, ed. Jan
      1992, pp.243–66, balances the lyrical with the threatening.

49   Teltscher, pp.4–5, 109–56, 229–55.

50   Arabshahid dynasty reg.1511–1817. Bregel 2003, p.57; Bregel 2007, p.60.

51   Bregel 2003, pp.58, 66; Bregel 2007, p.60; Allworth 1990, 1994 *passim*; Holzwarth,
      passim.

52   After Shibani Khan, the conqueror of Timurid Central Asia. See Bregel 2003, p.50.

53   Ibid., pp.52–58.

54   Bregel, 2004c, pp.96–98; Bregel, 1991, pp.416–17, 417–18 ('Mangit'), 418–19
      ('Mangits').

55   Holzwarth, pp.193–99.

56   Beneveni, pp.124–25. One faction supported the khan, another Samarqand, and
      another was against both these. Any alliance with Russia was seen as disadvanta-
      geous by some factions (Poujol, p.249).

57   Howorth, vol.2, pp.912–15; Lockhart 1938, pp.163–96; Avery, pp.42–44; Perry
      1993, pp.854–55; Bregel 2003, p.58; Axworthy 2009, pp.222–28 (greatly derived
      from Lockhart). For eighteenth-century sources, see Fraser, pp.223–26; Hanway,
      vol.2, pp.513–15; Cook, vol.2, pp.389–90; Jones 1773, pp.98–102.

58   *Russko-Turkmenskie Otnoshenia*, doc.40.

59   Hanway, vol.1, pp.515–16, note c.

60   Lockhart 1938, p.120.

61   Howorth, vol.2, p.918 (on Abul'Gazi Badadur Khan).

62   Georgi 1780–83, vol.2, p.166.

63   Ibid., pp.166–67.

64   Bregel 2003, pp.60, 62; Bregel 1988.

65   See Efremov, pp.105–12 for the rise of Rahim Biy and the strength of his successor
      Daniyal Ataliq.

66   Sela, p.5; Holzwarth, pp.202–3.

67   Geiss, pp.128–29.

68   Bregel 2003, pp.58, 60.

69   Georgi 1780–83, vol.2, p.130.

70   Forster, p.196.

71   Bell, pp.42–43.

72   Ibid., p.45.

73   Spilman, pp.8–10; cf. Hanway, vol.2, pp.20–21 for European goods and Persian money.

74   Probably a type of tiger.

75   Hanway, vol.1, pp.346–51.

76   Hanway, vol.1, p.352.

77   Ibid., pp.352–55.

78   Ibid., p.355.

79   Ibid., pp.355–56.

80   Ibid., p.138.

81   Ibid., pp.133–34.

82   Ibid., p.135.

83   Ibid., pp.136–38.

84   Ibid., p.134.

Introduction

The multi-ethnic, multi-tribal nature of the Central Asian regions discussed in this section has already been mentioned. British travellers referred to town-dwelling Khivans (sometimes as Chisinskys) and Bukharans in general, and singled out the nomadic Kazakhs (Kirgeese), Arak and Karakalpak Tatars, Turkmen (Turkumanians, Turkumans) and Uzbeks (Usbeck). They encountered these peoples in varied circumstances, whether peaceful and protective, threatening or neutral.

The travellers provide a broadly accurate idea of the distribution of the nomadic groups: the Kazakhs of the Orenburg and Yaik area; the Karakalpaks on the east shore of the Aral Sea, within sight of Samara in the early eighteenth century; the Aral Tartars on the south shore; and the Turkmen along most of the Caspian's east coast. In Gmelin's day Turkmen were said to extend from Astarabad to Khiva.[1] Bruce, on the other hand, writing about the early eighteenth century, divided the east coast into Turkmen and, below the Gulf of Alexander, Uzbek tribal territory. He may have been repeating what he was told at the time, or he may have used the label Uzbek for other Turkmen tribal peoples, labelled as Uzbek in early maps. Later observers such as Woodroofe, however, mentioned Uzbeks even on the south-east Caspian coast, rather than traditionally inland.

Eighteenth-century British sources give no details about tribal groups, their organisation, rivalries or alliances. The intimidating tactics of the Karakalpaks were noted by Bell and (particularly of the Turkmen) by Bruce. The merchants only mentioned hordes ('hordas'), who killed the old and captured the young. Again nothing was said about semi-nomadic groups or settled farmers. Although some Kazakh tribal customs were described by academicians, those of Turkmen or Uzbeks are only glimpsed in published eighteenth-century Russian sources (Gmelin was occasionally more thorough). Early nineteenth-century Russian and European sources[2] and indigenous ones, such as *Firdaws al-iqbal*,[3] still gave only a general picture, with tribes mentioned incidentally in the context of politics, feuds, rebellions or war.

Kazakhs

The Kazakhs descended from Turkish and Mongol tribes of the Dasht-i Qipchaq and were linked to the Uzbeks and the Kirghiz. Their mixed origin and composition, which confused academicians,[4] are still debated today.[5] The academicians, however, focused on the contemporary social organisation and customs of the Lesser and Midddle Hordes, with which the Russians had dealings (the Great Horde in Semirech'e was too remote).

The hordes were composed of 'branches' (tribal units or confederacies).[6] The Lesser (or Junior) Horde, known as 'Kiptschious' (Qipchaq), was divided into two 'stocks': the Altschinsk (?) and the Dschatyr (Zheti-Ru). The Middle Horde had four branches: Naimani (Nayman), Arguinzi (Arghyn), Onvak (?) and the Qipchaq.[7] Each of these branches was subdivided into 'ulusses', and each 'uluss' had its own 'aimaks' or nobles. Each horde was thought to contain about 30,000 habitations (and cavalry), although Georgi admitted that this figure was speculative.[8] Nobles were divided into classes: sultan (highest), *bu* (*biy*, descended from a sultan or famous warrior) and *godsha* (lowest, of good family).[9] The number of slaves owned was a mark of status.[10] Each family or 'aimak' elected its own elder, whose status was determined by wealth and the will of the people. Equally, the khan's authority depended on the goodwill of the people. Edicts were obeyed only if convenient.[11]

General assemblies were convened only in the face of major battle.[12] Kazakh laws were founded partly on the Koran and partly on 'the usage of their ancestors'. Equally, religion was nominally Muslim (but with few mullahs), and with divination and magic playing a central role.[13] The Kazakhs were considered rich compared to other nomads but lived a 'frugal' pastoral life, based on tending their herds of horses, sheep and some camels, and spoils from raids and wars.[14] They were regarded by the Russian state not as evil or bloodthirsty but as acquisitive, self-interested and 'passionately fond of uncontrolled liberty'.[15] Misdemeanours such as robberies were attributed to lack of civilisation, which would be rectified under Russian influence.[16] The Kazakhs were also reputed to be clean, hospitable, kind to their slaves, affable and high-spirited[17] (see pp.219-20).

Among the Kazakhs

They live in tents made of wooden stakes, and covered with a felt of camel's hair; this they fix or remove with great ease, whenever they change their quarters, and they never stay above two or three days in a place. They feed on horse-flesh, mutton and venison, and drink fermented mare's milk to excess; so that they often intoxicate themselves with it. They have no grain, nor any kind of bread. When they go upon an expedition, they take a small quantity of cheese, which they call CRUTE; this being dissolved in water, is their chief sustenance during their journey. Money is hardly known among them; their riches consist in cattle, fox, and wolf furs, which they exchange with their neighbours for cloaths, and other necessaries. What little religion they have, is MAHOMMEDANISM, and their language has great affinity with that of the TURKS. They are a strong robust people, but rude, ignorant, and treacherous. They are very civil to strangers, whilst they continue under their protection; for they esteem it the greatest dishonour to affront a guest: but no sooner is he departed, than his professed friend and protector will sometimes be the last person to rob him, and happy if he escapes without being made a slave.

These KIRGEESES TARTARS have very little sense of many atrocious crimes, particularly robbery. Their ordinary punishment in this case, is only restitution to the person robbed; and for murder the loss of their goods; sometimes indeed for the latter, the criminal and his whole family, are delivered up to slavery to the relations of the deceased.[18]

(Thompson and Hogg, in Hanway, 1740)

Karakalpaks

The nomadic and semi-nomadic Turkic Karakalpaks (meaning 'Black Caps'), first named as such at the end of the seventeenth century, were associated with the Sir-Darya and north-east of the Aral Sea. They were relatively powerless in the face of greater forces, such as the Kazakhs or Kalmyks, by whom they were buffeted and oppressed. While sharing some of the same enemies as the Kazakhs, such as the Oirats and Kalmyks, they were obliged to comply with the Kazakh khans and pay tribute. They were thus compelled to treat with the Russians and/or to intermittently ally themselves with the Bukharans and Khivans. In the second half of the eighteenth century they were driven further south to Khorezm and Bukhara, and eventually came under Qongrat control.[19]

The Karakalpaks were semi-agriculturalists and reputed to be more peaceful, hardworking and compliant than other nomads.[20] They served Russia out of necessity at certain times, such as against the Kalmyks in their exodus of 1771, and made trade arrangements with the empire. According to disingenuous Russian sources, the 'weight of bondage' was felt less by them than by other peoples.[21]

The Karakalpak threat

This tribe of TARTARS is not very considerable, and when their chiefs are united, which seldom happens, can scarce raise above ten or twelve thousand men, who are all mounted on horse-back; because, in their long marches to rob and plunder their neighbours, nothing but horse could be of any use. They live always in tents, with their flocks, removing from place to place, as led by inclination or necessity. Their weapons are bows and arrows, and sabres; some of them use fire-arms. While we were at SAMARA, the inhabitants were alarmed by the approach of two or three thousand people, who encamped about three miles distant. From one of the towers I could plainly see their camp, and them riding about it. As they had not artillery the garrison was in no danger, though so weak however, that it durst not at this time attack them. The people were obliged to keep a constant watch to defend their cattle.[22]

(Bell in Samara, 1716)

Turkmen

The name 'Türkmen' was first applied in the tenth century to part of the Turkic Oghuz people in Central Asia, even though some Oghuz were attested there earlier. They belonged to a confederation of nomadic tribes that had spread west from eastern steppes bordering the Islamic world in the tenth century. Some remained in the Caspian region and Khorasan, while others branched westwards to Iraq, Syria and Anatolia.[23] By the early sixteenth century the Ersari occupied much of west Turkmenia, with the Salur[24] and the Chawdor[25] in the Mangyshlak area. Within this group were also the Teke and Yomut[26] tribes. In the eighteenth century the Sarik[27] were dominant between Khorezm and Merv, and the Chawdor and Yomut (and sometimes the Teke) in Khorezm and up towards the Aral Sea, with some Teke moving towards Khorasan.[28]

These tribes traced their genealogy to the mythical Oghuz Khan, the progenitor of twenty-four Oghuz tribes.[29] They were like a kaleidoscope: younger groups emerged from bigger ones, most were disunited except by necessity,[30] while some were mixed, compelled to move and sometimes split by outside pressure or environmental problems, such as lack of water. Some, such as the Ersari, became partly sedentary and worked on irrigation on the Amu Darya, or on limited agriculture and fishing on the Caspian coast.[31] Others lived by animal husbandry, trading, raiding and capturing slaves. They were a constant threat to caravans. Their local social structure remained tribal and, if large and strong, autonomous.[32] Weaker tribes were at the mercy of stronger ones and/or ruling states.[33] Some, such as the Yomut, had a complex relation with Khorezm: they interfered in Khorezmian politics and were sometimes enrolled in their wars or forced to pay tribute and punished if they did not give support when needed, but also used each other when in need of refuge.[34]

Turkmen involved in the trade of Mangyshlak port were the best known to Russians, with whom they had had longstanding contacts. Their life and customs were discussed by Gmelin on his second Persian journey in 1772–74 (fig.17). Mangyshlak was also a general meeting point for the tribes. Gmelin mentioned five Turkmen tribes of the Esen-eli from Mangyshlak area (Abdall/Abdal; Büruntschuk, Igdür/Ighdir; Tschandü/

fig.17

Chowdor; Bulsatschi/ Bozachi).[35] The Abdal were the biggest, number-ing about 1000, and richest.

In total the tribes comprised some 2,500 families and were apparently united through necessity rather than friendship. Their conditions were harsh: under threat from the Khivans, they wandered in small groups, because the land was infertile and there was little water. Gmelin strug-gled to define their political organisation. Their leaders (elders known as *ak-sakal*, or white-beards) were chosen or even self-appointed, but the duration of the position was arbitrary and relied on the goodwill of the tribe. Some of the elders sent as envoys were appointed from St Petersburg; the Russians wanted the position to be hereditary, with limited success.[36]

Communications from the Mangyshlak Turkmen leaders to Russian officials regarding trade were full of assurances of peace and friendship, reminders of services rendered, reports of disagreements with Khiva and other neighbours, complaints about bad treatment from officials and requests for protection, and even the possibility of becoming subjects (1767).[37] A fort or permanent trading post to secure the Turkmen against the Kirghiz or Khivans had been requested and considered several times in the eighteenth century. [38] It had never been built, even though Gmelin, who envisaged a Caspian trading company, recommended the idea.[39] The Bekovitch-Cherkassky episode had involved some compliant Turkmen,[40] but others proved antagonistic.[41] A fort with a garrison was finally established in 1834, as a precursor to the Russian conquest.[42] The Turkmen living on Nephtenoy (Chelekan) island in Gmelin's time (for protection against the Persians) consisted of three tribes (Takejaumut, Gokscha, Ogurjali), of which the Takejaumut were the most powerful. Unlike the Mangyshlak Turkmen, they raided each other for cattle and slaves, as living conditions were so harsh.[43] Although the Turkmen tribes professed to be Sunni Muslims, their 'religious zeal was not very great'.[44]

Gmelin also gave details on the tribes' genealogy, dress and appearance.[45] His observations show how varied, complex and changeable the life of such nomads and semi-nomads was, and how elusive their history in the eighteenth century.

'Fierce free-booters'

We learned that a party of fifty Turcoman horses, had yesterday passed under the walls of Towrone, in the way to their own country. The fierce free-booters who wage a common war on the Persians, enslave as well as plunder those who fall on their hands. To prevent an escape, the captives are sent into the interior parts of the country, where they are employed in tending the numerous droves of cattle and horses, with which Tartary abounds. They are also occasionally sold to the Kalmucks, the most rude and savage of all the Tartar races. A slavery with these is spoken of with horror, and accounted worse than death. The Turcomans of this day are a tribe of no important note; and their military operations are directed chiefly to the attack of caravans and defenceless villages. They are no longer that great and powerful people which produced a Zingis and a Timur; the conquerors of Asia, whose posterity were seen in this country, seated on the most splendid throne of the world. It is now received as a general position of history, that those immense bodies of soldiers which spread over and ultimately subdued the dominions of Rome, under the name of Goths and Vandals, were the Tartars of Bochara, Khieva and the shores of the Caspian. The present chief of the Turcoman tribe, resides at Bochara, and excercises a very limited power. The Tartars of the more eastern regions, the modern conquerors of China, who may be ranged under the common designation of Kalmucks and Mongols, are divided into various roving herds, and would seem to be no longer a cause of dread to the southern nations of Asia.[46]

(Forster, Khorasan, 1784)

Uzbeks

The Uzbeks were tribes of Turco-Mongol origin from the Great Steppe of Dasht-i-Qipchaq (from the Emba east to the Ob). In the fifteenth and early sixteenth centuries they had conquered and moved some of their tribes into parts of Transoxiana and founded branches of the Shaybanid dynasty in Khiva and Bukhara, then expanded to Balkh and Khorasan.[47] According to Central Asian sources, there were thirty-two (some sources said ninety-two) tribes in total. The actual number appears to have been around thirty.[48] As already mentioned, in the eighteenth century rival military chiefs from the Manghit and Qungrat tribes gradually gained control of Bukhara and Khiva respectively, in positions (e.g. *ataliq*, *amir*) over which there was always great rivalry,[49] and which resulted in new dynasties. The Ming tribal dynasty was founded in Khoqand at the end of the century.[50] Tension between Chingisid and later dynastic sovereigns, Islam and tribal traditions persisted.[51] There is evidence from eighteenth- and early nineteenth-century indigenous sources that tribal chieftains were granted positions from the centre (when it was strong) or that representatives of the tribes were reconfirmed with a new accession,[52] but the power of the Uzbek tribes in maintaining or disrupting the state was considerable. When Russia proposed a trade agreement with Bukhara, for example, Daniyal biy ataliq replied that he needed the consent of the tribes before he could agree.[53]

There were branches of nomadic and semi-nomadic Uzbeks, such as the Khitay-Qipchaq, who had only partially adapted to sedentarisation and pursued pastoralism.[54] About these less seems to be known. They lived on their tribal territories, which in the nineteenth century lay in three main areas: Khorezm (dominated by the Qongrat, Manghit and Qangli); Bukhara and Mavarannahr and a little to the south-east and east (dominated by the Manghit, Saray and Qipchaq); and east of the Sir Darya and beyond (the Ming, Yüz and Qipchaq).[55] These tribes were ruled by their chieftains (*biy*), whose power depended on the acknowledgement of tribal followers.[56] Stronger chieftains had small fortresses.[57] The Khivan khan's ambassador's simple gifts to the Russian ambassador (a hawking glove, small knife, etc.) were symbolic of this nomadic society.

Moral judgements about these peoples were both given and implied by the travellers. The Kazakhs were reputedly strong, robust and civil to strangers but potentially treacherous, rude and ignorant, without a sense of crime. Such views roughly corresponded with the academicians'. The merchants made a point of distinguishing the real nomadic life of the Kazakhs with the more settled ways of the urban Khivans and Bukharans. The Khivans were considered the worst: they were allegedly dangerous, cunning, treacherous and crafty. Although more civilised and polite than the Khivans, the Bukharans were said to be cowardly, cruel, effeminate and perfidious. For Hanway, the people of Khiva and Bukhara were remarkable for their vivacity and love of liberty but had no sense of danger.[58] In contrast, he considered the Sarts (see p.213, otherwise not mentioned by the travellers) to be 'civilized, trading Tartars'.[59]

These were inherited western attitudes. To Jenkinson, the Bukharan khan had been 'barbarous' but just.[60] For the editor of Ebulgazi Bahadur Khan's *A General History of the Turks* (English translation in two volumes, 1729–30), for example, the people of the 'Bucharias' were rapacious, warlike, turbulent, restless and courageous.[61] For William Jones, they were merely 'warlike'. More positive or neutral views emerged as the century progressed. The *Universal Traveller* called the Bukharans 'civilized', through commerce,[62] and the *Encyclopaedia Britannica* of 1797 described them as 'addicted to commerce', 'tolerant' and 'not wanting in politeness'.[63] Georgi painted an ideal picture of Bukhara, noting its religious toleration, that the khans were 'not given to luxury', the 'schools' were famous throughout the Tartarian nations, and even their merchants were versed in Arabic. He reported that their priests were highly respected, that the people were hard-working (but weakly) and treated slaves as family members, and that, because the climate was as favourable to Venus as it was to Bacchus, they delighted in moderate sobriety.[64]

This glowing account of a Bukhara Georgi had never visited, which Bukharans would probably never read and which was obtained from Bukharan informants,[65] was partly aimed at promoting trade relations and possible alliance, but it may also express a genuine respect for 'schooling'. Settlers and merchants from Bukhara in Russia were said to preserve their national character but to be upright, modest, clean, sober and sensible.[66]

Passages by Bell and Forster illustrate the difference between two distinct types of travel writing at different times of the century. Bell's is a straightforward description of what he encountered on his route to Astrakhan. Forster, on the other hand, having left India where he knew orientalists such as William Jones and his circle, was keen to show off his knowledge of history, the passing of empires and the celebration of Timur.[67] It is ironic that, while Timur was promoted at a popular level in eighteenth-century Central Asia (and the Volga-Urals),[68] he was being used officially as an example of a successful ruler and empire-builder by British orientalists and the East India Company.[69] Forster nevertheless confused Turkmen with Uzbeks and associated them with the Vandals and the Goths, essentially grouping all Tatars from the east together.[70]

ENDNOTES

1   Gmelin 2007, p.244.
2   E.g. Efremov, pp.56–61, 65–66, 116, mentions nomadic Kirghiz (Kazakhs) around the Russian border and around the Syr Daria and Kashgar, or Kazakhs and Turkmen bringing cattle, firewood and grasses to Khiva. Muraviev (in *Russian Missions*) mentions Turkmen spreading from the Caspian to the frontiers of Khiva, subdivided into 'an infinite number of branches', each of which elected its elder. Those of Balkhan were the Kelte, Kirindjik, Teke. The latter were the most addicted to pillage (pp.75–79). Those to the south-east of the Caspian were the sway of Persia (*Russian Missions*, p.69). Burnes mentions the Ersari and Salur in passing (Burnes, vol.1, pp.336, 343) and the Turkmen from the River Atrek north. The powerful Teke were independent of Persia, whereas the Goklan were unwilling subjects (Burnes, vol.2, pp.100, 109–17). Burnes also gives a useful list of Uzbek tribes and their 'chiefs' (ibid., p.374).
3   Bregel 1999, pp.67–68; see also Ebulgazi Bahadur, *passim*.
4   Pallas thought they were Turkic, but from the west (Pallas 1788–93, vol.1, p.611). Georgi writes that they were first heard of when Russian began to conquer Siberia, but that some of their own traditions placed them as descending from the Crimean khans (Georgi 1780–83, vol.2, pp.242–43).
5   Bregel 2003, p.71; Geiss, *passim*.
6   Geiss, p.42, argues for confederacies because the composition of tribes changed, with some of their sections disappearing while new ones emerged.
7   Some of these names correspond to early twentieth-century ones (Bregel 2003, p.38; Geiss, p.42).
8   Georgi 1780–83, pp.250–51.
9   Pallas 1788,Vol.1, p.621; Georgi 1780-83, Vol.2, pp.257–258.
10 Pallas 1788, Vol.1, p.275.
11 Georgi 1780-83, Vol.1, p.258.
12 Pallas 1788–93, vol.1, p.622; see also Georgi 1780–83, pp.258–59.
13 Pallas 1788–93, vol.1, pp.618–21. Pallas names five ranks of soothsayers.
14 Ibid., pp.623–28. Pallas and Georgi (1780–83) also describe dress, dwellings, food, physical appearance and burial customs.
15 Georgi 1780–83, p.275.
16 Ibid., p.256; Pallas 1788–93, p.623.
17 Georgi 1780–83, p.256; Pallas 1788–93, p.612.
18 Hanway, vol.1, p.348.
19 Barthold; *Istoria uzbekskoi SSR*, vol.1, pp.59–63; Khodarkovsky 2002, *passim*; see also Howorth, vol.2, pp.1056–61 for references to early Russian sources and Vambéry.
20 Georgi 1780–83, vol.2, pp.172–76.
21 Ibid., p.176.
22 Bell, pp.28–29.
23 Kellner-Heinkele 2000, pp.682–85; Bregel 2003, p.72.
24 Leiser, p.1005.
25 Bregel 2004(a), p.168.
26 Kellner-Heinkele 2004(b), p.838.
27 Kellner-Heinkele 2004(a), p.706.
28 Bregel 2003, p.72.

29   E.g. Ebulgazi Bahadur Khan, vol.1, pp.10–21; Gmelin 2007, pp.278–79; Bregel 2003, p.72; Geiss, pp.46–49.

30   Markov, pp.333–34; Geiss, pp.41, 49–50.

31   Bregel 1981, pp.5–37.

32   For the patrilinear tribal and kin-based organisation of nomadic societies, see Geiss.

33   Sneath (2007), *passim*, argues against the top-down power of states on tribal societies, and argues for horizontal power structures based on local 'aristocracies'.

34   Bregel 1988; Kellner-Heinkele 2000, p.684.

35   Most of these names can be matched in Bregel 2003, p.71.

36   Gmelin 2007, pp.279–83.

37   *Russko-turmenskie otnoshenia*, e.g. docs 2, 8, 10, 12, 46, 48, 50, 69.

38   Ibid., docs 40, 53, 66, 67, 72, 79.

39   Gmelin 2007, p.283.

40   *Russkie-turkmenskie otnoshenia*, docs 8, 12.

41   Ibid., doc. 21.

42   Bregel, 1991, pp.415–17.

43   Gmelin 2007, pp.284–85.

44   Ibid., pp.280–81.

45   Ibid., pp.278–79, 281–82.

46   Forster 1808, vol.2, letter 14, pp.194–96.

47   Bregel 2003, pp.50–56, map 20.

48   Bregel 2000, p.20; Bregel 2003, p.70; Holzwarth 2004, pp.118–23 (on the thirty-two and ninety-two tribes). Beneveni, p.124, gives the number as thirty-two, amounting to a total of 90,000 in battle. Burnes, vol.2, p.374, lists more than twenty mixed groups, including Turkmen, Kalmyks and Persians.

49   Holzwarth 2004, pp.105–18.

50   Bregel 2003, pp.60, 62.

51   Geiss, p.127.

52   Bregel 2000, pp.22, 25–26, writing about the Tuhfat al-khani, Taj al-tavarikh, Majma' al-arqam.

53   Holzwarth 2004, p.118; *Istoriia uzbekskoi*, vol.3, p.152.

54   Holzwarth 2004, p.110 and *passim*, for the 'military estate'.

55   Bregel 2003, map 71.

56   Geiss, p.126.

57   Beneveni, pp.124–25; Bregel 2003, p.70.

58   Hanway, vol.2, p.202.

59   Hanway, vol.1, p.15.

60   'Voyage of Anthony Jenkinson from Moscow to Bokhara', in Hakluyt, p.86.

61   Ebulgazi Bahadur, vol.2, e.g. pp.427, 429, 456.

62   Carver, 1779, p.20.

63   *Encyclopaedia Britannica*, vol.3, pp.766–67.

64   Georgi 1780–83, vol.2, pp.134, 144–45.

65   Ibid., p.129.

66   Ibid., pp.148–53.

67   The second volume of Forster's book (in letter form) was compiled from his notes after his death in 1791 (de Lima Martins, 2004), but the references to Timur etc. ring true to late eighteenth-century orientalism from Calcutta (Teissier 2009, pp.133–47).

68 Sela, p.128ff.
69 Teissier 2009, pp.140–41.
70 This was probably informed by William Jones's discourses on the three distinct branches of Asian nations and languages: Arab, Persian and Tatar (Jones 1793, diss. 3–6, on the Hindus, Arabs, Tartars and Persians, pp.70–153). The Tatars were linked to the Goths etc. by certain orientalists in the eighteenth century; see Teissier 2004, p.513 (with references). The successive empires and peoples of Central Asia were in fact well known to orientalists (as were 'deserted cities' near the Caspian), see e.g. d'Herbelot de Molainville, *passim*; Jones 1773, pp.xxiii–xxvii.

CONCLUSION

The travellers knew they were writing for one of the eighteenth-century's most popular literary genres.[1] Such travel accounts were expected to instruct and entertain, with authors asserting the veracity of their observations and apologising for their plainness of style.[2] Some travellers focused on certain parts of their journey. Thus Bell wrote about his trip to Persia and then China via Siberia, having professed his specific desire to visit 'parts of Asia, at least those parts which border on Russia'.[3] Others, such as Bruce, Hanway and Cook, unimpeded by pressures of print length, described their wider experiences, including travel via Europe. Hanway and Cook inserted sections of other diaries, historical dissertations and even 'moral reflections' in their accounts. This compulsion to describe 'all' does not detract from the quality of travellers' observations, although it may explain some of the borrowings from earlier travellers when preparing for publication (as in Bruce). The length of some of these works may have also have meant that details were overlooked by geographical compendia or general readers (see below).

The travellers in this anthology witnessed key stages in the history of the expansion of the Russian Empire, its conflict with neighbouring powers and its trade relations with Britain. They shed light on places and the environment, peoples and their customs, and on social and military history. The reliability of the travellers' observations is variable. Many of Bruce's observations on places and peoples, for example, were taken from Olearius, whereas his reports on military campaigns generally tally with other contemporary accounts. Cook's personal dates may be confused at times, but his details on Astrakhan, the Kalmyks and parts of the Caucasus provide corroborated, first-hand information. Equally, Hanway's account of the John Elton affair and British expectations of Persian trade via Russia remain a major primary source for this period. Equally, Parkinson's unedited observations on Sarepta, Astrakhan and the Caucasus remain fresh, and unique for a British traveller.

The travellers were not historians, however (with the exception of Forster, who was associated with the Asiatic Society of Calcutta), nor linguists. They were writing within the constraints of the time and of language, and there were many things they disregarded or did not inquire into, such as literary or oral traditions, which would be of interest to us today and which are being revealed by modern scholarship.[4] With regard to peoples, their entries range in nature from anecdotal evidence on, for example, encounters with various 'Tartars', to customary, formal evaluations. In contrast to personal and anecdotal evidence, which brings people to life and has the ring of truth to it, their formal appraisal of the non-

Slavic indigenous people they encountered belonged to an eighteenth-century convention that classified peoples in stages from 'rudeness' to 'refinement' and whose purpose was ultimately to distance and separate. Previous travellers' and informants' opinions were also expressed.

The impression given could, therefore, be both positive and negative,[5] even in formal evaluations, such as Bell's and Cook's on the Daghestanis. Although they felt sympathy for the Kalmyks, for example, this did not affect their rating the Kalmyks as inferior to the Tatars of Kazan or Astrakhan.[6] Some of this distancing was benevolent in spirit (as in Bell or Parkinson), but the goals of taming and civilising were never in question. The travellers had little idea of what we now define as 'culture' in relation to the indigenous peoples they encountered. As with the Russian standpoint, their assumption was that others' way of life was (and should be) capable of change.[7]

Western attitudes to Islam in the eighteenth century were varied, ambivalent and generally negative, particularly when associated with the Ottoman or Persian empires rather than the Arabs. Muhammed was regarded as an impostor, adventurer or heretic, who could even so be admired for his achievements. The faith itself was respected because it proclaimed one god, was not idolatrous, believed in a holy book and encouraged learning and cleanliness.[8] Nevertheless, the *Encyclopaedia* stated that, because it had been won by the sword (unlike Christianity), it was not of divine origin and therefore false. The 'causes of its progress', partly attributed to infighting among Christians, was something to be observed.[9] 'Mahommedanism', therefore, was both a fact of history and close to being taboo. Thus the travellers appear virtually neutral about 'Mahommedanism' in Russia or on its borders, while being positive about the Tatars of Kazan and Astrakhan. An exception was Hanway, who ridiculed the 'awful tone of their priests', stated that Muslims deviated from the laws of god and nature with regards to polygamy, and vigorously defended Christianity.[10]

At the same time, the travellers questioned the Russian state, which was supposed to be responsible for progress. With the exception of stereotypical admiration for Peter the Great (see accounts by Perry, Bell, Bruce and Cook), much was made of the corruption of governors, the people's poverty, the Church's ignorance, the luxury of the court and the despotic system in general. Antagonism towards the Orthodox creed (see Perry, Cook and Hanway), seen as a deviation from the true faith, equalled or even displaced hostility towards Islam (except for Hanway). It was not all rhetoric; those in Russian service had great problems, not only in getting paid but in obtaining permission to leave the country (Perry, Bruce, Cook). They were left feeling like hostages, while others either experienced difficulties at the hands of officialdom or witnessed corruption or cruelty first-hand.[11]

The travellers indirectly conveyed the impact of empire on areas and peoples encroached upon. They attested to massive disruption and damage to indigenous ways of life, impoverishment caused by the co-opting of élites, enforced Christianity and officialdom, divisive policies, colonisation, resettlement and appropriation of nomadic lands. But they also observed enrichment (e.g. Tatar merchants), the growth of multi-ethnic, multi-religious towns and settlements, and personal advancement in the state. Most of the travellers experienced Russia before the British Empire in India was a solid reality, and there are no obvious parallels made between the empires, even by Bell or Cook, who published long after their travels, or even by Parkinson writing at the end of the century. There are references to the passing of great empires, however, and criticism of Russian ways served as an example, while always implying British superiority.

The British travellers' observations sometimes tally with those of Russian academicians. Parkinson, for example, met Pallas, who deepened the quality of his observations. Others knew learned men, such as Tatischev, and all would have been in contact with interpreters or governors with local knowledge, who were in positions to influence. Forster's diatribe against the Kalmyks, for example, suggests local or fashionable views of the time. Yet many comments contrast with the academicians', such as those on the Cheremis, Chuvash and Mordvin, or on certain 'Tatars' of Kazan and Astrakhan. The academicians had their own constraints; they were expected to enquire into and report on the natural and human resources of the empire for practical purposes of exploitation and assimilation, or to 'enlarge the bounds of science and extend the knowledge of useful arts among the natives', as Coxe explained.[12] All academicians needed interpreters. Thus their knowledge, including that of languages or written or oral culture, was tailored and limited.

Although much was written on customs and social organisation, there is comparatively little in-depth coverage of the peoples in question, except by a few dedicated men, including Müller, Pallas and foreign prisoners of war, such as Strahlenberg, notably on the Kalmyks and Siberia,[13] and to some extent Gmelin, Pallas and Güldenstadt on the Caucasus. While Georgi wrote knowledgeably on the history of 'Tartars' and mentioned 'learning' among the Tatars of the Volga-Ural region, he did not elaborate beyond stating that historical manuscripts were common in their homes. It is as though, in this case, as long as the *status quo* in relation to the state was upheld, 'culture' was irrelevant. The language of the official evaluation of some peoples, with suggestions that they were deeply primitive and/or dangerous (e.g. Gmelin on the Daghestanis), was also highly charged and subjective.

Despite the existence of private and institutional collections in Russia at the time, and diplomatic gifts, excavations and local archives that could have aroused scholarly interest in Asiatic cultures, there was no impetus from the state for such work or groups of people fuelling such interests.[14] Some Islamic manuscripts, given as gifts, were deposited in the College of Foreign Affairs in St Petersburg,[15] but there seems to have been no scholarly interest in them. The museum and library of the Academy of sciences included a vast collection of Chinese 'books' (but apparently no Islamic manuscripts); ethnographic collections of clothes, arms, implements and 'idols'; coins including Golden Horde and Tatar ones; 'ornaments' from Siberia; and natural curiosities, ores, anatomical specimens and so on.[16] The focus was very much on material objects, so that the preservation of monuments and the plundering of Siberian tombs for gold was encouraged, but the learning of languages was promoted only to serve communication and assimilation. Some manuscripts, however, were translated for potentially pragmatic reasons, such as the *Darband-namah* at the time of Peter the Great's invasion of Daghestan.[17] There was limited mixing, in contrast to late eighteenth-century British India, of the pragmatic with the cultural.[18]

Russia at this time was still preoccupied with researching its own history and historiography,[19] but the lack of knowledge of other people's texts and cultural conventions had negative repercussions throughout the eighteenth century and contributed to the difficulties of early Russian rule in Central Asia.[20] Academicians' illustrations, following eighteenth-century conventions, reinforced objectification rather than remoteness. Although such illustrations accurately depicted clothes, and even attempted to show physiognomy and sometimes natural 'habitat', or hints of local landscape, 'natives' were portrayed as decorative and mute as figurines (see e.g. figs 4, 5 and 7). Only in some of the illustrations from Pallas' last journey in the Caucasus and Crimea in 1793–94 are indigenous peoples and landscapes shown more realistically.[21] None of the travellers, except for Hanway, illustrated their books, and he did not focus on the indigenous peoples of Russia, preferring to show events in Persia.[22] In his only half-page illustration representing Kalmyks, who are shown attacking Russian soldiers,[23] they are virtually unrecognisable.

The style and attitude to content of the travellers' writing changed during the eighteenth century. The use of italics and capitals for proper names, and references to the Royal Society earlier in the century (e.g. Perry, Bell), gave way to the lengthy discursions of Hanway and Cook, and the more relaxed, personal diary-like entries of Parkinson. Whether these would have kept their freshness if he had worked on them himself for publication is uncertain, although the weight given to personal experience was an increasing feature of later eighteenth-century travelogues.[24] Forster's travels were presented as personal letters. What became nineteenth-century stereotypes of the beauty of Caucasian nature and women were already present in these (and earlier) travellers' writings, but no such romance was found in Central Asia at the time.

The reception of the travellers' publications in Britain was varied. Perry's work was chiefly admired for the way it contrasted a barbarous Russia with the achievements of Peter the Great.[25] Bell's *Travels* became a classic, appreciated and used by Gibbon [26] and widely quoted in geographies.[27] Cook's book was panned by the literati, although his observations on Astrakhan, the Kalmyks or the Karakalpaks were, with Hanway's, also edited and reproduced.[28] Geographies nevertheless tended, as the century advanced, to focus on growing or disintegrating empires (Ottoman, Persian, Indian, Chinese, Russian and, indirectly, British) or sensational explorations, such as the voyages of Captain Cook. The peoples and places fought over by these empires were recognised as having histories, written traditions or 'an ancient manner of living', but these could be legitimately subsumed or reduced by generalisations. In *A New and Complete System* (1779), for example, the section on 'Tatary' concludes that the Western Tatars are all ultimately defined by love of the horse and of robbery (of each other and of their neighbours).[29] New information on 'Bucharia', such as given in Hanway, is not mentioned in general geographies. This treatment both helped form and reflect the public mood for empire-building.

The travellers' contribution to knowledge was substantial, although piecemeal. With regard to peoples, it provided much anecdotal information, although its formal perspectives on indigenous peoples and Russians generally consolidated the notion of the innate backwardness of these societies compared to those of the west. It was entirely due to these travellers that this information could be disseminated. It was picked up by historians, such as Gibbon, used empirically and sensitively, and incorporated to varying degrees into geographies and other compilations. The major contributions of the travellers' work, however, lie not only in the partial answers they provide but also in the questions they compel one to ask, not only about times they were writing in but also about the future. Whereas modern frontiers and nations in the regions covered by this book are partially artificial, there is nothing artificial about the multifarious trading and prospecting interests of major powers, the balancing of allegiances, and the tensions between ethnic groups and elites that beset these regions in the eighteenth century and endure in new forms today.

ENDNOTES

1   As attested by the contents of private and circulating libraries of the time, e.g. Brewer, pp.167ff, 181. History and geography were the two other most popular genres.

2   E.g. Bell, pp.xiv–xvi; Cook, vol.1, p.7. There is a large literature on various aspects of travel writing (e.g. in relation to ethnography, empire, the novel); see e.g. Pratt; Lach and van Kley; Elsner and Rubiès; Hulme and Young; Vivies.

3   Bell, pp.xiii–xiv.

4   E.g. Frank 1996 and 1998; Sela.

5   For this vocabulary among the academicians, see Slezkine 2001, pp.27–57.

6   The *Encyclopaedia Britannica*, however, taking its cue from Pallas, stresses their 'many good qualities' (1797, vol.9, pp.423–24).

7   Geraci, p.145.

8   Teissier 2004, pp.521–22.

9   *Encyclopaedia Britannica* 1797, vol.10, pp.465–66.

10   Hanway, vol.1, pp.172–85, 268.

11   For attitudes towards Russia and personal difficulties, see e.g. Perry 1716, pp.8–14, 56, 256–58; Bruce, pp.296–97; Hanway, vol.1, pp.95–96, 103, 109; Cook, vol.1, pp.287–88 and vol.2, pp.92, 138–48; Parkinson, pp.149–50, 168.

12   Coxe 1784, p.399.

13   Witsen's *Noord en Ooost Tartaryen* (1692, rev. 1705) and Strahlenberg's *An Historico-geographical Description* ... (Eng. edn 1736) stimulated both Müller's work in the *Sammlungen Historische Geschichte* (1732–64) and Pallas's *Sammlung Historischer Nachrichten über die Mongolischen Völkerschaften* (1776).

14   Tolz, p.56.

15   E.g. the *Darband-namah*, presented to Peter the Great in 1722 (Storey, vol.1, p.423).

16   Coxe 1784, pp.355–82; for translations of Chinese works, see Tooke 1800, vol.3, p.320; Neverov, pp.54–61.

17   Storey, p.424.

18   Teissier 2009, pp.140–44.

19   See Black, pp.199–213 (Müller and Russian historiography) and *passim* for Tatischev; Coxe 1784, pp.436–39 (Müller and Tatischev) and pp.355–56 (chronicles in the library of the Academy of Sciences). See also Tooke 1800, pp.311–14.

20   Morrison, pp.286–87.

21   Pallas 1812, e.g. pls xviii–xx, xxii–xxv.

22   See Hanway, vol.2, 'Explanation of the Copper-Plates ...'.

23   Ibid.,, p.1.

24   E.g. Vivies, pp.109, 105–12 and *passim*.

25   Cross 2000, pp.46–48.

26   Gibbon 1995, vol.3, p.1197 (for references).

27   E.g. Payne, vol.1, pp.254–55, 257.

28   E.g. Bankes, vol.1, pp.133–34, 136–38 (virtually the same material appears in Middleton, 1779); Payne, pp.254, 257–58 (which also includes Pallas's observations); *Encyclopaedia Britannica* 1797, vol.1, pp.412–13. For Hanway in Rennel, see index.

29   Middleton, p.54.

Bibliography

Abbreviations

CHI   *The Cambridge History of Iran*, 7 vols. Cambridge: Cambridge University Press.

DNB   *Dictionary of National Biography*. Oxford: Oxford University Press [online edn used].

EI   *Encyclopaedia Islamica*. New edn Leiden: Brill.

Russian   *Russian Missions to the Interior of Asia*, Nazarov, F. et al.

Missions   London: Sir Richard Phillips & Co. [trans. from German].

Primary sources

Astley, T., 1745. *A New Collection of Voyages and Travels: Consisting of the Most Esteemed Relations which Have Hitherto Been Published in Any Language*. London.

Atlas général et élémentaire de l'empire de toutes les Russies, 1795. Moscow.

Atlas imperii russici: nova tabula geographica: imperii russici in gubernia, 1787. St Petersburg.

Azbuka tatarskovo iazyka, 1778. Moscow.

Bailly, J. S., 1777. *Lettres à Voltaire*, viii, *Lettre sur l'origine des sciences et sur celle des peuples d'Asie*. London.

Bankes, T., 1791. *A New and Authentic System of Universal Geography*. London.

Bell, J., 1763. *Travels from St Petersburg in Russia to Various Parts of Asia*. Glasgow. 1764, Dublin.

Beneveni, F., 1986. *Poslannik Petra I na vostoke: posol'stvo Florio Beneveni v Persiyu i Bukhara v 1718–1725 godakh*, ed. N.A. Khalfin and V.G. Bolovnikova. Moscow.

Bowles, T. and Bowles, J., 1736. *Atlas minor*. London.

Bruce, P. H., 1783. *Memoirs of Peter Henry Bruce, Esq. a Military Officer in the Services of Prussia, Russia and Great Britain*. London.

Burnes, A., 1973. *Travels into Bokhara and a Voyage on the Indus*. Karachi: Oxford University Press.

Carver, J., 1779. *The New Universal Traveller*. London.

Castle, J., 1784. 'Journal von der aᵒ 1736 aus Orenburg zu dem Abul Geier Chan der Kirgis = Caysak Tartarischen Horda ... Journal 1736–37', in *Materialien zu der Russischen Geschichte: Seit dem Tode Kaisers Peter des Grossen*. Riga.

Chappe d'Auteroche, A., 2004. *Voyage en Sibérie fait par ordre du roi en*

1761, ed. M. Mervaud. Oxford: Voltaire Foundation [first published 1768].

Chardin, J., 1686. *The Travels of Sir John Chardin into Persia and the East Indies*. London.

Churchill, A. and Churchill, J., 1704. *A Collection of Voyages and Travels, Some Now First Printed from Original Manuscripts*. London.

Clarke, E.D., 1816. *Travels in Various Countries of Europe, Asia and Africa*. London.

Cook, J., 1997. *Voyages and Travels through the Russian Empire, Tartary and Part of the Kingdom of Persia*, 2 vols, ed. A.L. Fullerton. Newtonville, MA: Oriental Research Partners [first published 1770].

Coxe, W., 1780–87. *Account of the Russian Discoveries between Asia and America. to which Are Added, the Conquest of Siberia and the History of the Transactions and Commerce between Russia and China*. London.

—— 1784. *Travels into Poland, Russia, Sweden and Denmark, Interspersed with Historical Relations and Political Enquiries*. Dublin.

Craven, E., 1789. *A Journey through the Crimea to Constantinople*. London.

d'Herbelot de Molainville, B., 1697. *Bibliothèque orientale, ou dictionnaire universel contenant tout ce qui regarde de la connoissance des peuples de l'Orient*. Paris.

de Lisle, G., 1723. *Carte des pays voisins de la Mer Caspienne*. Paris.

de Quincey, T., 1948. *Revolt of the Tartars or, Flight of the Kalmuck Khan and His People from the Russian Territories to the Frontiers of China (Illustrated by Stuart Boyle)*. London: Dropmore Press.

Derrick, S., 1762. *A Collection of Travels, thro' Various Parts of the World: But More Particularly, thro' Tartary, China, Turkey, Persia and the East Indies*. London.

Duff, W., 1773. *The History of Rhadi, the Hermit of Mount Arrarat: An Oriental Tale*. Dublin.

Dunns, S., 1788. *A New Atlas of the Mundane System of Geography*. London.

Ebulgazi Bahadur, Khan, 1729–30. *A General History of the Turks, Moguls and Tatars, Vulgarly Called Tartars*, 2 vols. London [Eng. trans. of seventeenth-century *Shajare-i Turk*].

Ellis, G., 1788. *Memoir of a Map of the Countries Comprehended between the Black Sea and the Caspian: With an Account of the Causasian Nations and Vocabularies of the Languages*. London.

Encyclopaedia Britannica, 1797. 19 vols, with suppls. Edinburgh.

Efremov, P., 1786. *Rossiskovo unter-ofitsera Efremova nin kollezhkovo assesora deciatiletnie stravnstrovanie i prikliuchenie b Bucharii, Chiv, Persii i Indii*. St Petersburg.

Falk, J.P., 1785–86. *Topographische Kenntnisse der Russischen Reichs*. St Petersburg.

Forster, G., 1808. *A Journey from Bengal to England through the Northern Part of India, Kashmire, Afghanistan, and Persia and into Russia by the*

Caspian Sea, 2 vols. University of Michigan Library [reprint].

Fraser, J., 1742. *The History of Nadir Shah (Formerly Called Thomas Kuli Khan) the Present Emperor of Persia to which Is Prefixed a Short History of the Moghol Emperors*. London.

Fuchs, K., 2005. *Kratkaia istoria goroda kazani*. Kazan: Izdatelstvo 'Zhien' [reprint; first published 1817].

Georgi, J.G., 1775. *Bemerkungen einer Russischen Reich, im Jahre 1772– 1774*. St Petersburg.

—— 1776–77. *Beschreibung aller Nationen des Russischen Reichs, ihrer Lebensart, Religion, Gebrauche, Wohnungen, Kleidungen und übrugen Merkwürdigkeiten*, 2 vols. St Petersburg.

—— 1780–83. *Russia: Or a Compleat Historical Account of All the Nations which Compose that Empire*. London.

Gärber, I.G., 1728. 'Opisanie stran i naradov bdol zapadnogo berega Kaspiiskogo moria', in Kosneva and Khacheva, pp.60–120.

Gordon, A., 1755. *The History of Peter the Great, Emperor of Russia*. Aberdeen.

Gmelin, J.G., 1751–52. *Reise durch Sibirien von dem Jahr 1733 bis 1743*, 4 vols. Göttingen [repr. Paris, 1767].

—— 1770–74. *Reise durch Russland zur Untersuchung der drey Natur-Reiche*, 4 vols. St Petersburg.

Gmelin, S.G., 2007. *Travels through Northern Persia 1770–1774*, ed. and trans. W. Floor. Washington: Mage Publishers.

Güldenstadt, J.A., 1787–91. *Reisen durch Russland und im Caucasischen Gebürge*. St Petersburg.

Guthrie, M., 1802. *A Tour Performed in the Years 1795–6 through the Taurida, or the Crimea, the Ancient Kingdom of Bosphorus … .* London.

Hakluyt, R., 1598. *The Principal Navigations*. London.

—— 1985. *The Principal Navigations, Voyages, Traffiques and Discoveries of the English Nation*, ed. J. Beeching. London: Penguin.

Halley, E., 1687. 'An Estimate of the Quantity of Vapour Raised out of the Sea by the Warmth of the Sun …', *Philosophical Transactions* 16, pp.366–70.

—— 1690–91. 'An Account of the Circulation of the Watry Vapours of the Sea', *Philosophical Transactions* 16, pp.468–73.

Hanway, J., 1753. *An Historical Account of the British Trade over the Caspian Sea: With a Journal of Travels from London through Russia into Persia*, 4 vols. London.

Harris, J., 1705. *Navigantium atque itinerantium bibliotheca: Or a Compleat Collection of Voyages and Travels*. London.

Hill, A., 1710. *A Full and Just Account of the Present State of the Ottoman Empire in All Its Branches: With the Government and Policy, Religion, Customs*. London.

Jones, Sir W., 1773. *The History of the Life of Nader Shah, King of*

Persia. London.

—— 1789. 'Discourse 3: On the Hindus', *Asiatic Researches* 1, pp.343–55.

—— 1790. 'Discourses 4–6: On the Arabs, Tartars and Persians', *Asiatic Researches* 2, pp.5–53.

—— 1790. 'Discourse 5: On the Tartars', *Asiatic Researches* 2, pp.88–114.

—— 1799. 'L'Histoire de Nader Chah', in *The Works of Sir William Jones*. London.

Kabardino-Russkie Otnoshenia, 1957. Moscow: Izdatelstvo Akademii Nauk SSR.

Kazakhsko-Russkie Otnoshenia v XVIII–XIV veka (1771–1867 godi), 1964. Alma-Ata: Izdatelstvo 'Nauka'.

Khalit, I., 2006. 'Tatarskaia mechet: neskolko slov o tipologii i etapax razvitia archetipa', in *Mecheti v dukhovnoi kulture Tatarskovo naroda (XVIIv-1917g)*. Kazan: Institut Istorii Sh. Mardjani, pp.73–92.

Klaproth, J.H., 1834. *Dr J.A. Güldenstadts Beschreibnung der Kaukasischen Lander*. Berlin.

—— 2005. *Travels in the Caucasus and Georgia*. London: Elibron Classics [reprint].

Krasheninnikov, S.P., 1755. *Opisanie zemli Kamchatki*. St Petersburg.

le Bruyn, C., 1737. *Travels into Muscovy, Persia and Part of the East Indies*. London.

—— 1759. *Mr Cornelius Le Brun's Travels into Muscovy, Persia and Divers Part of the East Indies*. London.

Ledyard, J., 1966. *John Ledyard's Journey through Russia and Siberia 1787–1788*. Madison: University of Wisconsin Press.

Lepekhin, I.I., 1774–83. *Tagebuch der Reise durch verschiedene Provinzen des russischen Reiches in der Jahre 1768–1769*. Altenburg.

—— 1795. *Drevniia zapiski po raznim provinziam russiskovo gosudartsva 1768 i 1769 godu*, vol.1. St. Petersburg.

Lerch, J.J., 1776. 'Nachricht von der Zweite Reise nach Persien von 1745 bis 1747', in *Bussching's Magazine für die Neue Historie und Geographies* 10. Hamburg.

MacCartney, G., 1768. *An Account of Russia in 1767*. London.

Materiali po istorii yzbekskoi, tadzhikskoi i turkmenskoi SSR, pt 3 of *Materiali po istorii narodov SSR*, 1933. Leningrad: Akademii Nauk.

Middleton, C.T., 1779. *A New and Complete System of Geography*. London.

Moser, J., 1796. *The Hermit of Caucasus, an Oriental Romance*, 2 vols. London.

Müller, G.F., 1760. 'Nachricht von dem Gold: Sande in der Bucharen,' *Sammlung Russischer Geschichte* 4. St Petersburg.

—— 1762. 'Auszug aus dem Tage-Buche des ehmahliger Schif-Hauptmanns und iesignen geheimen Raths und Gouverneurs von Sibirien, Hernn Fedor Ivanovitch Soimonov, von seiner Schillart auf der Caspischen See', *Sammlung Russischer Geschichte* 7, pp.155–319.

—— 1791. *Opisanie zhivuschchikh kazanskoi gubernii iazycheskich iako to Cheremis, Chuvach i Votiakov*. St Petersburg.

Nazarov, F., Akovlev, P. L. and Muraviev, N. N., 1823. *Russian Missions into the Interior of Asia*. London: Sir Richard Phillips and Co.

Olearius, A., 1669. *The Voyages and Travels of the Ambassadors Sent by Frederik, Duke of Holstein, to the Great Duke of Muscovy and the King of Persia*. London.

—— 1967. *The Travels of Olearius in Seventeenth Century Russia*, ed. S.H. Baron. Stanford, CA: Stanford University Press.

Pallas, P.S., 1771–76. *Reise durch verschiedene Provinzen des russischen Reichs*, 3 vols. St Petersburg.

—— 1776–1801. *Sammlungen historicher Nachrichten über die mongolischen Volkerschaften*, 2 vols. St Petersburg.

—— 1788–93. *Voyages de P.S. Pallas en différentes provinces de l'empire de Russie, et dans L'Asie septentrionale, traduit de l'Allemand par Le C. Gauthier de la Payronie*, 5 vols. Paris [Fr. trans. of Pallas 1771–76].

—— 1799–1801. *Observations faites dans un voyage entrepris dans les gouvernements mérididionaux de l'empire de Russie dans les années 1793–94*, 2 vols. Leipzig.

—— 1812. *Travels through the Southern Provinces of the Russian Empire, in the Years 1793 and 1744*. London.

Parkinson, J., 1971. *A Tour of Russia, Siberia and the Crimea 1792–1794*, ed. W. Collier. London: Frank Cass and Co.

Payne, J., 1791. *Universal Geography Formed into a New and Entire System*. London.

Perry, J., 1716. *The State of Russia, under the Present Czar*. London.

Petis, F., 1722. *The History of Genghizcan the Great, First Emperor of the Antient Moguls and Tartars; in Four Books ... Collected from Several Oriental Authors*. London.

Potocki, J., 1980. *Voyage dans les steppes d'Astrakhan et du Caucase*. ed. D. Beauvois. Fayard.

Purchas, S., 1625. *Pilgrimes*. London.

Reineggs, J. and von Biberstein, F.A.M., 2005. *General, Historical and Topographical Description of Mount Caucasus*, 2 vols. London: Elibron Classics [reprint of 1807 edn].

Rennel, J., 1800. *The Geographical System of Herodotus Examined, and Explained, by a Comparison with Those of Other Ancient Authors and with a Modern Geography*. London.

Richardson, W., 1784. *Anecdotes of the Russian Empire*. London.

Rukavin, K., 1839. *Putescheshtvie iz Orenburga b Khivu Samarkago Kuptsa Rukavina, b 1753 godu, c priubshcheniem raznikh izvesti o Chiv c otdalennikh vremen donin*, ed. S. Russov. St Petersburg: Tip. Ministerstva vnutrennikh del.

Russko-turkmenskie otnoshenia (b. XVIII-XIX v.v.), 1963. Ashkhabad.

Rychkov, P., 1767. *Opit kazanskoi istorii drevnikh i srednikh vremian sochinei P. Rychkovim*. St Petersburg.

Sinclair, S.J., 1787. *General Observations Regarding the Present State of the Russian Empire*. London.

Soimonov, F.I., 1763. '*Opisanie kaspiiskago moria ...*', ed. G.F. Müller. St Petersburg.

—— 1765. *O torgakh za Kaspiiskoe mope drevnikh, sreidni i noveischikh*. St Petersburg.

Spilman, J., 1742. *A Journey through Russia into Persia: By Two English Gentlemen*. London.

Strahlenberg, P.J., 1736. *An Historic-Geographical Description of the North and Eastern Part of Europe and Asia, but More Particularly of Russia, Siberia and Great Tartary*. London.

The Compleat Geographer: or, the Chorography and Topography of All Known Parts of the Earth. London, 1709, 1723.

Tooke, W., 1799. *View of the Russian Empire: During the Reign of Catherine, the Second, and to the Close of the Eighteenth Century*. London.

—— trans. and ed.,1800. *The Life of Catherine II, Empress of Russia, with a Correct Map of the Russian Empire*, by J.H. Castera, 3 vols. Dublin.

Turnerelli, E., 1841 (reprint 2005). *Kazan i eio zhiteli*. Kazan: Domo Globus.

White, J., 1783. *Institutes, Political and Military Written ... By the Great Timour ... First Translated into Persian by Abu Taulib Alhusseini, and thence into English*. Oxford.

Witsen, N., 1692. *Noord en oost Tartaryen*. Amsterdam.

Secondary sources

Aalto, P., 1996. 'John Bell's (1691–1780) Notes from His Journeys in Siberia and Mongolia', *International Journal of Central Asian Studies* 1 [online edn cited].

Abdullin, K., 1988. *Istoria kazanii*. Kazan.

Alexander, J.T., 1982. 'Pugachev, Emel'ian Ivanovich', in *The Modern Encyclopaedia of Russian and Soviet History*, ed. J.L. Wieczynski, vol.30, pp.72–79.

Algar, H., 1993. 'Nakhshbadiyya', *EI* 7, pp.934–36.

Alishev, S., 1997. 'Veleno b Kazani bit sukonnomu deli', *Echo Vekov* 3/4, pp.54–55.

Allen, W.E.D., 1956. 'The Sources for G. Deslisle's "Carte Des Pays Voisins de la Mer Caspienne" of 1723', *Imago Mundi* 13, pp.137–50.

Allsen, T.T., 1997. 'Saray' *EI* 9, pp.41–44.

Allworth, E., 1990. *The Modern Uzbeks, from the Fourteenth Century to the Present*. Stanford, CA: Hoover Institution Press.

—— 1994. *Central Asia, 130 Years of Russian Dominance: A Historical*

Overview. Durham and London: Duke University Press.

Appleby, J.H., 1997. 'The Royal Society and the Tartar Lamb', *Notes and Records of the Royal Society of London* 51, pp.23–24.

—— 2001. 'Mapping Russia: Farquharson, Delisle and the Royal Society', *Notes and Records of the Royal Society of London* 55(2), pp.191–204.

—— 2004(a). 'Anthony Jenkinson', *DNB*.

—— 2004(b). 'Henry Farquharson', *DNB*.

—— 2004(c). 'James Spilman', *DNB*.

—— 2004(d). 'John Perry', *DNB*.

Arapov, A., 2006. *Historical Monuments of Uzbekistan*. Tashkent: San'at.

Atkin, M., 1980. *Russia and Iran 1480–1829*. Minneapolis: University of Minneapolis Press.

—— 1988. 'Russian Expansion in the Caucasus to 1813', in *Russian Colonial Expansion to 1917*, ed. M. Rywkin. London and New York: Mansell Publishing, pp.139–87.

Avery, P., 1991. 'Nadir Shah and the Asfarid Legacy', *CHI* 6, pp.3–62.

Axworthy, M., 2009. *Sword of Persia: Nader Shah, from Tribal Warrior to Conquering Tyrant*. London and New York: I.B. Tauris.

Azamatov, D., 1996. 'Russian Administration and Islam in Bashkiria (18th–19th Centuries)', in Kemper, von Kügelgen and Yermakov, pp.91–112.

Babadzanov, B.M., 1996. 'On the History of the Naqsbandiya Mugaddiya in Central Mawara'annahar in the Late 18th and Early 19th Centuries', in Kemper, von Kügelgen and Yermakov, pp.385–414.

Baddeley, J.F., 1908. *The Russian Conquest of the Caucasus*. London and New York: Longman's, Green & Co.

Bagrow, L., 1956. 'Italians in the Caspian', *Imago Mundi* 13, pp.3–10.

Ballaster, R., 2005. *Fabulous Orients: Fictions of the East in England 1662–1785*. Oxford: Oxford University Press.

Barrett, T., 1995. 'Lines of Uncertainty: The Frontiers of the North Caucasus', *Slavic Review* 54/3, pp.578–601.

—— 1999. *At the Edge of Empire: The Terek Coassacks and the North Caucasus Frontier 1700–1800*. Boulder, CO: Westview Press.

Barthold, W., 1978. 'Karakalpak', *EI* 4, pp.610–11.

Barthold, W. and Bennigsen, A., 1965. 'Daghistan', *EI* 2, pp.85–89.

—— 1978. 'Kazan', *EI* 4, pp.849–50.

Barthold, W. and Golden, P.B., 1978. 'Khazar', *EI* 4, pp.1172–81.

Barthold, W. and Quelquejay, C.,1960. 'Burtas', *EI* 1, pp.1337–38.

Barthold, W. and Wixman, R., 1978. 'Karakalpak', *EI* 4, pp.610–11.

Bartlett, R., 1979. *Human Capital, the Settlement of Foreigners in Russia 1762-1804*. Cambridge: Cambridge University Press.

Bassin, M., 1991. 'Russia between Europe and Asia: The Idelogical Construction of Geographical Space', *Slavic Review* 52(1), pp.1–17.

Bennigsen, A., 1964. 'Un Monument populaire au Caucase au XVIIIe siècle: La 'Guerre Sainte' du Sheikh Mansur (1785–1791), page mal connue et controversée des relations Russo-Turques', *Cahiers du Monde Russe et Soviètique* 5, pp.159–205.

—— 1978. 'Kasimov', *EI* 4, pp.723–24.

Bennigsen-Broxup, M.B., 1996. 'Introduction: Russia and the North Caucasus', in *The North Caucasus Barrier*. London: Hurst, pp.1–17.

Benzing, J., 1993. *Bolgarisch-Tschuwasschische Studien*, ed. C. Schonig. Wiesbaden: Harrassowitz.

Berry, C.J., 1997. *Social Theory of the Scottish Enlightenment*. Edinburgh: Edinburgh University Press.

Black, J.L., 1986. *G.F. Müller and the Imperial Russian Academy*. Kingston, Montreal: McGill-Queen's University Press.

Black, J. L., Buse, D.-K. and Moessner, V. J., 1989. *G.F. Müller and Siberia 1733–1743*. Kingston, Ontario: The Limestone Press.

Bobrovnikov, V., 2006. 'Islam in the Russian Empire', in *Imperial Russia 1689–1917*, vol.2 of *The Cambridge History of Russia*, ed. D. Lieven, pp.203–23.

Bosworth, E., 2004. *The New Islamic Dynasties: A Chronological and Genealogical Manual*. Edinburgh: Edinburgh University Press.

Bower, D.R. and Lazzerini, E.J., eds, 2001. *Russia's Orient: Imperial Borderlands and Peoples, 1700–1917*. Bloomington, IN: Indiana University Press.

Brancaforte, E.C., 2003. *Visions of Persia: Mapping the Travels of Adam Olearius*. Cambridge, MA: Harvard Universities Press.

Brandes, D., 1993. *Von den Zaren adoptiert*. Munich: R. Oldenbourg Verlag.

Bregel, Y., 1981. 'Nomadic and Sedentary Elements among the Turkmens', *Central Asiatic Journal* 25, pp.5–37.

—— ed. 1988. *Firdaus Al-Iqbal: History of Khorezm*, vol.28 of *Islamic History and Civilization*. Leiden, New York, Copenhagen and Cologne: Brill.

—— 1991. 'Mangishlak', *EI* 6, pp.416–17.

—— 2000. *The Administration of Bukhara under the Manghits and Some Tashkent Manuscripts*. Bloomington, IN: Indiana University Press.

—— 2003. *An Historical Atlas of Central Asia*. London: Brill.

—— 2004(a). 'Cawdor', *EI* 12, pp.168–69.

—— 2004(b). 'Inak', *EI* 12, pp.419–20.

—— 2004(c). 'Ataliq', *EI* 12, pp.96–98.

—— 2007. *Documents from the Khanate of Khiva (17th–19th Centuries)*. Bloomington, IN: Indiana University Press.

Brewer, J., 1997. *The Pleasures of the Imagination: English Culture in the Eighteenth Century*. London: Harper Collins.

Breyfogle, N.B., Schrader A. and Sunderland, W., eds, 2007. *Peopling the Russian Periphery*. London and New York: Routledge.

Burton, A., 1993. *Bukharan Trade 1588–1718*. Bloomington, IN: Indiana University Press.

Bushkovitch, P., 2001. *Peter the Great: The Struggle for Power 1671–1725*. Cambridge: Cambridge University Press.

Busigin, E.M. and Zorin, N.V., 1984. *Etnografia narodov srednevo povolzhia*. Kazan: Kazan University.

Canard, M., 1988. *Ibn Fadlan: voyage chez les Bulgares de la Volga, traduit de l'Arabe*. Paris: Sindbad.

Carlyle, E.I., 2004. 'John Elton' (rev. S. Searight), *DNB*.

Chaucer, G., *The Canterbury Tales*, trans. D. Wright, 1985. Oxford: Oxford University Press.

Christian, D., 1998. *A History of Russia, Central Asia and Mongolia*. Oxford: Blackwell.

Crews, R.D., 2006. *For Prophet and Tsar: Islam and Empire in Russia and Central Asia*. Cambridge, MA: Harvard University Press.

Cross, A., 1997. *By the Banks of the Neva*. Cambridge: Cambridge University Press.

—— 2000. *Peter the Great through British Eyes: Perception and Representations of the Tsar since 1698*. Cambridge: Cambridge University Press.

Curtin, P.D., 1984. *Cross Cultural Trade in World History*. Cambridge: Cambridge University Press.

Dale, S., 2002. *Indian Merchants and European Trade 1600–1750*. Cambridge: Cambridge University Press.

Dawson, C., 1955. *The Mongol Mission*. London and New York: Sheed and Ward.

de Madariaga, I., 2002. *Russia in the Age of Catherine the Great*. London: Pheonix.

di Cosmo, N., 1989. *A Russian Envoy to Khiva: The Italian Diary of Florio Beneveni*. Wiesbaden: Harrassowitz.

Dudoignon, S., Ishakov, D. and Mohammatshin, R., 1997. *L'Islam de Russie: conscience communautaire et autonomie politique chez les Tatars de la Volga et de l'Oural depuis le XVIIIe siècle: Actes du Colloque International de Qazan, 29 Avril–1 Juin 1996*. Paris: Maisonneuve et Larose.

Dudoignon, S. and Komatsu, H., eds, 2001. *Islam in Politics in Russia and Central Asia (Early Eighteenth to Late Twentieth Centuries)*, London: Keegan Paul.

Dunlop, J.B., 1998. *Russia Confronts Chechnya*. Cambridge: Cambridge University Press.

Elsner, J. and Rubiès, J.-P., 1999. *Voyages and Visions: Towards and Cultural History of Travel*. London: Reaktion.

Erofeeva, I., 1999. *Khan Abulkhair: Polkovodets, pravitel i politik*. Almaty: 'Sanat'.

Fechner, M., 1978. *Velikie Bulgary, Kazan, Sviask*. Moscow: Vzdatelstvo 'Iskusstvo'.

Ferrier, R., 1986. 'Trade from the Mid 14th Century to the End of the Safavid Period', in *CHI* 6, pp.412–90.

Forsyth, J., 1992. *A History of the Peoples of Siberia*. Cambridge: Cambridge University Press.

Frank, A., 1996. 'The Development of Regional Islamic Identities in Imperial Russia: Two Commentaries on the Tavarikh-I Bulgariya of Husrmaddin Al-Muslimi', in Kemper, von Kügelgen and Yermakov, pp.113–28.

—— 1998. *Islamic Historiography and 'Bulghar' Identities among the Tartars and Bashkirs of Russia*. Leiden: Brill.

—— 2000. 'Historical Legends of the Volga-Ural Muslims Concerning Alexander the Great, the City of Yelabuga, and Bachman Khan', in *Revue des Mondes Musulmans et de la Méditerranée* 89–90, pp.89–107.

—— 2001. *Muslim Religious Institutions in Imperial Russia*. Leiden: Brill.

—— 2003. 'Islamic Transformation on the Kazakh Steppe, 1742–1917: Toward an Islamic History of Kazakhstan under Russian Rule', in T. Hyashi, *The Construction and Deconstruction of Natural Histories in Slavic Eurasia*. Sapporo: Hokkaido University, Slavic Research Centre.

Frye, R., 2005. *Ibn Fadlan's Journey to Russia*. Princeton: Markus Wiener Publishers.

Fedorov-Davidov, G.A., 1984. *The Culture of the Golden Horde Cities*. Oxford: British Archaeological Reports (BAR).

—— ed. 1987. *Gorod Bolgar: Ocherki istorii i kul'tury*. Moscow: Nauka.

—— ed. 2001. *Gorod Bolgar: Monumentalnoe stroitelstvo, arkhitektura, blagoustroitsvo*. Moscow: Nauka.

Gammer, M. and Wassertein, D.J., eds, 2006. *Daghestan and the World of Islam*. Helsinki: Academia Scientarum Fennica.

Garrard, J.G., 1973. *The 18th Century in Russia*. Oxford: Clarendon Press.

Gasanov, M., 2001. 'On Christianity in Dagestan', in *Iran and the Caucasus* 5, pp.79–84.

Garzavina, A.V. and Novitskaya, I.A., 2005. *Znamentie liudi o Kazani i Kazanskom krae*. Kazan: Izdatelstvo 'Zhiem'.

Geiss, P.G., 2003. *Pre-Tsarist and Tsarist Central Asia*. London and New York: Routledge, Curzon.

Geraci, R., 2001. 'Russian Orientalism at an Impasse: Tsarist Education Policy and the 1920 Conference on Islam', in Bower and Lazzarini, pp.138–61.

Geraci, R.P. and Khodarkovsky, M., 2001. *Of Religion and Empire*. Ithaca and London: Cornell University Press.

Gibbon, E., 1995. *The History of the Decline and Fall of the Roman Empire*, 3 vols, ed. D. Womersley [1st edn 1776–88]. London: Penguin.

Giliazov I.A., 1997. 'Le Role de l'Islam dans l'évolution des structures de la société tatare, de la conquête de Qazan au réformes de Catherine II (1552-1788)', in Dudoignon, Ishakov and Mohammatsin, pp.15–25.

—— 2002. 'Tatarskie slobodi goroda Kazani vo vtoroi polovinie XVI-seredine XIX v.v.', in Salikhov, Khayrutdinov and Guliazov, pp.60–75.

Gilmanov, A.D., 2002. 'Osovennosti formirovanaia staro-tatarskoi slobodi goroda Kazani', in Salikhov, Khayrutdinov and Guliazov, pp.22–60.

Golden, P.B., 2000. 'Tartar', *EI* 10, pp.370–71.

Goldenburg, L.A. and Postnikov, A.V., 1985. 'Development of Mapping Methods in Russia in the Eighteenth Century', *Imago Mundi* 37, pp.63–80.

Grau, C., 1963. *Der Wirtschaftorganisator, Staatsman und Wissenschaftler Vasilij N. Tatiscev 1686–1750.* Berlin: Akademie Verlag.

Greaves, R., 1991. 'Iranian Relations with the European Trading Companies, to 1798', *CHI* 7, pp.350–73.

Halkovic, S., 1985. *The Mongols of the West.* Bloomington, IN: Indiana University Press.

Harrison, R., 2004. 'John Bell' (rev. P. Carter), *DNB*.

Helimski, E., Kars, U. and Schotschel, M., eds, 2005. *Mari und Mordwinnen im heutigen Russland: Sprache, Kultur, Identitat.* Wiesbaden: Harrassowitz.

Hellie, R., 1984. 'Tatischev, Vasili Nikitich', in *The Modern Encyclopaedia of Russian and Soviet History*, ed. J.L. Wieczynski, vol.38, pp.190–96.

Herzig, E., 1991. *The Armenian Merchants of New Julfa, Isfahan: A Study in Pre-Modern Asian Trade.* Unpublished D.Phil. thesis, University of Oxford.

—— 2008. *On the Brink of the Modern: The Julfa Armenians and Their World.* Paris.

Hodgen, M.T., 1964. *Early Anthropology in the Sixteenth and Seventeenth Centuries.* Philadelphia: University of Pennsylvania Press.

Howorth, H., 2005. *The History of the Mongols from the 9th to the 19th Century.* Elibron Classics [first published 1880].

Holzwarth, W., 2005. 'Relations between Uzbek, Central Asia, the Great Steppe and Iran, 1700–1750', in *Shifts and Drifts in Nomad-Sedentary Relations*, ed. S. Leder and B. Streck. Wiesbaden: L. Reichert.

Hrbek, I., 1960. 'Bulghar', *EI* 1, pp.1304–8.

Hughes, L., 2000. *Russia in the Age of Peter the Great.* New Haven and London: Yale University Press.

Hulme, P. and Young, T., 2002. *The Cambridge Companion to Travel Writing.* Cambridge: Cambridge University Press.

Ibneeva, G.V., 2006. *Puteschestvia Ekaterini II: Opit 'ocvoennia' imperskobo prostranstva.* Kazan: Kazan University Press.

Immerwahr, R., 1972. '"Romantic and its Cognates" in England, Germany and France before 1790', in *'Romantic' and its Cognates: The European History of a Word*, ed. H. Eichner. Manchester: University of Toronto Press, pp.17–97.

Ishakov, D., 1997. '"L'Identité Bulgare" en question: Islam et ethnicité chez les Tatars de la Volga et de l'Oural au XVIIIème siècle', in Dudoignon, Ishakov and Mohammatshin, pp.73–88.

Istoria uzbekskoi SSR, 2 vols, 1955–56. Tashkent: Izdatelstvo akademii nauk Uzbekskoi SSR.

Iurchenkov, V.A., 1997. *Istoria mordvoskogo kraia b zapadnoi istoriografii XIII-XVII v.v.* Saransk [dissertation].

Jackson, P. and Morgan, D., 1990. *The Mission of Friar William Rubrick.* London: The Hakluyt Society.

Jean, M., 1992. *Le Voyage en Asie centrale et au Tibet.* Paris: Robert Laffont.

Kahan, A., ed., 1985. *The Plow, the Hammer and the Knout.* Chicago: Chicago University Press.

Kalinin, N.F., 1955. *Kazan.* Kazan: Tatgosizdat.

Kappeler, A., 2001. *The Russian Empire.* Harlow: Longman.

Kara, G., 2005. *Books of the Mongolian Nomads: More than Eight Centuries of Writing Mongolian.* Bloomington, IN: Indiana University, Research Institute for Inner Asian Studies.

Karaeva, L.M., Anisimova, L., Bonara, G.L., Franchi, C. and Plakhov, V.V., 2005. *Tesori della steppa di Astrakhan.* Milan: Fondazione Internazionale Accademia ARCO.

Kazemadeh, F., 1991. 'Iranian Relations with Russia and the Soviet Union, to 1921', in *CHI* 7, pp.314–49.

Kellner-Heinkele, B., 2000. 'Türkmen', *EI* 10, pp.682–85.

—— 2004(a). 'Sarik', *EI* 12, pp.706.

—— 2004(b). 'Yomut', *EI* 12, p.838.

Kemper, M., 1998. *Sufis und Gelehrte in Tartarien und Bashkirien, 1789–1889.* Berlin: Klaus Schwarz.

Kemper, M., von Kügelgen, A. and Yermakov, D., eds, 1996. *Muslim Culture in Russia and Central Asia from the 18th to the Early 20th Centuries,* vol.1 of *Islamkundliche Untersuchungen.* Berlin: Klaus Schwarz.

Khachikian, S., 2001. 'On the Commercial Activities of an 18th-Century New Julfa Merchant: Sarhad Bandurean in Amsterdam', *Iran and the Caucasus* 5, pp.27–42.

Khayrutdinov, R., 1997. 'Les Problèmes d'integration de l'aristocracie Tatare Musulmane dans la "noblesse de service" Russe, après les réformes de Catherine II', in Dudoignon, Ishakov and Mohammatshin, pp.131–53.

—— 2001. 'The Tartar Ratusha of Kazan: National Self-Administration in Autocratic Russia, 1781–1855', in Dudoignon and Komatsu, pp.27-42.

Khlebnikova, T.A., 1987. 'Istoria, arkheologischeskogo izuchenna bolgarkogo gorodishcha. statigrafia. topografia', in Fedorov-Davidov 1987, pp.32–88.

Khodarkovsky, M., 1992. *Where Two Worlds Met: The Russian State and the Kalmyk Nomads, 16001771.* Ithaca and London: Cornell University Press.

—— 1997. 'Ignoble Savages and Unfaithful Subjects: Constructing Non-

Christian Identities in Early Modern Russia', in Bower and Lazzarini, pp.9–26.

—— 1999. 'Of Christians, Enlightenment and Colonialism: Russia in the North Caucasus 1550–1800', *Journal of Modern History* 71, pp.394–430.

—— 2001. 'The Conversion of Non-Christians in Early Modern Russia', in *Of Religion and Empire*, ed. R.P. Geraci and M. Khodarkovsky. Ithaca and London: Cornell University Press, pp.115–43.

—— 2002. *Russia's Steppe Frontier: The Making of a Colonial Empire, 1500–1800*. Bloomington, IN: Indiana University Press [pb. edn. 2004 cited].

Khudiakov, M.G., 1991. *Ocherki po istorii kazankogo khanstva*, Moscow: 'Insan'.

Kidd, C., 1999. *British Identities before Nationalism; Ethnicity and Nationhood in the Atlantic World*. Cambridge: Cambridge University Press.

King, C., 2008. *The Ghost of Freedom: A History of the Caucasus*. Oxford: Oxford University Press.

Kniazhetskay, E.A., 1964. *Sudba odnoi karti*, Moscow: Uzdatalstvo Sozialno-Ekonomicheskoi Literaturi 'Misl'.

Knysh, A., 2000. 'Ushurma, Mansur', *EI* 10, pp.920–22.

Kosneva, M.O. and Khacheva, K.M., 1958. *Istoria, geografia i etnografia dahestana*. Moscow.

Kügelgen, A. von, 1996. 'Buchara im Urteil europäischer Reisender des 18. Und 19. Jahrhunderts', in Kemper, von Kügelgen and Yermakov, pp.415–30.

Kügelgen, A. von, Yermakov, D. and Frank, A.J., eds,, 1998. *Muslim Culture in Russia and Central Asia: Inter-regional and Inter-ethnic Relations*, vol.2 of *Islamkundliche Untersuchungen*. Berlin: Klaus Schwarz.

Kühlewein, G., 1865. 'Notes of the Intercourse of Russia with Khivan, Appendix IV', in *The Russians in Central Asia* …, trans. J. and R. Mitchell. London: Stanford, pp.536–52.

Lach, D.F. and van Kley, E.J., eds, 1993. *Asia in the Making of Europe*. Chicago and London: University of Chicago Press.

Latham, R., 1958. *Marco Polo: The Travels*. Harmondsworth: Penguin.

Layton, S., 1994. *Russian Literature and Empire: Conquest of the Caucasus from Pushkin to Tolstoy*. Cambridge: Cambridge University Press.

Leder, S. and Streck, B., 2005. *Shifts and Drifts in Nomad-Sedentary Relations*. Weisbaden: L. Reichert.

Leiser, G., 1995. 'Salur', *EI* 8, pp.1005–6.

Lemercier-Quelquejay, C., 1996. 'Cooptation of the Elites of Kabarda and Daghestan in the Sixteenth Century', in *The North Caucasus Barrier*. London: Hurst & Co., pp.18–44.

Levi, S., 1999. 'India, Russia and the Eighteenth-Century Transformation of the Central Asian Caravan Trade', *Journal of the Social and Economic*

History of the Orient 42(4), pp.519–48.

—— 2007. 'The Ferghana Valley at the Crossroads of World History: The Rise of Khoquand, 1709–1822,' *Journal of Global History* 2(3), pp.213–32.

Levi, S. and Sela R., eds, 2010. *Islamic Central Asia: An Anthology of Historical Sources*. Bloomington, IN: Indiana University Press.

Lima-Martins, L. de, 2004. 'George Forster', *DNB*.

Literature of Travel and Exploration: An Encyclopaedia, 2003. New York and London: Fitzroy Dearborn.

Lockhart, L., 1938. *Nadir Shah: A Critical Study Based Mainly upon Contemporary Sources*. London: Luzac and Co.

—— 1958. *The Fall of the Safavi Dynasty and the Afghan Occupation of Persia*. Cambridge: Cambridge University Press.

Lysenko, L.M., 2001. *Gubernatori i general-gubernatori rossiskoi imperii*. Moscow: Izd-vo Megu.

MacGregor, A., 2007. *Curiosity and Enlightenment: Collectors and Collections from the Sixteenth to the Nineteenth Century*. New Haven and London: Yale University Press.

McLaughlin, S., 1972. '"Russia", in *'Romantic' and its Cognates: The European History of a Word*, ed. H. Eichner. Manchester: Manchester University Press, pp.418–74.

Mamedova, G., 1989. *Russkie konsuly ot Azerbaidzhane, 20–60 e gody XVIII veka*, Baku: Elm.

Markov, G.E., 2001. *The Social Structure of the Nomads of Asia and Africa, Studies on Central Asian History in Honor of Yuri Bregel*. Bloomington, IN: Research Institute for Inner Asian Studies.

Martin, J., 1995. *Medieval Russia, 980–1584*. Cambridge: Cambridge University Press.

Matthews, D.J. and Bukhavaen, R., 2000. *Historical Anthology of Kazan Tatar Verse: Voices of Eternity*. Richmond: Curzon.

Maykhametshin, D.G. and Khakumzianov, F.S., 1987. *Epigraficheskii pamiatniki goroda Bulgara*. Kazan: Tatarskoie Krivznoe Uzdatelstvo.

Minorsky, V., 1986. 'Kuban', *EI* 5, pp.287–88.

Mitchell, J. and R., trans., 1865. The *Russians in Central Asia ....* London: Stanford,

Mitter, P., 1992. *Much Maligned Monsters: A History of European Reactions to Indian Art*. Chicago and London: University of Chicago Press.

Morrison, A., 2008. *Russian Rule in Samarkand 1869–1910*. Oxford: Oxford University Press.

Moseley, C.W.R.D., 1983. *The Travels of Sir John Mandeville*. Harmondsworth: Penguin.

Neverov, O., 1985. 'His Majesty's Cabinet and Peter I's Kunstkammer', in *The Origins of Museums: The Cabinet of Curiosities in Sixteenth and Seventeenth Century Europe*. Oxford: Clarendon Press, pp.53–61.

Nigmanova, G.G., 2002. 'Sennaia ploschad b Kazani: Istoria formirovania zastroiku', in Salikhov, Khayrutdinov and Guliazov, pp.80–112.

Nikitine, B. and Bosworth, C.E., 1995. 'Rasht', *EI* 8, pp.449–50.

Nizami, K.A., 1993. 'Nakshbandiyya' (in India), *EI* 7, pp.937–39.

Nogmanov, A., 1997. 'L'Evolution de la législation sur les Musulmans de Russie, de la conquête de Kazan à la guerre de Crimée (1552–1853)', in Dudoignon, Ishakov and Mohammatsin, pp. 115–30.

—— 2005. *Samoderzhavue i Tatari*. Kazan: Tatarskoe Knizhnoe Izdatelstvo.

Ocherki istorii SSR. 1953. Moscow: Nauka.

Ocherki istorii kalmytskoi ASSR. 1967. Moscow: Nauka.

Ostrovski, P., 1998. *Muscovy and the Monguls*. Cambridge: Cambridge University Press.

Ostrumov, V.P., 1978. *Kazan: Ocherki po istorii goroda i ego architekturii*. Kazan: Izdatelstvo Kazankogo Universitata.

Pedersen, J., 1971. 'Ibn 'Arabshāh', *EI* 3, pp.711–12.

Perry, J.R., 1993 'Nadir Shah Afshar', *EI* 7, pp.853–56.

Phillips, E., 1995. *The Foundation of Russia's Navy: Peter the Great and the Azov Fleet, 1688–1714*. Westport, CT, and London: Greenwood Press.

Pollock, S., 2006. *Empire by Invitation? Russian Empire-building in the Caucasus in the Reign of Catherine II*. Doctoral dissertation, Harvard University.

Ponjol, C., 1993. *L'Ambassade à Boxara de Florio Beneveni*. Paris: Peeters.

Porter, R., 2001. *Enlightenment: Britain and the Creation of the Modern World*. London: Penguin.

Postnikov, A.V., 2000. 'The Russian Navy as Chartmaker in the Eighteenth Century', *Imago Mundi* 52, pp.79–95.

—— 2003. 'Volga River', in Speake, pp.1250–54.

Pratt, M.-L., 1992. *Imperial Eyes: Travel Writing and Transculturation*. London: Routledge.

Putnam, P., ed., 1952. *Seven Britons in Imperial Russia, 1698–1812*. Princeton, NJ: Princeton University Press.

Quelquejay, C., 1960. 'Ceremiss', *EI* 1, pp.20–21.

Richardson, J., 1777–78. *A Dissertation on the Languages, Literature and Manners of Eastern Nations*. Oxford.

Rockhill, W.W., ed., 1900. *The Journey of William of Rubruck to the Eastern Parts of the World 1253–55, as Narrated by Himself, with Two Accounts of the Earlier Journey of John of Pian De Carpine*. London: Hakluyt Society.

Romaniello, M.P., 2007. 'Grant, Settle, Negotiate: Military Servitors in the Middle Volga Region', in Breyfogle, Schrader and Sunderland, pp.61–80.

Rorlich, A.-A., 1986. *The Volga Tatars: A Profile in National Resilience*. Stanford: Hoover Institution Press, Stanford University.

Runni, A., 1928. 'Alexander at the Caspian Gates', *Transactions and Pro-*

ceedings of the American Philological Association 59, pp.130–63.

Rywkin, M., 1988. *Russian Colonial Expansion to 1917*. London and New York: Mansell.

Salikhov, R.R., Khayrutdinov, R.T. and Guliazov, I.A., 2002. *Tatarskie slobodi kazani: Ocherki istorii*. Kazan: Uzd-vo In-ta Istorii.

Salikhov, R. R. and Khautpudinov, P. P., 2005. *Istoricheskie mecheti kazani*, Kazan: Tatarskoe Knuzhnoe Izdatelstvo.

Sanukov, K., 2005. 'Historische Voraussetzungen der Nationalen Identifikation', in *Mari und Mordwinen im heutigen Russland: Sprache, Kultur, Identität*, ed. E. Helimski, U. Kahrs and M. Schötschel. Wiesbaden: Harrassowitz, pp.1–22.

Savory, R.M., 1986, 'Kizil-bash', *EI* 5, pp.243–45.

Schamilöglü, U., 1990. 'The Formation of a Tatar Historical Consciousness: Sihabäddin Märcani and the Image of the Golden Horde', *Central Asian Survey* 9, pp.39–49.

Sela, R., 2004. *Central Asia in the 18th Century: The Age of Introspection*. Michigan: UMI Microform.

Shafranovski, K.I., 1954. 'Rukiopichie karti kaspiiskovo moria F.I. Soimonova', in *Geograficheskii Sbornik*, vol.3. Moscow and Leningrad: Izdatelstvo Akaemii Nauk SSR, pp.100–16.

Sixsaidov, A.R., 1996. 'Sammlungen arabischer Handschriften in Dagestan', in Kemper, von Kügelgen and Yermakov, pp.297–316.

Slezkine, Y., 1994. *Arctic Mirrors: Russia and the Small Peoples of the North*. Ithaca: Cornell University Press.

—— 2001. 'Naturalists Versus Nations: Eighteenth-Century Russian Scholars Confront Ethnic Diversity', in Bower and Lazzarini, pp.27–57.

Smirnov, K.A., 1960. *Velikue Bolgari*. Moscow: Izdatelstvo Akademii Nauk SSSR.

Sneath, D., 2007. *The Headless State: Aristocratic Orders, Kinship Society, and Misrepresentations of Nomadic Inner Asia*. New York and Chichester: Columbia University Press.

Spain, J., 2004. 'Bruce, Peter-Henry', *DNB*.

Speake, J., ed., 2003. *Literature of Travel and Exploration: An Encyclopaedia*. New York and London: Fitzroy Dearborn.

Spuler, B., 1960. 'Astrakhan', *EI* 1, pp.721–22.

—— 1965. 'Gilan', *EI* 2, pp.1111–12.

Stevens, C.B., 2007. *Russia's Wars of Emergence, 1460–1730*. Marlow: Pearson.

Storey, C.A. 1970, *Persian Literature*, vol.1. London: The Royal Asiatic Society of Great Britain and Ireland.

Subrahmanyan, S., 1995. 'Review of Dale, 1994', *Bulletin of the School of Oriental and African Studies* 58(2), pp.390–91.

Sunderland, W., 2004. *Taming the Wild Field: Colonization and Empire on the Russian Steppe*. Ithaca: Cornell University Press.

Tardy, J., 1982. 'A Contribution to the Cartography of the Central and Lower Volga Region', in *Chuvash Studies*, ed. A. Róna-Tas. Budapest: Akadémiai Kiadó, pp.179–222.

Tatischev, V.N., 1950. *Izbrannye trudy po geografii Rossii*. Moscow: Gos. Izd-vo Geog. Literatury.

Taylor, J.S., 2004. 'Hanway, Jonas', *DNB*.

Teissier, B., 2004. 'Asia in 18th-century Edinburgh Institutions: Seen or Unseen?', *Proceedings of the Society of Antiquaries of Scotland* 134, pp.499–556.

—— 2009, 'Texts from the Persian in Late Eighteenth-century India and Britain: Culture or Construct ?', *Iran* 47, pp.133–47.

Teltscher, K., 1997. *India Inscribed: European and British Writing on India, 1600–1800*. Delhi: Oxford University Press.

Ter-Sarkisiants, A. E., 2007. 'Sixteen Hundred Years of Armenian Writing', *Anthropology and Archaeology of Eurasia* 46(1), pp.75–94.

Thadeu, E.C., 1984. 'Tatischev, Vasili Nikitich', in *The Modern Encyclopaedia of Russian and Soviet History*, ed. J.L. Wieczynski, vol.38, pp.196–200.

Tolz, V.L., 2008. 'European, National, and (Anti-)Imperial: The Formation of Academic Oriental Studies in Late Tsarist and Early Soviet Russia', *Kritika: Explorations in Russian and Eurasian History* 9(1), pp.53–81.

Toomer, G.J., 1996. *Eastern Wisedome and Learning: The Study of Arabic in Seventeenth-Century England*. Oxford: Clarendon Press.

Vambéry, A., 1864. *Travels in Central Asia*. London: John Murray.

Vasary, I., 1995. 'Noghay', *EI* 8, pp.85–86.

Vasmer, R. and Bosworth, C.E., 1991. 'Māzandarān', *EI* 6, pp.938–39.

Vivius, I., 2002. *English Travel Narratives in the 18th Century: Exploring Genres*. Ashgate: Aldershot.

Werth, P., 2003. 'Coercion and Conversion: Violence and the Mass Baptism of the Volga Peoples, 1740–55', in *Kritika: Explorations in Russian and Eurasian History* 4(3), pp.543–69.

Zahidullin, I., 1997. 'La Conversion à l'orthodoxie des Tatars de la region Volga-Oural, aux XVII–XVIIIe siècle, et ses causes èconomiques et sociales', in Dudoignon, Ishakov and Mohammatshin, pp.27–64.

Zelkina, A., 1996. 'Islam and Society in Chechnia: From the Late Eighteenth to the Mid-Nineteenth Century', *Journal of Islamic Studies* 7(2), pp.240–64.

—— 2000. *In Quest for God and Freedom*. London: Hurst and Co.

ILLUSTRATIONS

Figures

Cover   Nomads by the Akhtuba River. From P.S. Pallas, *Travels through the Southern Provinces of the Russian Empire, in the Years 1793 and 1744* (London, 1812), pl.6. Bodleian Library, Oxford.

1   Ground plan of the colony of Sarepta, showing its regular layout within the fortress on the banks of the Sarpa. From J.G. Gmelin, *Reise durch Russland zur Untersuchung der drey Natur-Reiche*, vol.2 (St Petersburg, 1774), table 2. Bodleian Library, Oxford.

2   *View of Astrakhan from the north-west.* From J.G. Gmelin, *Reise durch Russland zur Untersuchung der drey Natur-Reiche*, vol.2 (St Petersburg, 1774), table 44. Bodleian Library, Oxford.

3   Cheremis female with traditional high headdress. From J.G.Georgi, *Beschreibung aller Nationen des Russischen Reichs, ihrer Lebensart, Religion, Gebrauche, Wohnungen, Kleidungen und übrugen Merkwürdigkeiten*, vol.1 (St Petersburg, 1776), pl.11. Bodleian Library, Oxford.

4   Tatar female from Kazan. From J.G. Georgi, *Beschreibung aller Nationen des Russischen Reichs, ihrer Lebensart, Religion, Gebrauche, Wohnungen, Kleidungen und übrugen Merkwürdigkeiten*, vol.1 (St Petersburg, 1776), pl.27. Bodleian Library, Oxford.

5   Tatar male from Kazan. From J.G. Georgi, *Beschreibung aller Nationen des Russischen Reichs, ihrer Lebensart, Religion, Gebrauche, Wohnungen, Kleidungen und übrugen Merkwürdigkeiten*, vol.1 (St Petersburg, 1776), pl.26. Bodleian Library, Oxford.

6   Astrakhan Tatars weaving, with looms, a bow and a musical instrument. From J.G. Gmelin, *Reise durch Russland zur Unter-suchung der drey Natur-Reiche*, vol.2 (St Petersburg, 1774), pls 4 and 5. Bodleian Library, Oxford.

7   Nogay female Tatar with a characteristic nose-ring. From J.G. Georgi, *Beschreibung aller Nationen des Russischen Reichs, ihrer Lebensart, Religion, Gebrauche, Wohnungen, Kleidungen und übrugen Merkwürdigkeiten*, vol.1 (St Petersburg, 1776), pl.30. Bodleian Library, Oxford.

8   Interior of Indian 'temple' at Astrakhan, with priest and worship-

pers. From P.S. Pallas's *Travels through the Southern Provinces of the Russian Empire, in the Years 1793 and 1744* (London, 1812), pl.9. Courtesy of the Taylorian Slavonic Library, Oxford. Photograph Roger Tomlin.

9   Interior of the main Armenian church in Astrakhan, with veiled Armenian ladies in the foreground. From J.G. Gmelin, Reise durch Russland zur Untersuchung der drey Natur-Reiche, vol.2 (St Petersburg, 1774), pl.8. Bodleian Library, Oxford.

10   Armenian male in shift and full dress. From J.G. Gmelin, *Reise durch Russland zur Untersuchung der drey Natur-Reiche*, vol.2 (St Petersburg, 1774), pl.6, Bodleian Library, Oxford.

11   Kalmyk females beside encampment. From P.S. Pallas, *Travels through the Southern Provinces of the Russian Empire, in the Years 1793 and 1744* (London, 1812), pl.5. Courtesy of the Taylorian Slavonic Library, Oxford. Photograph Roger Tomlin.

12   Kalmyk males beside encampment, with camels in the background. From P.S. Pallas, *Travels through the Southern Provinces of the Russian Empire, in the Years 1793 and 1744* (London, 1812), pl.4. Courtesy of the Taylorian Slavonic Library, Oxford. Photograph Roger Tomlin.

13   Monuments at the site of Bulgar. From P.S. Pallas, *Voyages de P.S. Pallas en différentes provinces de l'empire de Russie, et dans L'Asie septentrionale*, vol.5 (Paris, 1793), pl.8. Courtesy of the Taylorian Main Library. Photograph Roger Tomlin.

14   Circassian princess with male figure. From P.S. Pallas, *Travels through the Southern Provinces of the Russian Empire, in the Years 1793 and 1744* (London, 1812), pl.18. Courtesy of the Taylorian Slavonic Library, Oxford. Photograph Roger Tomlin.

15   Mounted Circassian nobleman. From P.S. Pallas, *Travels through the Southern Provinces of the Russian Empire, in the Years 1793 and 1744* (London, 1812), pl.20. Courtesy of the Taylorian Slavonic Library, Oxford. Photograph Roger Tomlin.

16   View of Baku on the Caspian. From J.G. Gmelin, *Reise durch Russland zur Untersuchung der drey Natur-Reiche*, vol.3 (St Petersburg, 1774), pl.9. Bodleian Library, Oxford.

17   Turkmen encampment. From J.G. Gmelin, *Reise durch Russland zur Untersuchung der drey Natur-Reiche*, vol.4 (St Petersburg, 1774), pl.6. Courtesy of the Taylorian Slavonic Library, Oxford. Photograph Roger Tomlin.

Maps

Biographical notes

Rulers of eighteenth-century Russia

Peter I (the Great)	1682–1725
Catherine I	1725–27
Peter II	1727–30
Anna	1730–40
Ivan VI (Anna Leopoldovna regent)	1740–41
Elizabeth	1741–62
Peter III	1762
Catherine II	1762–96
Paul	1796–1801

British travellers

Bell, John (b. Antermony, Stirlingshire, 1691; d.1780). Doctor, diplomat and merchant.

Bell was introduced to the Russian court by the tsar's chief physician, Robert Erskine. He travelled as a doctor and diplomat on missions to Persia (1717–18), China (1721–22) and Darband (1722). After a spell in Scotland, he returned to St Petersburg in 1734. In 1737 he was involved in Russian diplomacy in Constantinople, where he continued working as a merchant until 1746. He then returned to Scotland, having married, and settled on his estate in Antermony.

Source: R. Harrison, 'John Bell' (rev. P. Carter), *DNB*.

Bruce, Peter-Henry (b. Westphalia, 1692; d.1757). Military engineer.

Bruce grew up in Germany and Scotland. He entered the Prussian army and campaigned in Europe before entering Russian service in 1711 as a company captain of artillery and an engineer. In 1720 he became captain of a company of the Astrakhan regiment. He left Russia in 1724, forfeiting his pay and estate in St Petersburg. Bruce worked as an engineer on Providence Island and Charles Town from 1740 to1745. After his return to Scotland, he was involved in both engineering and campaigning against the Young Pretender.

Source: J. Spain, 'Bruce, Peter-Henry', *DNB*.

Cook, John (b. Hamilton, 1712; d.1790). Doctor.

Cook came to Russia in 1736, where he was accredited by the Medical Chancery in St Petersburg and became physician to Prince M.M. Golytsin.

He was attached to the Admiralty in Astrakhan as a doctor when Golytsin became governor (1740–41), and stayed on under V.N. Tatischev (1741–45). Cook accompanied an expedition to Persia in 1745–46. He then served under Count Lacy at Riga and escaped from Russia in 1751.
Source: J. Cook, ed. A.L. Fullerton, 1997, pp.xxi–lxxi [first published 1770].

Elton, John (d.1751). Sea captain and merchant.
In the 1730s Elton was chiefly involved in promoting the idea of British trade with Persia via Central Asia and Russia. In 1741 he accepted a commission from the Persian ruler Nader Shah to become his chief shipbuilder on the Caspian, to the great disapproval of both the Russians and the British Russian Company, which led to a suspension of British trade on the Caspian. Elton settled in Resht and, following Nader Shah's death in 1747, was murdered there in 1751.
Source: E.I. Carlyle, 'John Elton' (rev. S. Searight), *DNB*.

Forster, George (b. *c.*1752; d. Nagpur, 1791). East India Company civil servant and writer.
George is chiefly known for the publication of his travels during 1782–84 from Calcutta to Europe, and his *Sketches of the Mythology and Customs of the Hindoos* (London, 1785). He subsequently returned to India and in 1787 was employed by Lord Cornwallis as a negotiator and surveyor, and became resident at the court of Raja Raghoji Bhonsla.
Source: L. de Lima Martins, 'George Forster', *DNB*.

Graeme, Mungo (d. *c.*1743–47). Merchant.
In 1736 Graeme was engaged for six years as a merchant apprentice to George Napier, merchant in St Petersburg, with his uncle Sir Henry Stirling providing security. He was involved with John Elton's plan for the Caspian trade, and travelled with him down the Volga to Astrakhan, but in 1740–41 was left stranded in Resht in a dispute with Elton over unpaid bills. These bills were eventually settled, and Graeme left Resht for Astrakhan, where he set up business with other merchants and expected to return to Persia. By 1742 he was on his way to Moscow, owing Napier far more than Sir Henry Stirling's pledge of security. The dispute over the liability of his debts was carried on to the next generation.
Sources: National Archives of Scotland GD 24/1/454 1–33; GD 1/850/37.

Hanway, Jonas (bap. Portsmouth, 1712; d.1786). Merchant, philanthropist and writer.
Hanway worked as a merchant at the English Factory, Lisbon from 1729 to 1743. He joined the Russian Company in 1743, hoping to engage in British trade with Persia via the Caspian. This venture ultimately failed.

Hanway returned to England in 1750 and worked on Russia Company business until 1764. He entered government service in 1762 and worked at the Victualling Board. He founded the Marine Society's Ship School in 1777. Hanway promoted Christian mercantilism, was a member of the Society for the Propagation of Christian Knowledge and was involved in much philanthropic activity (e.g. hospital and penal reform, foundlings, prostitutes, poor boy apprenticeships, clothing for navy recruits). After the publication of his travels in 1753, he wrote numerous pamphlets on his various causes, as well as an account of a journey from Portsmouth to Kingston-upon-Thames (1756).
Source: J.S. Taylor, 'Jonas Hanway', *DNB*.

Hogg, Reynold. Merchant.
Hogg traded in in Russia in the 1730s and 1740s, where he seems to have been part of George Napier's circle of merchants in St Petersburg. Hanway published an account of Hogg and Thompson's journeys to Khiva and Bukhara.

Perry, John (b. Rodborough, Gloucestershire, 1669/70; d.1733). Hydraulic engineer and writer.
Perry served as ship's captain and hydraulic engineer in Britain and the West Indies before being recruited by Peter the Great in 1698. In Russia he worked on the Volga–Don canal, as comptroller of Russian maritime works, including building dams and docks to render the Don more navigable and constructing a canal to link the Neva and the Don. He was forced to leave Russia in 1712, having been largely unpaid for his services. Back in Britain he worked on the embankment at Dagenham, on Dover harbour, at Dublin harbour, on making the River Ouse navigable and on draining the Lincolnshire fens.
Source: J.H. Appleby, 'John Perry', *DNB*.

Parkinson, John (b.1779; d.1808). Fellow of Magdalen College, Oxford and Rector of Brockelsby, Lincolnshire.
Parkinson is chiefly known from the modern edition of his *A Tour of Russia, Siberia and the Crimea 1792–1794*, an account of his travels as tutor and companion to Edward Wilbraham-Bootle (later Lord Skelmersdale).
Sources: Parkinson, ed. W. Collier, 1971, p.xiv; Lincolnshire Archives, Dixon papers 16/6/14–16/6/24-25).

Spilman, James (bap. Yarmouth, 1680; d.1763). Businessman, officer in the Russia Company and diplomat.
Spilman came to Russia around the turn of the century on tobacco business and was admitted to the Russia Company in 1711. He became senior English merchant there, and was appointed to the Company's

Court of Assistants. He returned to England in 1721 but continued to be involved as an auditor and consul at the Russia Company's Court of Assistants. Spilman helped to draw up the Anglo-Russian Treaty of Commerce (1732–34) and a memorandum on importing Persian silk through Russia (1735). He became a director of the Bank of England and a Fellow of the Royal Society (1734), and published an account of Elton and Graeme's travels down the Volga.
Source: J.H. Appleby, 'James Spilman', *DNB*.

Thompson, George. Merchant.
Thompson was apprenticed to George Napier in St Petersburg 1730s and traded in Russia in the 1730s and 1740s.
Source: National Archives of Scotland GD 1/850/31.

Woodroofe, Thomas. Ship's captain, cartographer and associate of John Elton.
Woodroofe commanded the *Empress of Russia*, built by Elton and Woodroofe in Kazan, which he sailed down the Volga to Astrakhan. He accompanied Elton to Persia, and was partially successful in trading wool in exchange for raw silk. Extracts from Woodroofe's journal were published by Hanway in his 1753 account of British trade in Russia.
Source: Hanway, 1753.

INDEX

The index includes names used by travellers